FOR KENT AND COUNTRY

FOR KENT AND
COUNTRY

Kent's Cricketers in the Great War 1914–1918

PAUL LEWIS

Reveille
PRESS

Reveille Press is an imprint of
Tommies Guides Military Booksellers & Publishers

Gemini House
136–140 Old Shoreham Road
Brighton
BN3 7BD

www.tommiesguides.co.uk

First published in Great Britain by
Reveille Press 2014

For more information please visit
www.reveillepress.com

A catalogue record for this book is available
from the British Library

ISBN 978-1-908336-63-7

Cover design by Reveille Press
Typeset by Vivian@Bookscribe

Printed and bound in Great Britain

Dedication

With thanks to my wife Patricia, and our son
Adam, for supporting me throughout the writing
of this book, which is written in the memory of
the men of the Kent Elevens who served their
country.

CONTENTS

FOREWORD

As we reflect on the full enormity of the First World War one hundred years on it is hard to imagine what an impact it must have had on Britain and Kent. Today we are insulated and isolated from the larger scale conflicts around the world so it is increasingly important that we remember the sacrifices made by previous generations as they faced up to the ghastly challenges the "Great War" inflicted upon our country.

Kent and our cricketers played a full part. It is humbling to think that young men who underpinned great years of cricket at Canterbury also served fully in the war. Cricketing heroes such as Woolley, Hutchings and Cornwallis were also truly heroic in a military context. Valentine Fleming, my Great Grandfather, died whilst serving with the Oxfordshire Hussars in the first war and Michael Fleming, my Grandfather, was mortally wounded whilst serving with the Ox and Bucks in the retreat to Dunkirk so I appreciate and reflect regularly on the ultimate sacrifice.

As a soldier of more modest record myself, having been commissioned into the Royal Green Jackets, I can fully appreciate the characteristics that would have made these men excellent in both sporting and military contexts; The true sense of camaraderie and team spirit that only the threat of the ultimate sacrifice and great hardship can engender, the desire to win yet the maintenance of a great value base even under enormous pressure and so much more.

In sport we often trot out platitudes linking the games we play with the reality of conflict. How often do we hear sportsmen and women talking about "battles" and tough matches being like "a war"? In reality nothing could be further from the truth. This is a very important book for many reasons not least because it reminds us that there was a generation of Kent cricketers who really were prepared to make the ultimate sacrifice and who represented Kent with such pride and skill.

Matthew Fleming
London, January 2014

PREFACE

This book covers the events of the Great War of 1914 to 1918, relating the story of the military service and wartime deeds of the men who played for the Kent County Cricket Club Elevens. The idea for the book began with simple curiosity about the men named on the Blythe Memorial at the St Lawrence Ground. A service is held annually by the Supporters' Club to honour those Kent players who gave their lives in the two World Wars. Originally erected in the memory of Colin Blythe, it also names those others who fell in WWI and was later adorned with the names of the casualties of WW2. Other than one or two well-known players, I could find little in print about any of them. Who were they? What did they do in the War? How did they die? Having set out to research those men, curiosity got the better of me and I began looking for information about other players who served and lived to tell the tale. The 1915 Blue Book was a good source of information, the Committee Report naming many of those serving and their regiments. Derek Carlaw very kindly took the time to fill in the gaps in the list of names I had identified, and then the research took off. Information was gathered from the men's military files and regimental war diaries at the National Archive, from promotions announced in the London Gazette, announcements in *The Times* and other newspapers, Wisden Obituaries, from genealogy websites, the Commonwealth War Grave Commission, club histories and military histories. Librarians at schools and Universities were plagued with requests for assistance, which was given without question, and in several cases I was lucky enough to be put in contact with player's relatives, who were all incredibly helpful. The book is written with the intention of being a permanent remembrance of the men's deeds and the role each played in this monumental conflict. I hope I have done them justice.

ACKNOWLEDGEMENTS

Without the kind and unquestioning help of a large number of people this book would not have come to publication. The fact it covers both military and cricketing history, required calls for assistance to be made to numerous cricket clubs, military institutes, schools, universities, museums, photographic archives and other individuals. The following list hopefully catches them all, and I can only apologise to anyone I have missed. A special thank you goes to Kent's Derek Carlaw, Howard Milton and David Robertson, who were extremely helpful whenever I hit a brick wall, and also to Mathew Fleming for agreeing to write the Foreword. He was possibly the last Kent player to serve as a soldier and his comments are particularly pertinent. I would also like to express gratitude to the late Mike Spurrier who was most helpful and encouraging as I started the research. Information and assistance was also forthcoming from the following:

Relatives of former players: Philippa Williams, Pat Bryan, Hedley Prest and Ivo Longfield.

Librarians, Archivists and other Staff at the following Schools: Jackie Wilkie at Aldenham; Clare Bradley at Bradfield; Catherine Smith at Charterhouse; Jill Barlow at Cheltenham; Charles Knighton at Clifton; Calista Lucy at Dulwich; John Malden at Durham; Elaine Mundill at Glenalmond; John Hamblin at Lancing College; William Durran at Loretto; Ian Quickfall at Malvern; Terry Rogers at Marlborough; Clare Sargent at Radley; Jo Outhwaite at Rugby; Sarah Davies Jones at St. Andrew's; Julian Girdham of the Old Columban Society (St. Colomba's); Martin Clifford at St. Edmund's; Chris Tavare at Sevenoaks; David Pickard at Sutton Valance; John Brown at Taunton; Beverely Matthews at Tonbridge; Jerry Rudman at Uppingham; Ben Lewsley at Wellington; Elizabeth Wells at Westminster; Suzanne Foster at Winchester.

University Archivists: Robin Adams at Trinity College, Dublin; Sian Astill and Emma Harrold at Oxford University; Jacqueline Cox at Cambridge University.
Archivists at the Colleges of Oxford University: Elizabeth Boardman at Brasenose College; Judith Curthoys at Christ Church College; Robin Darwall-Smith for Magdalen and University Colleges; Jennifer Thorp at New College; Michael Riordan at St John's College; Emma Goodrum at Worcester College.

Archivists at the Colleges of Cambridge University: Robert Athol at Jesus College; Jayne Ringrose at Pembroke College; Fiona Colbert at St. John's.

Museums, Libraries and Archives: Deborah Saunders at Kent History and Library Centre; Staff of the National Archives; Giles Guthrie at The Queen's Own Royal West Kent Regimental Museum; Lauren Jones at The Royal Engineers Museum, Library and Archive; Nigel E Montagu of the Institution of Royal Engineers; Andrew Hudson at Folkestone Library; Gill Neal at Wiltshire and Swindon History Centre; Michel Brideau at Library and Archives Canada; John Endicott at Kent Police Museum; Boris Mollo and David Whitehouse at Kent & Sharpshooters Yeomanry Museum; Philip Mather at The Fusilier Museum Bury; Anthony Morton at The Royal Military Academy Sandhurst; Johannes Moosdiele at Bayerisches Hauptstaatsarchiv in Munich; Elizabeth Taylor at the National Portrait Gallery; Richard Dabb at the National Army Museum; Lorna Llewellyn-Jones at the Naval Historical Branch of the MOD; Neil Robinson at the MCC; Berni Metcalfe at National Library of Ireland; John Gibbons Studios; Roger Mann; John Lloyd at The Household Cavalry Museum; The Commonwealth War Graves Commission; Martin Starnes at the History Centre Surrey; Paul Evans at the Royal Artillery Museum; Richard Long-Fox at The Rifles Berkshire and Wiltshire Museum; Major Robin WB Maclean at The Royal Scots Dragoon Guards Museum; The Red Cross Society.

Others: Lord Walpole; Andrew Renshaw; Neil Harris (OUCC Scorer); Shaun Caveney; Phil Spain; Bill Horsley; Barry Hollis at Kent Media Group; Rev. Paul Ormrod and Peter Shaw (St. Peter's, Formby); Jonathan Tapp; David Armstrong; Graham Sacker; all the members of the Great War Forum who gave so much help; Bob Sellwood; Jane Jones; Judith Johnson.

INTRODUCTION

The Great War of 1914-1918 saw the introduction of the tank, trench warfare, poisonous gas, flamethrowers, the widespread use of the machine-gun, the decline of the importance of cavalry and the increased use of the aeroplane. Playing their part in the greatest conflict the world had seen, Kent's cricketers were present throughout and helped shape history, as several major empires came to an end, and the world map was redrawn at the cost of millions of lives. This book looks to record the role of the cricketers in this conflict. Those who served were not all in the 1914 XI's, indeed many had finished playing for Kent before the outbreak of war, and a number would first represent the County in the years that followed.

The book covers a number of different aspects to the war. Some of the cricketers were already serving, so an outline is given of their military associations prior to the war, for regulars, territorials and reservists. The volunteers are then reviewed, describing some of the differences between officers and the ranks and file, and what the introduction of conscription meant in 1916. Details are given of the units the men served with in the different branches of the three forces. The cricketers joined the army, navy and air force, and served as infantry and cavalry, as machine-gunners, artillery, engineers, drivers, medics and instructors. They served as Privates and Staff Officers, and a number served together.

Descriptions of the different theatres of war are provided to put each man's whereabouts in context, and to demonstrate their involvement in so many major events and battles. This includes the Western Front, Gallipoli, Egypt and the Western Desert, Palestine, Mesopotamia, Salonika, the Caucasus and also the Home Front. Each man's individual story is shared, covering their lives in general, helping us to understand what these men were prepared to sacrifice. How men from all walks of life faced the same risks of death on a daily basis. Those who paid the ultimate sacrifice are listed in a Roll of Honour, and those who were wounded are named, as well as the awards they received. The many memorials to the fallen are examined, both at home and overseas, including Kent's own Blythe Memorial at the St Lawrence Ground, and the book closes with a brief review of the legacy of the war and what followed.

Every effort has been made to cover all First XI players who served in any capacity. Second XI players are also included but, in an effort to avoid unmanageable numbers, subject to certain criteria; if they played during the 1914 season; were related to, or serving in the same units as, others being researched; were referenced in the Committee Meeting minutes during the War years; or are named on the Blythe Memorial. Most of Kent's cricketers and staff played their individual roles in the four years of conflict, whether militarily or otherwise. Fighting in distant lands, many performed acts of bravery, now long forgotten. Hardships were endured and battles were fought. Medals were won and lives were lost. In addition to those who died, many more were wounded, and the memories of battle and the carnage witnessed, of friends and comrades lost, undoubtedly stayed with the survivors for the remainder of their days. There are no individual stories for those who did not serve in the armed forces or the Red Cross, and for good reason. There is little information, for example, that can be given about the Special Constables as no records remain, but they are referenced in the Home Front summary.

The players who appeared in the 1914 First and Second Elevens are shown in Tables 1 and 2, together with details of the theatres of war they served in. 'Home Service' is used to denote where a man was not posted overseas or returned from an overseas posting to serve in the UK. 'Not Established' is used where it is known a man did serve overseas, but exactly where has not been uncovered. For those not joining the armed forces but who served in some other capacity, their occupation is indicated, and where no information was found of a man's wartime whereabouts, they are marked 'No record'. The men who served in the Royal Navy (RN), Royal Naval Reserve (RNR), Royal Naval Air Service (RNAS), Royal Naval Volunteer Reserve (RNVR), Royal Flying Corps (RFC) or Royal Air Force (RAF) are marked as such. Tables 3 and 4 provide details of the men who either finished playing for Kent before 1914, or made their debut after 1918. Those who died in service are marked in bold type.

Table 1 – First XI Players of 1914

PLAYER	KENT CAREER (1ST XI)	SERVICE	THEATRES OF WAR SERVED IN
C Blythe	**1899 – 1914**	**Army**	**Western Front**
DW Carr	1909 – 1914	Army	Egypt, Home Service
AP Day	1905 – 1925	Army	Home Service
SH Day	1897 – 1919	No record	–
WJ Fairservice	1902 – 1921	Army	Home Service
A Fielder	1900 – 1914	Non-military	Special Constable (UK)
AP Freeman	1914 – 1936	Non-military	Special Constable (UK)
HTW Hardinge	1902 – 1933	RNAS, RAF	RNAS , RAF
CE Hatfeild	**1910 – 1914**	**Army**	**Gallipoli, Egypt, Palestine, Western Front**
WE Hickmott	1914 – 1921	Army	Western Front
JC Hubble	1904 – 1929	Non-military	Special Constable, VTC
FH Huish	1895 – 1914	No record	–
E Humphreys	1899 – 1920	RNR, RN	RNR, RN

PLAYER	KENT CAREER (1ST XI)	SERVICE	THEATRES OF WAR SERVED IN
DW Jennings	**1909 – 1914**	**Army**	**Western Front**
FH Knott	1910 – 1914	Army	Western Front, Salonika
JR Mason	1893 – 1914	RNVR	RNVR
WA Powell	1912 – 1921	No record	-
WGM Sarel	1912 – 1914	Army, RAF	Western Front, Home Service, RAF
J Seymour	1902 – 1926	Non-military, RAF	Special Constable (UK), Home Front
LHW Troughton	1907 – 1923	Army	Western Front
GWE Whitehead	**1914**	**Army, RFC, RAF**	**Western Front**
FE Woolley	1906 – 1938	RNAS, RAF	RNAS, RAF

No information was found to determine unequivocally the wartime whereabouts of Sam Day, Fred Huish and William Powell. It is not certain that they did not serve; simply that evidence to the contrary has not been discovered. Fred Huish was well over the recruitment age limit from the outset, although it did just catch up with him in 1918, but no records have been discovered as to whether he was called for a medical. William Powell and Sam Day were both within the age limits for volunteers, but no record was found of a military connection. Public School Registers and University Alumni typically recorded whether their pupils served, but Malvern College has no record of Sam Day having done so. There are entries in *The War List of the University of Cambridge (Carey 1921)* for all the Kent men who attended the University pre-war, other than Day, and it seems very likely he did not enlist. He was a teacher / headmaster before and after the war, and may have continued in that role during the intervening years, some teaching roles being treated as reserved occupations.

Table 2 – Second XI Players of 1914

PLAYER	KENT CAREER	SERVICE	THEATRES OF WAR SERVED IN
WH Ashdown	1920 – 1937 (1st XI)	Army	Home Service
JL Bryan	1919 – 1932 (1st XI)	Army	Gallipoli, Egypt, Western Front
RT Bryan	1920 – 1937 (1st XI)	Army	Western Front
GC Collins	1911 – 1928 (1st XI)	No record	–

PLAYER	KENT CAREER	SERVICE	THEATRES OF WAR SERVED IN
JC Colquhoun	1914 – 1921 (2nd XI)	Army	Western Front
PW Cook	1914 – 1921 (2nd XI)	No record	-
CK Douglas	1913 – 1923 (2nd XI)	No record	-
F Dutnall	1919 – 1920 (1st XI)	Army	Home Service
GH Heslop	**1914 (2nd XI)**	**Army**	**Western Front**
CP Johnstone	1919 – 1933 (1st XI)	Army	Western Front, Home Service
AF Leach-Lewis	1911 – 1922 (2nd XI)	Army	Gallipoli, Egypt
LJ le Fleming	**1897 – 1899 (1st XI)**	**Army**	**Western Front, Home Service**
FS Lowe	**1914 (2nd XI)**	**Army**	**Western Front**
A Povey	1921 – 1922 (1st XI)	Army	Western Front
LM Powell	**1914 (2nd XI)**	**Army**	**Western Front**
CES Rucker	1914 (2nd XI)	Army	Gallipoli, Western Front, Home Service
A Smith	1911 – 1914 (2nd XI)	Army	Not established
AO Snowden	1911 (1st XI)	Army	Home Service
FN Tuff	**1911 – 1914 (2nd XI)**	**Army**	**Gallipoli**
GJV Weigall	1891 – 1903 (1st XI)	Army	Home Service, India
JHE Whitehead	**1912 – 1914 (2nd XI)**	**Army**	**Home Service**
GEC Wood	1919 – 1927 (1st XI)	Army	Gallipoli, Egypt, Mesopotamia, Caucasus
CT Wycherley	**1913 – 1914 (2nd XI)**	**Army**	**Mesopotamia**

Those men who appeared for both XI's in 1914 are detailed in Table 1. Where players of the 1914 2nd XI did not make the 1st XI that year, but did so either before or after 1914, the years they represented the 1st XI are shown; otherwise their 2nd XI career span is indicated. George Collins, Percy Cook and Claud Douglas were all of military age, but no service records or details of their whereabouts during the war years were found. Douglas appears in *The Register of Tonbridge School from 1861-1945 (Furley 1951)* but his entry gives no military details, and he has no entry in *Tonbridge School and the Great War of 1914-1919 (Tonbridge School 1923)*.

Table 3 – Players who last appeared for Kent before the 1914 season

PLAYER	KENT CAREER (1ST XI UNLESS STATED)	SERVICE	THEATRES OF WAR SERVED IN
PC Baker	1900 – 1902	Army	Home Service
BD Bannon	1895 – 1900	Red Cross	Western Front
RB Bannon	1902 – 1904 (2nd XI)	Red Cross, RNVR	Western Front
K Barlow	1910	Army	Home Service
EM Blair	1893 – 1900	Army	Egypt, Home Service
RNR Blaker	1898 – 1908	Army	Western Front
M Bonham-Carter	1902	–	Air Ministry
HM Braybrooke	1891 – 1899	–	Hospital Commandant
SW Brown	1899	RN	RN
EW Dillon	1900 – 1923	Army	Gallipoli, Egypt, Palestine
AH du Boulay	**1899**	**Army**	**Western Front**
AC Edwards	**1895 – 1897 (2nd XI)**	**Army**	**Western Front**
LB Friend	1886 – 1887	Army	Ireland, France
AW Fulcher	1878 – 1887	RNR	RNR
EA Fulcher	1909 (2nd XI)	Army	Western Front
HH Harington	1897	Army	Home Service
GRC Harris	1870 – 1911	Army, VTC	Home Service
HS Hatfeild	1911 – 1913 (2nd XI)	Army	Western Front, India
WC Hedley	1888	Army	Home Service
G de L Hough	1919 – 1920	Army	Western Front, Home Service
CVL Hooman	1910	RNR	RNR
CS Hurst	1908 – 1927	–	Ministry of Munitions
FV Hutchings	1901 – 1905	Army	Home Service
KL Hutchings	**1902 – 1912**	**Army**	**Western Front**
WEC Hutchings	1899	Army	Egypt, Western Front
HM Lawrence	1899	Army	Gallipoli, Egypt, Palestine, Western Front
J le Fleming	1889 – 1899	Army	Home Service
FB Leney	1905	Red Cross	Western Front, Egypt
ROH Livesay	1895 – 1904	Army	Western Front
CHB Marsham	1900 – 1922	Army, RAF	Gallipoli, Egypt, Palestine, Home Service, RAF

PLAYER	KENT CAREER (1ST XI UNLESS STATED)	SERVICE	THEATRES OF WAR SERVED IN
FWB Marsham	1905	Army	Western Front
JE Mason	1900	RNVR, Army	RNVR, Home Service
WT Monckton	1911 – 1913 (2nd XI)	Army	Western Front
PE Morfee	1910 – 1912	RFC, RAF	Western Front
TE Pawley	1880 – 1887	–	Treasurer Kent Hospitals
W Pearce	1878	–	Chemical Manufacturer
F Penn Jr *	1904 – 1905	Army	Western Front, Home Service
HEW Prest	1909 – 1922	Army	Western Front
HJB Preston	1907 – 1913	Army	Gallipoli, Egypt, Palestine, Syria
EH Simpson	**1896**	**Army**	**Western Front**
KS Singh	1901 – 1902	Indian Medical Service	Not established
RT Thornton	1881 – 1888	Red Cross	Western Front
JSR Tufton	1897 – 1898	Army	Western Front
HS Walpole	**See note below ****	**Army**	**Western Front**
EA Willson	1898	Army	Home Service
CN Woolley ***	1906 – 1908 (2nd XI)	Army	Western Front
CR Worthington	1898	Army, CAMC	Western Front

* Frank Penn Jr is referred to as 'Jr' in a cricket context, as his father also played for Kent. For the purposes of this text he is referred to as Frank Penn throughout.

** HS Walpole is included on the strength of his Wisden Obituary which states he played for the Kent 2nd XI. The Club has no record of his having played, and his grandson, the current Lord Walpole, confirmed the family had no knowledge of his doing so. It is entirely possible Wisden made an error in the obituary but, as it has not been confirmed either way, it was decided a better option to include him in this work than not to.

*** The forename of CN Woolley is spelt Claud or Claude depending on the source, but his birth index and early census records use the spelling 'Claud', and this has been used throughout.

Table 4 – Players who first appeared for Kent after 1918

PLAYER	KENT CAREER (1ST XI UNLESS STATED)	SERVICE	THEATRES OF WAR SERVED IN
AF Bickmore	1919 – 1929	Army	Western Front
N Boucher *	1924 – 1925 (2nd XI)	Army, RFC, RAF	Western Front, Home Service
S Boucher	1922	RN	RN
CJ Capes	1923 – 1928	Army	Mesopotamia
WS Cornwallis	1919 – 1926	Army	Western Front
BS Cumberlege	1923 – 1924	Army	Western Front
SE Day	1922 – 1925	Army	Western Front, Home Service
EW Dilnot *	1914 – 1919 (C&G)	Army	Western Front
W Dutnall	1923	Army	Home Service
AJ Evans	1921 – 1928	Intel att'd RFC, RAF	Western Front, Palestine
CLD Fawcus	1924	Army	Home Service
GN Foster	1921 – 1922	Army	Palestine, Western Front
EJ Fulcher	1919	Army	Western Front
AC Haywood *	1920 – 1922 (2nd XI)	Army	Home Service, India
B Howlett	1922 – 1928	Army	Western Front
CS Marriott	1924 – 1937	Army, RAF	Western Front, Home Service, RAF
GA Simpson	1929 – 1931	Army	Western Front
HJ Taylor	1922 – 1925	Army	Gallipoli, Egypt, Palestine
JR Tylden	1923	Army	Gallipoli, Egypt, Western Front

* Of the 2nd XI players referenced in this table, Noël Boucher is included on the grounds his brother is included as a 1st XI player, and Noël himself went on to be Club President. Archie Haywood was mentioned in the 1915 Committee report as being one of the Young Players who had enlisted. EW Dilnot is the only Club and Ground player referenced, having been mentioned in the Committee notes of 1917.

The histories of Kent CCC have something of a gap in the records between 1914-1918 and 1939-1945 due to fixtures being suspended. Hopefully this book will fill the gap for the Great War years, and serve as a permanent reminder of the deeds performed by those players on the battlefields, and of those who gave their lives for their country.

CHAPTER ONE:
MOBILIZATION, VOLUNTEERING AND CONSCRIPTION

When the 1914 cricket season opened, the Kent team was enjoying an unprecedented period of success. Having won the Championship four times in eight years, hopes were high for a fifth title. Ted Dillon had resigned the captaincy after leading the team to win the Championship in 1913, and Lionel Troughton was promoted from 2nd XI Captain to replace him. Despite the fact that he was uncapped and not even assured of a place on merit, Troughton had captained the 2nd XI quite capably in the preceding years, and the appointment was a popular decision. Amongst the amateurs that had played under Dillon, a good number appeared with Troughton in 1914; Douglas Carr, Arthur and Sam Day, Eric Hatfeild, Freddie Knott, Jack Mason, William Powell and Bill Sarel. There was also by now a strong core of professionals in the side, and more coming through the Tonbridge Nursery where Gerry Weigall had been the coach since Captain McCanlis retired in 1912.

At the beginning of May the professional and colt players were called to the Nursery for a pre-season gathering. Many of the better established cricketers had spent the previous months engaged in coaching roles, and Blythe missed the gathering as he had not returned from such an appointment in Birmingham. Frank Woolley and Bill Fairservice had spent the winter in sunnier climes, the former on tour with England in South Africa and the latter coaching in India. Ted Humphreys and William Hickmott had been with Pelham Warner at Leeds (Kent), whilst Fielder, Hardinge and Fairservice (once he returned from India) had just finished coaching various young gentlemen at the Angel Ground. James Seymour had been engaged at Tunbridge Wells and Jack Hubble working with the young Forsters at Rumwood Court.

Gerry Weigall had been busy talent-spotting, and as a result there was also a group of young amateurs present at the practice. It was hoped the youngsters might support the Club and Ground, 2nd XI and even possibly the 1st XI in 1914 or subsequent seasons. Amongst these hopefuls were George Whitehead of Dartford, the captain of the Clifton College XI, Jack and Ronnie Bryan from Beckenham, both in the Rugby XI of which Jack was captain, and George Heslop of Sevenoaks who was captain of the Lancing College XI. Con Johnstone, another member of the Rugby XI, was due to assist Pelham Warner that month and was also suggested as a potential future Kent player. There were others, but these young men were the ones who did play during the course of the summer. Following the fixture at the Parks toward the end of May, Oxford fast bowler Charles Rucker was also spoken of as a potential future player, qualifying by birth and residency.

There were several new additions to the professionals, including a trio of 16 year olds: Ernest Dilnot from Ramsgate, Archie Haywood of Eltham and Bill Ashdown from Lewisham. Of the previous years' players, Preston had headed to Lancashire, and George Collins was on the Lord's staff whilst recovering from appendicitis, but was to be made available if required. The six foot 22 year-old bowler Alex Smith was thought to have improved over the past year, and there were high hopes for Bill Hickmott. David Jennings had already appeared in the 1st XI and 17 year old Frank Dutnall was expected to follow suit. Tich Freeman's mastery of the googly held him in good stead for the future and Charles Wycherley was selected to replace Smith for engagement at Canterbury.

The year began with mixed fortunes, and as Kent went into their tenth Championship match at Gloucester on 29 June, they had won five, drawn two and lost two. On the day the match began the newspapers reported the assassination of Archduke Franz Ferdinand, heir to the Austro-Hungarian throne, in Sarajevo. Many causes contributed to the Great War, and this event is generally accepted as having been used as the excuse Germany

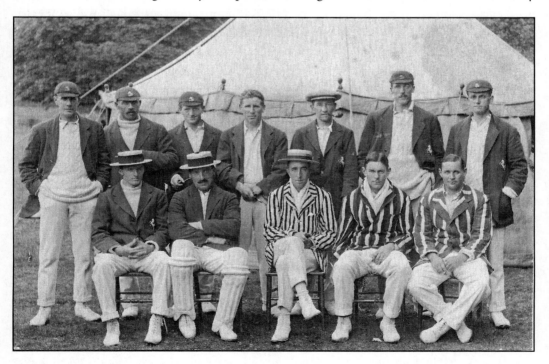

Kent team of 1914. Back row: Fairservice, Fielder, Hardinge, Humphreys, Hubble, Woolley, Blythe. Seated: Seymour, Huish, Troughton (Capt), AP Day, SH Day.

required to push things along. On this day however, no-one could have foreseen just how close the greatest conflict the world had seen actually was. What unfolded in the next four weeks became known as the 'July Crisis', as the diplomats of Austria-Hungary, Russia, Germany, Britain and France sought a solution. When Austria-Hungary declared war on Serbia at the end of July, the chess pieces of Europe began to move into place.

Russia started to mobilize on 29 July, the German Empire on 30 July and France on 1 August, the same day that Germany declared war on Russia. The United Kingdom declared war on Germany on 4 August when no assurance was forthcoming that Belgian neutrality would be respected.

The declaration of war came at the beginning of Canterbury Week, and financially the event was ruined. The town was decorated for the Week, mostly before the crisis took shape, and although the cricket was well attended, the spectators' minds were distracted. The *Kent Messenger* reported a lack of the usual gaiety associated with the event, and an air of depression among the supporters. The well-known families of Kent were absent, the military tents were much quieter than usual, and talk was less of cricket, and more of the continuous rail traffic heard at night, and of the militarization of Dover. The traditional balls fell victim and were cancelled, and the theatre performances by the Old Stagers were cancelled due to the mobilization of cast members, the first time in their 72 year history the group had not appeared during Canterbury Week. Fred Lowe, who had made his 2nd XI debut during July, had been playing his fourth game against Essex at Leyton. He was in the Army Reserve and his battalion, the 1st Buffs, received their orders to mobilize on Tuesday 4 August. Allan Leach-Lewis and Eric Hatfeild, who were both members of the Royal East Kent Mounted Rifles, also received orders to report to their regiment as it mobilized.

There were still eight Championship games to play, and when the Committee met on Tuesday the decision was made to stick to the existing fixture programme, but that there be no catering for the public at Dover. As more troops mobilized and Dover became an armed camp, it was agreed that the matches due to be played there against Lancashire and Worcestershire should be transferred to Canterbury, and further financial loss was incurred as a result. The Committee Report for 1914 noted that August's cricket was overshadowed by the War. Of the nine games were played during the month, four were won, four lost, and the honours shared once. Gates were affected as the population occupied themselves in assisting the Military Authorities, and facilities for travel to the grounds were reduced.

'Tich' Freeman, Bill Hickmott and George Whitehead were the three players who made their County Championship debuts in the 1914 season, and all three did so in the matches that followed the declaration of war. The 2nd XI had seen the debuts of the amateur hopefuls Jack and Ronnie Bryan, George Heslop, Con Johnstone and Charles Rucker, and also of the young professional Bill Ashdown. At the end of the season Kent had won 16 of their matches, drawn five and lost seven, giving them third place in the Championship, and the 2nd XI finished fifth in the Minor Counties Championship, with four wins, four losses and two draws. Such matters would however have seemed less important than usual, as the summer ended under the cloud of war, with all eyes on Europe.

Photo]   Fielder.   Seymour.   Hubble.   Hearne.   Woolley.   Jennings.   Freeman.   Fairservice.   *[Mockfo*
                  Hui-h.   A. P. Day.   L. H. W. Troughton (*Capt.*).   Hardinge.   Blythe.

A Kent side of 1914, including Blythe and Jennings who enlisted together and were both killed during the war. Troughton, the team captain, was to spend a year in captivity

OLD SOLDIERS

When Britain mobilized her forces in August 1914, there were a number of former, existing and future Kent cricketers serving in the Regular Army, the Reserve or the Territorial Force, and many more had passed, or were passing, through some form of military training in schools and universities. Four of those soldiers were Royal Engineers.

NOTES ON THE ROYAL ENGINEERS

A strong relationship existed between the Royal Engineers and the cricket clubs in Kent at the end of the 19th Century. The School of Military Engineering had been established at Chatham in 1812 and the RE Cricket Club began playing at the local Garrison Ground circa 1863. The team played a full fixture list each year and, although their greatest rivalry was

against the Royal Artillery, they also played host to the MCC and the wandering clubs, I Zingari, Band of Brothers and Free Foresters. In this way several cricketing engineers encountered Lord Harris and other Kent players, and were invited to appear for the County. Their military commitments limited their ability to play, and although Friend, Blair, Hedley and du Boulay all played with much success for the RE side, they collectively represented Kent just 18 times.

Lovick Friend sitting in front of Lord Harris, on the occasion of the RE versus I Zingari fixture of 1874. Reproduced by permission of the Institution of Royal Engineers.

BOER WAR 1899–1902

The second Boer War, also known as the second South African War, was fought between 1899 and 1902, and quickly caught the public's imagination. Thousands of young men flocked to join up in scenes that were repeated on a grander scale in 1914. Of those cricketers serving prior 1899 a good number took part in the campaign, including John Tufton, Robert Livesay, Lawrence le Fleming, Herbert Harington, Walter Hedley and Arthur du Boulay. Not all made it to South Africa. Arthur Edwards served in the Mediterranean, guarding Boer prisoners, and when the war was over John

Lord Harris (left) with the officers of the Royal East Kent Mounted Rifles in 1900.

Tufton did likewise at St. Helena. During the campaign Everard Blair remained at the RMA Woolwich as an Instructor, and Lovick Friend stayed in Egypt, having served in Kitchener's Nile Expedition in 1898. Lord Harris also missed out. He was elected to sit on a committee considering the future of the Yeomanry, and when he was finally released and travelled to South Africa as AAG to the Imperial Yeomanry in 1901, the fighting was all but over.

The war also encouraged several more of our subjects to volunteer. Hervey Lawrence and Bill Sarel joined Militia units but transferred to the regulars once in South Africa. Charles Worthington joined a Volunteer Company, and served a full twelve months, but Frank Penn joined the Royal Fusiliers too late to be posted and at the end of 1902 transferred to the Yeomanry. Francis Marsham was another who joined the Militia in 1901 but did not serve overseas. The men who did fight in South Africa were no doubt able to draw on their experiences during the Great War despite the differences between the two battlefields, and most were to hold senior positions during the latter conflict.

1902–1914 RESTRUCTURING THE ARMY

The British Army had undergone a number of reforms in the years preceding the Boer War, but the conflict had highlighted the fact that several shortcomings remained in a rapidly changing world. There had been a less than satisfactory system of supplying reserves to South Africa and it was also apparent that, whilst its forces were overseas, the country would have been hard pushed to defend itself against an invasion. The Esher Committee was established in 1902 by Royal Commission and its report was published two years later, recommending reform within both the Army and War Office. With the Army Chiefs opposing what they perceived to be unnecessary changes, implementation was slow but, in a way, inevitable. Richard Haldane, who was appointed War Secretary in the Liberal Government of 1905, was a secret supporter of the need for reform, and in his new role he brought about changes between 1906 and 1909 that shaped the British Army of 1914.

The Boer War had highlighted the need to be able to mobilize an Expeditionary Force quickly, and Haldane's reforms allowed that to be done in 1914, even though 60% of the BEF was made up of men in the Reserve. Haldane created the Special Reserve using existing Militia units, and he also created a Territorial Force (TF) from the Volunteers and Yeomanry. The thinking was that in the event the BEF was deployed overseas, the TF would act jointly with the Reserve as a Home Force, and at the same time would undergo training that could make them battle-ready within six months.

There were different components of the Reserve Force. Fred Lowe enlisted as a regular with the 1st Buffs in 1907, and joined the Army Reserve in 1912. This Army Reserve was for men who had already completed a term of service, and Lowe joined to see out the last few years of his engagement. Tufton and Sarel joined the Special Reserve in 1909, and were both liable to be mobilized in 1914. The Special Reserve was different in that men could enlist in it without having previously served, and could be mobilized with the other forces. Officers who retired could join a different reserve, the Reserve of Officers, and could also be mobilized. Harington had joined the Reserve of Officers in 1904 on his retirement, and Livesay joined in 1914 after spending five years as an Adjutant of the newly created OTC, although his retirement was to prove quite brief.

The Suffolk regiment in which Hervey Lawrence served was typical of Territorial units, including the Yeomanry. The men were required to attend annual training of ten parades, each of one hours duration, and a fortnight summer camp. There were also shooting practices and competitions, social gatherings, occasional war games, annual dinners and other such events. The Territorial cricketers were thus often absent from their teams during the period the summer camps were held. Eric Hatfeild was once such example, being unavailable for part of the summer of 1914 due to his commitments with the Royal East Kent Mounted Rifles. Other cricketers of the Yeomanry who received their orders to mobilize were Allan Leach-Lewis, Keith Barlow, James Tylden and Cloudesley Marsham.

Haldane also created OTCs, the Officer Training Corps, of which there were 23 new Senior OTC Divisions created in Universities, 166 Junior Divisions in Public Schools, and an Inns of Court OTC associated with the legal profession. This was achieved by reorganizing school cadet corps and university rifle corps. Many of Kent's amateur players passed through OTCs whilst at school and/or university, giving them a taste of the military early in life. Examinations were taken and cadets could earn certificates A and B. Certificate A was primarily for the Junior Division, and B for the Senior Division. Those earning Certificate B were entitled to a commission in the Special Reserve of Officers or the TF.

MOBILIZATION

We can now look at the whereabouts of our serving cricketers on 4 August 1914, the day Britain's forces were mobilized. This can be split between those in the Regular Army, the Territorials, the Yeomanry and the Special Reserve.

REGULAR ARMY

Reservists

PLAYER	YEAR JOINED RESERVE	ORDERS ON MOBILIZATION
HH Harington	1904 (Reserve of Officers)	Appointed Staff Captain in Reserve of Officers
WGM Sarel	1909 (Special Reserve)	Transferred to 10th Rifle Brigade
JSR Tufton	1909 (Special Reserve)	Appointed APM in 6th Division in 1915
FS Lowe	1912 (Army Reserve)	Recalled to 1st Buffs, joined the BEF
ROH Livesay	1914 (Reserve of Officers)	Recalled as GSO2 in 48th Division

Whilst the Regular Army that formed the BEF and headed to France included a number of reservists, the Special Reserve took over control of Home Defence, and supplied reinforcement drafts to the regulars.

Territorial Force

PLAYER	SERVING WITH	YEAR APPOINTED	POSTING ON MOBILIZATION
AH du Boulay	1st London Division (Adjutant)	1909	Remained UK until June 1915
HM Lawrence	5th Suffolk (Adjutant)	1911	Remained in UK until August 1915
Lord Harris	4th Buffs Hon. Colonel	1908	Not posted, honorary position only

The Territorials were not bound to serve overseas, having been created as a Home Defence Force, but Kitchener was open to transferring TF units to the New Armies for service overseas once they were fully trained. Du Boulay remained with the 1st London Division whist its battalions were gradually attached to other Divisions, and once it was eroded he joined the 33rd Division, part of the New Armies, accompanying them to France. Following mobilization, Lawrence's battalion was asked to volunteer to serve overseas, and three quarters of the men did so. Once fully trained and recruited to strength, they embarked for Gallipoli, where many of the Territorials, including the Yeomanry, were to be tested.

Yeomanry (Territorial Cavalry)

PLAYER	UNIT SERVING WITH	YEAR JOINED	POSTING ON MOBILIZATION
AF Leach-Lewis	REKMR (1)	Joined 1904	Part of SEMB (2)
CHB Marsham	West Kent Yeomanry	Joined 1906	Part of SEMB
JR Tylden	REKMR	Joined 1909	Part of SEMB
K Barlow	REKMR	Joined 1911	Part of SEMB
CE Hatfeild	REKMR	Joined 1913	Part of SEMB

1. REKMR the Royal East Kent Mounted Rifles
2. SEMB the South Eastern Mounted Brigade

The South Eastern Mounted Brigade was a Yeomanry Brigade formed as part of the Territorial Force (TF) in 1908 by the Haldane Reforms. As with the rest of the TF, its members were under no obligation to serve overseas. Prior to the war only 7% of TF men had signed the obligation as an advance agreement to serve overseas, but in August 1914 all were asked again. Returns varied from unit to unit, and although there were few cases of all the men agreeing, there was generally a good response. The cricketers in the Kent Yeomanry all responded with a 'yes', as did Hervey Lawrence with the Suffolks. The men who did agree were formed into 1st line units e.g. the 1/1st West Kent Yeomanry, and those who were unwilling were formed into new 2nd and 3rd line units for training and use as depots e.g. the 2/1st REKMR and 3/1st Kent Cyclist battalions. When the SEMB was posted to Gallipoli, it was made up of the first line units of the REKMR, the West Kent Yeomanry and the Sussex Yeomanry.

Indian Army
Shumshere Singh was serving as a Captain with the Indian Medical Service at the time war was declared, although his precise whereabouts are not known.

VOLUNTEERS
Despite popular opinion that the war would be over by Christmas, Field Marshal Lord Kitchener, the Minister of State for War, believed it would take at least three years to defeat the German forces. The famous 'Your Country Needs You' and 'Your Country Wants You' posters bearing his image were part of a recruitment drive for volunteers that ended only when conscription was introduced in 1916. Initially there was no shortage of candidates,

the first few months seeing the greatest patriotic surge of men enlisting, and it was during those months, August to November 1914, that most of Kent's cricketers stepped forward. In time, when more recruits were needed, the age and height limits were extended and the initial call for single men was relaxed to include married men. At the outset volunteers had to be between 19 and 30 years old, but by 1916 this was 18 to 41 years, and in April 1918 a further extension took the upper age limit to 50 years.

A recruitment poster that appeared in the Kent Messenger in August 1914. Image Courtesy Kent Messenger.

Although not actually serving prior to the War, future Kent Captain Johnny Evans had been identified as a suitable candidate for the Intelligence Corps, and was commissioned just two days after Britain joined the fray. He seems to have been the first of our men to have landed in France, some days before any of the Regulars embarked with the BEF.

Only three of our volunteer cricketers actually accompanied the BEF to France before the end of 1914. In addition to Evans, Jack Bryan enlisted as a Private in the Honorable Artillery Company and Barry Cumberlege was commissioned in the ASC and joined the supply column of the new Third Cavalry Division as it was sent to relieve Antwerp. Most other men underwent months of training with their new units and did not see action until 1915. Similarly the men of the Yeomanry who had volunteered to serve overseas were put through a long period of training to bring them to battle readiness, most waiting almost a year before departing for Gallipoli.

Some volunteers joined the Territorial Force, although this was not actively encouraged as Kitchener was seeking to build completely new armies rather than expand what already existed. The threat of invasion was however a serious concern and Territorial units were required for Home defence, whilst regular troops were used to form the BEF. Some who joined Territorial units also signed to serve overseas, Con Johnstone and Frank Tuff amongst them. In 1915 John le Fleming and Gerry Weigall, both well into their forties, joined the Kent Cyclist Battalion which was a part of the TF, serving with the second and third line to train and recruit younger volunteers and Geoffrey Foster did likewise with the East Riding Yeomanry. A number of Kent's cricketers joined the Kent Fortress Engineers (KFE), another branch of the territorials; Colin Blythe, David Jennings, Claud Woolley, Henry Preston, Bill Fairservice and Arthur Povey probably selected the KFE for no reason other than they were recruiting in their home town of Tonbridge, although all had skills useful to the regiment.

Men volunteered where they were living, working, attended school or were born: Ken Hutchings the Liverpool Regiment, George Wood the Gloucestershire Regiment, Charles Marriott the Lancashire Fusiliers and Freddie Knott the Wiltshire Regiment being good examples. Former soldiers were called upon to add much needed experience in Kitchener's New Army battalions, and Arthur Corbett Edwards, who had resigned his commission in 1901, was recalled to the Royal West Kent Regiment and granted the rank of Temporary Captain. At the other end of the spectrum, age limit restrictions prevented Ronnie Bryan from enlisting, although once he turned 17 he was eligible for the TF which had a lower minimum age requirement. He was posted to a 'Provisional' battalion, manned by those too young, or not fit enough to serve overseas, and once he came of age he joined a regular battalion to serve in France.

The number of volunteers dried up during 1915, Douglas Carr being one of Kent's last when he joined the Army Ordnance Department in September, although Walpole might count as the last as he took his medical to join the Inns of Court OTC during December. As a last ditch attempt to avoid the introduction of conscription, men were encouraged to join the Derby Scheme, whereby those eligible to serve could register to be called up as and when required. Dick Blaker, Ernest Simpson and Erasmus Willson, all outside of the original age restrictions, but eligible following the extension of the upper limit, enlisted during the period the Derby Scheme ran. They were attested as Privates in the Reserve and were then sent home, to be posted a few months into 1916. Arthur Day and Arthur Snowden both followed the same route, Day not mobilized until January 1917 and Snowden even later, in June 1918. The scheme was unsuccessful in engaging the numbers required and the Military Services Act subsequently introduced conscription in 1916, so ending the process of volunteering as the first batch of conscripts were summonsed in March.

As has been noted, the territorial soldiers were under no obligation to serve overseas, at least not until conscription was introduced. When that happened in 1916, the territorial men were required to sign an Imperial Service obligation to serve abroad, putting them on an equal footing with the conscripts.

Before leaving the subject of volunteering, it should be remembered that the call to the colours was answered across the Empire and elsewhere. Charles Worthington, who had emigrated to British Colombia, joined the Canadian Expeditionary Force in 1916 at the age of 39 and fought in France. Gerard Simpson, who was living in Argentina, returned to England and joined the RFA to serve in France. Volunteers of another kind also stepped forward. Frederick Leney was older than the maximum age limit for military service and instead joined the British Red Cross. He was 39 years old when he arrived in France in January 1915. Bernard and Raymond Bannon, also exceeded the age limit and joined the French Red Cross as ambulance drivers, subsequently serving in France. Richard Thornton put them all to shame when he volunteered for the French Red Cross at the age of 61 and converted his own car into an ambulance which he drove across France in June 1915. Other men served at home with the Volunteer Training Corps, which was a sort of 'Dad's Army' raised independently of the Army, and funded voluntarily. Lord Harris commanded the Kent contingent, and John le Fleming spent the first seven months of the war as an instructor with the VTC before joining the Kent Cyclists. Jack Hubble also spent time with the VTC after failing his medical.

OFFICERS AND OTHER RANKS

In the early part of the War officers were almost exclusively recruited with a Public School background, and the lower ranks from humbler beginnings. So it was that the amateur cricketers generally sought commissions, whilst the professionals enlisted in the ranks.

Amateurs and the Public Schools (Officers)

Many of the amateurs were able to obtain the commissions they sought straight away, but the natural home of the professional players, 'the ranks', was also the starting point for a number of players of officer material. Initially there were simply not enough officer vacancies available to appoint men to, and many joined units in the rank of Private and sought commissions as they became available. Jack Bryan seems to have been the only Kent player to have fought in the line both in the ranks and as an officer.

Three of Kent's amateurs who volunteered. Marsham (centre), already serving with the Yeomanry, quickly signed to serve overseas, whilst Troughton (left) and Dillon (right) enlisted in the same battalion of the Royal Fusiliers in September 1914

Public School Battalions found themselves in the odd position of having thousands of potential officers serving in the ranks, the Royal Fusiliers being a good example. The huge numbers of volunteers saw that particular regiment form four Public Schools Battalions at Epsom in September 1914; the 18th, 19th, 20th and 21st Battalions. Initially serving with 18th Battalion as Privates were Dillon, Troughton and Sydney Day, two of the three ultimately obtaining commissions in other regiments. The vacancies for commissions that did become available were partly a result of the deaths of so many young men in France and Flanders as the fighting continued, but also from the building of Kitchener's New Armies. These were each 100,000 men strong and are often referred to as K1, K2, K3, K4 and K5.

The creation of each one brought new opportunities for men to apply for commissions. The transition of men from Private to Officer continued throughout the War. In August 1915 William Hutchings enlisted as a Private whilst seeking a commission, and Charles Worthington, having joined the CEF in 1916 and fought in France as a Private, later put his medical training to good use by obtaining a commission into the Canadian Army Medical Corps. From early 1916 many other officer candidates passed through Officer Training Corps, training as Privates before being commissioned, including 'Derby Scheme' men Arthur Day, Dick Blaker and Ernest Simpson.

Junior officers, that is to say 2nd Lieutenants, Lieutenants and Captains, suffered appalling casualty rates which were higher in comparison to the men they were in charge of. They were typically first over the top, leading their men on the battlefield and on trench raids, performing reconnaissance and covering withdrawals. Whilst it is impossible to compare the casualty rates of the cricketers on the basis of junior officers versus other ranks, it can be seen from the numbers that died and were wounded, that they were certainly not employed in a safe role. Ten out of the sixteen players who died in service were junior officers killed in action. Two of them had returned to the front having recovered from previous wounds. Of the twenty-four men who were wounded in action, the vast majority were junior officers. Gerald Hough, Con Johnstone and Charles Rucker all survived being wounded twice.

Not all the men joined the Army, and some of the older players offered their services to the RNR and RNVR. Jack Mason and his brother James both served with the RNVR, whilst Arthur Fulcher and Charles Hooman opted for the RNR.

Public Schools and Universities – the OTCs

Many of the cricketers were educated at the top schools of the country, and a good number attended Oxford and Cambridge. As a result of the Haldane Reforms, most of these schools and the Universities had their own Officer Training Corps (OTC) which was designed to give young men a taste of the military. Jack Bryan wrote that when he joined the Honourable Artillery Company as a Private in 1914 he had received a Certificate A from Rugby OTC, making him more experienced than most of the other ranks, who presumably came from a non-Public School background. James Tylden's WW2 papers refer to his having served in the Rugby School OTC circa 1906, but at that time it was the pre-Haldane Rifle Corps, forerunner to the OTC. Others who benefitted from OTC training included Leonard Powell at Loretto, George Whitehead in the Clifton Engineer Corps, Jack Capes at Malvern, Eric Bickmore also at Clifton, George Heslop in the Lancing College OTC, George Wood the Cheltenham College OTC, James Colquhoun the Glenalmond OTC and Charles Marriott first with St Columba and then Dublin University OTC. There were of course plenty more who had completed their education before the OTCs were introduced, but it is likely some had experience in the school cadet corps that preceded the OTC. Horace Walpole and Ted Dillon both passed through the Inns of Court OTC, which was originally part of the London Territorial Force and predominantly connected with men employed in the law courts.

Professionals and the Tonbridge Nursery (Other Ranks)

In addition to the amateurs biding their time waiting for a commission, quite a few of the professionals enlisted in the ranks. The men who came through the Tonbridge Nursery were engaged as 'Young Players', receiving coaching and providing services to the first team players, typically bowling at them. They were farmed out to play for other clubs in the County, who would pay their expenses, allowing them to gain valuable match experience. Many found their way into the 1st XI and, as we have seen, the seasoned players often took on coaching roles themselves. As paid employees of Kent County Cricket Club they found themselves under some pressure from their employer to answer the call to arms, and those who did not were written to by the Committee, requesting explanations. Volunteers were granted some financial incentive, in that the Club offered to make up the difference between what the men would have received as standard pay, and what they actually received in Army pay and allowances.

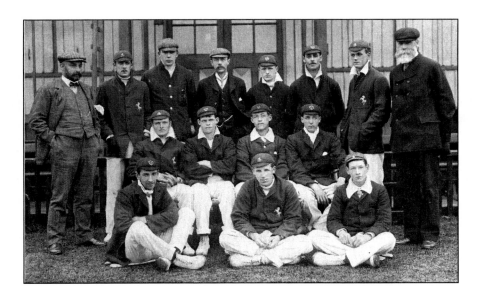

The Young Players and Professionals of the Kent Nursery circa 1906 including Fairservice, Hardinge, Fielder and Blythe in the back row, Seymour, Preston and the Woolley brothers seated middle row, and Hubble and Humphreys front.

Blythe, Jennings, Preston and Claud Woolley enlisted together in the Kent Fortress Engineers (KFE), all of them products of the Nursery and good friends. These men, and the others who lived in and around Tonbridge, not only played cricket together. Local newspapers carried regular reports of their exploits in the local Tonbridge football team. Jennings' brother Thomas, who trialled for Kent but later played for Surrey, joined the four Kent players at the recruiting office, and Charles Woolley, the brother of Claud and Frank, enlisted in the KFE about ten days later. Arthur Povey and Bill Fairservice were to follow suit in the coming months, Povey actually recruited by Colin Blythe.

KENT CRICKETERS JOIN THE ENGINEERS.

The first cricketers to enlist with the Kent Fortress Engineers. From Left to Right: Thomas Jennings, Henry Preston, David Jennings, Colin Blythe and Claud Woolley. Reproduced by the kind permission of Fraser Beale

Fred Lowe became the only Young Player to join the mobilization of the BEF, and also became the first casualty amongst the County's cricketers when killed near Armentières in October. Three players quickly joined the Royal West Kent (RWK) Regiment, Charles Wycherley enlisting in September, and Bill Hickmott and Alex Smith in the first weeks of the war. The younger players were unable to volunteer immediately due to the age restrictions, but later in the war Archie Haywood joined the Kent Cyclist Battalion (KCB), Ernest Dilnot the Royal Artillery and Bill Ashdown the Rifle Brigade. Horace Taylor, who played for Kent after the war, volunteered with the West Kent Yeomanry in August 1914 and served under Cloudesley Marsham.

Kent legend Frank Woolley is known to have attempted to join his brothers and fellow cricketers in the KFE, but was turned down for medical reasons, eventually being accepted to join the Royal Naval Air Service toward the end of 1916. This was after conscription was introduced, but as he was medically exempt he effectively volunteered again. The Dutnall brothers, Frank and William, volunteered and served on the Home Front. Frank joined the Buffs in 1915, employed as a clerk in the Cavalry Record Office, and his brother William seems not to have attested until 1917 when he joined the RGA. His papers reveal he suffered the same problem as Frank Woolley, namely compacted toes, and that he actually applied to follow Frank into the RNAS before being posted to the Artillery. With a C grade medical category it is likely he had applied earlier in the war but was judged to be unfit. The Military Service (Review of Exceptions) Act 1917 reviewed men previously classed as unfit, and the timing makes it probable Dutnall was recalled for a further medical and passed fit for Home Service at the second time of trying.

It is not clear when Ted Humphreys volunteered. He had two service numbers, one for the RNVR and the other a replacement for when he was called up for service, but no date is given other than that for his RN service commencing in February 1917. Percy Morfee was conscripted into the RFC in 1916, Stevens Brown the Navy in 1918 and Percy Baker the Army in April 1918, the extended age limits finally catching up with the three men. Wally Hardinge was one of those written to by the Club enquiring as to his support for the colours, and he volunteered for and served with the RNAS from 1915. Several players who did not pass through the Tonbridge Nursery also served as 'Other Ranks'. Percy Baker and Arthur Snowden had both attended Public School but neither man was commissioned, age and/or medical categorization the likely reasons. Baker did not enlist until 1918 when, aged 44, he joined the 18th Essex and then transferred to the RASC, whilst Snowden joined the Inns of Court OTC as a Private in December 1915. Erasmus Willson, who was 36 in 1914, joined the 2nd battalion London Regiment in December 1915. These last two men, Snowden and Willson, joined through the Derby scheme, enlisting just before conscription was introduced.

Of the players the Club wrote to early in 1915, Frank Woolley, Fairservice, Humphreys and Hardinge all went on to serve, but there were others who did not. Age, height, fitness and marital status were all factors. Fred Huish was 45 at the end of 1914, well over the age limit, and only just inside when it was increased to 50 years in 1918. 'Tich' Freeman was unsurprisingly under the standard height, and also explained to the Committee that he had a wife and child to keep. James Seymour also had marital responsibilities and a motor business in Pembury to look after, whereas Jack Hubble cited a variety of reasons in his response to the Club, and had failed his medical. Arthur Fielder joined the Kent Constabulary as an auxiliary policeman, and it seems that Freeman, Seymour and Hubble served as Special Constables, and Hubble also spent time in the Volunteer Training Corps. Seymour was to join the RAF later in the war.

RMA, RMC AND THE NAVAL COLLEGE

Under war conditions, and with most of our men volunteering for the duration of hostilities, the majority who were given commissions went straight into service. There were some exceptions who passed through the Royal Military Academy at Woolwich and the Royal Military College at Sandhurst. Woolwich gave more of a technical grounding and was typically where men of the Royal Engineers and Artillery were schooled, whereas Sandhurst trained officers for the more traditional regiments. In the pre-war years Everard Blair, Arthur du Boulay, Lovick Friend and Walter Coote Hedley all passed through RMA Woolwich and joined the Royal Engineers on leaving. Cornwallis and Robert Livesay had passed through Sandhurst before gaining their commissions into the Scots Greys and Royal West Surrey Regiment.

During the war Charles Fawcus and George Whitehead passed through the RMA into the Artillery, and Bernard Howlett and Jack Capes both through the RMC into the Royal West Kent Regiment. In the same way that some post-war University degree courses were shortened, so too were courses held at the RMA and RMC. This was in part due to the ability to train men for a specific war, and not a wide range of military deployments, but also it was not feasible to wait so long for men to be trained. Whereas Capes passed through Sandhurst in six months and Whitehead passed through Woolwich in about eight months, in the pre-war years du Boulay had spent almost two years at Woolwich. Several men also spent time as Instructors at the colleges. When LJ le Fleming had recovered from his second Blighty wound he was appointed commander of an intake of cadets at Sandhurst. Livesay and Blair had been Instructors there, pre-war, and Friend had held a similar role at the RMA during which time he was in charge of Cadets Haig, Rawlinson and Maude.

Cricketers undoubtedly prefer dry land to play on, but Sidney Boucher, who would play a single game for Kent after the war, had chosen a life on the seas for his career. He was at the Royal Naval College Osbourne in 1914, moving to the RN College at Dartmouth a month after fighting broke out, and was appointed a Midshipman in 1915 at which time he joined the Grand Fleet. Other Kent players served with the various branches of the Navy, but Boucher was the only RN Officer among them.

CONSCRIPTION

Once conscription was introduced, younger men leaving school or university had no choice but to enlist. These are obviously men who appeared for Kent after the War was over, and include among their number Jack Capes who was age 18 in 1916, passing from the Malvern OTC into the RMC Sandhurst and then commissioned to the RWK. Bernard Howlett who turned 18 at the end of 1916 also went into Sandhurst in 1917 and like Capes was commissioned in the RWK. Charles Fawcus came of age in 1916 and passed through Woolwich to join the Royal Garrison Artillery. Sandhurst and Woolwich were one route to a commission, but men could alternatively pass through the OTCs, as Blaker, Arthur Day, Ernest Simpson and Walpole did. It has already been mentioned that Percy Morfee, Stevens Brown and Percy Baker were conscripts, and Seymour appears to have also been conscripted to serve with the RAF. Thomas Hugh Pitt Beeching also deserves a mention. He was to appear in the Kent XI 1920-21, and passed through Sandhurst in 1918 but was not commissioned into the RWK until after the Armistice. He went on to serve with distinction in Italy during WW2.

CHAPTER TWO:
WHO DID THEY SERVE WITH?

Kent's cricketers served in the Army, Navy and Air Force in a variety of roles, although predominantly in the Infantry, and their ranks stretched from lowly Private to appointments as Staff Officers. For a variety of reasons many served in more than one regiment and others in more than one service. The majority served with the British forces, but a small number were involved with the ANZACs, the New Zealand Division, the Indian Cavalry, the Indian Army Medical Corps and the Canadian Expeditionary Force.

HEADQUARTERS AND STAFF OFFICERS

The British Forces were divided into various units, and the Order of Battle of the Army describes that structure. At the very top was the GHQ, and this cascaded down through Armies, Corps, Divisions, Brigades, Battalions, Companies, Platoons and Sections to the individual soldiers. Kent's cricketers served on the HQ's at all levels and in many different theatres of war. Around a dozen served on battalion HQ's of whom Troughton, Hervey Lawrence, the le Fleming brothers, Dillon, Penn and Livesay all spent time as Commanding Officers. Livesay and Lawrence both commanded Brigades, and eight men served with Divisional HQs. The Corps HQs were also well represented and du Boulay and Livesay both served with Army HQs. At the top of the tree each force had its own GHQ, one for each of the Home Force, British Expeditionary Force (BEF), Egyptian Expeditionary Force (EEF), Mesopotamian Expeditionary Force, Salonika Army and so on. The Egyptian Expeditionary Force was for some time split into Eastern Force and Western Force, dealing with operations either side of the Suez Canal. Blair was with Eastern Force HQ in Egypt, Leach-Lewis with Western Force and later with EEF HQ, as was Ted Dillon when he joined the Intelligence Department in 1917. Sarel, Hedley and Harington were all employed at some time with the War Office, the GHQ in London.

CAVALRY

In August 1914 the cavalry contingent of the BEF consisted of a single division made up of four brigades, plus a separate independently operating fifth brigade. By the end of 1914 there were five cavalry divisions available. The 2nd Cavalry Division was established in France during September, and the 3rd Division was created in England, crossing the Channel during October. The two Divisions of the Indian Cavalry Corps also arrived in

France during October, and were officially renamed the 4th and 5th Divisions towards the end of 1916.

Frank Penn served with the 1st, 2nd and 3rd Cavalry Divisions at different times, Francis Marsham with the 1st and 2nd, Stanley Cornwallis with the 2nd and Barry Cumberlege with the supply column to the 3rd. Herbert Hatfeild arrived in France from India with the 1st Indian Cavalry Division which was later renamed the 4th Cavalry Division. All the men were in France before the end of 1914, and Penn, Cornwallis and Hatfeild had to learn to play a dual role, in mounted or dismounted capacity depending on the situation. In fact many men of the cavalry and yeomanry found themselves in the trenches acting in an infantry role and some, including Penn, were converted to Machine Gun units later in the war when that weapon came to the fore. Although tanks and aeroplanes also changed the way armies operated, the cavalry were still a valued resource, in particular when the fighting became mobile. They were used far more effectively in the eastern theatres of war where the front was mobile, and were also vital to the success in Afghanistan in 1919, where Hatfeild's regiment was in the thick of the action. Edward Fulcher volunteered and joined the cavalry in 1914, but was not posted to France until the autumn of 1916 when he joined the 11th Hussars in the field. Back in England, Frank Dutnall was employed with the Cavalry Records Office at Canterbury, administering the affairs of the Dragoons and Lancers regiments.

YEOMANRY

The Yeomanry was the territorial arm of the Cavalry, although few had the opportunity to fight as anything but infantry. A number of the men covered by this book were pre-war members of the East and West Kent Yeomanry, and Geoffrey Foster was to volunteer with the East Riding regiment during October. All of the cricketers of the Yeomanry began their war at Gallipoli except Barlow, who remained in the UK as second in command of the 3/1st East Kent, and Foster who served on the Home Front as Adjutant with a second line battalion until proceeding overseas at the end of 1917.

Notes on the South Eastern Mounted Brigade (SEMB)

The SEMB was created in 1908 as part of the Haldane Reforms, and formed part of the Territorial Force, drawing on units from Kent, Sussex and Surrey, including the East and West Kent Yeomanry. On 4 August the orders to mobilize were received, and the squadrons of both of Kent's Yeomanry Regiments began to gather at their individual headquarters. The four squadrons of the Queen's Own West Kent Yeomanry (QOWKY), including Cloudesley Marsham, moved to Maidstone where they occupied a school. Parties were sent out to obtain mounts, and within three days the horses had been bought, collected and branded in the school orchard. Many had never been ridden which must have made for an interesting 35 mile journey to Canterbury on 9 August. Horace Taylor joined them there after enlisting at the end of the month. Meanwhile Barlow, Hatfeild, Tylden and Leach-Lewis were ordered to Canterbury with the Royal East Kent Mounted Rifles (REKMR) on 4 August, to concentrate in the Broad Oak area. The Secretary of State for War, Viscount Milner, owned Sturry Court, and soon gave over the house and grounds to the use of the Regiment. Equipment was scarce as the BEF had priority for most of what was available, and the REKMR was not fully equipped and mounted until October. By then both Kent Regiments had lost men who transferred to obtain commissions, and those who did not agree to serve overseas, were used to form the new second line. Third line units were also formed, and Barlow served with the 3/1 REKMR.

Cloudesley Marsham (centre) with two fellow officers – prior to being posted to Gallipoli. Reproduced by permission of Kent & Sharpshooters Yeomanry Museum

There followed a period of training and work on coastal defences, and Marsham and Taylor's regiment moved into newly erected huts at Westbere. The men were keen to get to grips with the enemy and during the summer they agreed to serve overseas as dismounted troops if required. During May the SEMB Sports were held at Canterbury, attended by Lord Harris and leading families of the county. The competition was keen, and the REKMR carried off the prize for Best Troop under Lieutenant Tylden. Frank Tuff was commissioned into the REKMR during June, and in September orders were issued to prepare to move, and equipment was issued. This included sun hats which would have given the cricketers some idea of where they were headed. On 22 September the SEMB travelled to Liverpool by train to embark on the White Star liner the "*SS Olympic*", an older sister of the "*Titanic*", and within two days were sailing towards the Mediterranean. At that time there was nothing to stop the men smoking on deck or singing and there was no proper black out. Their destroyer escort, leaving them at Gibraltar, messaged "Good bye and good luck. You are looking like a gin palace!"

Spirits were undoubtedly high, but the cricketers soon found just how serious the war was about to become when the liner stopped to pick up the survivors of a French trawler, sunk by a German submarine. Only two hours later they narrowly missed being hit by a torpedo themselves. If this ship had been lost it would have been a severe blow, and not only to Kent CCC. There were 8,000 men on board, practically all that were to make up the 74th (Yeomanry) Division. The ship arrived at Mudros on 2 October and the two Kent Regiments were soon directed to Gallipoli. Marsham and Tylden both initially stayed at Mudros with the Yeomanry Base Depot, whilst the main force landed on 7 October, disembarking at Lancashire Landing, Cape Helles. They heard the sounds and saw the flashes of exploding shells as they made their way to their bivouac area.

Frank Tuff was fatally wounded at Gallipoli, and when the Peninsula was evacuated at the end of the year the remaining men concentrated in Egypt to recover from the harsh conditions they had experienced. Tylden left to take up an appointment with 42nd Division HQ whilst the remaining cricketers found themselves involved in the Western Desert campaign against the Senussi tribe. When that was over they were ordered east of the Suez Canal as the British headed across the Sinai Desert to push back the Turkish forces, and press on into Palestine. The two Kent regiments were merged into a single battalion in early 1917, the 10th Buffs, or to give the full title, the 10th (Royal East and West Kent Yeomanry) Battalion, the Buffs. The creation of the new battalion brought the remaining cricketers under one umbrella, although around the time of the 2nd Battle of Gaza, Marsham left for England due to sickness, and two months later Leach-Lewis took up an appointment with the Eastern Expeditionary Force HQ. Eric Hatfeild and Horace Taylor fought on in Palestine, and were then ordered to France. When Taylor returned to England to enter a cadet course, Hatfeild was the only cricketer left. He was killed in action in September 1918.

INFANTRY

Although the Army had many component parts, it was the infantry that were needed to physically capture and occupy enemy territory, and they were needed in large numbers to do so. They held their own positions against determined attacks, were subjected to shelling, machine-gun fire, snipers, gas and flame throwers. They went over the top in attack and caught the enemy unawares during trench raids. They cleared enemy positions with rifles, pistols, bayonets, bombs, fists and feet. Sometimes they received the protection of the cavalry, tanks, aircraft and machine-gun fire, but on the ground they fought for their own lives, and the lives of the men they served with. Of all the branches of the forces, the infantry got their hands dirty more than anyone else. Almost thirty of the cricketers who volunteered served as infantry, a higher percentage than served with any other branch of the forces, and to that number can be added the cavalry who fought dismounted and the yeomanry who fought as infantry.

The regiments of Kent were well represented, in particular the Royal West Kent Regiment with which the following served: Eric Fulcher (1st Battalion), Charles Wycherley and Charles Capes (2nd Battalion), Ted Dillon (2/4th Battalion), Noël Boucher and Walter Monckton (3/4th Battalion), John le Fleming (4th Reserve Battalion), William Hickmott and Gerald de Lisle Hough (6th and 8th Battalions), Bernard Howlett (7th Battalion), Arthur Edwards (8th Battalion), James Whitehead (9th Battalion) and Alex Smith (Battalion unknown). Fewer served with the Buffs, initially just Fred Lowe and later in the war Eric Hatfeild, Cloudesley Marsham, Taylor and Leach-Lewis became members of the new 10th Battalion that was created from the Kent Yeomanry regiments.

Aside from the regiments of Kent, the cricketers represented a number of other regional units, joining up in the places they were schooled, living or working, whilst others joined more prestigious regiments. Colquhoun and Johnstone followed remarkably similar paths: both initially joined a County of London Battalion of the Territorial Force, signed an obligation to serve overseas, were commissioned into the Highland Light Infantry, were injured, returned to England to join HLI Reserve Battalions and underwent Medical Boards at Edinburgh. Other men served in the same battalions, such as Edwards and Hough, whose story is told in their joint entry in a later chapter. Five other cricketers served with the Rifle Brigade, three of them in the same battalion.

Notes on the Rifle Brigade

When war was declared Bill Sarel was serving with the 5th (Reserve) Battalion, a depot /

training unit, and he transferred to the 10th Battalion in November 1914. Lionel Troughton had answered the call to the colours and joined one of the University and Public School battalions, the 18th Battalion Royal Fusiliers, in September 1914. He obtained a commission into the 10th Battalion Rifle Brigade in March 1915, on the recommendation of Sarel, who knew him well. Charles Rucker joined the ranks of the 10th Battalion Royal Fusiliers in August 1914, and was commissioned into the Rifle Brigade in October, joining the 15th Battalion. He served in Gallipoli whilst attached to the 1st Battalion Royal Dublin Fusiliers, before returning to England as a casualty. Having recovered he joined the 10th Battalion Rifle Brigade in France during November 1915.

The 10th Battalion came into being as part of Kitchener's second New Army (K2) in mid-September 1914 hot on the heels of the first 100,000. After initial training the men were soon firing their first musketry courses at Blackdown, although restricted to two companies at a time due to shortage of rifles. By March 1915, when Troughton was commissioned, the battalion was training on Salisbury Plain and remained there until July when they received orders for France. Travelling by train from Amesbury to Folkestone, Sarel in command of half of the Battalion, they sailed to Boulogne and joined III Corps, settling into the line near Laventie in August. The men were not only linked by their service in the same battalion. By coincidence it was in the match between Kent and Oxford in 1914 that Troughton and Sarel made their highest first class scores, the game also marking Rucker's first class debut. The match is, however, more likely to be remembered for the debut of another Kent cricketer, 'Tich' Freeman.

The fourth Kent player to serve with the Rifle Brigade was Dick Blaker who joined the Army Reserve at the end of 1915. Posted to the 10th Battalion Royal West Kent Regiment, he obtained a commission into the Rifle Brigade in November 1916. Due to a debilitating attack of influenza he was destined to spend more time in hospital than at the front, but was eventually posted to the 13th Battalion, arriving in France in September 1918. Despite his war being short-lived, he still found time to earn the Military Cross. Bill Ashdown was the last to serve with the Rifle Brigade, enlisting once he was old enough to do so, and serving with a reserve battalion.

THE ROYAL ARTILLERY

Throughout the Great War the big guns churned up the landscape, typically during the long bombardments that preceded each major offensive. The Artillery that handled the heavy weaponry consisted of three branches, the Royal Horse Artillery (RHA), the Royal Field Artillery (RFA) and the Royal Garrison Artillery (RGA). Kent's cricketers served with each.

The RHA gave support to the cavalry with its light mobile guns, and the only Kent man falling under their command was Jack Bryan, but then only as part of one of the infantry battalions that the Honourable Artillery Company (HAC) supplied. Bryan's service with the HAC lasted only a few months before he was wounded and he was subsequently commissioned into the Manchester Regiment. The RFA brigades were responsible for the medium sized guns which were the largest by numbers, and typically horse-drawn. George Whitehead joined the RFA on leaving Woolwich in 1915, and was involved in the bombardments at Loos and the Somme. Eric Bickmore was commissioned into the RFA from Sandhurst in 1918, and posted to the 52nd Division Ammunition Column which carried the ammunition and artillery to where it was needed. Gerard Simpson joined the RFA in 1915 and was quickly posted to France, where he was attached to the RHA as part of the ammunition column of the 2nd Indian Cavalry Division.

The RGA began the war as a small formation as the Army did not have many large calibre guns but many more of these weapons were manufactured as the war progressed. Ernest Simpson was commissioned into the RGA Reserve in 1916 and, having gone through an anti-aircraft course, was posted to the 201st Anti-Aircraft Section on arrival in France, serving with several other AA Sections thereafter. Ernest Dilnot served with an RGA Siege Battery in France and Belgium, and William Hutchings served with the Army Service Corps Motor Transport, helping to move the big guns of a siege battery around. William Dutnall was also with the RGA in an Anti-Aircraft Brigade in the UK, and when Charles Fawcus passed out of Woolwich, he was commissioned into the RGA in late 1918 and served in India after the Armistice.

MACHINE GUN CORPS

Machine Guns were in use from the start of the war, but it took the British a little while to recognise the value of this particular weapon. Tactics were developed throughout the conflict, a Machine Gun Corps was created in 1915, and the weapons were developed to equip new Machine Gun Companies and Battalions. In the latter part of the war some cavalry and yeomanry units were converted to Machine Gun units as use of the weapon was increased. The machine-gun could be used to harass the enemy, whereby fire was trained on specific areas to prevent them moving freely, and could also be used to create barrages to cover Infantry advances or retreats. Some thought the thousands of rounds being sent over the horizon were a waste of time, but German statements after the war gave evidence to the contrary, confirming the devastating impact it had.

Jack Bryan was trained on machine-guns and, having been within the MG unit of his Manchester Battalion, was a prime candidate for the MG Company of his Brigade. Later in the war when cavalry and yeomanry units were converted, Geoffrey Foster found the East Riding Yeomanry merged into 102nd Battalion MGC, and when the Life Guards became the Guards MG Regiment, Frank Penn served with and then commanded the 4th Battalion. Harold Prest of the Berkshire Regiment was seconded to the Lewis Gun School in France in 1917, where he was Chief Instructor in teaching tactics to the recruits, and George Wood spent a short time as MG Officer with his Brigade at Gallipoli when the existing officer went sick.

Jack Bryan (seated centre) with the Machine Gun Company he commanded. His sleeve insignia show he was Lieutenant at the time, dating the photograph after August 1917, and in France or Belgium. Reproduced by the kind permission of Pat Bryan

ROYAL ENGINEERS

Perhaps amongst those not given as much credit as deserved, the RE was vital to all other branches of the Army. Providing the means for the war to be fought, they constructed roads, railways, bridges, all manner of structures, shelters and fortifications, established water supplies and were involved with signalling, transport, balloons and tunnels. They were very often involved in work on the front line, such as the bridging work undertaken during the last Hundred Days, and also some of the last to leave positions during a retreat when tasked with demolition work, as seen during the Retreat from Mons and again in spring of 1918 during the German *Kaiserschlacht* offensive.

Four of Kent's cricketers were with the RE prior to the War, but only Blair served overseas with them between 1914 and 1918, holding senior positions around work on the Suez canal defences, and overseeing the construction of the water pipeline toward Palestine. Walter Hedley ran the Geographical Section at the War Office, supplying maps of the front, Friend was otherwise engaged in Ireland, and du Boulay took on a Divisional HQ role. After Sydney Day recovered from wounds received in France, he was employed with the Inland Waterways and Docks section of the RE at Richborough, involved in the transportation of supplies to France. More of Kent's cricketers served with the Kent Fortress Engineers, a Territorial arm of the RE, and several went on to serve with RE Field Companies. Blythe and Claud Woolley were instead attached to the 12th King's Own Yorkshire Light Infantry, a Pioneer battalion that was used by the Fifth Army for work on light railways.

Notes on the Kent Fortress Engineers (KFE)

Among the first to volunteer for service after the outbreak of War were Colin Blythe, David Jennings, Henry Preston and Claud Woolley, who enlisted together in 1/1 Company of the Kent Fortress Engineers (KFE) at Tonbridge. During October, having had their initial training, the men were ordered to the 'Woodlands' Depot in Gillingham. Accompanying them was David Jennings' brother Thomas, who trialled for Kent but played for Surrey after the War, later becoming an umpire. The *Kent Messenger* recorded that Blythe proposed a sweepstake, the winner to be the first to secure promotion, and he would have won quite easily, being made Corporal within a fortnight. It was in fact Corporal Blythe that recruited Arthur Povey during January 1915, about the time the Club wrote to Kent's non-serving players. Povey's papers noted his trade as 'painter', as did those for Preston and Jennings, whereas Woolley was a 'fitter', and Blythe had trained with his father as an engineer. Another Tonbridge man, Bill Fairservice, was on the list of 'non-serving' players written to by the Club in early 1915 asking what they were doing to help. He did join the KFE but left for the Military Police several years later and did not serve overseas.

During September 1915 Blythe, Woolley and David Jennings, and possibly some of the others, were transferred to 2/7th Company, formed from the reserve company they initially joined. Their new unit was well prepared for them. In May an appeal had appeared in *the Kent & Sussex Courier* for old cricket balls to be sent to the Company which was based at Pier Road, Gillingham. There were ample opportunities for the men to play cricket in the summers of 1916 and 1917, and the KFE cricket side they formed included all the Kent men except Preston who departed for Gallipoli in September 1915. Blythe and Woolley were not posted overseas until September 1917, David Jennings in January 1918 and Povey April 1918. As the Fortress Engineers were part of the Territorial Force (TF), the men had initially signed up for one year of Home Service, or until the TF was disembodied, should the war last longer. The Military Services Act of January 1916 altered the landscape by introducing conscription and compulsory service overseas. This meant the Territorials were asked to sign Imperial Service Obligation forms, thereby agreeing to serve abroad as required. Most of the Kent men signed theirs at Minster in January 1916, although Preston had voluntarily signed his before the Act was introduced.

The Fortress Engineers stationed at home were part of "Southern Army Home Force" working on coastal defence, training and bridge building. The huge loss of life in the Battle of the Somme in 1916 gave rise to a desperate need to bolster the Armies in France and Flanders. RE units were looked to for likely candidates, not only for service with Field Companies, but also to fill the gaps in other regiments. In early 1917, some 5,000 RE Territorials were drafted and by August a further 8,000 were earmarked for transfer to needy units. The three original KFE Companies became RE Field Companies and were sent overseas, extra companies being raised to replace them. Blythe and Claud Woolley were attached to the King's Own Yorkshire Light Infantry (KOYLI), to use their engineer skills in work on light railways.

Of the Kent Fortress Engineers, Colin Blythe and David Jennings gave their lives for their country. Claud Woolley was injured by the same shell that killed Blythe, and saw further service in France before he returned home in 1919. Although Frank Woolley was found unfit when he first tried to enlist with the KFE, his brother Charles joined and was badly wounded at Gallipoli when serving in the same unit as Preston, and the fourth Woolley brother Frederick is also said to have served with the KFE, but remained in England working with his father. Preston survived Gallipoli and the campaigns in Egypt, Palestine and Syria, and Povey returned safely from service in France during 1918.

SUPPLY LINES

The sourcing, procuring, storing and issuance of arms, ammunition and all other equipment, was dealt with by the Army Ordnance Department (AOD) and Army Ordnance Corps (AOC), the former being for officers and the latter for soldiers. The stores in England were predominantly at Woolwich, but later spread elsewhere as the huge volumes produced required greater space. Didcot was one of the new stores and Douglas Carr spent some time there, although he was initially posted to Egypt, where he served with the AOD. Carr later came under the command of the RAOC (Royal Army Ordnance Corps) when the AOD and AOC merged in 1918.

The logistics of moving men and materials to the front were huge. The Army Service

Corps (ASC) was tasked with operating Base Depots, transporting men and horses, and running mechanical transport parks and ammunition parks amongst other things. Barry Cumberlege was with the Mechanical Transport (MT) in France and Belgium, whilst Percy Baker and Frederick Hutchings did similar work on the Home Front. William Hutchings was also with the MT but attached to the Royal Garrison Artillery, helping to move the big guns, and Eric Bickmore served with 52nd Divisional Artillery Column, transporting ammunition to forward positions. James Mason served with the Forage Committee of the ASC, procuring supplies for men and horses.

TRAINING BATTALIONS AND TRAINING SCHOOLS

With the introduction of conscription, a system of training officers was required. February 1916 saw the introduction of that system, by which all candidates were required to have served in the ranks or passed through an Officer Training Corps (OTC), and then attended a four month course at one of the Officer Cadet Battalions (OCB). The OCBs were also referred to as Officer Training Battalions (OTBs), were numbered 1-24 and located throughout the UK. There were also another half a dozen Officer Cadet Schools specifically dedicated to the Artillery. A number of Kent's cricketers served with, or passed through, these training units.

Those who passed through the training battalions before being commissioned were Dick Blaker, Arthur Day, Ernest Simpson, Eric Bickmore and Walpole, whereas Horace Taylor was in the middle of his course when the war ended and was demobilized without completing the course. Arthur Day had trained with the Garrison OTB at Jesus College, Cambridge and subsequently became an officer with No.15 OTB at Romford, this being the 2/28th London Regiment (Artists Rifles). He was later joined by Erasmus Willson who served as a Private with the same unit. Arthur Snowden served with No.14 OTB, which was the Inns of Court OTC, based at Berkhamstead, and Con Johnstone became an instructor with No.6 OTB at Balliol College, Oxford after he had recovered from his second 'Blighty' wound.

Men also continued to train as officers at RMC Sandhurst and RMA Woolwich throughout the war, and when Lawrence le Fleming returned to England to recover from his second wound, he was recalled to Sandhurst and trained cadets for 18 months until returning to France in 1917. Other players were employed at specialist training facilities in France. As has already been noted, Harold Prest was Chief Instructor at the Lewis Gun School in France, and later instructed at the Lewis Gun Branch of the school at Quesques. Having been wounded with the Highland Light Infantry, James Colquhoun was appointed an Instructor at the Physical and Bayonet Training School at St. Pol and once the Americans began to arrive in France, Robert Livesay served for a time on the Staff at the American

Staff School that was established. After Noël Boucher had recovered from the wounds he received when his aeroplane was brought down, he became a flying instructor in England.

MEDICAL CORPS

The Great War brought casualty numbers to a level that shocked the nation as hospitals were quickly filled with the wounded and maimed returning from the front. A system was established whereby men were treated at a chain of medical facilities starting at the front, starting with assessment at aid posts. Those cricketers who were wounded passed along such a chain of medical stations, the worst cases returning to England for treatment of what became known as 'Blighty' wounds.

Whilst there were no Kent players with the Royal Army Medical Corps (RAMC), Charles Worthington served with the Canadian contingent (CAMC) and Kanwar Shumshere Singh with the Indian Medical Service. Details of Singh's service have not been found, but Worthington had initially served on the Western Front with the Canadian infantry, before obtaining a commission in the CAMC. He spent some time treating casualties in England before returning to the front in 1918, where he was attached to a Canadian Division as a Medical Officer during the 100 Days Offensive.

RED CROSS

Four Kent players served with the Red Cross, Frederick Leney the British Red Cross and the Bannon brothers and Richard Thornton the French Red Cross. They were all over the maximum age for volunteers in 1914 and decided to offer their services in another way. The British Red Cross raised funds to provide transport for the wounded, to organise convalescent homes and to help supply hospitals. They also set up centres to record those wounded and missing in France, and this is where Leney fitted in. He acted as a searcher in France and then Egypt, visiting hospitals to interview patients and trying to trace those men missing in action, something the Red Cross still does to this day. Bernard and Raymond Bannon became ambulance drivers in France, and both worked through the horrors of the Battle of Verdun during which it is estimated there were close to a million casualties, half of them French. Thornton served with the French Red Cross for almost four months in 1915 at the age of 61.

ROYAL NAVY

Sidney Boucher, Stevens Brown, and Ted Humphreys were the three Kent men who served with the Royal Navy during the war. Boucher had been studying at the RN College prior to the war, and joined *HMS Colossus* on appointment as Midshipman in 1915. Much of the naval activity reviewed took place around, or close to, the British Isles because the British

Navy effectively blocked in the German Navy by sealing off the Channel and the North Sea. Boucher spent most of his war stationed in Scapa Flow, and took part in the Battle of Jutland in 1916. Ted Humphreys served on the Coastal Motor Boats that were part of the Dover Patrol, preventing the enemy using the Channel. He found himself involved in the raids on Zeebrugge and Ostend in 1918. Brown only served from July 1918 when the upper age of conscription was lifted far enough to include him, and he was based at Stratford for the duration of his service.

RNVR AND RNR

When it was created in 1859 the Royal Naval Reserve (RNR) was made up of professional seamen from the merchant navy and fishing fleets, and later took in trainee officers, whereas the Royal Naval Volunteer Reserve (RNVR) mainly comprised civilian volunteers who had no naval experience. Arthur Fulcher and Charles Hooman both served with the RNR, and whereas Fulcher had plenty of sailing experience it is not apparent what experience Hooman had, if any. Fulcher spent time on patrols in the Hebrides, a part of the blockade, whilst Hooman also served on armed ships which were used to stop and search neutral shipping. The Mason brothers, James and Jack, both served with the RNVR although James transferred to the Army Service Corps after spending a few months with an anti-aircraft unit. Jack Mason did not actually begin his service until 1917 when he joined the Hydrophone service, using underwater listening devices to trace German submarines. Raymond Bannon also transferred to the RNVR after serving with the Red Cross.

RNAS

Two Kent men served with the Royal Naval Air Service (RNAS), but neither flew, being involved in other sides of the service instead. Wally Hardinge joined in 1915 and served as a mechanic, for some time with the Armoured Car Division. Frank Woolley, having failed to pass his medical to join the Fortress Engineers, was adjudged fit by the Navy and joined the RNAS in 1916. He served on a motor boat, picking up downed airmen from the sea, before being stationed at Queensferry where he saw out the war in the employment of Admiral Sir John de Robeck who had played for Devon and MCC. When the RNAS and RFC were merged to form the RAF in 1918, both Hardinge and Woolley were transferred to the new service.

ROYAL FLYING CORPS AND ROYAL AIR FORCE

Three Kent players actually flew with the RFC/RAF, although quite a few more served under the force toward the end of the war as it was expanded. Johnny Evans, Noël Boucher and George Whitehead all began serving with other units and later trained to fly. Percy

Morfee joined the RFC as a conscript and served in France as an air mechanic. Frank Woolley and Hardinge were automatically transferred into the RAF from the RNAS in April 1918, and Cloudesley Marsham, Charles Marriott, James Seymour and Bill Sarel all served in the RAF in England toward the end of hostilities.

CHAPTER THREE:
THEATRES OF WAR

The mention of WW1 usually stirs images of men fighting in the trenches on the Western Front, of mud and water-filled shell holes, and of men going over the top. The Western Front was without a doubt the largest theatre of war as far as British troops and Kent's cricketers were concerned, but other theatres of war also worthy of review. Some men served at Gallipoli, in Egypt, Palestine, Salonika, the Caucasus and Mesopotamia, and quite a few fought on more than one front. Rather than trying to combine the events of all the theatres of war into a single timeline, each one is treated individually, recording where each man played his part. It should be made clear that what follows is not a complete history of the war and all its theatres, but is simply intended to give some context as to the whereabouts of the cricketers during the conflict. The entries for each player's service will provide a chronological order of events for that individual.

WESTERN FRONT 1914

Our cricketers were involved from the off. Eight of them embarked for France by the end of the year, and three were wounded, one killed and another returned to England due to an accident, all in the space of a few months. The BEF were on the back foot from almost the moment they engaged the Germans, forced to retreat as the French withdrew, back from Mons to the Marne. Turning the tables they then forced the Germans back to the Aisne where the enemy dug in, and trench warfare began. The line quickly spread northwards in what was termed the Race to the Sea, and that line was fought over for the next four years. Our men were involved in all the major stages of the fighting up to the end of 1914, and the following year would see many more arrive, not only on the Western Front, but also on the other fronts that opened around the globe.

The BEF Lands in France

When they invaded France, the Germans were essentially following the *Schlieffen Plan*, the aim of which was to quickly defeat France in the west, to allow the movement of troops to meet any threat from Russia, so avoiding a war on two fronts. The British therefore needed to act quickly as German troops poured into France, and the British Expeditionary Force (BEF) was soon mobilised and started crossing the Channel. The British Army was highly trained, but numbered only around 250,000 men; small-fry in comparison to the large conscripted armies of France and Germany. Johnny Evans, a future Kent captain, was the first Kent player to arrive in France on 12 August, attached to the Intelligence Corps, a part of GHQ. The Expeditionary Force, drawn from the existing Regular Army in the UK, consisted of six Infantry Divisions and a Cavalry Division, plus support units such as artillery and supply columns. Due to fears that Germany might land an invasion force on the English coast, several Divisions were initially retained in the UK. The Cavalry Division consisted of four Brigades, and Frank Penn arrived in France on 16 August serving with 4th Brigade. There was also an additional independent 5th Cavalry brigade with which another future Kent captain, Stanley Cornwallis, arrived in France on 17 August.

Mons to the Marne

The BEF quickly pushed across France to meet up with the French forces. On reaching the Mons Canal on 23 August they were greeted with the news that the French Fifth Army was retiring, which left the British with no option but to do likewise. The BEF was soon engaged with the German forces, as they carefully retired in two columns, representing I Corps and II Corps, commanded by Douglas Haig and Horace Smith-Dorrien. Cornwallis was with the Scots Greys, tasked with protecting I Corps throughout the retreat, and Penn was with the Household Cavalry Composite Regiment, aligned with II Corps. Whilst I Corps crossed the River Sambre, II Corps was slowed down by congestion on the roads and bridges, and Smith Dorrien chose to make a stand at Le Cateau to buy time. Penn took part in the battle on 26 August in which the British force suffered heavy casualties, but achieved its objective in delaying the German advance. On the II Corps front the bridges over St Quentin Canal were blown and I Corps prepared to act similarly over the Sambre. Four long, bloody years were to follow before Penn crossed that river again, heading in the opposite direction.

The retreat continued across the Oise, and then the Aisne, but all the while the Allies continued to show dogged resistance, not allowing the enemy an easy advance. On 28 August the Scots Greys, including Cornwallis, and the 12th Lancers inflicted heavy losses on the Germans, and on 29 August the French made their own attack at St Quentin. The BEF reached the outskirts of Paris on 2 September, the whole force crossing the Marne, blowing bridges, and guarding crossing points, Cornwallis doing so at St Jean. At this point the retirement slowed down. The French counter-attacked on 5 September at the Battle of the Marne, and the Germans now made a tactical error. Although approaching Paris in accordance with the *Schlieffen Plan*, they swerved away to try and envelop the retreating French forces, and in doing so exposed their right flank. After a long retreat the Allies seized their chance and made a rapid advance. The Germans, themselves now in danger of encirclement, beat a hasty retreat to the River Aisne.

The Battle of the Marne gave some idea of the scale of the fighting to come, with 2 million men clashing on the battlefield, and over five hundred thousand casualties across both sides. On 8 and 9 September the Allies secured crossings over the Marne, Penn crossing at Azy and Cornwallis leading his squadron in the advance back toward the Aisne. Francis Marsham landed in France about this time, and seems to have joined the staff of one of the cavalry brigades. By 14 September most of the BEF had crossed the river but found the Germans had dug in to face them. Cornwallis was wounded in the fighting that followed, and returned to England to recover, that same day marking the stabilisation of the battle line. Fred Lowe, now in France with the Buffs in 6th Division, was involved in the fighting at Vailly, and Penn in that near Pargnan. Sir John French, Commander of the BEF instructed his force to dig in – the nature of the war was about to change from mobile to static.

News that Cornwallis was wounded appeared in 'The Graphic' at the end of September 1914, his picture middle right

Race to the Sea

The next stage of the war became known as the 'Race to the Sea', a series of attempts by each side to outflank the other, extending the front line all the way to the coast. The fighting from 25 September to 18 October included the Battles of Albert, Artois, La Bassee, Messines, Armentières, and Yser. Fred Lowe was killed on 18 October in fighting near Beaucamp Ligny, south of Armentières, the first Kent player to give his life during the war. Lawrence le Fleming reported for duty with the 1st East Surrey Regiment during October and was wounded during the Battle of La Bassee just three days after his arrival. As the Race to the Sea headed north, the front reached Ypres, just inside the Belgian border. Ypres was strategically important, being the last point protecting the ports of Calais and Boulogne, and this area saw some of the most severe fighting over the next four years. It fell under British command when the BEF was relocated from the Aisne to Flanders to hold the extreme left of the Allied line in early October.

Ypres

The famous Ypres Salient was created during the First Battle of Ypres (19 October – 22 November) after which the Germans held the high ground on three sides of the city, a position they maintained for most of the war. As the fighting raged, Penn was in the trenches at Messines and Wytschaete during the second half of October and into November. Barry Cumberlege arrived in Belgium in October with the Motor Transport Section of the 3rd Cavalry Division, sent to assist the city of Antwerp which was under siege. Antwerp fell before they arrived and the Division instead found itself taking part in the fighting around Ypres, including the Battles of Langemarck, Gheluvelt and Nonne Bosschen. Despite numerous attacks, the line was somehow held. Away from the Ypres front, Jack Bryan arrived in France with the Honourable Artillery Company during September. After a period of training he moved up to the line, and was wounded by a shell fragment north of La Bassee on 14 November, and was evacuated to England.

Those men of the BEF who saw service up to 22 November, the end of First Ypres, were recognised after the war as being eligible for the 1914 Star medal. Those who survived the war would call themselves the 'Old Contemptibles', a reference to the Kaiser's reported description of General French's 'contemptible little army'. From the end of Ypres through the winter of 1914-1915 the front line stabilised, reinforcements arrived from England, and India Corps arrived from the East. Herbert Hatfeild arrived in France as part of the latter on 10 November, with the 1st King's (Dragoon) Guards (1st KDG) in the 1st Indian Cavalry Division.

Winter 1914/1915

As winter set in, both sides set about reinforcing their positions and more men headed across the Channel. John Tufton joined 6th Division HQ in February, and Robert Livesay reported to 48th Division HQ in March. Le Fleming returned to France, still with the East Surrey Regt., but now commanding the 2nd Battalion, whilst Cornwallis and Evans also re-joined their units in France during December, Cornwallis having recovered from his wounds, and Evans from a motorcycle accident at the end of September. In a non-military capacity, Frederick Leney joined the Red Cross and travelled to France in January 1915 acting as a searcher. Operations were kept up against the enemy during these months, but there were no major offensives.

WESTERN FRONT 1915

The year 1915 was to see offensives launched by both sides, and our expanding group of fighting cricketers were involved in the two Allied Offensives, Neuve Chapelle and Loos, and also the German offensive that became Second Ypres. At the end of the year two had been killed, four wounded, and one returned to England suffering shell shock. For Penn and Cumberlege the year started in the miserable trenches of Flanders where the land was low lying and sub-surface water rose rapidly in wet weather, making the trenches difficult to drain. The conditions could however, be just as challenging elsewhere. During January Herbert Hatfeild was in the trenches at Festubert, in the Artois region, where the flooding was so bad the works were abandoned.

Neuve Chapelle

Hoping to drive the Germans back from the territory they had occupied, the Allies planned an attack at Neuve Chapelle at the beginning of March, the aim being to breach the German line and exploit this with a rush on Aubers Ridge and Lille, an important German communication centre. Before the offensive began, the RFC was used to photograph the entire First Army front, the first time aerial photography had been used so prominently in a major offensive. On his return to France, Evans had been attached to the Royal Flying Corps (RFC) as an observer with No 3 Squadron, and the job of aerial photography was given to his Squadron jointly with No. 2 Squadron. The battle opened on 10 March and in the early stages went very well, more shells being fired in the first thirty-five minutes of the opening bombardment than in the entire Boer War. The aerial photography proved useful and Neuve Chapelle was captured, but the new positions the Germans took up were less easily pinpointed. Hatfeild and Cornwallis both joined the general advance with the cavalry, waiting in vain for the chance to exploit the situation, but following a failed German counter-attack on 12 March, the British abandoned the venture. As the battle-weary 1st Highland Light Infantry (HLI) came out of the line, Con Johnstone joined the battalion as part of a draft.

The British line was extended during April 1915, around the Ypres Salient as far as the Ypres-Poelcapelle road, and from this time until the end of the War the Salient was held by British troops. In addition to the few who had already spent time in the Ypres line, many more of Kent's cricketers would become familiar with this sector in the forthcoming years. In spring of 1915 the trenches were in a very poor state, the dead from the fighting of 1914 still lay unburied in places, and many more lives would soon be lost there. Thousands would be wounded too, and Le Fleming was amongst them. He received his second 'Blighty' wound during April when shot in the foot by a sniper near Zonnebeke, and was soon crossing the Channel once again. Further south of the salient lay Hill 60, which had been captured by the Germans in 1914 during the *Race to the Sea*, and which was hotly contested throughout the war. The British captured the peak on 17 April have blown five mines beneath it, and the Germans drenched the area in gas before launching a counter-attack to reclaim it on 5 May. The 1st RWK were among the battalions involved in the battle and suffered heavily, Frank Tuff's brother amongst those killed, and Eric Fulcher one of the reinforcements sent to bring the battalion back to strength.

Second Ypres

Second Ypres began on 22 April when the Germans released gas along a four mile front held by the French, followed by an artillery bombardment. The French broke, leaving a gap in the salient, but the Germans were slow to follow up, perhaps wary of their own weapon. This was fortunate for the Allies who rushed up reserves to cover the gap, and Canadian troops launched a counter attack. Cornwallis and the Scots Greys helped reinforce the line, manning the trenches for 20 of the 28 days the battle lasted. Penn, another cavalry man, was also in the Ypres line, although the Life Guards were not provided with gas masks until 8 May, the Allies struggling to keep up with the new tactics employed by the Germans. Francis Marsham joined the newly formed 9th Cavalry Brigade as they were ordered to the front at Elverdinghe. A second gas cloud was released on 24 April forcing the British back, and attack and counter-attack followed through to 1 May. During that time men were moved to Ypres from elsewhere on the front to relieve the situation, including Johnstone with 1st HLI, and Hatfeild with 1st KDG. Johnstone's stay was brief; he was shot in the neck in a trench near Hill 29 on 1 May, suffering a punctured lung.

The British made a deliberate withdrawal to the Frezenburg Line on 1 May, and exactly one week later the Germans launched an attack on the new positions. After repulsing two attacks a further withdrawal was made, and during the fighting Penn was in the trenches near Hooge, Cumberlege was nearby with the 3rd Cavalry Supply Column and Francis Marsham with 9th Cavalry Brigade. Further withdrawals followed as the Germans kept up the pressure, and even more reinforcements were directed to Ypres to plug the line.

Eric Fulcher moved there with the 1st RWK, new arrival Leonard Powell joined the 1st Gordon Highlanders at Hooge, and Tufton moved to the Salient with 6th Division from the Armentières area. When Second Ypres officially ended on 25 May, the Allies had suffered around 70,000 casualties. Attritional fighting continued. Herbert Hatfeild was at Hooge when the 1st KDG tenaciously defended the Chateau from a fierce German attack, and on 17 June, less than a month after his arrival at the front, Powell was killed by a shell in the Ypres trenches.

New entrants to the front included Gerard Simpson during March to serve with the RHA as part of the 2nd Indian Cavalry Division Ammunition Column, and Raymond Bannon who joined the Red Cross during May to work as an ambulance driver. Richard Thornton also arrived in France, driving hundreds of miles in his converted car to serve with the French Red Cross. Ken Hutchings arrived in France at the end of April and joined the 2nd Royal Welsh Fusiliers in the line at Bois Grenier. That same month there was a joint British and French offensive north of Arras, the 2nd Battle of Artois, but little progress was made, and none of the cricketers appear to have been involved.

Loos

The offensive at Loos in the autumn was planned to coincide with a French attack in Artois, and a second French offensive in Champagne. Loos was to be the largest operation undertaken by the British, and all efforts were made to pave the way for success. More New Army Divisions were sent to France during the build-up, from July to September, bringing a number of our cricketers with them. In July six Divisions arrived, one of which was the 20th Light Division including William Sarel and Lionel Troughton with the 10th Rifle Brigade. Gerald Hough and Arthur Edwards of the 8th RWK accompanied the 24th Division in August, one of the two Divisions arriving that month, and the 26th Division was one of five that arrived during September, including Freddie Knott with the 7th Wiltshire. That same month George Whitehead joined the Royal Field Artillery in the Loos area, and during August Bernard Bannon arrived in France to serve with the French Red Cross.

Whitehead was with the 75th Brigade RFA, one of many engaged in shelling the German positions four days before the battle, but the British bombardment proved to be too weak due to lack of shells, with the result that little of the wire was cut. The British also used gas for the first time, installing 5,500 cylinders in front trench positions. The gas was released at 05.30 on 25 September, but met with little success, the wind not carrying it as hoped. As the attacking battalions took up their positions, Ken Hutchings waited with the 2nd Royal Welsh Fusiliers at Cambrin in support to the 1st Middlesex. A quantity of the gas was released in Hutchings' sector, where it hung in the air in front of the British trenches. The attack began at 06.30 and despite heavy losses Loos was captured, but the success was not exploited. Whilst the fighting went on, Eric Fulcher was at Carnoy with the 1st RWK ready to support any success, Hatfeild and Francis Marsham were on standby with the cavalry, and Cumberlege was with the 3rd Cavalry Division Supply Column as they joined the attack. Further north at Laventie Sarel and Troughton were involved in a support attack by the 20th Division, the objective being to prevent the Germans moving reserves to Loos, and Knott was with the 7th Wiltshire, in support of the French attack, though not called into action.

When the battle resumed on 26 September, the Germans were well prepared to repulse any advance. The twelve attacking battalions that day suffered 8,000 casualties out of 10,000 men in the space of four hours. This attack drew in several New Army Divisions who were hurried up to the line as the first day's fighting closed, some only reaching their positions a short while before their zero hour. One of these was the 24th Division, in which Hough and Edwards were serving with the 8th RWK. Of the 25 Officers and 800 men of the 8th RWK who went over the top, only one officer and 250 men remained effective, Edwards among those killed, and Hough one of the wounded. By 28 September the British were, in places, back at their starting positions and had suffered 20,000 casualties. The Germans attempted to regain some lost ground on 8 October with a major offensive but had to abandon the attack after suffering heavy losses. On that day Ken Hutchings stood to with the Welsh Fusiliers on the Loos-Hohenzollen Line, ready to repel the Germans, but saw no action. One last attack by the British on 13 October met with failure and the Loos Offensive finally came to a close. Evans was awarded the Military Cross for his part in the battle as an Observer with No 2 Squadron.

Elsewhere on the front Tufton was at Ypres with 6th Division who were involved in the fighting around Hooge during July that saw the first use of flamethrowers. In September Leney left France to carry out Red Cross work in Egypt, and James Colquhoun arrived at the beginning of October, posted to the 10th HLI in the 9th Scottish Division at Ypres. He suffered a bullet wound to his wrist just three weeks later and was evacuated to England. Ken Hutchings returned to England after falling sick at the end of October, and Penn, Francis Marsham and Cornwallis spent the end of the year in winter billets with their cavalry units.

Winter 1915/1916

There were to be no further major engagements for the British until the following July, but there was enough fighting on the front to keep the men busy, and many reinforcements arrived over Winter and Spring, earmarked to help with the next big push. During November Charles Rucker, having recovered from wounds received at Gallipoli, joined Sarel and Troughton with the 10th Rifle Brigade in the Armentières area. Rucker was quickly into action, awarded the Military Cross for his part in a trench raid in December, whilst Sarel returned to England suffering from nervous exhaustion. Gerard Simpson also returned to England having injured himself when trying to put a fire out. Freddie Knott left France as the 26th Division departed for Salonika, whilst Arthur du Boulay arrived from England with HQ of 33rd Division during November, and George Heslop landed with the 16th Middlesex, as part of the same Division. During January the London Gazette announced that Tufton was awarded the DSO, and later in the month Heslop was wounded in the trenches at Bethune during a German artillery bombardment. February found Troughton and Rucker posted to Ypres, where Whitehead had spent the winter. The trenches were in an appalling condition, the severe cold and flooding combining to make life miserable for the inhabitants.

WESTERN FRONT 1916

There were no major offensives involving the British in 1916 until the Somme, which then took up most of the second half of the year. Kent's cricketers were present on this sector of the front from the first day of the offensive through to the last. By the year's end two had been killed, five wounded and another taken prisoner of war, and the Somme sector accounted for all bar two of the wounded.

As always, the lack of an offensive did not equate to a quiet time for soldiers. During February, near Vermelles in the Loos region, the Scots Greys exploded a mine beneath the German line and captured the resulting crater. For his part in fighting off the German counter-attack, Stanley Cornwallis was awarded the Military Cross. A week later the Germans launched a massive attack on the French part of the line further south, starting the Battle of Verdun which did not end until December and cost each side over 300,000 men killed. Both Bernard and Raymond Bannon served with the French Red Cross during that battle, ferrying wounded Frenchmen to hospitals. In March Charles Marriott was posted to the 16th Lancashire Fusiliers in the Somme area, and Charles Rucker was wounded at Ypres, returning to England after having his left leg amputated. April saw the arrival of Sydney Day as a reinforcement for the 17th Royal Fusiliers, and William Hutchings was transferred to France from Egypt, serving with the with the ASC and attached to a Royal Garrison Artillery Siege Battery. The last Kent player to arrive in France in preparation for the Somme Offensive was Harold Prest, joining the 2nd Royal Berkshire as a reinforcement at Albert during May. Lovick Friend also arrived in France at this time, but in a non-combatant role, taking over the position of President of the Claims Commission. In the King's Birthday Honours announced in June, Francis Marsham was awarded the Military Cross.

Somme

The early part of 1916 was spent reorganising the BEF. When the Germans attacked Verdun in February the French withdrew their Tenth Army from Arras and the British line was again extended. Reinforcements arrived, Divisions regrouped and six new Corps were formed. Haig would have preferred an attack in Flanders but agreed to the French request to attack on the Somme as part of a co-ordinated summer offensive. The German attack at Verdun made the British offensive all the more vital, but also reduced the planned French participation, there being 13 French and 20 British Divisions allotted to take part. Preparations began on a grand scale to allow the large forces to assemble in the Somme area, and a number of mines were dug under the German positions. Bapaume was designated the major objective, about seven miles behind the German lines.

A week-long bombardment preceded the attack, during which time William Hutchings was at Albert with the Siege Battery he was attached to and, as the German positions were pounded, Evans flew with the RFC, spotting German gun positions to allow the artillery to range their guns effectively. Penn, Francis Marsham and Cornwallis moved forward and waited with their cavalry units, hopeful of a breakthrough the next day that would allow them to exploit behind the German line. Meanwhile Livesay was temporarily with the HQ of Third Army which had several Divisions at the northernmost part of the attacking line. Overnight the infantry were moved up into their jumping off positions, convinced that few of the enemy could have survived the seven days of shelling. Zero hour on 1 July was 07.30. At 07.20 a number of large mines were blown, including a 40,000 pound one at the Hawthorn Ridge Redoubt, and two more were fired at 07.28 near La Boiselle.

First Day of the Somme

At 07.30 thousands of British and French troops went over the top. To the north of the Albert-Bapaume road the attack was almost a complete failure. George Heslop was with the 16th Middlesex in the 29th Division attacking from Beaumont Hamel to the Hawthorn Redoubt, the explosion of the mine there signalling the British advance. They followed the first line at 07.55 and shortly afterwards Heslop was cut down and killed in a hail of German machine-gun and artillery fire. Astride the Albert-Bapaume road the attack also failed despite the two mines fired at La Boiselle. Here Charles Marriott was with the Lancashire Fusiliers in the 32nd Division attacking Thiepval, and Harold Prest with the Royal Berkshires in 8th Division attacking Ovillers. Only at the southern part of the attacking line was there greater success. During the day Evans flew counter-battery work, directing fire on to German gun positions and also flying reconnaissance over Bapaume and further down to Cambrai. Eric Fulcher was with the 1st RWK who were intended to be part of a support attack at Wailly, further north near Arras, but this was cancelled.

Somme Continued

The first day of the Somme had resulted in a fifth of the attacking force being killed,

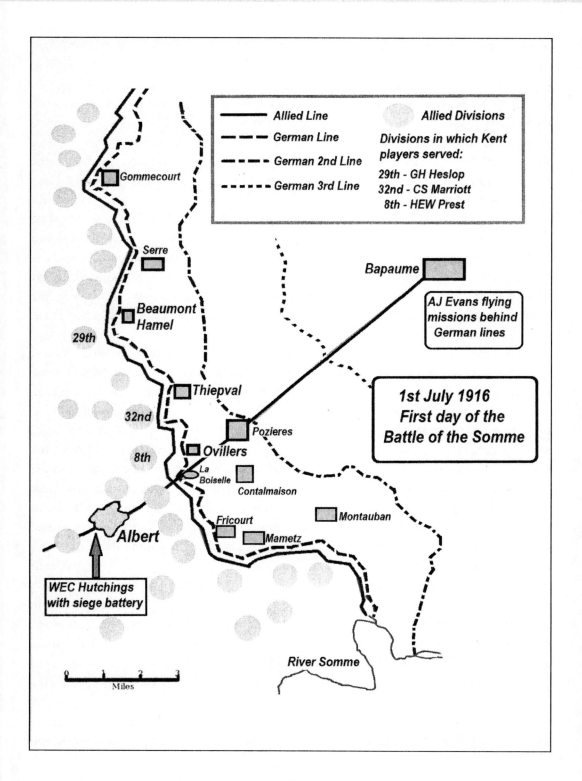

Legend:
- Allied Line
- German Line
- German 2nd Line
- German 3rd Line
- Allied Divisions

Divisions in which Kent players served:

29th - GH Heslop
32nd - CS Marriott
8th - HEW Prest

Gommecourt

Serre

Beaumont Hamel

29th

Bapaume

AJ Evans flying missions behind German lines

Thiepval

32nd

Pozieres

8th

Ovillers

La Boiselle

Contalmaison

Montauban

Fricourt

Mametz

Albert

1st July 1916 First day of the Battle of the Somme

WEC Hutchings with siege battery

0 1 2 3
Miles

River Somme

including sixty per cent of the officers involved. British casualties totalled approximately 20,000 killed, 35,000 wounded, 2,100 missing and 600 taken prisoner, the heaviest ever suffered by the British Army. Opinions vary, many believing the attack was a failure, and others that the distraction from Verdun meant it achieved its aim. Either way, the battle was resumed the following day.

Although the Germans had been stunned by the scale of the attack, the British were possibly more shocked by their losses and were slow to progress. Whilst the French pressed on with success in the south, the British offensive turned into a series of small scale local actions. Many regiments had been left badly understrength and reinforcements were needed quickly. Among the drafts that arrived was Gerald Hough to join the 6th RWK which had suffered 375 casualties in an attack on Ovillers on 3 July. Ken Hutchings had joined the 12th King's (Liverpool Regiment) during May as a replacement for one of the battalion's officers wounded in the line at Ypres, and he was soon heading south to the Somme. Robert Livesay joined the Staff of the NZ Division, responsible to the Commanding Officer for the conduct of operations and was instrumental in the Division's operations on the Somme in the coming months.

The Fourth Army was finally ready to resume the offensive on 14 July. The objective was to capture the German second defensive position, along the ridge from Pozieres, south east towards Guillemont and Ginchy, including Longueval adjacent to Delville Wood. Beyond, on the ridge, lay High Wood. The Battle of Bazentin Ridge left the British with a foothold in High Wood and in the days that followed the fighting for it raged, as well as for Delville Wood and Longueval. The cavalry had a role in the plans but, as Francis Marsham found, there was little more to do than send patrols out. Flying a reconnaissance behind Bapaume on 16 July, Evans was forced to land when his engine cut out, and he and his pilot were taken prisoner. Eric Fulcher took part in an attack on High Wood with 1st RWK on 23 July, and was also involved in the fighting around Longueval, and then in support to an attack made on Delville Wood on 30 July. Sydney Day was also involved in the fighting in the area with 5th Trench Mortar Battery in 2nd Division. There was no significant success in the northern sector of the line during the first few weeks of July, but Ovillers was finally captured on the 16th, and Pozieres soon after. Hough went into the trenches at Ovillers and was wounded a second time during a German bombardment on 5 August. As the line was bolstered, Troughton and the 10th Rifle Brigade moved into the trenches at Hebuterne, between Gommecourt and Beaumont Hamel on 27 July, and Ken Hutchings spent time in the Somme front line during August. George Whitehead moved near Acheux with the RFA on the first of the month.

It was now accepted that a breakthrough was unlikely, but fighting continued in the form of small actions and attritional warfare. There were the usual movements of men, and several of our cricketers departed or arrived. Tufton moved to the Somme area from Ypres with 6th Division HQ, whilst Worthington crossed the Channel with the 102nd Battalion of the Canadian Expeditionary Force on 12 August, to be stationed in the Ypres area. Horatio Walpole also arrived as reinforcement to the 1st Coldstream Guards at Morlancourt. William Hutchings moved with his unit to north-west of Fricourt which had been captured on the second day of the Somme Offensive, whilst his brother Ken and Lionel Troughton moved with the 20th Division towards Guillemont at the end of the month.

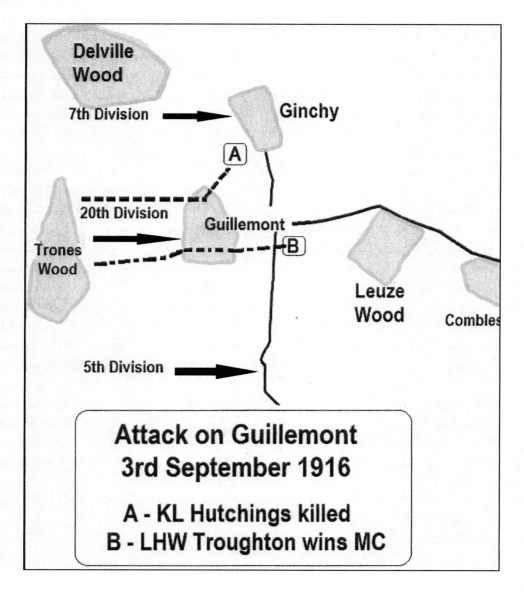

Guillemont and Ginchy

The capture of Guillemont and Leuze Wood was deemed strategically necessary to straighten out the line, and the village had been subjected to a number of attacks from the end of July through August. Although the station was captured and the line advanced, the village proved elusive. The 20th Division was tasked with attacking Guillemont on 3 September, with 5th Division to their right attacking Falfemont Farm and Leuze Wood, and 7th Division to their left attacking Ginchy. Troughton was awarded the Military Cross for his bravery in the attack. His brigade pushed through beyond Guillemont to face Leuze Wood, whilst the 47th Brigade also pushed through the village to the left of Troughton's position. Hutchings' battalion then moved forward and dug in on a line facing Ginchy. The 7th Division had however not taken their objectives and the Germans at Ginchy threatened the flank of 20th Division, making several determined counter-attacks. During that fighting Ken Hutchings was killed. The Division's losses were very heavy; Troughton was one of only two officers in his battalion to come through unscathed. Ginchy was subsequently captured on 9 September by the Irish Guards.

Debut of the Tank, the Battle of Flers-Courcelette

On 15 September the advance was continued by eleven British Divisions on the Flers-Courcelette sector of the Somme front, supported by their new secret weapon – the tank. Of the 49 tanks available, 32 made it to the start line and only 25 saw action. Those allocated to the Ginchy section, where Walpole was with the Coldstream Guards, did not arrive. Still in its infancy, the tank was plagued by mechanical failures and many machines became bogged down in mud or shell holes, but those that did take part helped the advance and the British made gains across the length of the front attacked. Edward Fulcher, who had arrived in France just days before, was with the Hussars near Leuze Wood, waiting to exploit any breakthrough, but was stood down when it became apparent there was to be no opportunity for cavalry. Francis Marsham's cavalry brigade was similarly disappointed.

This battle was also the first major Western Front action for the NZ Division, Robert Livesay playing a major role in the planning of divisional operations that saw them capture the Switch Line west of Flers. The Canadians took Courcelette and the British finally captured High Wood after two months of trying. The battle finished on 28 September, but it was during the opening day's fighting that Walpole was wounded, shot in the forearm just three weeks after joining his battalion, the wound severe enough to warrant evacuation to England. Herbert Hatfeild was with the cavalry at Mametz on 25 September, their HQ in Trones Wood, waiting to exploit any breakthrough in the southern part of the British line but, as the success failed to materialize, he and the KDG returned to billets.

Last Phase of the Somme

The Battle of the Somme moved into its final phase toward the end of the month. On 26 September Gough's Reserve Army launched its first major offensive since 1 July, the 18th Division capturing Thiepval, the 11th Division Mouquet, and the Canadians pushed the line 1000 yards forward from Courcelette. Close to Thiepval, Worthington joined the 102nd Battalion CEF attack on Regina Trench on 21 October, but only part of the trench-works was captured. The gains were subsequently lost and hotly contested for some time, the Canadian 4th Division finally capturing Regina Trench on 11 November. Worthington was not in the attack on that final successful day, instead his unit acted as stretcher bearers and provided carrying parties around Bailey Wood. Prest took part in the 2nd Royal Berkshire attack on Zenith Trench on 23 October, and again the day after, both times failing to capture the enemy positions. Zenith was near le Transloy, between Bapaume and Combles.

The Battle of the Ancre was the final large British attack of the Battle of the Somme. A seven day preliminary bombardment was made, and the attack put in along the Ancre River north of Thiepval on 13 November. The 51st Division captured Beaumont Hamel after a mine was exploded beneath the Hawthorn Ridge Redoubt, 135 days after Heslop was killed attacking the same place. St Pierre Divion and Beaucourt were also captured, threatening the German hold on Serre. Five Divisions were in the attack, Sydney Day with 5th Brigade in 2nd Division advancing along the Redan Ridge. Day's brigade formed up in no man's land and got into the German trenches easily, pressing forward trench by trench, but ending up so depleted in numbers they had to fall back and consolidate. On 14 November the 2nd Division attacked Munich Trench, and a number of casualties were caused by inaccurate barrage or 'friendly fire' in modern terms. Only small numbers reached the objective and had to retire to Wagon Road. During that days' fighting Day was wounded, shot through the arm and back, and he was soon heading back to England. Below Thiepval Marriott was back on the Somme with the 16th Lancashire Fusiliers, in support to a proposed 56th Brigade attack, although this was postponed due to heavy rain.

Haig was happy that the Somme Offensive was now finished, but Gough argued for one last effort. The attack on the 18 November started during a sleet storm and the participating Divisions struggled to make progress in the poor weather. The 32nd Division attack on Munich and Frankfort Trenches was made in the face of heavy machine-gun fire and many of the men who actually reached Munich trench were captured. A party of the 16th Highland Light Infantry was cut off in Frankfort Trench where they bravely held out until 21 November when, running out of ammunition, they surrendered. Not knowing the fate of this party, Marriott's battalion was sent to try and rescue them on 22 November, a day too late. The Lancashire Fusiliers were involved in hand to hand fighting with the enemy but, finding no trace of the Highlanders, were forced to retire.

Winter 1916/1917

As was the case each winter the front saw no major actions, though each side was active in shelling the other. The cavalry, Penn, Hatfeild, Edward Fulcher, Francis Marsham and Cornwallis, went into winter billets, using the opportunity to train and reorganise. Troughton spent the winter in the Somme region, his battalion out of the line much of the time, reorganising and training the reinforcements that arrived to bring their depleted numbers back up to strength. A number of Kent players were still in England, sick or wounded (le Fleming, Colquhoun, Johnstone, Sarel, Rucker, Day and Walpole) but there was one new arrival to the front when Ernest Simpson landed in France during October with the 201st Anti-Aircraft Section of the Royal Garrison Artillery. Con Johnstone returned in November, and was attached to the 17th Lancashire Fusiliers at Arras, whilst Whitehead went in the opposite direction in December, back to England to recover from a case of appendicitis. He was joined by Eric Fulcher who was suffering from pneumonia in January, and Cornwallis who went on leave to get married. Frank Penn was awarded the Military Cross in the New Year's Honours, and in February Marriott returned to the Somme with the 16th Lancashire Fusiliers. The winter was one of the worst experienced during the war, and Marriott suffered the consequences, slipping on an ice covered board and injuring his elbow. As he returned to England to recover, Worthington also headed back, having received a commission in the Canadian Army Medical Corps (CAMC). The beginning of 1917 also saw the arrival in France of Pat Morfee who was employed as a mechanic with an aircraft depot.

WESTERN FRONT 1917

During the course of 1917 two Kent players were killed, four wounded and one taken prisoner. It was year of Allied offensives, and the cricketers took part in all the major ones undertaken by the British, namely Arras, Messines, Third Ypres and Cambrai. The year did however begin with some major German activity.

Operation Alberich – German Withdrawal

Over the course of the autumn of 1916 and the winter months, the Germans had constructed the Hindenburg Line behind their existing lines. In March 1917 they withdrew to this new strong and heavily fortified line, and in doing so shortened the front by 40 km and gave up more French territory than the Allies had gained since September 1914. The surrendered territory was deemed a fair exchange for the freeing up of 13 Divisions, especially as the land given up was not simply left intact. On 9 February they embarked on a scorched earth policy. Roads and railways were put out of action, trees were cut down, buildings destroyed, water sources polluted and booby traps laid. The bulk of the German forces were behind the Hindenburg Line by 20 March.

The advancing Allies found the enemy ensconced in their new, well-chosen and well-fortified defensive positions, and began to take stock of the work required to rebuild the infrastructure. Hatfeild advanced with the Dragoon Guards, and Prest with the 2nd Royal Berkshire, the latter joining a successful attack on the German positions at Bouchavesnes on 4 March. Marriott was back in France, and as his battalion moved forward they engaged a German rear-guard at Savy Wood near St Quentin. March also saw the arrival in France of the 42nd Division, bringing James Tylden with the Staff, and Jack Bryan with the 127th Brigade Machine Gun Company (MGC) from Egypt.

Arras

The Battle of Arras was launched simultaneously with the French Nivelle Offensive further south, and was designed to take the German high ground and also draw German troops from the area of the French attack. The Canadians were to advance north on the Vimy Ridge, the British in the centre astride the Scarpe river, and a combined British and Australian force faced the southern part of the line. The preliminary bombardment began on Vimy Ridge on 20 March and the rest of the line on 4 April. Two and a half million shells were fired, predominantly on a narrow 11 mile front, destroying German trenches before the attack began on 9 April. The First Battle of the Scarpe, fought in extreme cold and falling snow, was over by 14 April, with most objectives gained. During the battle Cornwallis was in charge of a working party, tasked with erecting bridges over captured trenches to ease the cavalry advance. The cavalry however found no chance to exploit the position and Penn, Edward Fulcher and Francis Marsham had to return to billets. The Canadian Corps captured the crest of Vimy Ridge, a 4,000 yard advance, and Tufton joined the push forward with 6th Division. Arthur du Boulay was with 33rd Division HQ as they also took part in the battle, and William Hutchings was to the north-west of Arras as Senior MT Officer at First Army Dumps.

The push to the east of Arras continued on 15 April, even though it was clear the Nivelle Offensive was failing. This second phase of Arras took in the Battle of Lagnicourt, Second and Third Battles of the Scarpe, Battle of Arleux and the Battle of Bullecourt. Some ground was taken but there were no significant gains and heavy losses were incurred before the offensive drew to a close about 16 May. By this time Jack Bryan was in the line at Havrincourt towards Cambrai, as was Troughton, whilst Cornwallis, Penn and Hatfeild were all with the Cavalry in the Somme area. Johnstone was further south at St Quentin, and Marriott was now in the waterlogged trenches at Nieuport at the northernmost part of the line. Prest had left his battalion after being appointed Chief Instructor at the XV Corps Lewis Gun School in France.

Messines

The largest offensive of 1917 was still to come, but several more events took place to pave the way. Following the failure of the 'Nivelle Offensive', the French Armies had become demoralised and mutinous during May. The attack on Messines was designed to relieve pressure on the French by drawing German resources north to Flanders. The tactical objective was the German held ridge, running north from Ploegsteert through Messines and Wytschaete to Mt Sorrel. The success of the operation would deny the Germans the high ground south of Ypres. Livesay played his part on the Staff of the NZ Division, planning their role in the attack, and Cumberlege was with ASC MT HQ supporting II ANZAC, the southernmost of the attacking Allied forces. The attack began on 7 June with the detonation of 19 mines, destroying the German front line and allowing the Allies to secure the ridge with infantry, cavalry and tanks. Noël Boucher, who had arrived in France the previous month, was performing reconnaissance duties with the RFC to spot German positions. Further advances followed, and Livesay's Division pushed forward on either side of Messines after the initial attack, whilst William Hutchings was with his unit organising siege parks and the movement of vehicles for battery and supply columns.

Operation Hush

German forces had occupied most of the Belgian coast after the Race to the Sea in 1914, using the ports for submarines and ships. This position had always been a thorn in the British side, threatening the Channel Ports and therefore the safety of the BEF in France and Flanders. Operation Hush was a proposed landing on the Belgian coast and a breakout attack from Nieuport and Yser, to capture the entire Belgian coast as far as the Dutch border. The plan was never to come to fruition as the Germans, having detected the British takeover of Yser, made a pre-emptive attack in July, destroying all but one bridge over the river, and overwhelming the British battalions in the area. Hush was cancelled and fighting continued in the area for some time. Marriott was in Nieuport with the Lancashire Fusiliers when, on 22 July, he was affected by Mustard Gas which was a new introduction to the front, and he was evacuated to England.

During June and July Walter Monckton arrived in France with the 3/4th RWK in the Arras region, and Lawrence le Fleming returned from England, taking over command of the 9th East Surrey Regt. Meanwhile Johnny Evans crossed the Swiss border, after escaping from the German POW Camp he was being held in.

Third Ypres – Passchendaele

The Third Battle of Ypres is often referred to as Passchendaele, the name of the village much of the fighting was centred around. The Allied objectives were the high ground and ridges to the south and east of Ypres, the Passchendaele – Staden Ridge, and it was hoped that an offensive here would relieve pressure on the French and loosen the German grip on the Belgian coast. The ground was naturally swampy and unusually wet weather made it worse, flooding shell holes and leaving it in a state unsuitable for the use of tanks. When the battle was over, it had accounted for the deaths of two Kent players, and left two more wounded.

The fighting took the form of three distinct phases, the first of which began on 31 July with the Battle of Pilckem Ridge, during which the Allies advanced to the Steenbeck River, but the Germans regained ground with a counter-attack. Edward Fulcher fell ill around this time and returned to England on 11 August. That same day Troughton went into the line with the Rifle Brigade near Pilckem, and on 14 August his battalion attacked in the Steenbeck Valley. Two days later, there was little success when the British attacked Langemarck and they were forced back to their start lines. Further subsidiary actions followed until the end of August, whilst the French launched the 2nd Battle of Verdun further south. On 24 August Tufton's Division relieved the Canadians on the Hill 70 front, and reinforcements began to move towards Ypres from other parts of the line to join the effort. Ernest Simpson was in Ypres with his anti-aircraft unit, and 42nd Division moved to the region, bringing Tylden and Jack Bryan to Poperinghe. Livesay was with the NZ Division around Passchendaele during August, as was Cumberlege with their Supply Column, and William Hutchings was organising motor transport in the area throughout the battle.

The weather improved during the second phase of the battle, and consequently the British had more success. It opened with the Battle of Menin Road Ridge on 20 September, the Allies capturing most objectives on a 14,500 yard front and beating off the German counter-attack that followed. Troughton took part in the 20th Division attack on Langemarck, leading his battalion to the capture of all their objectives bar one, which was taken in a follow up attack. The Germans made a counter-attack on 25 September, but the following day the British regained lost ground in the Battle of Polygon Wood. Du Boulay joined V Corps HQ during the fighting towards the end of September, and as this phase of the battle came to an end, Ernest Simpson was wounded near Vlamertinghe by a German aircraft bomb. He died from his wounds on 2 October in hospital at St. Omer.

Herbert Hatfeild returned to India with the Dragoon Guards at the end of September, but there were also new entrants to the front, Colin Blythe and Claud Woolley landing at Boulogne on 26 September to join the King's Own Yorkshire Light Infantry (KOYLI). James Colquhoun also returned to France about this time, joining the 2nd Highland Light Infantry near Bethune. At the start of October Tylden and Jack Bryan accompanied 42nd Division to Nieuport, and Monckton moved with the 3/4th RWK northeast of Langemarck, employed in digging roads under Royal Engineer supervision. Blythe and Claud Woolley joined the 12th KOYLI at Ypres and were set to work on the light railways at the front, and whilst Cornwallis also moved to this sector, there were few opportunities for the cavalry to exploit.

The third phase of Third Ypres saw the rain return and a consequent lack of success. Livesay's NZ Division was involved in the First Battle of Passchendaele on 12 October which was fought in heavy rain, and the modest gains achieved were lost to a counter-attack. Following fighting in the Houthulst Forest on 22 October, Con Johnstone joined his battalion at a rest camp, and received his second Blighty wound when hit in the chest by a shell fragment on 29 October. The Second Battle of Passchendaele was launched on 26 October; the Canadian Corps had been transferred to Ypres to capture Passchendaele Ridge, but exceptional German resistance left the Allies short of their objective. Luck would have it that the rain stopped between 3-5 November, the dry conditions assisting the advance to the point that Passchendaele was captured on 6 November. The final action to gain control of the high ground north of the village began on 10 November, the success of this signalling the end of the Third Ypres campaign. Just two days before, on 8 November, Colin Blythe was killed and Claud Woolley amongst the wounded when a shell exploded by their working party behind the British line.

Cambrai

As Third Ypres drew to a close, Haig believed the Germans would now expect the British to settle into winter rest, and that an unexpected attack with large numbers of tanks might achieve a surprise breakthrough. Cambrai seemed the ideal place to do that, as occupation of the Bourlon Ridge would threaten the German line to the north. The combination of surprise, sound-ranging enemy guns (a technique championed by Walter Hedley in 1915) and new shell fuses that did not crater the ground so leaving a clear path for tanks, proved successful on 20 November, and the Hindenburg Line was penetrated. Troughton was with 20th Division as it forced its way through La Vacqurie, then advanced to capture a bridge across the St Quentin Canal at Masnieres. In the centre the cavalry passed through late and in small numbers, and were thus forced back by the enemy. Francis Marsham was with 2nd Cavalry Division HQ and Cornwallis with the Scots Greys, both close to Masnieres, waiting for the instructions to cut the Germans off by advancing east of Cambrai, but the Germans reinforced so quickly the opportunity was missed.

A greater advance had been made in six hours than three months at Ypres, and with half the casualty rate, but the all-important Bourlon Ridge had not been reached. Troughton's battalion entered Crevecour on 21 November but the British advance slowed after the first day, and the enemy brought forward large numbers of reinforcements. On 23 November the British attacked into Bourlon Wood and the Ridge, the latter being captured at huge cost, but the Wood remained elusive. A final British effort was made on 27 November, and

Walpole joined the Guards attack on Bourlon Wood and Fontaine. Although some men reached their objectives, their numbers were so depleted they were forced to retire. The following day the offensive ended, the British ordered to lay wire and dig in, whilst the Germans fired some 16,000 artillery shells into Bourlon Wood.

The advance of the German counter-attack on 30 November was unexpectedly swift, despite a determined British resistance. The HQ of 6 Division, where Tufton was based, was shelled three times that day as the Germans threw everything at the British line, much of which was overrun, and Troughton was among the prisoners taken. Counter-attacks were made by the Guards, and the arrival of tanks and nightfall allowed the line to be temporarily held. Walpole was with the Coldstream Guards as they were pushed up near Gouzeaucourt Wood to face the Germans, but despite the temporary blocking of the enemy advance, the hold on Bourlon Wood was precarious. On 3 December, the Germans captured La Vacquerie and Haig ordered a withdrawal from the salient created by the initial breakthrough, Du Boulay retreating to the Flesquières Line with V Corps.

WESTERN FRONT 1918

The last year of the War was to see a major offensive by the Germans in spring-time which was followed by an Allied advance that continued through to the Armistice. Five more cricketers were killed, another died as a result of the influenza epidemic and two were wounded. The Germans planned their offensive in an attempt to strike a decisive blow before the newly arriving Americans gave the Allies a decisive numerical superiority. They were suddenly at a temporary advantage themselves, with 50 Divisions being freed for use from the Eastern Front when the Russians signed the Treaty of Brest-Litovsk. Before the German offensive began William Hutchings was injured and returned to England on sick leave, and Ernest Dilnot and David Jennings both arrived in Belgium and were posted to the Ypres sector, Jennings attached to 206th Field Company and Dilnot to 242 Siege Battery RGA.

'Kaiserschlacht' – the Spring Offensive

The Allies expected a German attack in the early part of 1918, but believed it could be contained. *Kaiserschlacht* (Kaiser's Battle), also known as the Spring Offensive, was made up of four German attacks; the first, codenamed 'Michael', being the main thrust, followed by three subordinate attacks 'Georgette', 'Blucher-Yorck' and 'Gneisau' designed to stretch the Allied forces across the entire front and pierce the line at key points. Michael was launched on the Somme front on 21 March 1918 in the area left behind following the German withdrawal to the Hindenburg Line the prior year, and where the Allied defences were incomplete.

The main attack was launched from Arras to just south of St Quentin, falling against the British Third and Fifth Armies. Nearly the entire British front line fell that morning during bitter hand to hand fighting and over 20,000 men were taken prisoner. When Lawrence le Fleming went out in the mist to reconnoitre his battalion's front with another officer near Villecholes, a machine-gun opened up, killing him instantly. Large parts of the Fifth Army fell back, and so began what was effectively the first mobile warfare since 1914, reminiscent of the retreat from Mons. On the right the Third Army fell back to avoid being flanked, including du Boulay with V Corps HQ, The fighting turned into a series of isolated incidents and actions, with a real risk that the Third and Fifth Armies might become separated. Some British units stood firm, some were wiped out. Francis Marsham was with 2nd Cavalry Division HQ at St Quentin, and was appointed GSO1 during the first week's desperate fighting. Cornwallis was with 5th Cavalry Brigade HQ as they attempted to delay the enemy crossing the St Quentin Canal, and Livesay was with 61st Division as they fought a successful retreat over the Somme with Fifth Army. Tylden and Tufton were driven back with 6th Division and dug in on a new line.

Reserves were thrown into the fray wherever possible. Walpole joined the Coldstream Guards as they pushed up to the front line on the left wing of the Third Army near Arras and Jack Bryan was rushed to the front with his MG Company in buses to help hold the line near Bapaume. In the ensuing chaos of the retreat they had no transport and had to carry their guns and ammunition everywhere. Cumberlege had the task of supporting Third Army with the NZ MT Company, not an easy task with an ever changing front line. The British were in full retreat again on 23 March as the Germans broke through the Crozat Canal at Jussy. Elements of Cornwallis' brigade attempted to hold the Canal for some time but were eventually compelled to make an orderly retreat. Ludendorff thought he had broken the British lines and implemented the second phase of his plan, one German Army continuing westwards whilst another rolled northwards toward Arras and St Pol, the latter place being where James Colquhoun was based at the Physical and Bayonet Training School. The School was evacuated when it was subjected to shelling and Colquhoun and his fellow instructors stood to in battle order.

By nightfall of 24 March the British had lost the line of the Somme and Bapaume was evacuated. Bryan was in action near Bapaume and, his battalion being split up, he and his unit ended up fighting a rear-guard action with the 1st Irish Guards near Avette. Haig considered it vital to hold Amiens due to its value as a rail centre and many reserves were positioned to protect it. On 28 March the Germans launched Operation Mars around Arras in an attempt to widen the breach in the Allied lines, but the 29 attacking Divisions were defeated in a day, and during that time Du Boulay was with V Corps HQ organising the British engagement with the enemy. The Michael offensive was all but over by 5 April, with Arras and Amiens still in Allied hands. One side effect of the German Offensive was that the RAF Depots, one of which Morfee was serving at, were moved nearer to the Channel ports.

The movement of troops to defend Amiens had left parts of the front in Belgium vulnerable and on 9 April the Germans launched 'Georgette' around the area of the La Bassee Canal and spread northwards. Dilnot's RGA Brigade was forced to pull back from Kemmel and reinforced the line near Voormezeele, firing at the advancing Germans from their new position. Fighting still continued on the line of the Michael offensive, and that same day Walpole was killed by a shell which landed in his trench near Boiry St Martin, south of Arras. The next day David Jennings was gassed whilst near Bienvillers, also south of Arras – he was evacuated to England and died in August. Meanwhile the defenders of Armentières were forced to withdraw and the Germans also captured the Messines Ridge. Yet more new arrivals and transferred troops were moved into the area to help reinforce and hold the line. Arthur Povey arrived in France to join the Royal Engineers near Bethune just as heavy fighting was breaking out, and Livesay was transferred to the same area, having withdrawn with 61st Division across the Somme during the Battle of St. Quentin. About this time Monckton transferred to the 9th West Riding Regiment and moved to the Ancre front where his new battalion was recovering from the mauling they experienced in the first part of the offensive.

With desperate fighting all over the front, Haig made his memorable order of the day on 11 April, saying "With our backs against the wall and believing in the justice of our cause, each one of us must fight on to the end". The Allies doggedly met the German attacks, Tylden and Tufton involved with 6th Division during the battles of Bailleul and Kemmel Ridge. When 'Georgette' ended on 29 April, the Germans occupied a vulnerable salient, the British having strategically withdrawn from much territory won during Third Ypres which was deemed unimportant in comparison to the key places they had prevented the Germans from capturing. 'Blucher-York' was launched in May and although the Germans made gains they were halted, and 'Gneisau' failed within three days during June. The Germans tried one last attack on 15 July, the *Second Battle of the Marne*, hoping to draw Allied reserves south, but a French counter-attack forced them back. Hervey Lawrence was wounded during that fighting and was subsequently awarded the bar to his DSO.

By August 1918 the initiative was passing to the Allies. They had been bolstered by the arrival of American troops and the British Army had also been reinforced by men from Palestine and Italy, as well as large numbers of troops held back in Britain by Prime Minister Lloyd-George. These additional men replaced the losses of 1917 and the Spring Offensive, putting the Allies in a position to be able to consider their own attack. Eric Hatfeild, Geoffrey Foster and Hervey Lawrence had all arrived from Palestine during May and June, and Povey and Ronnie Bryan from England during April. Taylor had also arrived in France from Palestine, but soon departed for England after being accepted for an Officer Cadet course. As the German offensive drew to a close at the end of June, Monckton joined 17th Division HQ as Education Officer, and Eric Fulcher returned to France from sick leave in July followed shortly by Claud Woolley who had recovered from the wounds he received during Third Ypres. Frank Penn joined the newly created 4th Battalion Guards MG Regiment during August, having arrived back in France from four months in England.

The Hundred Days Offensive

A large number of Kent's cricketers were to play a part in the last few months of the war, this final phase generally being referred to as *The Hundred Days Offensive*, although it was not a specific event or strategy, simply a title since given to a sequence of actions, events and Allied victories. The *Kaiserschlacht* had been halted and the Allies considered their options. Haig persuaded the French to agree to push the Germans back from their still threatening position, by striking east of Amiens, on the Somme but south-west of the area attacked in 1916. This was the point the British and French Armies joined, and would allow them to co-operate. The German defences here were relatively weak and the country-side was ideal for the use of tanks.

Amiens and the Second Somme

The Battle of Amiens (1918) was launched on 8 August and simultaneously the French commenced the Battle of Montdidier further south. Dilnot had moved to Amiens several days before and his siege battery opened fire that morning to support the Canadian Corps attack on the Villers-Bretonneux front. Both Francis Marsham (GSO2) and Cornwallis (GSO3) were with Cavalry Corps HQ, the Corps being tasked with gaining possession of the old Amiens line. The advance of ten Allied Divisions and 500 tanks caught the Germans by surprise, and as their line broke the tanks attacked the rear positions. At the end of the day a 15 mile gap had been created in the line, 330 guns captured and 17,000 men taken prisoner. Total German losses were 30,000 compared to the Allies 6,500. Ludendorff called this "the Black day of the German Army". The seven mile advance in one day was one of the greatest of the war, and it continued for three days before the Allies began to outrun their supplies and artillery. Du Boulay was now on the Staff of Third Army which was heavily involved in the fighting, and as the Germans retreated from the salient they had created during *Michael*, Jack Bryan helped to harass them with the 42nd MGC and Eric Hatfeild pushed forward across the River Lys with the Buffs in 74th Division.

On 21 August Haig launched the Battle of Albert (1918), a fresh offensive by the Third Army between the Ancre and the Scarpe, and the start of the Second Somme (1918).

During the preceding night Jack Bryan and his battalion fired their machine-guns to cover the sound of the tanks being brought forward, and during the battle fired a barrage onto German positions to support the attacking infantry. Bryan was awarded the Military Cross for his role in fighting off a German counter-attack near Miraumont on 22 August. Albert was captured on 23 August, and the 2nd Battle of Bapaume saw the Fifth Army capture that town on 29 August, Eric Fulcher being awarded the Military Cross for his role in the attack with the 5th Division. The NZ Division also took part in the battle, and Cumberlege was with the Divisional MT Company, providing transportation support.

Advance to the Hindenburg Line

With the German line broken, a number of battles took place as the British pushed on to the Hindenburg Line, and the front was widened by the First Army during the 2nd Battle of Arras. This opened on 26 August with the Battle of the Scarpe (1918), during which Bickmore was with the 52nd Division Ammunition Column (DAC) and Povey was with 9th Field Company. Eric Hatfeild joined the Buffs attack on the German positions on Canal du Nord and pushed onwards once a crossing was made. Bernard Howlett, having joined the 7th RWK in August, was with them as they captured Sailly Saillisel on 1 September, about 10 km south of Bapaume. The following day the Battle of Drocourt-Queant began at the northernmost section of the Hindenburg Line, the Germans overwhelmed by the Canadians within two days, Povey and Bickmore both taking part with their units and Francis Marsham and Cornwallis with the Cavalry Corps. Jack Bryan pushed forward with his Machine Gun Battalion, providing covering fire for the advancing Infantry, whilst his brother Ronnie Bryan was in the Lens sector with the 9th Sussex. As the French also approached the Hindenburg Line, Dick Blaker arrived in France to join the 13th Rifle Brigade just west of the St Quentin Canal, and George Whitehead returned to the BEF but now as a pilot attached to the RFC.

Battles of the Hindenburg Line

Haig had been wary of a making a direct attack on the Hindenburg Line, but news of the Third Army victory at Havrincourt, which was attacked on 12 September, changed his mind. When he launched the Battle of Epehy on 18 September, the Fourth Army approached along the St Quentin Canal, and an Allied victory was quick in coming, and 11,750 prisoners taken. Eric Hatfeild was awarded the Military Cross for his role in the attack near Templeux Gerard, and just three days later he was killed in an attack at Hargicourt. Monckton was with 17th Division which also took part in the Battle of Epehy, and Tylden and Tufton's 6th Division took part in the advance, attacking the high ground overlooking St Quentin. Eric Fulcher had moved into the trenches with the 1st RWK near

Havrincourt Wood after the village was captured, and they spent several days trying to advance as the Corps attacked along the line on 25 September.

French and American troops to the south commenced the Meuse-Argonne Offensive and to the north the Fifth Battle of Ypres was launched by British and Belgian troops, meeting much success. On the Hindenburg Line, heavy fighting centred around the Canal du Nord region on 27 September, Jack Bryan, Penn, Monckton, Foster, Eric Fulcher and Povey all joining the push, and the following day the Germans began to fall back toward the St Quentin Canal. As the Allies broke through in several places, Tylden and Tufton pushed through with 6th Division and Penn's MG battalion provided covering fire for the advancing Guards Division. Dilnot was providing supporting fire with his siege battery for IX Corps, and as the 50th Division advanced, Claud Woolley's Field Company helped put bridges across the Canal, their crossing made on 4 October. Blaker crossed the Canal the same day with 13th Rifle Brigade, where they took a support role to the Royal Fusiliers attack on the new German positions. Francis Marsham and Cornwallis were also involved with the Cavalry Corps. The pressure was maintained with several divisions attacking the third line defences of the Hindenburg Line, one such attack made by 24th Brigade which was now commanded by Livesay. A total break in the line was achieved on 5 October.

On 8 October the Battle of Cambrai (1918) was launched and, led by the Canadian Corps, the British First and Third Armies broke through. Charles Worthington was back in France with the Canadian Army Medical Corps attached to the Canadian 2nd Division which took part in the battle, and Livesay's brigade was again in the thick of things, pushing on to the St. Quentin Canal, whilst Cumberlege was with the NZ MT Company. Dilnot was still with his siege battery firing in support to the IX Corps advance. Geoffrey Foster moved to Cambrai with the 102 MG Battalion in the days that followed and, as Monckton and 17th Division soon found, the Germans in the Canal du Nord region were withdrawing.

Beyond the Hindenburg Line

Having been forced out of the Hindenburg Line the Germans had taken up new positions on the River Selle, and the British relentlessly pushed toward them. Ronnie Bryan moved east of the St Quentin Canal with the 9th Sussex to occupy Cauroir, his brother Jack Bryan pushed forward with the 42nd MG Battalion after a two week break out of the line, and Foster took up position with 102nd MG Battalion to cover the infantry crossing of the river. The Battle of the Selle lasted 17 to 25 October, the attack launched against a ten mile front south of Le Cateau. The objective was to reach a line between Valenciennes and the Sambre – Oise Canal, which would put the Allied artillery within range of the key German railway centre at Aulnoye.

Crossings were forced over the river in the first days of the Battle of the Selle, and Le Cateau was captured after severe fighting. Povey and Claud Woolley played a part with the RE, both men's Companies bridging the river for the Infantry to cross, whilst Dilnot was with the artillery, providing covering fire for IX Corps. Foster and Jack Bryan covered the infantry with their MG Battalions, Blaker was with the 13th Rifle Brigade in the attack on Briastre and Cumberlege was with XXII Corps Motor Truck Company supporting the attack. Howlett was with 7th RWK to the south of Le Cateau fighting their way over the River Richemont, with the aid of wooden bridges they carried up with them, then pushing into the Mormal Forest. As Foster found, the Germans were not entirely finished, his MG battalion having to fight off two German attacks near Querenaing on 28 October. They were however still on the back foot and were gradually forced back to the Sambre-Oise Canal, within the area of the Mormal Forest. As the Battle of the Selle ended the British entered the forest after them.

By strange coincidence, far away in Belgium on the day the Battle of the Selle opened, George Whitehead was shot down and killed whilst flying operations near Lauwe, and on the last day of the battle Arthur du Boulay died from influenza contracted whilst with Third Army HQ. During the latter part of October much fighting had taken place elsewhere on the front. Following 5th Ypres in Belgium, the Battle of Courtrai had seen the Allies capture Roulers, Ostend, Lille, Douai, Bruges and Zeebrugge. By 20 October the Dutch border had been reached.

Final Push

Haig now planned for one last push to defeat the German Army on their latest line, and to gain the desired jumping off positions to achieve this, the city of Valenciennes needed to be taken. The Battle of Valenciennes began on 1 November, Foster's battalion providing covering fire for the infantry, and Povey and his Field Company supporting the Canadians who took part in the main assault. The attack was hugely successful, the Germans rapidly retired from the city, and the Allies moved forward again, ready for Haig's planned offensive on the Sambre. North of Valenciennes, Livesay was leading 24th Brigade towards Mons with the 8th Division, and further south Howlett, Jack and Ronnie Bryan, Blaker, Eric Fulcher, Tylden, Tufton and Penn were now all in the Mormal Forest as the British prepared to advance again.

The Battle of the Sambre opened in the early hours of 4 November and, despite heavy German resistance, progress was made. Just south of Le Quesnoy, which was captured by the NZ Division, Blaker took part in the attack on Louvignies with 13th Rifle Brigade, and was awarded the Military Cross for his bravery. Howlett and the 1st RWK followed the three tanks allotted to them into the battle, the Germans scattering into the forest in disarray. Ronnie Bryan and the 9th Sussex attacked the high ground North of Wargnies le Petit and Wargnies le Grand, forcing the Germans to retreat, and Penn's MG Battalion covered the advance of the Guards Division. Dilnot's siege battery provided supporting fire to the infantry of IX Corps as they forced a crossing. The Allies pushed on over the Sambre, Jack Bryan and the 42nd MG Battalion doing so on 7 November, and it was clear that the Germans were now close to defeat.

The advance across the entire front was relentless up until 11 November when the Armistice came into effect. Orders were received to cease hostilities at 11.00.

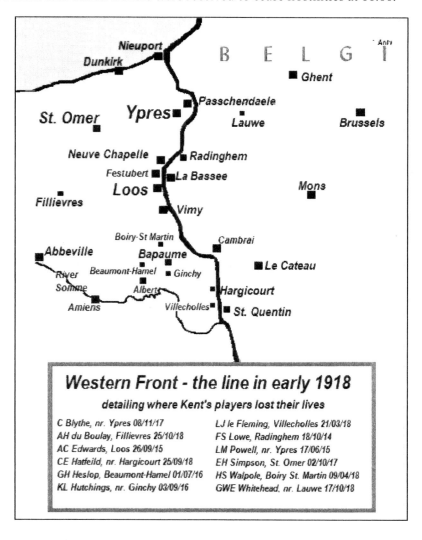

Western Front - the line in early 1918

detailing where Kent's players lost their lives

C Blythe, nr. Ypres 08/11/17

AH du Boulay, Fillievres 25/10/18

AC Edwards, Loos 26/09/15

CE Hatfeild, nr. Hargicourt 25/09/18

GH Heslop, Beaumont-Hamel 01/07/16

KL Hutchings, nr. Ginchy 03/09/16

LJ le Fleming, Villecholles 21/03/18

FS Lowe, Radinghem 18/10/14

LM Powell, nr. Ypres 17/06/15

EH Simpson, St. Omer 02/10/17

HS Walpole, Boiry St. Martin 09/04/18

GWE Whitehead, nr. Lauwe 17/10/18

The casualties on the Western Front 1914-1918

ARMY ON THE RHINE

Although the guns fell silent as the Armistice came into effect, Peace Terms were still to be signed. German troops had two weeks to withdraw behind their borders, and Allied troops moved into Germany in December. Livesay, Tufton, Tylden, Ronnie Bryan, Worthington, Edward Fulcher and Penn all joined the move into enemy territory as part of the Army of Occupation, and the British Army on the Rhine was established in March 1919. The Treaty of Versailles was signed on 28 June 1919.

GALLIPOLI

Twelve of Kent's cricketers took part in the eight month long Gallipoli campaign, at the end of which one had been killed, one wounded and many others had succumbed to the dysentery, diarrhoea and other sicknesses that were prevalent on the peninsula. There were a number of factors which contributed to the Allied decision to embark on the campaign in the Dardenelles, and the delay in actively doing so was because there were probably just as many reasons not to open a second front. At the beginning of 1915 the fighting in France was at a stalemate, and capturing the Gallipoli Peninsula was seen as an opportunity to take Constantinople, put pressure on Germany, and ultimately shorten the war. The biggest downside was the need to divert vital troops and supplies away from the Western Front. This is perhaps why we find that so many of the cricketers in the Yeomanry and other Territorial Forces, who were until this time training in England, were blooded on this front. Those in favour of the campaign won the argument, although initially it was thought a naval bombardment would suffice, with troops only required for the subsequent occupation.

The failed naval action took place in March 1915, and the landing of troops in April. At Helles on the tip of the peninsula, a predominantly British and French force landed, whilst an Australian and New Zealand force landed 14 miles further north at an area that became known as ANZAC. Unfortunately the naval action in March had alerted the Turks, who had quickly reinforced the area and the landings were strongly opposed, both forces being pinned back close to the coastline. During May to July all efforts to break out were beaten back. It is not clear when Charles Rucker arrived on the peninsula, but he was the first Kent player at Gallipoli and also the first casualty. He was wounded at Helles at the end of June whilst attached to the 1st Dublin Fusiliers, and was subsequently evacuated to England.

With the Allies struggling to break out of their foothold on the coast, many reinforcements were sent in August as part of a major effort to push inland. Hervey Lawrence landed at Suvla with the 1/5th Suffolk and went straight into the attack, and George Wood, having landed at Helles during July, moved with the 7th Gloucesters to join the attack at ANZAC. Ted Dillon was with the 2/4th Royal West Kent Regiment who landed at Suvla on 10 August with the 53rd Division, but the battle had effectively been decided in the preceding two days and the new troops were also confined to a narrow area on the coast. Supplies had to be shipped from Mudros on the Island of Lemnos, and throughout the campaign the lack of essentials was problematic, in particular fresh water. Dysentery was rife and sickness levels high. These factors, combined with the horrific casualty rate from any offensive action, plus the constant shelling, left most units far below strength.

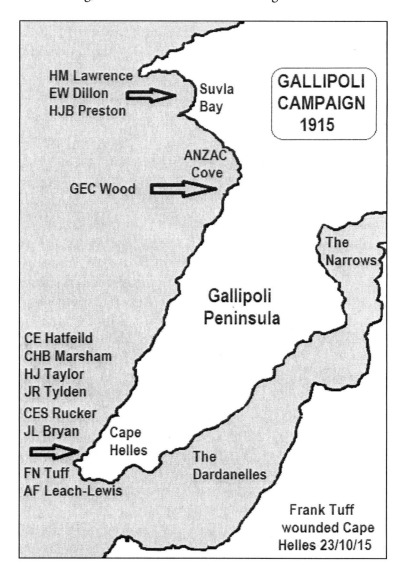

Gallipoli – where the Kent players landed

During September Britain promised to provide assistance to Serbia. This effectively doomed the Gallipoli campaign as the level of reinforcements required for success was never going to be made available. It was evident the Turks would soon have greater supplies of heavy guns which would destroy the British positions, and one last effort was planned to break out. Jack Bryan arrived as a reinforcement to the 1/5th Manchesters at Helles during September, and the South East Mounted Brigade (SEMB) landed at Helles in October to support the planned attack. Accompanying the latter were Frank Tuff, Allan Leach-Lewis, Eric Hatfeild and James Tylden with the Royal East Kent Mounted Rifles and Cloudesley Marsham and Horace Taylor with the West Kent Yeomanry. At about the same time Henry Preston and Charles Woolley sailed from England with the 1/1st Kent Field Company, landing at Suvla and attached to the ANZAC Corps.

The new arrivals dug in and the SEMB remained at Helles as winter approached. Only a couple of weeks after landing Frank Tuff was wounded by a cricket ball bomb, and died at the beginning of November in a hospital on Malta. In the middle of October Jack Bryan was evacuated suffering from jaundice, George Wood fell sick and also appears to have been evacuated, and Dillon left for England having injured his ankle. The Allied position was quite hopeless and after Lord Kitchener spent a week in November touring the battlefront, he recommended evacuation. The last few days of November saw thunderstorms and torrential rain followed by blizzards, snow and heavy frost. At Suvla alone there were 5,000 cases of frostbite, and 200 men drowned or froze to death. Lawrence and the 1/5th Suffolks suffered badly as much of their kit had been sent ahead of a planned move and they struggled to shelter from the weather, and Wood was lucky not to be in the trenches with his battalion as they were flooded out and several men died of exposure.

At the beginning of December the Cabinet agreed to the evacuation of Gallipoli. Careful planning and ingenious schemes, such as the self-firing rifle, ensured the evacuations were made without the loss of a single life. Suvla and ANZAC were evacuated first, Preston and Lawrence amongst the first to leave for Lemnos. They were followed by Leach-Lewis, Hatfeild, Tylden, Marsham and Taylor when Helles was evacuated several weeks later. The campaign had seen the British suffer over two hundred thousand casualties on the Gallipoli Peninsula, three quarters of which were accounted for by sickness such as dysentery, diarrhoea, and enteric fever.

EGYPT AND THE WESTERN DESERT

Egypt had been governed by Britain since 1882, and by 1914 had a garrison of some 5,000 troops, with both the Egyptian Army and Police being British trained. The country was a valuable source of supplies, the land bridge between Asia and Africa, and the Suez Canal was vital to linking Britain with the oil fields being developed in the Persian Gulf. The strategic importance of Egypt to Britain was huge, and although there was no immediate threat to the country upon the outbreak of war, there were concerns about sabotage to the Canal and possible invasion by Turkish forces. Troops were sent from Britain and then India to bolster the defences, and Britain declared war on Turkey on 5 November, 1914.

During 1915 many of Kent's cricketers who were evacuated from Gallipoli were moved to Egypt to regroup, re-equip and train, the size of the country being ideal for the purpose. This included West and East Kent Yeomanry troops Marsham, Hatfeild, Taylor and Leach-Lewis with the South East Mounted Brigade, Dillon with the Royal West Kent Regiment, Lawrence with 1/5th Battalion Suffolk Regiment, Preston with the Royal Engineers, and Tylden who had a new appointment with GHQ 42nd Division. Jack Bryan and George Wood, having both recovered from their illnesses, also re-joined their battalions in Egypt. William Hutchings was posted there in January with the ASC attached to a Siege Battery of the Royal Garrison Artillery, but was sent on to France by April, and Everard Blair arrived in January and took over duties as Chief Engineer, Cairo District. Frederick Leney moved to Egypt with the Red Cross in September and two months later Douglas Carr arrived, for employment with the Royal Ordnance Department at Alexandria.

Britain decided the best policy at that time was one of static defence. Any attack over the desert against the Turks required good water supplies, which at that time was impossible. Defence works were continued throughout the year, with forward positions being fixed some six or seven miles to the east of the Canal to put it out of range of any artillery the Turks might bring up. Canal duties were generally in the desert at the outposts and railheads, or on the bridgeheads and banks of the Canal itself, there being permanent pontoon bridges every ten miles along its length. Marsham, Dillon, Hatfeild, Tylden, Leach-Lewis, Taylor, Lawrence, Bryan and, very briefly, Wood all found their units employed on Canal Defences at some point, as did most men passing through Egypt. The reason Wood did not spend long in the Canal Zone was that he departed for Mesopotamia during February, part of the reinforcements sent to help the besieged force at Kut.

To the West of the Canal a threat was posed by the Senussi tribe in the Libyan Frontier area, when they alone answered the call to a Holy War that the Central Powers tried to instigate. It was considered possible that their actions might give rise to copycat behaviour and cause a general uprising in Egypt. British troops moved to the West of the Canal along the coast, and also some way inland near several oases, to answer the threat and reclaim captured ports. Dillon, Marsham, Hatfeild, Leach-Lewis, Taylor and Preston were all involved in those operations in which the Senussi were defeated.

During 1916 the Allied plans began to change from a policy of static defence to a more ambitious incursion into Sinai, to take El Arish and El Kossaima, and close in on the border with Palestine. As a solution to the problems of mobility and water supply, it was planned to build a railway and a water pipeline across the Sinai Desert from Qantara to El Arish, a large engineering project, to be undertaken in stages. Everard Blair, as Chief Engineer of Eastern Force, was responsible for the important pipeline, one of the largest single engineering undertakings in any theatre of the war, and a bold plan. Blair also designed an extension to the pipeline, which took it a further thirty miles to Rafah, and was constructed in 1917. Jack Bryan, Dillon and Lawrence spent time with their regiments providing protection for the advancing engineering works.

The Turkish launched the Battle of Romani in August 1916, and were beaten back and pursued to El Arish, Tylden being involved in that operation with 42nd Division. This was the last Turkish offensive against the Suez area, and the initiative subsequently passed to the British. By the end of the year the Sinai Peninsula was virtually clear and General Murray's plan to defend Egypt's eastern front by pushing the Turks to El Arish had been a success. An offensive into Palestine was now a possibility for the British Government to consider.

Marsham, Taylor, Dillon, Hatfeild and Preston, had all been involved in the Western Desert campaign against the Senussi, and subsequently moved to Canal Defence duties. Now they made the steady move eastwards to take part in the campaign in Palestine. Of the other cricketers, Leach-Lewis was attached to Delta and Western Force Headquarters, Douglas Carr was to remain in Egypt with the Ordnance Corps, Tylden and Jack Bryan moved with the 42nd Division to France at the end of February 1917, and Blair returned to the UK in March 1917. Later in the war Dillon was posted to Cairo with HQ of Economic Section in the Intelligence, and Johnny Evans spent a brief time there in 1918 with the RFC before moving into Palestine. Others spent leave and sick leave in the country, but most were to see little of Egypt again, as the focus switched to Palestine and, for others, to France.

PALESTINE

The hard-fought campaign in Palestine was responsible for one of our cricketers being wounded, one being taken prisoner, and quite a few cases of sickness. In January of 1917 the commander of the Egyptian Expeditionary Force, Sir Archibald Murray, was informed that any large scale operations were to be left until the autumn, and several Divisions were to be released for transfer to France. This included the 42nd Division, the departure of which took Jack Bryan and Tylden to the Western Front. Murray looked at what actions he might take with the remaining resources at his disposal, as a precursor to a later offensive into Palestine, and restricted his attention to the capture of Gaza, 20 miles north-east of the Palestine frontier and gateway to the Philistia Plain. The approach to the city was covered by the Wadi Ghazee, a watercourse entering the sea five miles south west of Gaza, and that was where the Turks had fallen back to, retiring again when the Allies approached.

Three Kent players were involved in the first attempt on Gaza which was made on 26 March. Dillon took part in the operations with the 2/4th Royal West Kent, part of 53rd Division, making a demonstration to the left flank; Lawrence with the same Division joined the attack commanding the 1/1st Cheshire; and Preston was with the RE, employed on water supplies and track maintenance as part of the main attack. This attempt on Gaza failed and the Turks improved defences and moved up reinforcements before the second British attempt at taking the city on 17 April. The second battle also ended in failure for the Allies. Dillon, Lawrence and Preston played similar roles to those they had in the first battle, and Hatfeild, Taylor and Marsham took part with the newly formed 10th Buffs, albeit in reserve with the 74th Division. A defensive policy then ensued until autumn, as both sides settled down to trench warfare. Dillon was wounded in June when a German plane dropped bombs on the relief column he was in.

Murray requested more infantry and artillery to pursue his aims, but following his failures at Gaza he was replaced as Commander-in-Chief of the EEF by Sir Edmund Allenby, who was ready to put his own plans into effect by August 1917. One of his first actions, designed to improve the morale of the troops, was to move GHQ from Cairo to Rafah in Palestine. Leach-Lewis who had been appointed DAAG Egypt in June 1917 was part of the restructured command. The enemy thought Beersheba an unlikely option for the British as it was far inland, surrounded by desert and therefore had little in the way of water supplies for an attacking force. Allenby, however, opted for a surprise attack at Beersheba, solving the water problem by having new pipelines secretly laid. A feint was planned against Gaza to keep the Turks thinking that was the intended target for a third time, whilst the main attack on Beersheba was set for 31 October.

Marsham had by now returned to England on sick leave, and Preston was in hospital in Alexandria, but Dillon, Lawrence, Taylor and Hatfeild took part with their respective regiments. The attack was a success and an encouraged Allenby ordered a full attack on Gaza. The infantry assault began on 1 November and the entire Turkish line from Gaza to Beersheba began to crack. When the British attacked at Sheria the Turks retreated, and Gaza soon fell. The next objective was Junction Station, the capture of which would cut the Turkish supply line, leaving them to rely on the road from Jerusalem. The Station fell on 14 November and Allenby now prepared his Divisions to take Jerusalem itself.

Dillon, Lawrence, Taylor and Hatfeild joined the advance into the Hills of Judea and more fresh troops were pushed up. Once their defences began to fall, the Turks withdrew from the city and it was captured on 9 December, Lawrence immediately leading his Battalion to post guards on the city gates. Two days later Allenby entered Jerusalem on foot as a sign of respect. Lloyd George had requested the city 'as a Christmas present for the British people' and Allenby had delivered. On the coast Jaffa was captured on 22 December.

At the beginning of 1918 it was clear that even more Divisions needed to be transferred to France, and Palestine was destined to receive no further assistance towards a grand offensive, although Allenby did continue the advance with the resources at his disposal. There were some new arrivals to the country in the early months of the year. Johnny Evans was posted to Palestine in January to command 142 Squadron, the RAF presence greatly supporting the men on the ground by performing observation duties and also carrying out some bombing raids. Geoffrey Foster also arrived in the region as part of one of the drafts to the 1/1st East Riding Yeomanry, designed to bring it up to strength before transferring to France. Dillon was transferred to the newly created Economic Section of Intelligence at HQ in Cairo, and he served on the Staff there until the end of the war.

During February the British entered Jericho and advanced towards Es Salt and Amman where the railway line came down from Damascus. The advance proved difficult and the troops withdrew to the Jordan Valley to reorganise, remaining there for seven months. Between the months of May and June four of the cricketers received their orders for France. Hatfeild and Taylor departed with the 10th Buffs and Lawrence with the 1/1st Herefordshire Regiment which he was now in command of. The 1/1st East Riding Yeomanry had been converted into a Machine Gun unit and Foster left for France with them during May.

Henry Preston was the single Kent cricketer remaining in Palestine, when he returned from sick leave during July. He saw out the end of the campaign with his Field Company in 54th Division, which had its proposed transfer to France cancelled. The final offensive began that autumn when the Battle of Meggido opened on 19 September as part of the coastal advance. The outskirts of Damascus were reached on 1 October, and the city was soon occupied as the remaining Turks retreated towards Aleppo. The Turks sought an Armistice, which came into effect on 31 October 1918, by which time Preston's unit was near Beirut.

MESOPOTAMIA

Only three of the cricketers took part in the campaign in Mesopotamia, but it claimed the life of one of them before it was finished. There were fears early in the war that British interests in the region might be threatened, in particular the oil fields in the Gulf which were vital to the Royal Navy. There was also the threat of the destabilisation of British interests in India, and the Indian Government despatched a mixed Brigade to Bahrain in the Persian Gulf, even before Turkey entered the war. The country was dependent upon the River Euphrates and River Tigris, along which most of the population lived, although neither was capable of carrying an army and movement on the water was restricted to small craft.

George Wood was the first Kent player to arrive in the region, but not until April 1916, and by that time much had happened. The Turks had been driven from Basra in November 1914, up both the Tigris and the Euphrates rivers, past Qurna and Kut as far as Ctesiphon, upon which the British advanced in November 1915. This had however not been a careful advance. The supply line stretched around 500 miles from base, and a high sick rate combined with battle casualties much reduced fighting numbers. Ctesiphon, only 14 miles from Baghdad, proved to be a step too far and the 8,000 strong British force had to retire to Kut, where, surrounded by Turks, they were under siege for five months. Wood was with the 13th Division, sent to help the force trying to relieve Kut, having been redirected from Egypt. He arrived at the end of four months of fighting but still had time to pick up a 'slight wound'. The relief force failed to get through in time, and the force at Kut was forced to surrender.

It was during the siege that Charles Wycherley also arrived in Mesopotamia, serving with 2nd Battalion RWK, based on the Euphrates some distance from Kut. The Euphrates was the shallower of the two rivers, less able to support transport, and was thus the quieter of the two, although there were some actions with the Arabs during 1916. Following the fall of Kut, the British reorganised, Major-General Maude took control in place of Major-General Townshend and the reasons for the previous failures were heeded. Rail and road links were improved, river transport augmented, supplies improved and troop numbers increased. This took much of the remainder of 1916 to complete. As a result of the difficulties in bringing supplies forward, there was a lack of hutted accommodation that was vital in the summer heat, and 13th Division with which Wood was serving was withdrawn to Amara.

With so few reserves available, Maude could not risk heavy casualties, and so favoured a methodical advance, clearing enemy concentrations on both sides of the Tigris towards Kut. The advance was still made quite quickly and the Turks withdrew beyond Baghdad, Wood pushing forward with 13th Division when Maude's army entered the capital on 11 March 1917. Further victories pressed the enemy to retreat to Kirkuk in April and, as the heat of summer approached, the British dug in to consolidate the ground they had gained.

Charles Capes arrived in Mesopotamia in May 1917 and, after a short bout of illness, joined 2nd RWK, the same battalion with which Wycherley was serving on the Euphrates. During June the two men moved with their battalion, as part of 17th India Division, concentrating around Baghdad on the Tigris. Wood was also in the same area with 13th Division, and the Allies and the Turks settled down to selecting defensive positions for the ensuing period of hot weather. Maude died of cholera in November and the offensive slowed down whilst his replacement, Major-General Marshall, settled in. January and February 1918 were relatively quiet months, but it was during January, whilst moving on the Tigris on the troop ship S-44, that Wycherley accidentally fell overboard and was drowned.

During the summer 39th Brigade was given orders to join Dunsterforce, and George Wood departed with them as they headed for the Caucasus. As the British renewed their offensive up the Tigris, the Turks continued to retreat, destroying the roads in their wake. The 17th Division advance was delayed as men were employed in repair work, and Capes was one of those assisting the Artillery move their guns forward. The Turks retired to Sharqat, and the 17th Division drove them from their positions on 28 October, Capes joining the charge on the Turkish positions during the battle. The pursuit was continued and just two days later an Armistice was signed at Mudros, the Turkish force surrendering unconditionally.

SALONIKA

Salonika was a very complicated front, the Allies landing there in 1915 as part of operations to assist Serbia. They were welcomed by the Greek Prime Minister, but not the King who wished to remain neutral. The Serbs had been forced to retreat into Albania, and British and French troops marched north to threaten the Bulgarian flank. The British were however under orders not to cross the Greek border, and the French went on alone. About this time, November 1915, Freddie Knott arrived with the 7th Battalion of the Wiltshire Regiment, the only Kent player to fight in this particular theatre of war. He was serving under the 26th Division which was transferred from France.

The early part of 1916 was spent fortifying the area, the men doing little but digging, earning them the nickname 'the Gardeners of Salonika'. A huge amount of barbed wire was used to create a bastion connecting the Vardar Marshes, the lake defences of Langaza and Beshik to the Gulf of Orfano and the Aegean Sea. Due to the amount of wire used the area became known as the Birdcage. Not to be outdone, the Bulgarian and Austro-Hungarian forces were fortifying the hills surrounding Salonika, and so the front was defined. The digging-in continued into the summer, and the original force was added to by the British, French, Serbians, Russian and Italians. Knott and his battalion settled into the line after taking over trenches from the French near Kalinova at the end of July.

The Allies were confident that Romania was about to declare its allegiance to their side, and prepared for an assault on the Bulgarian Army facing them. Greeks sympathetic to the Germans passed on intelligence about the Allied activity, and the Bulgarians made a pre-emptive strike on 17 August. Caught unaware the Allies were initially knocked back, but managed to hold a defensive line. During this time Knott and his battalion were in the fray near Tertre Vert, repulsing a series of attacks by the Bulgarians. The Allied counter-offensive in September made some ground, but the Bulgarians were in good defensive positions and the going was slow. Gains were made, although not on that part of the front where Knott was based, but his battalion did move up to Doiran during October where they reverted to trench warfare.

The early part of 1917 saw little fighting on the British part of the front. General Sarrail, the Frenchman commanding the Allied Forces (or Armée d'Orient) now had 24 Divisions at his disposal, and he started planning an Allied attack for April. The main part of the fighting was centred around Lake Doiran, where the British made good progress with their attack, and repelled strong Bulgarian counter-attacks. On 25 April 1917 Knott was wounded, his battalion suffering massive casualties when attacking the enemy after a three day artillery bombardment. He was not to return to the country and the outcome of the Salonika Front was determined in 1918 when, following an Allied Offensive, the enemy sought an Armistice.

Although no other Kent players seem to have been involved in this theatre, several references were found to associate Kent players with Salonika. The Bradfield College Register entry for Frederick Leney notes he served with the RAMC in Serbia, but makes no reference to his work with the Red Cross in France and Egypt. It is possible he did transfer from the Red Cross to the RAMC but no records have been discovered to confirm it. In *Tonbridge School and the Great War of 1914-1919*, there is mention that William Hutchings served in Salonika from October 1915 to March 1916; however his service papers place him in Egypt at that time. After the War ended Douglas Carr enquired whether he was eligible for a Salonika medal, probably on the basis he had assisted in supplying that front from Egypt, but presumably he had, or made, no claim as no medal was awarded.

CAUCASUS – DUNSTERFORCE

The Caucasus theatre of war and '*Dunsterforce*' are little known operations of the War, but were part of a number of secret missions designed to speed up victory by bypassing the Western Front. The Eastern Front had collapsed at the end of 1917 and when the Treaty of Brest-Litovsk was signed by Russia and the Central Powers in early 1918, Russia exited the war. This left Germany able to transfer large numbers of troops to the Western Front for their *Kaiserschlacht Offensive* during the spring. The sudden absence of the Russian line also presented problems in the East. Allenby's Mesopotamian forces were left exposed, and Germany was able to invade Southern Russia and the Caucasus to capture oil, minerals and other valuable resources. This opened a way around the Allied blockade of Germany and when the Turks began working along the Trans-Caucasus Railway to the oil rich region to the south, concerns were raised about the safety of Britain's Jewel in the Crown – India.

The strategic solution was to limit Turkish access to transportation routes leading south, in part by occupying the main cities on the Euphrates and Tigris. Allenby's force in Palestine was small, and the Russians were no more, so an obvious need arose to put a new force in the region. The Russians had been 100-200 thousand strong, but those numbers were not replaceable. It was decided that the best solution was to put in a smaller special force, well trained and very mobile. The 1,000 strong force which was raised under General Lionel Dunsterville, later called 'Dunsterforce' (or in some unkind cases, 'Dunsterfarce'), was mainly created from Canadian, Australian and South African Forces, all men with experience on the Western Front, many decorated, and all volunteers. The British contingent accompanying the volunteers was 39th Brigade under which George Wood was serving as Staff Captain, and which was over 2,200 strong.

The volunteers left London in January 1918 and arrived at Baghdad during March, this being where Wood was already stationed. Dunsterville meanwhile had reached Enzeli in February with an advance party but, with the Bolsheviks not willing to entertain them, they had to leave. Dunsterforce eventually occupied Enzeli (in Iran) in June, and sent smaller groups to Baku (in modern-day Azerbaijan) on the Caspian Sea by July. Baku was the main objective of the advancing Turkish forces, and once there Dunsterforce set about its work. The main objectives were to organise resistance from a range of ethnic groups in the Caucasus, mainly Georgians, Armenians and Assyrians. The rail routes were to be guarded and the route to India blocked. If possible independent nations were to be established, although that was a long term project.

Wood arrived at Baku on 24 August and his stay was short though not uneventful. The Turks were already shelling the town, and whilst Dunsterville attempted to negotiate with the local groups, his force made efforts to organise local resistance. Turkish attacks from 26 August were heavy and, with local forces unwilling to man the line, it was left to small groups of Allied troops to bear the brunt. They suffered heavily. When the Brigade withdrew on 14 September, it had only 892 effective rifles, less than the strength of a battalion. Wood, following several reorganizations, was acting as Brigade Major. Their position now untenable, the force left Baku after a major Turkish attack and sailed for Enzeli, arriving on 15 September. That same day the Turkish Army commenced a three day long massacre of Armenian civilians in Baku, resulting in 30,000 deaths. The Force was still at Enzeli when the Armistice between the Allies and Turks came into effect on the last day of October, and Wood returned to Baku when the city was occupied several days after the Armistice with Germany.

WAR AT SEA AND IN THE AIR

In the early part of the twentieth century flying machines were in their infancy, but both the British Army and Navy had an interest in flight, and each had a branch in the fledgling Royal Flying Corps (RFC). The Naval branch broke away to become the Royal Naval Air

Service (RNAS) in 1914, and the RFC and RNAS were merged in 1918 to form the Royal Air Force (RAF). These changes create a certain amount of overlap in the stories of the cricketers in those services, and it makes some sense to review them together. This section therefore covers the Kent's cricketers serving with the Royal Navy (RN), the Royal Naval Reserve (RNR), the Royal Naval Volunteer Reserve (RNVR), the Royal Naval Air Service (RNAS), the Royal Flying Corps (RFC) and the Royal Air Force (RAF).

1914 The Blockade and Control of the Seas

In August 1914 Britain moved quickly to gain control of the seas, and a series of naval battles were fought as the German fleet at sea was defeated. The Royal Navy's *Grand Fleet* was based at Scapa Flow; positioned to block the bulk of the German *High Seas Fleet* from leaving the North Sea, and limiting or preventing German merchant ships from importing vital war supplies. German vessels were detained in ports worldwide and other shipping was boarded and checked for war materials. The Dover Patrol was created to prevent enemy shipping passing through the Straits, and the Northern Patrol to stop them gaining access to the Atlantic by sailing around Scotland. Small vessels played an important role, and when Arthur Fulcher joined the RNR and was given command of the patrol boat *Hersilia*, he became the first Kent cricketer involved in the war at sea, stationed in the Hebrides.

Unable to use her fleet, Germany sent U-Boats out to attack British ships, and on 22 September U-9 torpedoed the British cruisers *Aboukir, Cressy and Hogue,* Ted Humphreys' brother Albert among the crew of *Hogue* that perished. Britain soon began looking for ways to combat the U-Boat threat, and this involved spotter planes from the RNAS as well as the usual patrol boats. In addition to enforcing the blockade, the Navy was able to use its firepower to assist the land forces early in the war. During October 1914 Admiral Hood, commanding Dover Patrol, was off Nieuport with a number of scout cruisers and destroyers. He directed fire on the German forces on land, in support of the Belgians who had just evacuated Antwerp. At this time Barry Cumberlege was on his way to Belgium with the 3rd Cavalry Division to help relieve Antwerp. In the next few days the British ships laid down such a murderous fire that the Germans retreated back behind the Yser.

Toward the end of the year James Mason joined the RNVR and was posted to the Anti-Aircraft (AA) Corps until March 1915. The RNVR AA Corps was, for a while, responsible for defending London from Zeppelin raids which began in 1915.

1915 U-Boat Campaign

Charles Hooman was appointed a temporary Assistant Paymaster in the RNR during February 1915 to serve on *Stephen Furness* in the mercantile fleet auxiliary. His ship was one of the smaller vessels used to stop and search neutral shipping as part of the blockade, taking on the role that Cruisers were reluctant to do as being stationary made them easier targets for U-Boats. Two months later Wally Hardinge joined the RNAS as a mechanic and cyclist with the Royal Naval Armoured Car Division. Experiments had been made with armoured cars on the continent to protect RNAS air bases, and much work was done in England in developing these. Naval cadet Sidney Boucher completed his training at Dartmouth during June and was appointed Midshipman, joining the Grand Fleet at Scapa Flow aboard *HMS Colossus*.

Having failed to gain control of the seas, Germany began a U-Boat campaign, attacking British shipping and hoping to lure out part of the Grand Fleet in order to cause as much damage as possible to it, and reduce Britain's numerical superiority. Both sides deployed mines for defence and offense, and casualties quickly mounted. Initially Germany waged 'restricted' submarine warfare, attacking only merchant ships belonging to Britain and her Allies, but early in 1915, with the blockade already taking effect, the Kaiser ordered unrestricted submarine warfare. The result was a large number of ships lost to the U-Boats, the most famous being the *Lusitania* in May 1915. Germany reverted to restricted submarine warfare that September.

1916 Battle of Jutland

The Battle of Jutland was fought on 31 May and 1 June 1916 in the North Sea near Jutland, Denmark. It was the largest naval battle, and only full scale clash of battleships, of WW1. In fact it was only the third ever fleet action between steel battleships, the two prior occasions having occurred during the Russo-Japanese war in 1904 and 1905. Sidney Boucher was serving on *HMS Colossus* during the battle, the ship taking several hits but fortunately suffering few casualties. The fighting between 250 ships and 100,000 men left some 6,000 British sailors dead. Although the losses were heavier than those the enemy suffered, Britain retained command of the sea, and Germany decided they could not afford another similar action.

1917 U.S.A. Enters the War

During November 1916 Frank Woolley commenced training with the RNAS, and in January 1917 Hooman became temporary Assistant Paymaster on the yacht *Eileen*. Whilst both men were settling into their new positions the Germans resumed unrestricted submarine warfare, and during April the USA declared war on Germany. It would take time for American troops and machines to make a meaningful difference, but Germany realised that if it did not defeat the Allies on the Western Front soon, then their own defeat was inevitable. It was during the following month, with the Allies morale lifted by thoughts of American support, that Able Seaman Ted Humphreys was attached to *HMS Arrogant*, the base flagship of the Dover Patrol, of which he was to be a part. Humphreys was soon serving in the Coastal Motor Boats that patrolled the coast, and was one of a small number based at Dunkirk for operations that side of the Channel. The threat from beneath the sea was still a major worry to the Allies and anti-submarine tactics involved spotting, ramming, bombing, torpedoes and depth charges. New ways of combating the threat were always being worked on. In June 1917 Kent veteran Jack Mason joined the RNVR and was posted to *HMS Tarlair*, a land based experimental station where underwater listening devices were developed to trace submarines.

1918 Zeebrugge and Ostend

Frank Woolley found himself stationed at Felixstowe in February 1918 where he was coxswain of a motor boat tasked with rescuing RNAS pilots who came down in the sea. The RNAS and RFC were merged to form the RAF from 1 April and Woolley and Hardinge became members of that force by default. At the same time the Royal Navy was planning an operation against the German-held ports of Zeebrugge and Ostend. They were the access points to the German submarine base at Bruges, and no attack could be launched on that base by water. The plan was to sink 'blocking ships' at the harbour entrances to prevent the submarines passage, similar to what had already been done at the entrance to Dover harbour earlier in the war to protect it. Most of the men involved in 'Operation ZO' were volunteers because the raids were considered so dangerous. The bulk of the attacking force left Dover on 31 May, but there was also a small contingent from Dunkirk involved, used at Ostend, and among their number was Ted Humphreys on one of the Coastal Motor Boats.

The Zeebrugge Raid is far better known than that on Ostend because it was successful. The ships were sunk as planned, albeit at the cost of many lives lost to the murderous German fire, and the survivors crawled back to Dover the following day to a hero's welcome. The Ostend survivors were not ignored but there was little to celebrate and, when written about, it has generally been as a footnote to Zeebrugge. The crews of the Coastal Motor Boats, including Humphreys, carried out their role bravely, creating a smokescreen, laying inshore buoys and collecting the surviving crew from the blockships, much of their work conducted whilst under fire.

Stevens Brown was called up in July 1918 to serve with the Royal Navy at Stratford. This was the former RNAS Experimental Station, but as the RNAS was no longer in existence, the work carried on there under the RN. Frank Woolley moved to North Queensferry on the Firth of Forth, where his motor boat was berthed by a balloon kite station. His papers confirm he was officially in the RAF from 1 April 1918, but in reality he was employed by Admiral Sir John de Robeck who was commanding 2nd Battle Squadron. The work of the Navy was less critical during the last few months of the war as advances on the Western

Front signalled the end was in sight. The German fleet was ordered to meet the British fleet in a last ditch attack at the end of October, but the mutinies at Wilhelmshaven and Kiel put paid to that. When the Armistice came into effect in November 1918 there were still concerns the Germans might not accept the terms the Allies were presenting. The German Fleet did however surrender itself on 21 November, and Sidney Boucher was present on that memorable occasion, on board *HMS Colossus*.

WAR IN THE AIR

The war in the air was predominantly conducted by the RFC in France, although the use of aircraft became prevalent in other theatres, and the RNAS also played its part. On the Home Front the RFC had training establishments and ground crews and, later in the war, home squadrons to defend against Zeppelin attacks. Due to the expansion of the RFC the training establishments also expanded rapidly, particularly toward the end of the war, and a number of Kent's cricketers served with those units in addition to three who flew as pilots.

The experiences of those cricketers who became pilots demonstrate just how dangerous their role was. Johnny Evans, who was employed with the Intelligence Corps, was attached to the RFC in February 1915 as an observer with No3 squadron. As has been referenced elsewhere he was involved with the new innovation of aerial photography, and was awarded his Military Cross for carrying out his duties despite being under fire during *Loos*. He was forced to land behind enemy lines during the Somme and was taken prisoner for the first time. Having escaped and been posted to Palestine, he was forced to land again, and became a prisoner of the Turks. Noël Boucher was involved in a number of combats in 1917 before his aircraft was shot down in flames, although he managed to land on the British side of the lines. Having served with the Artillery, George Whitehead applied to join the RFC whilst on sick leave. He was re-posted to the BEF toward the end of the war, now attached to the RAF, and was shot down and killed over Belgium during October 1918.

Anti-aircraft batteries were established to prevent or deter aircraft from getting close enough to spot artillery positions and other important locations. The batteries were placed at the front lines, and also sited to protect HQ positions in the rear and vital storage depots. Life was equally dangerous for the aircraft crew and the anti-aircraft units. Ernest Simpson was serving with a mobile anti-aircraft unit in France in September 1917, and was fatally wounded when their position was targeted by German aircraft bombs. Percy Morfee joined the RFC in February 1916 and he served in France from March 1917 as a mechanic, a little further behind the lines where the squadrons were based.

Others cricketers served with the RFC/RAF in one capacity or another. During September

1917 Charles Rucker was briefly the Officer in Charge of Messing at the School of Aerial Gunnery, as he recovered from the amputation of his leg. As previously mentioned Woolley and Hardinge joined by default when the RNAS was absorbed into the RAF during April, Hardinge going on to serve at the Cadet Brigade HQ at Hastings, and Woolley heading to Scotland to serve under the Commander in Chief at North Queensferry. A number of others joined after returning to England through sickness or being wounded. After recovering from being gassed Charles Marriott joined Hardinge at Hastings in July 1918, with the RAF Cadet Wing, and Cloudesley Marsham was posted to the RAF Cadet Brigade at St. Leonards following his return to England. Bill Sarel meanwhile, joined the Staff at the Air Ministry during September following his bout of nervous exhaustion. Although invalided, all these men had much experience that could be put to good use in training new recruits, and that experience was not ignored. James Seymour is also known to have served with the RAF in the latter part of the war, but no service details have been found.

INDIA AND AFGHANISTAN

Several men served in India and Afghanistan, but those places do not form part of the operational theatres of war of 1914-1918. India was part of the Empire, and naturally there was a need to defend it from unwelcome attention whilst regular troops were redirected to the Middle East and the Western Front. Herbert Hatfeild was stationed in India on the outbreak of war, and was part of the forces sent to France to support the BEF. Archie Haywood became one of the replacements sent to the garrisons of India, accompanying the 1/1st Kent Cyclists there. He saw some action during outbreaks of violence by local tribes, and was also part of British force used during the Third Anglo-Afghan War in 1919. Hatfeild returned to India in 1917 and also found himself in the thick of things during the Afghan War. The other cricketer stationed in that part of the world was Gerry Weigall. Once the training units of the Kent Cyclists were reduced, he was stationed in India and Burma, serving with the Bedfordshire Regiment.

ON THE HOME FRONT

The Home Front can be taken to include those who enlisted but saw only service in the UK, others who were attached to reserve units whilst recovering from illnesses or wounds received, and also those who saw non-military service. The time spent at home by those serving in a military capacity are covered elsewhere and, as it would add little to describe the Home Front in a similar way to the other fronts, this section is reserved to describe the non-military service of Kent's players. This covers those in Government work, munitions workers, the Special Constables and Hospital workers, and also takes a brief look at the Club itself.

Several of the cricketers became Special Constables. The first to be referenced as such was Arthur Fielder who was mentioned as serving as a Special Constable in the Committee meeting notes in December 1914. In early 1915 the Club wrote to the non-serving players asking for explanations, and at that time James Seymour was referred to as also being a Special Constable. The Club took a strong line on the players' contribution to the war, and Fielder's application for winter pay was refused in March 1916. One source also suggested that Freeman and Hubble served as Special Constables at some point, but unfortunately there are no records in existence to consult and so that has not been properly confirmed.

Several Kent players worked in the Government. Christopher Salkeld Hurst (Kent 1908-1927) held an appointment in the Public Trustee Office but on the outbreak of war he transferred to the Ministry of Munitions as a Secretarial Officer and remained there throughout, being awarded the OBE (Officer of the Civil Division) and Order de la Couronne (Officer Class) by the Belgians in 1919. Maurice Bonham-Carter (Kent 1902) was Private Secretary to Asquith on the outbreak of the war, and immediately involved in the political side of the conflict. He accompanied the PM around the country on official business and also visited the front line with him at Ypres during June 1915. He was married to Asquith's daughter Violet that same year, and in 1916 he accompanied the PM to Italy and then to Ireland following the Easter Rising. After Asquith was replaced as PM by Lloyd George at the end of 1916, Bonham-Carter became Asst Secretary of the Ministry of Reconstruction and joined the Road Transport Board in 1918. He was made KCB in 1916 as Asquith left his post, and Knight Commander, Royal Victorian Order (K.C.V.O.) in the Birthday Honours of 1917. As noted elsewhere Lord Harris continued to attend the House of Lords throughout the war as well as being involved as Vice-Lieutenant of Kent, in command of the Kent VTC and sitting on the East Kent Tribunal after the introduction of conscription.

Henry Mellor Braybrooke (Kent 1891-99) was the wartime commandant of Oakfield VAD Hospital at Hawkhurst and was awarded the MBE (Civil Division) in 1920. Tom Edward Pawley (Kent 1880-87) was Financial Organiser for the County War Fund, and greatly involved in the establishment of VAD Hospitals. In 1915 he also busied himself with an appeal for cricket equipment to send to the troops of the Kentish regiments. His obituary noted that his only son was killed in the war. William Pearce (Kent 1878) was a chemical manufacturer and MP in London. In an effort to promote co-operation of those involved in the industry during wartime, the Association of British Chemical Manufacturers was established, and Pearce became its first Treasurer in October 1916. In the Birthday Honours of 1915 he was honoured as a Knight Batchelor (Kt) which is not a part of the Orders of Chivalry.

The Club itself continued to operate as far as possible. The General Committee met annually to discuss affairs, and early on showed quite a hard line to its employees – the professional players. Those who were not quick to volunteer were written to demanding explanations, and encouragement to join the colours was given in the form of an offer to make up the difference between normal pay and army pay, and the discontinuance of winter pay for those who did not volunteer. The St Lawrence was occupied by the South East Mounted Brigade Field Ambulance by the end of 1914 and, although the centre strip was protected, men were drilled on the playing field, and horses were stabled on the south side of the ground. Open spaces were needed for use by the military and cricket grounds were apparently well suited for use. The Vines, Sevenoaks became a parade ground, with the pavilion used as a canteen, and the West Kent Yeomanry set up camp at Mote Park beside the cricket ground. Much work was needed to repair damages once the war was over and the Club looked to resume fixtures.

CHAPTER FOUR:
THE MEN

In compiling the individual stories for each man, two occasions arose where it seemed fitting to write a combined entry. The reason for doing so is the same in both instances; the men joined the same battalion, served together and, during major battles, one of each pair was killed and the other wounded. The men had such close ties that a joint entry seemed entirely appropriate. The first pairing is Colin Blythe and Claud Woolley, and the second is Arthur Edwards and Gerald Hough. The remaining entries are for each man's individual story, although for each set of brothers that are included, an introduction is given to avoid repetition of detail.

The rank given in the title for each man is generally that shown on the records for medal entitlements. Where there is no such record the rank nearest to the end of the war is given. Some men did obtain further promotions in the following years, and these are mentioned in the text, but the titles are designed to represent ranks obtained through service during the war.

PRIVATE PERCY CHARLES BAKER

Percy Baker was one of two brothers who played for Kent in the early 1900's, both of them prominent in club cricket with Beckenham. Born on 2 May 1874 at Bromley, Percy was the second son of Stockbroker Alfred John Baker and his wife Alice. He was educated at Uppingham from September 1887 and although the School Roll does not list him as having

secured a place in the XI, he did appear in the fixture against Haileybury College in June 1891. He was seemingly used to make up the numbers, listed as eleventh man but not bowling. On leaving school Baker went up to Christ Church College, Oxford in October 1892, and played in the Seniors' match in 1895. He was

Percy Baker enlisted in the Army Service Corps aged 43. Photograph courtesy The Roger Mann Collection

awarded his BA the following year and followed his father into the world of stockbroking. His success in club cricket earned a trial with Kent in 1900, and he was awarded his cap that year and appeared for the county on 41 occasions, accumulating 1,600 runs. His first class career came to an end in 1902, after which he continued in club cricket.

When war broke out Baker was, at 40 years old, outside the criteria for volunteers, and still outside the age range when conscription was introduced. It was not until April 1918, when the upper age limit was increased to 51, that Baker was called upon to serve. His papers show that he was deemed to have enlisted on 24 April 1918, but was not called to attest until 25 June in Central London. The following day Private Baker was posted to the 18th Battalion of the Essex Regiment, a Home Service Battalion that had been formed at Yarmouth in April for garrison duties, replacing the 15th Battalion which had been posted to France. He remained at Yarmouth for the last months of the War, then transferred to the Army Service Corps (ASC) Motor Transport Depot at Sydenham on 4 December. There he learnt to drive lorries and was for a while close to home, being based at Kelsey Manor, Beckenham. The Manor was home to a unit of the ASC and a hospital during the war years, its size, like many other such homes, proving useful to the authorities. Baker's service with the ASC was fairly brief, and he was demobilized at Wimbledon on 6 March 1919, last serving with 2 Company MT Depot, Sydenham. Baker died in Northwood Middlesex on 30 December 1939, just after the outbreak of WW2.

BANNON BROTHERS

Bernard Douglas and Raymond Blennerhassett Bannon were the first and second sons of solicitor James Norman Bannon and his wife Kate. Bernard was born at Goudhurst on 7 December 1874 and Raymond 23 October 1882 at New Romney. Both boys were schooled at Tonbridge, Bernard from 1890-94 and Raymond 1899-1901. During his time there Bernard was in the XI 1891-94, as Captain in his last two seasons, making an unbeaten 153 against MCC in 1893. Quite the sportsman, he also played in the Football XV 1891-3 as Captain in the last of those seasons, and was joint winner of the Athletic Points' Cup in 1894. He was also Head Boy 1893-94. Raymond followed his older brother's footsteps into Judde House at Tonbridge in 1899, and although he did not have quite the same success he was a school praepostor in his last year, 1901, and made the Cricket XI 1900-01.

Bernard made his Kent 2nd XI debut in 1893, whilst still at Tonbridge, and then went up to Oriel College, Oxford at the end of 1894. The following summer he made his first class debut for Kent against Sussex at Catford, but did not make the University XI until 1897, and was awarded his Blue in 1898 as well as his Kent Cap. He was also a Hockey Blue in 1897 and threw the hammer for Oxford in the Athletic meeting of 1898. His BA in Law was awarded that year and he followed his father in becoming a solicitor. In all he played

25 times for the county, accumulating 755 runs, with a high score of 78 against Lancashire at Canterbury in 1898. Meanwhile Raymond left Tonbridge in 1901 and appeared for the Kent 2nd XI on half a dozen occasions between 1902 and 1904, but made no scores of note. He also became a solicitor and practiced in the Malay States.

On the outbreak of war both Bernard and Raymond were outside the upper age limit for volunteers, and instead joined the Red Cross.

FRENCH RED CROSS DRIVER – BERNARD DOUGLAS BANNON

Bernard Bannon began working as a driver for the French Military Health Service in August 1915 in the Vosges sector, a mountainous area in the Alsace-Lorraine region. During April 1916 he moved to the Reillon Salient in Lorraine which was the scene of severe fighting. The use of flamethrowers and mines by the enemy combined to keep the Red Cross very busy in that area. The worst was however still to come.

Bernard Bannon served with the Red Cross during the Battle of Verdun. Photograph courtesy The Roger Mann Collection.

The Battle of Verdun started with a German attack in February 1916, and the resulting pressure on the French restricted the support they could provide for the Somme offensive that summer. Whilst the Somme was in progress, Germany launched a surprise push on the Verdun front on 1 August advancing toward Fort Souville. Attack and counter-attack followed, and Bannon was moved to Verdun to help with the casualties during September. Souville was a part of the inner ring of forts at Verdun, and its successful defence was a turning point in the battle. If it had fallen, Verdun would likely have followed. The following month Bannon moved to St. Mihiel, a salient within the French lines that blocked communication between Nancy and Verdun. This area was also the scene of very heavy fighting. It is estimated that over 150,000 French soldiers were killed at Verdun in 1916, and the numbers of wounded were much higher.

Bannon's work as with the ambulances was critical to the French, but at the end of 1916 his services seem to have ceased, and no records were found of further service during the war. He was resident at Holloway Sanatorium in Surrey when he died on 18 December 1938, and his effects were left to Raymond.

LIEUTENANT RAYMOND BLENNERHASSETT BANNON

Raymond seems to have beaten his brother to France by several months, arriving in May 1915 from the Federated Malay States. From 2 June he served as a motor ambulance driver with a French Division, and was employed in the same sectors as Bernard, namely the Vosges region, Lorraine and then Verdun. His service with the Red Cross also finished at the end of 1916, and in December he was recorded as sailing from London to Singapore. Six months later, on 15 June 1917, he was employed with the Royal Naval Volunteer Reserve, for service under the Admiralty Intelligence Division with the temporary rank of Lieutenant. Unfortunately the records are quite unclear as to what his role was, but he sailed from Singapore to New York in October 1917, where he remained for five months before sailing on to Liverpool. Back in England he remained with the RNVR until the end of the war.

Bannon returned to the Malay States in early 1919, his demobilization taking effect from the date of his arrival, which was 2 March. He resumed his work as a solicitor and in 1923 became a Member of the Federal Council of the Federated Malay States with the courtesy rank of 'Honourable', a position he held for five years. In 1929 he was married to Margaret Hibbert, and settled on a farm in Hampshire. During WW2 he spent the years 1941-43 in Egypt and was awarded the Order of the Nile 2nd Class for his services to the Government. Post-war he and his wife settled on Jersey in the Channel Islands. Raymond Bannon died on 30 April 1957 at St Peter, Jersey, and his wife died on 17 May. By a strange quirk of fate Raymond's sister Mabel died in June and another sister Hilda died in July.

CAPTAIN KEITH BARLOW

Keith Barlow was born at Essex Villas in Kensington on 27 August 1890, second son of Alice Mary and Edward Percy Barlow, the Chairman of Wiggins Teape, a paper manufacturer. He was a pupil and boarder at Wootton, near Dover, but later had a private tutor after suffering very poor health. During the years 1910 to 1911 Barlow spent time at his father's mill in Dover, as did Ken Hutchings who apparently "worked" there whilst being sponsored by Barlow's father. It was hoped Hutchings might play a role in the company, whilst being free to play for Kent but, though popular, he was apparently not suited to the paper making business. Barlow played for the 1st XI in May 1910, against Oxford and then Cambridge University, scoring 5 and 0 in the first and 6 in the latter. Higher and more useful scores were made in the 2nd XI fixtures he played between 1909 and 1913, and it was in 1913 that he married Elsie Muriel Allen

Barlow applied for a commission in the Royal East Kent (Duke of Connaught's Own) (Mounted Rifles) (REKMR) in March 1911 and having been appointed 2nd Lieutenant he served with Lt. Leach-Lewis, 2nd Lt Hatfeild and 2nd Lt. Tylden. Barlow and his fellow officers were mobilised on 4 August 1914, assembling at Canterbury, where he was appointed Acting Captain on 30 October. The REKMR assisted with Kent's coastal defences and spent time in training. Barlow was second in command of the 3/1st REKMR and remained in England when the 1/1st embarked for Gallipoli in September. A Medical Board during November noted his chronic nephitis, an inflammation of the kidneys which he had suffered for twelve years, as well as a hardening of the arteries and high blood pressure. The Board declared him unfit for service, but he was thanked for his efforts at a time of crisis, and he relinquished his commission on account of ill health on 16 December 1915. The following year he was awarded a Silver War Badge, reserved for those wounded or invalided out of the forces whilst serving.

In May 1917 Barlow wrote to the War Office requesting re-examination in accordance with the Review of Exceptions Bill, to determine whether he was still deemed unfit for duty. The Military Service (Review of Exceptions) Bill, was designed to review medical exceptions and comb out men from industry, agriculture and the mines, to identify those who might be called for service. He attended a Medical Board at Caxton Hall in August but was found permanently unfit for any service. Barlow was appointed Chairman of Wiggins Teape in 1925 having been a Director since 1912. He was elected to the Kent CCC General Committee in 1920, and was treasurer of the Royal St George's Golf Club. He died on 5 April 1930 whilst living in Kensington, aged 39, and Lionel Troughton was among those who attended his funeral.

2ND LIEUTENANT ARTHUR FREDERIC BICKMORE

Arthur Frederic Bickmore was born in Tonbridge on 18 May 1899, second born son of Lilian

Middleton Fanny (née Barwell) and Arthur Lawrence Bickmore an Oxford graduate, schoolmaster, and for many years Headmaster of Tonbridge Preparatory School at Yardley Court. Bickmore attended his father's school and, although it typically fed into Tonbridge, he went on to Clifton College on a scholarship, where he made the Cricket XI. He was a talented batsman, and against Tonbridge in 1916 he made 103 out of 342 and then 86 not out, out of 139-3 declared, heading the yearly averages with 54.16. Playing as captain the following year he scored 32 and 47 against MCC and his average was 47.20.

Eric Bickmore at Clifton in 1916, the year before he enlisted. Copyright Clifton College.

The War came at an awkward time for Bickmore, as he would no doubt have headed to Oxford earlier than he did. Instead service beckoned. He served in the College Officer Training Corps (OTC) from September 1914, and during January 1917 he enlisted and was appointed a Private in the Royal Horse and Royal Field Artillery (RFA). Allocated to the Army Reserve, Bickmore applied for admission to an Officer Cadet Unit and was mobilised in December and attached to No.3 Officer Cadet School (OCS) at Weedon as a Gunner. He fell ill with influenza during the epidemic that swept Europe in early 1918 and, once recovered, was finally commissioned and appointed temporary 2nd Lieutenant in the RFA in June.

Bickmore was posted to France in August 1918, joining 2 Section of the 52nd Divisional Ammunition Column (DAC). The Column was part of the chain which brought ammunition from England to the front line. Ammunition was shipped to France to be stored at key locations, and was then carried by train to mechanized parks that moved supplies to refilling points. The DACs then used horsed wagons to bring their loads towards the front line. At the time Bickmore joined the DAC, the Allies were entering what became known as the *100 Days Offensive*. The 52nd Division took part in the *2nd Battle of Albert* during *Second Somme*, and Bickmore and the DAC would have been very busy arranging supplies to be taken to key points.

The Division took part in the *Battle of the Scarpe* at the end of August during the *Advance to the Hindenburg Line*. As the column was supplying a whole Division, they rarely stayed in one place for long, moving around the Division's sector as required. Working behind the lines did not remove the DAC men from danger, as they were well within reach of German artillery. On one occasion a shell killed 14 mules and wounded 23 other animals of Bickmore's column, disrupting the unit's ability to move their loads. On other occasions the shells injured and killed men in the camp.

Bickmore's unit continued their work as the Division advanced during the *Battles of the Hindenburg Line*, the *Battle of Canal du Nord* and the *Final Push* in November, occasionally carrying out the salvage of German guns as well as delivering supplies. Bickmore joined the advance into Belgium at Peruwelz on 10 November, and it was there, the following day, that orders to cease hostilities were received. Later in the day the Column moved to Sirault where they stayed until almost the end of the month. Demobilization began by New Year's Eve and Bickmore went to Calais on leave on 3 January, not returning to his unit until February. At the end of the month he relinquished his commission, was struck off the strength of 52nd DAC, and granted the rank of 2nd Lieutenant.

Back in England Bickmore had a trial with Kent and his debut followed on 9 June against Essex at Leyton. He was capped in 1920 and went on to play 48 matches for the county, with an average of 23.36 and a high score of 120 against Essex in 1922, an innings which included 20 fours. At Oxford he was at Magdalen College as a commoner, between 1919 and 1921, and seems to have sat one of the special war degrees, only at Oxford for two years as opposed to the usual three or four years. He was awarded his Blue as a freshman, and was also in the College's Association Football XI in 1919/20 and 1920/21. In 1921 he played against Australia twice, first for Oxford and then for Kent, playing a fine innings of 89 for the county.

Bickmore's position as a schoolmaster restricted his appearances for Kent. In January 1923 he became engaged to Lillias Elizabeth Lawson, and the couple were married at Parish Church, Tonbridge in April 1925. He and his brother Maurice were joint Headmasters at Yardley Court, providing scholarships to Tonbridge School, King's Canterbury and a Naval Cadetship during the 1930's. When he died, aged 79, in a nursing home at Tonbridge in 1979 he was the last surviving member of the 1920 Oxford side.

BRIGADIER-GENERAL EVERARD MCLEOD BLAIR

Everard McLeod Blair was born on 26 July 1866 in Bangalore, India, the son of Gustavus Frederick Blair, a Colonel in the Royal Artillery, and his wife Mary. At Cheltenham between January 1877 and July 1884, he represented the College at racquets and gymnastics, was Racquet champion in 1883, and made the Cricket XI in 1883 and 1884, playing against Marlborough both years. From Cheltenham he entered the Royal Military Academy (RMA) Woolwich in August 1884 where he won a prize for Gymnastics and played for the

Cricket XI. Against Sandhurst in 1885, he took 8 for 42 and 3 for 45, and also opened the batting but only made 6 and 0 not out, his partner scoring the 4 runs needed to record a 10 wicket victory.

Blair, pictured in the RMA XI that played Sandhurst in 1885. Supplied by the Sandhurst Collection, the owner of the copyright

Blair standing behind Jack Mason in the Blackheath side of 1901

Commissioned a Lieutenant in the Royal Engineers (RE) in February 1886, Blair was in the Cricket XI from that year until 1905. He was a more than useful bat, heading the averages in 1892, 1893 and 1897 and scoring over 500 runs in five separate seasons. He captained the side in 1892 and 1893, and also played rackets, winning the Army Doubles Championship on several occasions. In later years he suffered poor health and was unable to maintain the brilliance of earlier days.

Blair played only seven times for Kent between 1893 and 1900, five of the appearances in 1893. On the occasion of his debut against Gloucestershire at Bristol he made 61 out of 167, which remained his highest for the county. After 1893 he played once in 1896 and once in 1900. He became a member of the MCC in 1894, representing them in 1902 against Hertfordshire at Lord's, and occasionally played under the name of J. Forrest. He was posted overseas for a while, representing Hong Kong Cricket Club in five games between January 1890 and January 1891, and back in England was appointed an Assistant Instructor in Fieldworks at the School of Military Engineering, Chatham.

In March 1896 Blair was promoted to Captain and appointed Instructor at the RMA from August 1898 until July 1903. About the time he reverted to his Corps he went on sick leave for 12 months suffering neurasthenia. His wife submitted the medical certificates on his behalf, but it is unclear when he married Nora Gladys Dorothy Albertine, perhaps whilst on overseas service. During March 1904, he was promoted to Major, and in June 1912 he was made Lieutenant-Colonel.

The first year of war passed before Blair was ordered to Egypt. About the time he arrived at Alexandria, in January 1916, the RE Force was divided into Cairo and Alexandria districts for administration purposes, and he was appointed Chief Engineer Cairo District. Promotion to Colonel (and temporary Brigadier-General) followed in June, and he was made Chief Engineer No.3 Section Canal Defences, which ran from north of Ferdan to Port Said. The appointment ran until the end of February 1917, during which time he was Mentioned in Despatches.

The GHQ of EEF was transferred from Ismailia to Cairo during October 1916, and all troops east of the Suez became the Eastern Frontier Force. Blair became Chief Engineer and retained the rank of Brigadier-General. A month later he was put in charge of all water supply works from Qantara West to El Arish, an extremely important role. In order to allow the Allies to advance across the desert towards Palestine, it was necessary to build a railway and water pipeline to facilitate the movement of large numbers of troops. The pipeline was planned in four stages, to be laid between November 1916 and February 1917, and pipe-laying began that October, as Blair took up his appointment.

Blair was under huge pressure from the Staff to expedite the construction but, through no fault of his own, not all the correct diameter pipes were delivered. The use of slightly narrower pipes would ultimately result in the delivery of less water than desired, and Blair appears to have received criticism for this from his GOC, Lieutenant General Dobell. With the resources available to him Blair did however make a good job of it. Water was being delivered into the El Arish reservoirs by February 1917 and he was vindicated when Murray, the Commander-in-Chief, congratulated both the GOC and Blair as the completion of the pipeline meant a potential British offensive into Palestine was appreciably nearer. On 1 January 1917, whilst the pipeline was under construction, Blair was also honoured with the CMG.

Before the pipeline had been completed, an extension to it was authorised because local supplies between El Arish and Wadi Ghazee proved to be smaller than anticipated. The extension to Rafah was ordered during February 1917, and was designed by Blair. It covered an additional thirty miles to the original planned route and was completed later that year, after the first two Battles of Gaza. During March 1917, before the work was complete, Blair was ordered to report to the War Office. He sailed on the troopship "Arcadian" which was sunk the following month by a U-Boat, with 277 lives lost.

Back in England, Blair was employed with the RE on the London Defences, but in February 1918 a Medical Board at Caxton Hall deemed him unfit for service and recommended six months leave. He was suffering from neurasthenia, and a Medical Board in July 1918 found him permanently unfit. During August he was placed on retired pay, deemed eligible for the Silver War Badge, and was granted the honorary rank of Brigadier-General. His records show that his wife supported him throughout his illness, often dealing with the War Office when he was unable to do so. He lived in Bath during his retirement and died in St. Andrews Hospital, Northampton on 16 May 1939 aged 72.

LIEUTENANT RICHARD NORMAN ROWSELL BLAKER

Richard Norman Rowsell Blaker was born on 24 October 1879 the fourth child of Solicitor Harry C Blaker and his wife Edith (née Rowsell). Schooled at Westminster from September 1893 to July 1898, he was captain of the Cricket XI and Football team for four years. His

Blaker was awarded the Military Cross in 1918

run in the cricket eleven lasted from 1895 to 1898, as captain in the last two years. He went up to Jesus College, Cambridge in 1898, receiving his BA four years later, and his sporting prowess brought him Blues in cricket and football. He played in the XI against Oxford 1900-1902, and football 1899-1901, as captain in the last year. For Kent, between 1898 and 1908, he gained a reputation as both a hard-hitting batsman and a fine slip fielder.

'Dick' Blaker was awarded his county cap in 1900 and went on to help Kent to carry off the County Championship in 1906. He was a good fielder and able to throw the ball farther than most, perhaps with the exception of Ken Hutchings. Whilst at school at Westminster in 1898, aged 18, he threw a cricket ball 108 yards, breaking the school record. Blaker captained the Butterflies, toured West Indies with R.A. Bennett 1901/02, and appeared for Gentlemen of the South, Oxfordshire, MCC, London Clubs, the Civil Service and Blackheath. He also frequently played football for the Corinthians who had much success in those years. His career with Kent all but ended when he entered the Civil Service in April 1908, as a clerk in the Chancery Registrar's Office. That August he married Mary Kenyon Godby and the couple had three children. By 1911 he was Principal Clerk at the Chancery Registrar's Office, Law Courts.

Blaker was thirty-six years old when he attested during the Derby Scheme, and he entered the Army Reserve as a Private during December 1915. The following March he was posted to 10th Battalion Royal West Kent Regiment Depot, then transferred to the 12th Battalion, where he was appointed Lance Corporal during April, and Lance Sergeant in July. Having successfully applied for admission to an Officer Cadet Unit, he joined No 10 Officer Cadet Battalion at Gailes in Ayrshire at the end of July. After four months of training he was commissioned 2nd Lieutenant in the Rifle Brigade, but almost immediately fell ill with Influenzal Pneumonia. The illness was debilitating, and it was not until September 1918 that Blaker was posted to France to join the 13th Battalion Rifle Brigade, by now a Lieutenant, having been promoted that May.

The war had reached its last stage, the *100 Days Offensive,* and Blaker's battalion moved into the line at Vaucelles preparing to cross the St Quentin Canal. The crossing was made unopposed on 4 October, the enemy having withdrawn, and the battalion joined the attack at Briastre on 23 October, pushing the Germans back further before moving on to Neuville. Blaker and his battalion were then in reserve until the early days of November.

In researching this book I was lucky enough to make contact with a kind soul whose passion is the Rifle Brigade. He has in his library the original copy of an account written by Blaker, describing the events for which he was awarded the Military Cross, and was agreeable to for the account to be reproduced. The tale is unfortunately too long to be recounted in full, but hopefully the following extracts give some idea of just what the attack was like, and the bravery and luck that could be found on the battlefield. Blaker recalled:

The position the 13th R.B. had to attack was, first, a railway line (partly an embankment and partly a cutting); and secondly, orchards (both very strongly held – the orchards particularly so – according to our information).

We had orders to attack on the morning of the 4th November, 1918. Zero time was at 5.30 a.m. There were, as usual, countless conferences, until everyone was quite conversant with their duties, etc. We had some aeroplane photos which gave us a very fair idea what the country we were to attack was like – but the actual location of any machine guns in the orchards had not been reported.

I must say here that as we came through the country before reaching Neuville I always, when I got the chance, went and had a look at the positions over similar country which the Germans had been driven out of and got a good idea where they were likely to put their machine guns, etc.

We started off from Neuville at night, 12.15 a.m., to get to our positions, and after a tiring and muddy march over ploughed fields, and with a certain amount of shelling too, we were met a mile outside Ghissignies by guides from the Lincolns and taken to spots near our starting points.

Blaker and the others then took shelter in a stable, just 100 yards from the German positions. He went out to recce the area they were to attack, and then got his platoon in position. When the artillery barrage started they followed behind it toward the enemy line, and crawled under a hedge. Then:

As I went down the cutting (which was 15 feet) two Germans came out of a dug-out almost under my feet, I managed to kill them both, then I went over the single line and a German officer came out of a dug-out and fired at me from 5 yards but missed, I then killed him and went up the bank the other side and found my Sergt there firing at some Germans who were running away towards the orchards.

Blaker went on alone to "try to have a go at the machine-guns in the orchard" whilst his Sergeant went back to bring the other men forward. This involved Blaker walking through the British barrage.

As I said earlier, I had studied the positions where the enemy were likely to put machine guns and I now found this very useful. It was still fairly dark but beginning to get light.

I immediately saw in a corner of an orchard a place where it was practically certain there would be a machine gun and got there without being seen, and my surmise was right. I got right up to a machine gun dug out with two Germans on the look-out, but they had missed seeing me in the dark and also no doubt they didn't expect anyone so soon and were doing more sheltering than watching. On seeing me they immediately tried to put their hands down for their revolvers, but I killed them both before they could do so, as I was very close on them, thereupon yells came from the dug-out and I shouted "come-out," and out came five pretty scared looking Germans with "hands up."

I motioned them to go back through the barrage towards our lines, and after a slight hesitation, they had to do so. I then went to another likely place on my front and managed to do exactly the same as before to another machine gun crew. I then looked about but could see no more machine guns on my front.

Having cleared more Germans out of their holes, and sent them back toward the British line, he continued on alone until he came to a solitary house on the road. He spotted a crowd of Germans inside:

I don't know who was more surprised – they or I. Anyway I managed to pull myself together a bit quicker than they did and advanced just under the doorway holding a Mills bomb in my left hand and my revolver in my right, the only thing I could think of to say was "Kamerad," and so I said it, at the same time menacing them with my revolver. They didn't seem so very willing to surrender, so I repeated "Kamerad," and to my surprise and delight they "Kameraded," 2 officers and 28 other ranks. My idea is that they were holding a sort of conference, as the barrage was not then reaching them in full force. Both officers and three of the other ranks had Iron Cross ribbons on!

Having sent the prisoners back towards British lines he rounded up between 20 and 30 men from the dugouts and lined them up in front of the house, standing sentinel whilst waiting for his men to arrive.

The barrage knocked things about a good deal and the Germans got a bit uneasy at times and wanted me to go down with them into a cellar under the house and road, but I was not taking any risks. I got a small bit of shrapnel in the face whilst guarding them and one of them wanted to dress it, but again I was taking no risks, as my view of them would have been impeded.

At last to my relief I saw one of our men dodging along just by the road, and then another. I waved to them and think they saw me as they went back, and then the rest came along on to the road about 100 yards off with 2nd Lieut. Dion, "A" Co., and Sergt. Packer, together with about 14 men of my Platoon. I immediately marched the prisoners up to them and sent them off to the rear under escort and told 2nd Lieut. Dion that there were some revolvers and arms in the house and he went off with a few men and got them. I have in my possession now one of the German officer's revolvers from this house.

I found my Lewis gun and three of the team had been knocked out just before reaching the railway, but the rest of the Platoon had had very little opposition after getting over the railway, but the Platoons Nos. 14 and 16 on our right and left had practically been wiped out by machine gun fire from the orchards.

Blaker and his men then successfully pushed on to their final objective, slightly delayed by their own guns firing into their position. Once there:

..my servant, Tubbs, who had come up at the first objective, managed to get me some tea to drink (without milk), but still it tasted excellent as I was very tired and thirsty.

We hung on to this barn and our line until 9.30 at night, when orders came for us to march back to Beaurain, about nine and a half miles. Poor old infantry, after all that, we had to march back, absolutely dead tired too, however, we had to do it and we did.

The next day Blaker found:

....some pieces of shrapnel had gone right through my leather jerkin at the back, just missing my spine, and also a hole was blown right through the top of my torch which was strapped to my belt."

The London Gazette (*Issue 31680, 9 December 1919*) reported his Military Cross award:

"For most conspicuous courage and good work on 4th November, 1918 near Louvignies. While leading his platoon in the attack, he was temporarily cut off from it, and came single-handed on two enemy machine guns in action. He dashed between the guns, capturing them both and their teams. Seeing his men a short distance ahead, and held up by machine-gun fire from a house on their flank, he again single-handed took them in the flank, clearing the house and capturing two officers and 28 other ranks."

No mention of his cup of tea, and one can only wonder at the full stories that lay behind the bravery awards received by the other cricketers. Blaker's battalion was moved back to

Beurain the following day and remained there until 10 November when they moved to Caudry, arriving as the Armistice was announced. During December the Battalion moved to Belgium, and Blaker soon returned to England where he was officially demobilized on 12 February 1919. He resigned his commission in January 1920, retaining the rank of Lieutenant, and returned to work where he rose to Principal Clerk at the Supreme Court. He continued to play cricket for Blackheath and the Civil Service, was President of Sou'Westers CC 1932-1933, and maintained his association with Kent, serving on the Committee from 1946 to 1950, and as President in 1950, the year of his death. He died at Eltham Hospital on 11 September following an operation for peritonitis.

SERGEANT COLIN BLYTHE AND CORPORAL CLAUD NEVILLE WOOLLEY

Colin Blythe is one of the most famous of Kent's cricketers, whereas Claud Woolley is perhaps unknown to most Kent supporters. Claud did however pass through the Tonbridge Nursery and made a number of appearances in the 2nd XI before departing to Gloucestershire and finally settling with Northants. These two men were good friends, and were to enlist and serve together on the Western Front.

Claud Woolley and Colin Blythe, both products of the Tonbridge Nursery, served together on the Western Front. Image of Blythe reproduced by the kind permission of Kent County Cricket Club.

One of the all-time great left arm spin bowlers, Blythe played for the Kent 1st XI from 1899 until 1914. He was born on 30 May 1879 in Deptford, the first child of Walter and Elizabeth Blythe and, following his education at Duke Street Infants and Primary schools, he was apprenticed as a fitter and turner with his father at the Woolwich Arsenal. In 1897 he went to watch Kent play Somerset at the Rectory Field, Blackheath and, whilst there, took a turn in the nets. Captain McCanlis spotted something promising and Blythe was soon trialled at the Tonbridge Nursery, making his 2nd XI debut against Sussex at Hove during July 1898. The following year he was adjudged ready for a first team debut, which he duly made against Yorkshire at the Angel Ground, Tonbridge on 21 August, bowling Frank Mitchell with his very first ball.

Blythe was capped in 1900 and that same season he took 100 wickets, going on to achieve the feat in every season up to 1914, except 1901. One of Wisden's Cricketers of the Year in 1904, his highest season's haul was in 1909 with 215 wickets at 14.54. In 1907 he took 17 wickets in a day against Northants, and his 10-30 in the first innings of that match was a record for himself and Kent that still stands. In all he played 381 matches for Kent, claiming 2,210 wickets at 16.67, accumulated 195 five wicket innings and 64 ten wicket matches. His first Test appearance was in 1901/02 with McLaren's team in Australia, and his 100 Test wickets averaged 18.63. In the midst of his cricketing success Blythe was married to Janet Gertrude Brown at Greenwich on 11 March 1907 and the couple lived in Tonbridge.

Claud Neville Woolley found his cricketing success with Northamptonshire, and later as an umpire, but his career began when he passed through the Tonbridge Nursery around the same time as his younger brother Frank, and he played for the Kent 2nd XI eighteen times during the years 1906-1908. Claud was born in Tonbridge on 5 May, 1886, third son of Charles and Louisa Woolley. The boys' father was a dyer, cycle maker and agent and, as the automobile became popular, a motor engineer. Claud and his three brothers used to play on the tarmac area behind their father's workshop in Tonbridge, propping a board

Colin Blythe, left arm bowler but right handed bat

against the wall as a wicket, and taking turns with the bat. A few years later Claud joined the Tonbridge Nursery, and first played for the Kent 2nd XI in 1906, the year that Frank broke into the first team. Frank was, however, playing for the 2nd XI on the occasion of his brother's debut, against Middlesex 2nd XI at Lord's. Claud kept up with him as far as scoring runs went, making 24 and 4 to Frank's 6 and 21, but Frank settled any sibling rivalry by taking 9 wickets and holding 2 catches. A further four appearances came that season, six in 1907 and seven in 1908, but he struggled to stand out.

Claud made a decision to move on from Kent and joined Gloucestershire in 1909. He made his first class debut against Australia that August, but was unable to establish himself in the side. Another move in 1911 took him to Northamptonshire, as the professional at Lilford Hall, residence of Lord Lilford, the President of Northants Cricket Club. Both Claud and Lord Lilford made their first class debuts against the Indian tourists in July, the pair at the bottom of the batting order. Claud scored 1 not out, but marked his appearance with his maiden first class wicket, that of Mukandrao Pai. The following season, now qualifying for his new county by residence, he appeared for the 1st XI regularly, although it wasn't until 1913 and 1914 that his performances began to pick up. 1914 saw his maiden century against Somerset, 103 in 145 minutes, and he finished the season with 802 runs to his name.

On the outbreak of war Claud returned to his family home in Tonbridge and within a few weeks he, Blythe, Henry Preston and the Jennings brothers enlisted in the Kent Fortress Engineers (KFE). All the men cited skills useful to the KFE, Blythe having trained with his father as a civil engineer and Woolley working as a fitter in his father's workshop. The new recruits received their initial training at Tonbridge in No.1 Reserve Company, and in October 1914 were sent to the 'Woodlands' depot in Gillingham. Blythe and Woolley remained at Gillingham for over two years, appointed to 2/7th company which was formed in 1915 out of the reserve company they had been recruited into. Before the end of the year both men had been promoted to Corporal and Blythe was promoted again the following year, to Sergeant. As part of the Territorial Force they were employed to work on coastal defences, but when conscription was introduced at the start of 1916 they were required to sign Imperial Service Obligations. Once those forms were signed at Minster in January 1916 the cricketers were liable to be sent overseas.

Blythe and Woolley were however not destined to be posted to the Western Front until mid-1917, and in the interim they formed a KFE Cricket team, along with the Jennings brothers and Bill Fairservice. Earlier in the war some opinion had pushed for the cessation of cricket whilst men were dying at the front, but by now it was seen as a way of raising public morale. Their first game was against a Royal Engineers side and Blythe led the way, taking 3-33 and 4-3 as they won by an innings. In June 1916 the side beat South Africa at Gravesend, Blythe taking 7-36, and in August they played regular games at the Oval and

Lords. Meanwhile, across the Channel, the *Somme* Offensive had seen the loss of so many lives that it was only a matter of time before the KFE members posted to France.

In early 1917 Blythe and Woolley were amongst the Territorials identified for service overseas, and they spent the summer at a training camp in Marlow, Bucks. Whilst based there Blythe played his last game at Lord's, for the Army and Navy versus an Australian and South African side during August. His only wicket turned out to be his last, that of McCartney. Blythe had by now recognised his talents were waning, and spoke to Lord Harris about the matter, saying he did not think he could still spin the ball as well as in his prime, and would not be fit for the first eleven by the time the War was over. He applied for and received the position of cricket coach at Eton, intending to start his employment when hostilities ceased.

At this time both Blythe and Woolley were transferred to a Pioneer battalion, the 12th Battalion King's Own Yorkshire Light Infantry (KOYLI), and sailed for France on 25 September 1917. Having arrived in the Ypres sector they were sent with B Company to Watou for training in light railway construction. The Ypres Salient was overlooked by the Germans from the higher ground which gave them a natural advantage. The area had been subjected to so much shelling over the preceding years, that the drainage systems had been all but destroyed, stream and river banks broken, and the muddy ground was pocked with flooded shell holes and extremely hard to traverse. This made the movement of men and supplies very difficult and the engineers and pioneers were needed to lay and maintain the duckboard routes and light railway lines that enabled food and ammunition to be moved forward. The men often worked at night under cover of darkness, and although this was seen as less dangerous than the role of the infantry, the engineers suffered many casualties from shell fire, the railways visible to the Germans and constantly targeted.

Blythe and Woolley spent the following weeks working on the Wieltje (Forest Hall) and Bedlington lines as the *Third Battle of Ypres*, or *Passchendaele*, was fought. On 6 November the village of Passchendaele was finally captured by the Canadians in a fierce battle. Days later the ridge was secured, and the campaign was over by 10 November. Between those two events, on the evening of the 8 November, a shell landed behind the British lines, close to a party working on the line between Wieltje and Gravenstafel, which was at this time close to Pommern Castle. Three men were killed instantly, including Colin Blythe, and Woolley was amongst the injured. Whilst Blythe was buried at Oxford Rd Cemetery at Wieltje, Woolley was evacuated to England. Just how badly he was injured is difficult to say, his service records making no reference to the incident. Mourning the loss of his good friend, he was attached to the RE Base Depot whilst he recovered. The best part of a year passed before he was considered fit for duty again.

During July 1918 Woolley was posted to France for the second time, joining 447th Field

Company RE in 50th Division. The *100 Days Offensive* was underway, and as the Allies pushed up to the Hindenburg Line the Germans retired to the St Quentin Canal. The 50th was the only Division of XIII Corps in the line on 1 October, and it fell to them to make the crossing of the Canal at Vendhuille. Woolley's Company, together with the 446th, built a heavy bridge near the village, whilst two foot bridges and a pontoon bridge were erected by other units. This enabled XIII Corps to make rapid progress to the River Selle, which was crossed on 17 October. Twenty infantry bridges were put across at St. Benin and St. Souplet, four launched by Woolley's Company, and the infantry were again able to make a rapid crossing. By 21 October XIII Corps was in Reserve, and Woolley was granted 14 days leave to the UK from 29 October. This meant he was in England when the Armistice came into effect, and perhaps able to celebrate with his family. Having returned to France he was finally despatched to the UK on 7 March, 1919 and was demobilized during April.

Two months after his return to England, Woolley was back playing for Northamptonshire, and was a regular in the side until 1931. When he retired he had made more runs than any other Northants player, and scored over 1,000 runs in a season seven times between 1921 and 1929, being in the 900's on three other occasions. Against Worcestershire in 1921 he made 204 not out, and against Glamorgan had match figures of 10 for 52, his first and only ten wicket match haul. During his successful 1921 season he was apparently owed £70 in wages but, after he threatened to leave and join Kent, his grievances were dealt with.

Woolley went on to captain the first Northants team entirely made up of professionals, as they defeated Kent by 10 wickets in 1929. He also lay claim to being the first professional to captain Northants, and represented the Players in the drawn match at the Oval in July 1922. He scored some 15,000 runs for Northants in total, and took 352 wickets.

Northants had financial problems in 1931, and Woolley found himself released, at the age of 45. In *100 Greats: Northamptonshire County Cricket Club (Radd 2001: 128)* the author wrote that he would probably have been appointed coach if the finances were stronger, but instead he joined the first-class umpires list, officiating until 1949, including the Ashes Test at Lord's in 1948. His last years were spent as assistant groundsman at the County Ground. He was married to Constance May Taylor in Northampton in the latter half of 1926, and died at their home in Abington on 3 November, 1962, having survived Colin Blythe by forty-two years. Following his cremation at Milton, his ashes were scattered on the County Ground.

BOUCHER BROTHERS

Noël and Sidney Boucher were the sons of solicitor Franklin Coles Boucher and his wife Ada. Noël was born first on 22 December 1896 and Sidney on 17 September 1899 in Rochester. They were both educated at Dumpton House Preparatory School in Ramsgate, but whereas Noël went on to Tonbridge in 1911, Sidney entered the Royal Naval College at Osborne during September 1912.

LIEUTENANT NOËL BOUCHER

At Tonbridge from 1911-1915, Noël was in the Cricket XI 1914-1915 and a school prefect in his last year. When the school played Clifton in 1914 George Whitehead was opposition captain, and in 1915 Eric Bickmore opened for them. Boucher also joined the school OTC and left with the rank of Lance-Corporal in July 1915, to be commissioned 2nd Lieutenant in the 3/4th Royal West Kent Regiment, the same battalion Walter Monckton had joined the previous month. In April 1916 he was attached to the 4/4th reserve battalion and spent the next six months at Crowborough. The battalion moved to Tunbridge Wells by October 1916, and that same month Boucher, now a temporary Lieutenant, entered No.2 School of Military Aeronautics, a training school for the RFC based in Oxford. There he underwent preliminary training and was taught flight theory, including map reading, gunnery and mechanics.

Noël Boucher, captain of the St John's College XI in 1921. Reproduced by permission of the President and Fellows of St. John's College, Oxford (PHOTO I.D.13)

On 1 December 1916 Boucher was officially seconded to the RFC and continued his training for several months, qualifying as a Flying Officer at the end of April. On the last day of the month he left to join the Expeditionary Force, reporting for duty with 20 Squadron on 8 May. His new unit was tasked with carrying out reconnaissance duties behind enemy lines, photographing German positions and destroying aircraft. At the time Boucher arrived they were mainly flying FE2's.

During May and into June, Boucher put in 100 hours active flying time in the Ypres and Armentières areas, flying with his Canadian observer, Lieutenant NM Birkett. They had been credited with shooting down two German Albatros Scouts, one on 20 May and the second on 26 May, and were involved in reconnaissance duties as the Battle of *Messines* began. The crews reported back German gun positions, and also alerted the artillery when enemy infantry were seen in the open so that a crushing bombardment could be directed upon them. Messines was taken and the fighting over by 14 June. At this time Boucher's squadron was based at St. Marie Cappel aerodrome, just south of Cassel, and looking for any enemy build-ups or new defences in the wake of Messines.

On the evening of 17 June 1917 Boucher and Birkett set off on a Close Offensive Patrol, flying FE2D A6469. At about 18.30 as they were flying over enemy territory near Houthem, several miles south-east of Ypres, they were attacked by a number of Albatros Scouts. Their aircraft was badly damaged and set alight by Oberleutnant E Dostler of Jasta 6, and Boucher was shot in the stomach. In spite of his wounds, he managed to guide the aircraft back over the line, and crash-landed in the fields. *Tonbridge School and the Great War (Tonbridge School, 1923: 386)* recorded that Boucher suffered severe burns and he was evacuated to England on 23 June and admitted to hospital.

Boucher spent time in a Convalescent Hospital and, for administration purposes, was attached to 76th (Home Defence) Squadron. During that time the London Gazette announced he was promoted to Lieutenant effective 1 July. By early January 1918 he was deemed fit enough to begin flying again in a dual control aircraft, and within two months was able to undertake ordinary flying. On 1 April as the RFC and RNAS merged, Boucher became a Lieutenant of the new RAF (attached from the RWK). He did not return to active service, but instead became an Instructor and night pilot at Copmanthorpe near York through to February 1919, helping to train new pilots. His papers reveal he flew a wide range of aircraft and held a First Class Aerial Gunnery Certificate from Turnberry, which was one of two aerial gunnery schools in Ayrshire, open from 1917 to the end of the war.

Later in the year Boucher attended a course of instruction at the School of Wireless at Penshurst and returned to 76th Squadron on 21 October. Within weeks the war was over. Boucher was demobilized in February 1919, relinquished his commission in November 1920, and was appointed a Lieutenant in the TF. That year he went up to St. John's College at Oxford and left in 1921 with a BA, having been granted some dispensations for war service. The following year he resigned his commission in the TF.

In 1921 Boucher played for Mote, as did his brother, and in 1924 and 1925 he made several appearances for the Kent 2nd XI. Against Bedfordshire in 1924 he opened the batting and made 60, and the following year he opened with a young Les Ames against Surrey. He turned out on occasion for Yellowhammers, and played for Mote as late as 1934. In 1923 he was admitted a solicitor and was in practice at Rochester for many years. He married Edith Brice in 1927 and, living in Rochester, was made Clerk to City Magistrates and Deputy Coroner, positions he held into the 1960's.

During WW2 Boucher's talents were called upon again, and he was appointed Acting Pilot Officer in the RAF Volunteer reserve for service with the ATC. He continued in his practice after the war, and in 1963 was appointed President of Kent County Cricket Club and also of the Kent Law Society. Noël Boucher died on 27 July 1968 in London, and a service was held for him at Rochester Cathedral.

SUB-LIEUTENANT SIDNEY 'SAM' BOUCHER

During Sidney Boucher's time at Osborne he became Chief Cadet Captain, and during September 1914 moved on to the RN College at Dartmouth to continue his studies. He was appointed Midshipman from 30 June 1915, joining the dreadnought battleship *HMS Colossus*. The Navy had effectively gained control of the seas, and *Colossus* was part of the Grand Fleet stationed at Scapa Flow, blockading Germany to prevent its merchant shipping entering the Atlantic Ocean. The German Highs Seas Fleet was bottled up following the RN success at Heligoland Bight in August 1914 and had embarked on a campaign of restricted submarine warfare, attacking British merchant shipping. Boucher joined *Colossus* just a month after the passenger ocean liner *RMS Lusitania* was sunk with the loss of some 1,200 lives.

During May 1916 the British deciphered a German message with the help of a captured code book, and discovered the German High Seas Fleet was planning an action. Vice-Admiral Sir John Jellicoe led the Dreadnought Battle Fleet out of Scapa Flow to rendezvous with Vice-Admiral Beatty who had taken a group of scouting cruisers to make contact. Boucher was on board *Colossus* as she led 1st Battle Squadron, having been made flagship the previous November. Beatty's force engaged with the German scouting group but withdrew toward Jellicoe, the following Germans unaware that the British Battle Fleet was at sea. When Jellicoe deployed the fleet at 17.51, Boucher and *Colossus* were seventeenth in line, and the two forces, 250 ships in total, clashed between 18.30 and 20.30, directly engaging twice.

Jellicoe led the British fleet across the line of the German Fleet to form a 'T' shape, a tactical move that had met with success in the Russo-Japanese War. As the range closed, the *Colossus* opened fire at 18.30 but Scheer soon had his fleet performing an evasive move in order to flee. At 19.00 the British again crossed the 'T', and this time the Germans suffered heavily. Boucher was in the thick of the fighting with *Colossus* which fired on an armoured cruiser, *SMS Wiesbaden*, at a range of less than 10,000 yards. The German ship later sank after taking damage from several British vessels. *Colossus* also reported hits on *SMS Derfflinger* and at 17.16 was hit herself by heavy shellfire, suffering damage to the forward superstructure. Eventually the German fleet slipped away under cover of darkness, and Boucher spent a tense night on *Colossus* as the British tried to locate the enemy ships.

The battle over, Boucher returned to the UK where *Colossus* underwent a refit and finally returned to the Grand Fleet in September. During the following year Boucher studied and took exams as part of his progression towards a promotion to Lieutenant, was appointed acting sub-Lieutenant in January 1918 and confirmed in the rank in June. He moved with *Colossus* to Rosyth in April 1918, but there was little more action for him before the end of the war. He was however present on board *Colossus* on the occasion of the surrender of the German fleet on 21 November 1918.

Boucher was appointed Lieutenant in June 1920, and all his reports noted what a fine athlete he was, cricket being something of a speciality. Both he and his brother played for Mote in 1921, and his single appearance for Kent 1st XI came the following season against Hampshire at Southampton. On that occasion he bowled a few overs without success and only batted once as Kent won by 51 runs. His career obviously prevented him playing again, but he did meet with much success for the Navy, captaining the side for a number of years. Shortly before his first class debut Boucher had applied to go on a Physical and Recreational Training course, and by 1924 had qualified as a PT specialist. Between the wars he held many positions, both on shore and at sea, was promoted to Lieutenant Commander and was married twice, firstly to Phyllis Ellershaw in 1924, and then to Betty Holt in 1938.

In 1939 Boucher was Assistant Director of Physical Training and Sports, Admiralty and Secretary of the Sports Control Board. After war broke out he worked as liaison officer with the Army (Southern Command) until the beginning of 1941 when he was given command of the Destroyer *HMS Highlander*. Boucher was also commander of the 9th Escort Flotilla, and he continued to serve almost continuously at sea throughout the war. He was promoted to Captain in 1942 and shortly afterwards took command of *HMS Cormorant*, which was the RN base at Gibraltar, and where he was responsible for the large number of destroyers and smaller craft that passed though for repairs. During this time he was Mentioned in Despatches.

At the end of 1944 Boucher was appointed Captain of *HMS Tyne* and was Chief Staff Officer and subsequently Flag Captain to Rear-Admiral (Destroyers), British Pacific Fleet.

He was serving in the Pacific when the Japanese surrendered on 2 September 1945 and was subsequently awarded the CBE for distinguished services during the war. Boucher spent the following years as Senior Officer of the Reserve Fleet and then as Director of PT and Sports at the Admiralty. In January 1951 he was made Aide-de-camp to King George VI, and retired from the Navy that summer. The King died in early 1952, but Boucher lived on until 4 August 1963 when, aged 63, he passed away at his home, the aptly named Turret House in Wadhurst.

MECHANIC 2ND CLASS STEVENS WILLIAM BROWN

Stevens William Brown was born at Cliffe near Rochester on 15 April 1875, the son of builder George W Brown and his wife Harriet. He is referred to as Stephen William Brown until the 1911 Census, by which time the Stephen had become Stevens. Twenty years before, at the age of fifteen, Brown had followed his father into the building business, working as a cement labourer, there being a thriving cement and brickmaking industry in the area. Taken on at the Tonbridge Nursery in 1899, he was given the chance to play for the 1st XI three times that season, against Essex the MCC and Sussex. He was predominantly employed as a bowler, as were all the Nursery men, and took a handful of wickets but failed to impress.

Brown was with the Nursery in 1901, but that seems to have been his last season in the Kent ranks. By 1911 he was landlord of the Halfway House in Chatham, and on his conscription in 1918 his occupation was described as an 'engineer'. Perhaps his work directed him towards the Royal Navy, as he was employed as Mechanic 2nd Class from 26 July 1918 for the duration of hostilities. It should be remembered that Brown was beyond the age of volunteering in 1914 and just beyond the age of conscription in 1916. He became eligible for service when the Military Services Act of 1918 extended the conscription limits to capture men aged 41 to 50. Stratford, where Brown served, was an RNAS Experimental Station until April 1918 when the RNAS merged with the RFC to form the RAF. It was there that Wing Commander Brock had devised and tested the smoke screens used for the Zeebrugge and Ostend raids and was also where phosphorus grenades were developed and hydrogen gas produced for airships.

Brown's papers do not state what he actually did, but other first-hand accounts reveal that Stratford had a parade ground where the men spent their first weeks being drilled to get them into shape, and that is presumably how he began his service. The station had many smoke floats stored there, these being designed for use by dropping them over the side of ships to float on the water and provide cover. Brown would have taken his turn on guard duties to protect the stores of equipment and experimental designs. It is also possible he went out on night patrols if a mechanic was required to use the equipment under development, and quite possibly crossed the Channel to escort troop ships back to Dover. He was awarded the British War Medal and Victory Medal for his service after he was demobilized on 14 January 1919. Stevens Brown was aged 82 when he died on 21 October, 1957 at Watford.

BRYAN BROTHERS

Jack and Ronnie Bryan were the first and second sons of Emily Beatrice and Lindsay Edward George Bryan, a solicitor. The brothers were born in Beckenham, John 'Jack' Lindsay on 26 May 1896 and Ronald Thurston on 30 July 1898. They and their younger brother Godfrey were all left-handed and all played for Kent. Jack was described as a timid little boy when he started at St. Andrew's preparatory school in Eastbourne in 1907, but he soon found a liking for sports, captaining the 1st XI, and was also academically proficient, winning a scholarship to Rugby in 1911. Ronnie followed Jack to both schools, always a year behind. Members of Stallard House at Rugby, the brothers were both in the XI, and Jack was also a keen rugby player and represented the school in the Racquets Pairs.

Jack (left) and Ronnie Bryan (right) both fought on the Western Front

Ronnie made his mark as a bowler in 1913 and played each year until he left in 1915. As Captain in his final year, Jack led the side against Marlborough at Lord's in 1914, and in August he opened with George Whitehead for Lord's Schools against the Rest, scoring 122 in the second innings against a side that included Heslop and Capes. At the start of the 1914 season the brothers had attended the pre-season gathering of young amateurs and professionals at Tonbridge Nursery, and toward the end of August they both found places in the Kent 2nd XI, playing against Essex at Hythe. They were also both in the Club and Ground side against Merion toward the end of the month.

MAJOR JOHN LINDSAY BRYAN

Jack Bryan volunteered for service with the Honourable Artillery Company (HAC) on 26 August 1914, the day after the Merion match, subsequently serving as a Private in C Company. He wrote afterwards that, having achieved a Certificate A with the Rugby OTC, he was a little more experienced than most recruits. The 1st Battalion HAC did not depart with the initial BEF, but sailed for France on board the SS "Westmeath" on 18 September. The men's rifles had only arrived two days before and they had spent no time on the ranges, so they were allowed a few days on the ranges before moving to St. Omer toward the end of October to help construct the reserve line.

The following week Bryan was carried toward the front on a bus of the London General Omnibus Company. Employed on digging trench-works behind the firing line, the HAC were within range of the German artillery as Bryan found to his cost. On 14 November, as *Ypres* was drawing to a close, he was to the south at Rouge Croix near Neuve Chapelle, when wounded in the head and shoulder by shrapnel. He was taken to No.8 General Hospital at Rouen where a piece of shell was removed from his shoulder. This was a 'Blighty' wound, and Bryan returned to England on the 'Asturias', a hospital ship that had already carried Johnny Evans across the Channel, and would also evacuate Con Johnstone the following year. It was sunk in 1917 when torpedoed by the Germans without warning.

Initially sent to a school in Kemp Town, Sussex that was not really prepared for the new arrivals of wounded from the front, Bryan's father arranged his removal so that he was home for Christmas. During January he re-joined the HAC at Armoury House in London, but in February received a commission as 2nd Lieutenant in the 2/5th Manchester Regiment, backdated to 20 January. From May 1915 his battalion moved from Southport to Crowborough in East Sussex and it was here that he attended a Machine Gun course. The 1/5th Manchester battalion had landed at Cape Helles at the beginning of May 1915, in support of the initial Gallipoli landings, seeing its fair share of action and suffering heavily. With reinforcement drafts desperately needed, Bryan sailed from Southampton on the SS Mauritania on 28 August, reaching Lemnos after a five and a half day voyage. He then finished the journey to *Gallipoli* on a paddle steamer called 'Brighton' which amused him as the family lived in Sussex.

On reporting for duty Bryan was immediately attached to the 1/4th East Lancashire battalion but, in his own words, '*made a fuss*' as he had only agreed to serve overseas with his own regiment. A few days later he joined the 5th Manchester's, and was appointed Machine-Gun Officer, on the strength of the course he attended days before leaving England. His stay was brief although it did overlap with the arrival of the Kent cricketers of the Yeomanry who also joined the 42nd Division at Helles. Here Bryan commanded the extreme left hand machine-gun of the British Army, just above the beach, an honour he was to hold in two other theatres of war. Bryan left the peninsula on 27 October, evacuated to Mudros suffering from jaundice. He did not re-join his battalion until 28 December by which time they too were on Lemnos after the general withdrawal that month.

Bryan moved to, and remained in, *Egypt* until February 1917, during which time the machine-gun sections of the 5th, 6th, 7th and 8th Manchester battalions were brigaded into the 127th Brigade Machine Gun Company (MGC), Bryan in command of one section of men of his former battalion. Three weeks were spent at Mena by the Pyramids, before moving to Suez, where the remainder of the year was given to training and practicing operations. During this time Bryan spent his second stint in command of the left hand machine-gun of the British Army as part of the advance guard protecting the railway being built towards El Arish. He later recalled that he 'wangled a couple of courses in Cairo' scoring 100% on one of the more difficult papers. These were a Machine Gun Course and Machine Gun Tactics Course at Zeitoun, and he received his 'Distinguished' mark at the former. He also noted that there were many Band of Brothers players in the East and West Kent Yeomanry, and that he made a trip to Cairo to play cricket for the Division on the Gezira Club ground. It is likely some of the Kent players in the SEMB accompanied him.

Their training complete and the need for men on the Western Front quite urgent, the 42nd Division was ordered to France. Having landed at Marseilles in March they were soon re-equipped with new Vickers guns to replace their Maxims. Time was spent at various positions in the Somme sector, but on 26 May, Bryan's 21st birthday, he was hospitalised with PUO (pyrexia of unknown origin). His papers refer to it as 'trench fever', but whatever it was it put him in the same ward of the hospital at Rouen that he had been in during November 1914. Having re-joined his unit Bryan was promoted to Lieutenant on 1 August and headed north to Ypres at the end of the month. A lot of time was spent in the Nieuport area over the next two months, and it was here that Bryan was, for the third time, in command of the extreme left hand machine-gun of the Army, lapped by the sea at high tide.

During early 1918 Machine Gun Battalions were formed in Divisions, by bringing together the four Brigade MGC Companies into a single unit. Bryan's 127th MGC was absorbed into the 42nd MGC Battalion, together with the 125th, 126th and 268th MGCs, and was designated C Company. Just five days later on 21 March 1918, whilst the battalion were training, the German *Kaiserschlacht* was launched. Bryan was soon on his way to the front, ordered into the line north of Albert in the Somme region. The individual companies were attached to different infantry brigades, covering retirements, and in the general confusion Bryan's Company lost touch with the Battalion, ending up fighting a rear-guard action in the 31st Division area. The Division repulsed all attacks on 27 March, but suffered heavy casualties before being relieved two days later. As the German offensive continued, Bryan was appointed Acting Captain whilst second in command of a Company, and the threat of a German breakthrough gradually subsided.

Lieutenant Jack Bryan serving with the 42nd Machine Gun Battalion on the Western Front (left) and another snap of him taken during the war (right). Reproduced by the kind permission of Pat Bryan

The *Hundred Days Offensive* opened with the Battle of Amiens on 8 August, the beginning of the last stage of the War. Bryan's Company was in the thick of *Second Somme*, engaging hostile snipers, MGs, Trench Mortars and Artillery pieces to cover the advancing infantry and harass the retiring Germans. On the night of 20 August their machine-guns were fired at intervals to neutralize the sound of tanks moving forward for use in the *Battle of Albert* the next day. Albert was captured on 22 August, and Bryan played his part, a heavy barrage being put down by the artillery and MGs from positions in Munich Trench.

The Germans were now positioned at Miraumont and, following a heavy bombardment which included gas shells, they counter-attacked on 22 August. This attack was entirely broken up by the MGs, 36,000 rounds were fired and several hundred dead were afterwards counted in front of the MG positions. The MGs were also instrumental in the capture of 217 prisoners. For his role in the action, Bryan was awarded the Military Cross, the London Gazette (*Issue 31043, 29 November 1918*) carrying the following announcement:

> **Lt. (A/Capt.) John Lindsay Bryan, 1/5th Bn., Manch. R., T.F., Secd. 42nd Bn., M.G. Corps.**
>
> *Under very heavy fire he made a skilful reconnaissance and brought his guns into positions from which he broke up a counter-attack with heavy loss, and was able to cover the subsequent advance of our infantry. He displayed great ability in the way he handled his guns, and his coolness and courage under fire set a fine example to his men.*

Bryan modestly played down the award, writing '*got the MC, largely because I brought the earliest first hand news back to Brigade about what the situation was, but the citation does not say this!*' The following day the MGs together with the artillery fired upon the German positions, to prepare the way for fighting patrols, and within two days Miraumont was captured.

Joining the *Advance to the Hindenburg Line,* Bryan took part in the *Second Battle of Bapaume*, and harried the enemy as they fell back from Canal du Nord to their Hindenburg Line positions. A few days later the battalion was relieved and, during a fortnights rest, he attended a Company Commanders course at the MG School, Camiers, taking command of A Company on his return, through to the Armistice. His Company covered the attacking infantry during the *Battles of the Hindenburg Line* toward the end of the month and, when the German defences were breached, on *Beyond the Hindenburg Line*. He crossed the River Selle on 20 October using pack animals to carry guns and ammunition, and led his Company to take up positions on the high ground, engaging the enemy with considerable effect. They fired some 57,000 rounds to cover the 127th Infantry Brigade's advance.

The crossing of the River Sambre began in other sectors on 4 November, during which the war poet Wilfred Owen was killed, and Bryan's Division made their way forward the next day, having to use pack animals again to circumvent the craters blown in the roads by the retreating enemy. The Forest of Mormal was entered, entirely unsuitable for MGs due to the closeness of the country, but was cleared by nightfall, and the Sambre was crossed on 7 November. The MG battalion were withdrawn on 10 November, and the following day hostilities ceased at 11.00. Bryan was appointed Acting Major in command of a company on 24 November, and then moved with the Division to Velaine in Belgium in December, where the process of demobilization began. He relinquished his acting rank of Captain on 1 May 1919, but was a Captain with the Territorial Force Reserve for some time.

Bryan played several times for Kent in 1919 before going to St. John's College, Cambridge, where he read History and Mathematics and was conferred his BA in 1921. In his first year there he scored 83 in the Freshman's match and 97 for Perambulators against Etceteras, but the competition for places was so strong he was not to gain his Blue until 1921. Taking up a teaching position at his old school St. Andrew's, Bryan was only able to play for Kent in the holidays from 1922 until 1932, but did captain the side on a number of occasions. He was awarded his Kent cap in 1920, scored 6,174 runs for the county, and could also bowl. He took a wicket with his second ball in first class cricket against Essex at the Crabble in 1920, a wicket with his first ball for Cambridge, and also with his first ball for MCC, the only wicket he took in Australia. Wisden named him one of their five cricketers of the year in 1922, and the following summer he made a career best 236 out of 480 against Hampshire. He toured Australia with MCC 1924/25 but was unable to break into the Test side.

In 1927 Bryan was engaged to Irene Innes Pocock of Eastbourne in March, and married that summer, which also saw the one occasion the three Bryan brothers played for Kent in the same match, against Lancashire at Dover. His appearances for Kent were now second place to his career at St. Andrew's where he was a Master and Master-in-Charge of cricket. In September 1939 Bryan re-joined the Army. He was appointed Adjutant and served in France with the Manchester Regiment a second time, being Mentioned in Despatches at Dunkirk. Back in England he became an Instructor at the Eastern Command Infantry Company Commanders School and was promoted to acting Major. In May 1942 he was transferred to the Territorial Army Reserve of Officers, was posted to the RAC and held different commands through to 1945. He relinquished his commission in 1949, being granted the honorary rank of Major.

After the war Bryan was appointed Headmaster at St. Andrew's but had to step down on account of the ill health of his wife after a single term. As late as 1950 he turned out to play cricket for Eastbourne, and kept himself busy as President of the Old Contemptibles. He was the oldest living Kent cricketer and sole survivor of the 1921 Cambridge XI when he died on St George's Day in 1985 after a short illness.

LIEUTENANT RONALD THURSTON BRYAN

Ronnie Bryan, having just reached his sixteenth birthday, was not able to enlist in the Regular Army in autumn 1914. When he turned seventeen the following year he became eligible for the Territorial Force (TF), which had a slightly lower minimum age limit. He applied for a commission and was appointed 2nd Lieutenant with the Manchester Regiment on 1 October 1915. It seems he joined the 5th Battalion, in which his older brother Jack was serving, but would have been with the second or third line units, and the London Gazette announced he was seconded for duty with a Provisional Battalion. These units were for personnel of the TF who were not eligible to serve overseas, often for medical reasons or, as in Bryan's case, not meeting the minimum age. The London Gazette announced his promotion to Lieutenant on 1 July 1917, and it was not until 9 January 1918 that he was restored to the establishment, to serve with the Manchester Regiment.

On his arrival in France during April 1918, Bryan was attached to the 9th Battalion Royal Sussex Regiment, which was training at Friville in the Somme area. On 31 May the Germans fired around 400 gas projectors on to the Royal Sussex positions inflicting many casualties, and in June an outbreak of influenza severely weakened the unit, with 5 Officers and 250 men hospitalized. As the *Hundred Days Offensive* began Bryan's battalion moved to positions in front of Lens and made a successful raid on a German post, only to be raided themselves, during which one man was captured, two wounded and a machine gun lost.

His battalion took part in the *Battles of the Hindenburg Line*, gathering east of the St Quentin Canal and, having occupied Cauroir, were ordered to attack Cagnoncles the following day. No opposition was met initially, but the enemy were entrenched on the high ground to the north, and were soon shelling the British troops. After the hills were cleared Bryan's battalion were put in reserve and went into billets in the captured area. As the Germans retired to the line of the Selle River, and the British moved

A photograph of Ronnie Bryan taken during the war. Reproduced by the kind permission of Pat Bryan

Beyond the Hindenburg Line, Bryan's battalion was selected to support the main thrust of the attack, but the plans were cancelled. On 1 November they were ordered forward to the Mormal Forest where, probably unknown to Ronnie, his brother Jack was located with the 42nd Machine Gun Battalion. On 4 November Bryan joined the attack on the high ground North of Wargnies le Petit and Wargnies le Grand, in the northern extreme of the forested area. As the men moved to their assembly positions they came under a good deal of German shell and machine-gun fire, but forced the enemy to retire, capturing their objectives.

The battalion continued with the advance, occupying Bersillies on 9 November before going into billets. On the morning of 11 November they marched to Louvignies-Bavay, where at 10.00 orders were received that hostilities would cease at 11.00 that day. Germany had accepted the terms of the Armistice. The 9th Sussex then marched west towards the Belgian border, eventually based at Taintegnies where demobilization began, and where Christmas was spent. Volunteers were requested for the Army of Occupation on the Rhine and Bryan, having put his name forward, was transferred to the 4th Battalion Royal Sussex, reporting for duty on 21 March 1919 at Seelscheld in Germany. In June he moved to Hennef, preparatory to joining the Advance Guard into Germany in the event the Peace Terms were not signed. When the Treaty of Versailles was signed on 28 June, the men were finally stood down, and Bryan returned to England.

Kent against Warwickshire at Edgbaston in June 1920 was the occasion of Bryan's first class debut, and he appeared five times for the county that season. The following February he was transferred to the Territorial Reserve, able to turn his attention to his work and his leisure time to cricket. In 1927 he turned his attention to Cynthia Warren Hill, marrying her at St. Peter's Church, Broadstairs on Saturday 3 October. His appearances for Kent were limited due to his work with Lloyds Bank, and were mostly during his periods of annual leave, his weekends reserved for club cricket. He played periodically for Kent from 1923 to 1928, and then in 1937 shared the captaincy with Bryan Valentine, as the club struggled to find a successor to Chapman. It was that season he was awarded his county cap.

Ronnie Bryan served his country again during WW2, initially in the TA Reserve of Officers. Like his brother he was at Dunkirk with the Manchester Regiment and was appointed Lieutenant in the Royal Armoured Corps in 1942. He appeared in his last game for Kent in July 1945, a one day affair against Northamptonshire at Beckenham, in which he scored 52. In 1948 the London Gazette announced Major Bryan had been awarded the Bronze Star Medal, this being a meritorious award, primarily for US servicemen, but able to be awarded to any person who had served in or together with the US Armed Forces. Bryan died at Pevensey Bay, Sussex on 27 July 1970.

The brothers' father had been a Lieutenant-Colonel with the 5th Manchester Regiment, which explains why they both served with that particular unit.

LIEUTENANT CHARLES JOHN CAPES

Charles John Capes was born on 5 January 1898 at Forest Hill, London, first son of Matthew Charles Capes, a Master Printer, and Amy Capes (née Wright). He attended Heathfield School in Keston, Kent from 1904 until 1912 when he entered Malvern College, playing in the XI 1914-1915. In his first season Capes took 51 wickets including eleven against Repton, and he took nine against them the following year. He was a School Prefect and Head of House, played in the Football team, and was a Corporal in the Malvern OTC. Having passed the Army Entrance Exam, he was admitted into the Royal Military College at Sandhurst during April 1916. He was only there for six months, passing through one of the short courses, but still found time to make the XI, taking six wickets against Harrow in June.

Jack Capes served in Mesopotamia

Gentleman Cadet Capes was appointed 2nd Lieutenant in the Royal West Kent Regiment (RWK) on 27 October 1916. Following initial training he was sent to *Mesopotamia*, arriving at Basra in May 1917, where he joined Charles Wycherley in the 2nd Battalion. Just two weeks after his arrival he was admitted to hospital for a fortnight, suffering from sand-fly fever, and on being discharged was ordered upstream to join his unit. He finally reported for duty on 4 July at the Hinaidi Grove Camp where the battalion had recently joined the 17th India Division which was concentrating around Baghdad. The troops in Mesopotamia suffered a high rate of sickness and Capes was to prove no exception. On 17 October he was admitted to hospital for a second time, now in Baghdad, suffering from dysentery, and was not discharged until 8 November.

In December Capes moved to Akab, where his battalion took over part of the outpost line on the left bank of the Tigris, and the year ended quietly, the only contact with the Turks being a few deserters coming in. 1918 began as quietly as 1917 had finished, the 2nd RWK playing no part in the capture of Kifri, Tuz Kharmatli and Kirkuk during April and May. In March the battalion moved from Akab to Samarra where they remained for six months. During that time, on 27 April, Capes was promoted to Lieutenant and during May and June went on leave in India, re-joining his unit on the first day of July. The railway extension from Samarra to Tikrit was under construction, necessary to the plans for striking a final blow at the Turks, whose Sixth Army was entrenched across the Tigris some thirty miles upstream. When the works were completed, Capes and his battalion travelled by train to Tikrit, and on 21 October the 2nd RWK led the 34th Brigade advance upstream to Khan Suraimyah, a long march over very poor roads.

The Turks were pursued, but tended to retire without contact being made, until digging in at Sharqat. The 2nd RWK led the advance to that place and attacked on 28 October. Capes was with B Company which was deployed on the right, with C Company on the left. As they swept towards the Turkish front line they came under heavy and effective machine gun fire, but pressed forwards, knocking out the troublesome gun positions and reaching the Turk's second line. Capes led his Company as they stormed the redoubt on the cliff edge, and the position was taken and the British line consolidated. The battalion had lost a quarter of its strength in the attack, but took a large number of prisoners and captured 10 machine guns. They pressed forward the next day but on the morning of 30 October the bugle called "Stand Fast". The Turkish force of 8,000 men had surrendered unconditionally. The next day the Armistice was signed with Turkey and Capes moved back to railhead with his battalion and around 1,000 prisoners.

Returning to England in April 1919, Capes was struck off the strength of the Mesopotamian Expeditionary Force, and resigned his commission in November. He was recalled briefly in 1921 during the Emergency of the General Strike, but otherwise resumed civilian life. Most of his cricket post-war was for Beckenham, but he made his debut in the Kent 2nd XI in 1920 and played a handful of games in 1921 and 1923 before breaking into the 1st XI. He joined Kent's tour in Scotland in 1923, scoring 39 not out and taking 5-29 against Perthshire at Perth, and also appeared for Lord Harris's XI against the West Indies. His 1st XI debut came in 1923, and he was capped in 1927, playing until 1928 in a total of 33 matches, taking 55 wickets at an average of 25.10. His best score was 65 not out against Lancashire at Maidstone in 1928.

Capes was also a keen hockey player. He appeared many times for the South in international trial matches, and represented England in 1926. He was ill for some time before he died on 16 February 1933 at Ospedaletti in Italy, aged just 35. A memorial service was held at St. Bartholemew's in Sydenham the following week.

LIEUTENANT DOUGLAS WARD CARR

Douglas Ward Carr was born on 17 March, 1872 at Cranbrook in Kent, first born son of Mary and Thomas Arnold Carr, the vicar of the town. Carr was brought up there, and later lived at Marden when his father moved parish. There were only 85 pupils at Sutton Valance School when Carr attended, between 1886 and 1890, and competitive sport against other

schools was restricted to the seniors. He first played cricket for the school in 1887, was made vice-captain for the 1889 season, and in his last year came second in the batting averages and topped the bowling. He also played Rugby and Fives with some success, was made a prefect in 1889, and shone academically, winning several prizes on speech days and taking part in the debating.

After going up to Oxford in 1890 as a non-collegiate student, Carr migrated to Brasenose a year later, studying the Classics and receiving his BA in 1893. He played little cricket at Oxford after his first year there, having injured his knee playing football, but did appear in the 1891 Freshman's Match. He left to become a School Master and, following a phase of club cricket in Kent,

Carr served with the AOD in Egypt

132

he studied and mastered the googly. He was offered a trial with Kent on the strength of his bowling, and took 5 for 65 and 2 for 30 against his old University on his debut in May 1909, followed by eight wickets for the Players against the Gentlemen in July and seven wickets when the same sides met again several days later. This earned him an England call-up for the Fifth Test against Australia at the Oval.

Carr received his Kent Cap in his first season with the county, playing a few times as the side won the Championship, and was named one of the Wisden Cricketers of the Year in 1910 when he took 60 wickets as Kent retained the Championship. He had 8 ten-wicket matches and 31 five-wicket innings in his six years in the top flight, and his last match for Kent was against Surrey, finishing just three days before war was declared. Carr was well over the upper age limit for volunteers, but he applied to join the Army Ordnance Department (AOD) in September 1915, and was appointed Temporary Lieutenant. His application reveals that, in spite of his being a Schoolmaster, he was still required to have a referee to certify he had attained a good level of education. Having known him 17 years, and worked with him, the Headmaster of Stanmore Park School, Vernon Royle, recommended him as an 'excellent fellow'. Royle himself played cricket for Oxford University and Lancashire, and had toured with Lord Harris's team to Australia in 1878/9.

When war broke out there were existing peace time ordnance depots in Alexandria and Cairo to supply the occupying army, and Alexandria was identified as the Ordnance base for the Gallipolli campaign, tonnage shipped from there to Lemnos. It was to Egypt that Carr was posted in November, and it became his home for the next two years. The Gallipoli campaign was almost at an end, but there was strenuous work ahead. The men evacuated from the Dardanelles arrived in Egypt at the beginning of 1916 needing to be clothed and re-equipped. Stores evacuated from Gallipoli needed sorting, cleaning and mending, and transport needed to be found, a difficult task as little had been used on the peninsula and it had to be sourced from scratch. New operations planned for Salonika and Palestine also had ordnance requirements.

Egypt was the pivot between east and west campaigns, men passing through when transferring from one campaign to another, and its depots helped to relieve pressure on the establishments in the UK, notably Woolwich and Pimlico, by servicing most Eastern theatres and leaving England to concentrate on the Western Front. As the advance to Palestine continued, a new depot was opened at Kantara to avoid stretching supply lines too far, but by the time the offensive into *Palestine* began, Carr was on his way to the UK for three weeks leave. He sailed on 11 August 1917 and did not return. In February 1918 he was transferred to Home Establishment, serving in the London area as well as Section 18 RAOC (Royal Army Ordnance Corps) at Didcot, where he remained until the end of the war.

When hostilities ceased, the Ordnance work did not. Equipment stores had to be run down, sold off and destroyed over a long period of time, demobilized troops needed to be clothed and rather bizarrely, manufacturing contracts honoured. This entailed handling new supplies which would never be used. A Medical Board in November 1918 decided that Carr was unfit for general service, due to large varicose veins in both legs, and that he should have sedentary employment only. He was demobilized on 29 January, 1919. Douglas Carr died in a nursing home at Salcombe Hill, Sidmouth, Devon on 23 March, 1950.

TEMPORARY CAPTAIN JAMES CLIFTON COLQUHOUN

James Clifton Colquhoun, born on 1 December 1893 in Coatbridge, Lanarkshire, was the son of James Colquhoun, Gentleman. Educated at Trinity College Glenalmond, now known as Glenalmond College, from 1908 to 1912, he was wicket-keeper in the Cricket XI 1909 to 1912, as Captain in his last year. Working his way up from the 3rd XI to the 1st XI, he made a number of useful scores, including 93 against Edinburgh Academy in 1910. Colquhoun also represented the school at Rugby, Hockey and Fives, played Golf at St. Andrews, won the Hurdles in the 1912 School Games and was awarded his First XI Colours in 1910. Like many public schools Glenalmond had an Officer Training Corps, in which Colquhoun served for four years, making Sergeant by the time he left. He was returned 'efficient' four times, and obtained a qualification in Musketry.

Colquhoun in the Glenalmond XI in 1911. Reproduced by the kind permission of Glenalmond College

Colquhoun studied at Gonville and Caius College, Cambridge from 1912 and, having played for Tonbridge and Blue Mantles, made his only first class appearance in June 1914 for Gerry Weigall's XI against Oxford. He presumably impressed the Kent coach as he soon appeared for the Kent 2nd XI, and was in the side for all ten of their Minor Counties matches that year. He had some success but with Povey, Leach-Lewis and Wood available, he was not used as wicket-keeper. Against Monmouthshire in his first appearance he made 80, followed by 52 against Surrey, and he opened the batting on a number of occasions. His last match of 1914 was against Essex on 14-15 August, by which time the country was at war.

At the beginning of October 1914 Colquhoun enlisted as a Private in 2/28th County of London Battalion, the London Regiment (Artists Rifles). He joined as a Territorial to serve four years in the UK, but soon signed to serve overseas although his time with the Artists Rifles proved to be short. He received a temporary commission with the 13th (Service) Battalion of the Highland Light Infantry (HLI) during December. The 13th HLI, had been formed as part of K4, Kitchener's fourth new army, and was based in Gosport until May 1915. About this time they were made a Reserve Battalion, and moved to Stobs, a camp in the Scottish Borders. He remained there until 3 October 1915, when he embarked for France as part of a draft to the 10th HLI which had been decimated during Loos and was in dire need of reinforcements.

Having landed in France, Colquhoun moved to Ypres to join the battalion at their new posting. He reported for duty on 6 October, but his stay was brief. The Divisional front lay south of Zillebeke, extending from north of Hill 60 to south of the Ypres-Combines Canal near Ooshoek. Moving out of reserve on 16 October the 10th HLI took over part of the line. The trenches were in a very poor shape and pumps were of little use in battling the rain water, leading to a high rate of trench foot among the men. On 25 October whilst in the trenches, Colquhoun was shot in the right wrist and was evacuated to England. He was admitted to Palace Green Hospital in Kensington, which had opened that January as a special neurological hospital for Officers.

X-Rays showed there was no injury to the bone, and gradually Colquhoun began to regain his wrist movement. After time spent on light duties with the 13th Reserve Battalion at Catterick and then Leven near Fife when they relocated, he was scheduled to attend a Medical Board at Edinburgh but suffered a severe attack of bronchitis delaying a 'fit' verdict. In March 1917 he was appointed temporary Lieutenant, and was eventually ordered back to France, departing in September. This time he joined the 2nd HLI at Le Preol and spent some time in the trenches of the La Bassée Canal sector, but was transferred during November to HQ P&BT, the Physical and Bayonet Training School at St. Pol, where he was to be an Instructor.

The School had been established in 1914 when war was becoming more likely, and the instructors included several sportsmen, including boxers Jimmy Wilde and Bombardier Billy Wells. Two weeks after his arrival Colquhoun was transferred to the General List for duty as a Supervisor at the School and was appointed temporary Captain whilst in the role. When the German's launched the *Kaiserschlacht* on 21 March 1918, St. Pol was hit by long range shells and aircraft bombs as the Germans fired a million shells at the Fifth Army lines. The students and instructors vacated the town and, when they received reports of the extent of the German advances, stood to in battle order.

The school had been badly damaged by the shelling, and HQ was re-established near Abbeville, in the camp of the Fifth Army Artillery School, and later at Hardelot, quartered with the First Army Infantry School near Boulogne. New camps were erected and the school was back up and running by mid-May. The following month Colquhoun was appointed Assistant Superintendent and life was undoubtedly a lot quieter for him for the remainder of the war. He left for England on 21 November to serve with the Army Gymnastic Staff at Aldershot, until demobilized during February 1919.

In July 1919 he was married to Margaret Colquhoun Barry at Holy Trinity Church, Brompton, and was also awarded the MBE that year for his war services. He played in a trial match for Kent in August 1919, but only played three more times for the 2nd XI, all during 1921, and by 1929-30 was appearing for Cornwall. Colquhoun had attended the Royal School of Mines in 1919 and enjoyed a successful career in metallurgy. He was appointed Chairman of the Manganese Bronze and Brass Company from the 1930's until the 1960's and was Chairman of Lightalloys. James Colquhoun died in a London hospital on 9 February 1977, aged 83.

CAPTAIN WYKEHAM STANLEY CORNWALLIS

The future "Colonel the Right Honourable Lord Cornwallis KCVO, KBE, MC, DCL the second Baron of Linton, Her Majesty's Lord Lieutenant of Kent, and Custos Rotolorum from 1944", was born Wykeham Stanley Cornwallis at Linton Park on 14 March 1892. He was second son to Fiennes Stanley Wykeham, Baron Cornwallis of Linton, CBE, TD, DL Colonel of the Royal West Kent Yeomanry and Mabel Leigh, the Dowager Lady Cornwallis. His father was MP for Maidstone from 1888-95 and 1898-1900, Vice-Chairman of Kent County Council for twenty years, and created a Peer in 1927. Elder brother Fiennes Wykeham

Stanley Cornwallis, served on the Western Front from August 1914 to the end of the War

Mann Cornwallis was set to be 2nd Baron Cornwallis, so it was unlikely anyone foresaw Stanley surpassing his father's achievements, or gathering quite so many letters after his name, but fate had a hand when his brother was killed in Ireland in 1921 by the IRA.

Schooled at Ludgrove, where he captained the Cricket XI, Cornwallis went on to Eton in 1907. He did not make the XI whilst there but had some talent at the game. In *66 Years' Memories of Kent Cricket (Igglesden, 1947: 5)* the author recalled that Cornwallis' father had secured him some coaching at Linton during the summer holidays, and that Frank Woolley had remarked upon his potential for future success. At Eton he studied Military History, Maths and French and, expecting his elder brother to succeed his father, he opted for a military career, taking the Army qualifying exam and leaving Eton in 1910 to enter Sandhurst. The following September, Gentleman Cadet Cornwallis was appointed 2nd Lieutenant in the Royal Scots Greys, the 2nd Dragoons, promoted to Lieutenant in August 1912 and stationed at York until 1914. Passionate about horses, he was at home in the cavalry, and won a number of trophies for regimental events. His horse "White Knight" accompanied him to France, but was killed during the retreat from Mons.

The Scots Greys were mobilised on 4 August 1914, purchasing the horses they required from local hunts, and departed York eleven days later, Cornwallis with A Squadron. Having landed at Havre, Cornwallis advanced with the Greys to meet up with the French army. As they reached the French positions they found their ally retreating, and had to do likewise. The first taste of action for Cornwallis came on 22 August when the Greys engaged the enemy near Mons, fighting dismounted, and inflicting a large number of casualties on the Germans. The Battle of Mons was fought the next day, and the retreat soon followed. Vastly outnumbered, the two Corps of the BEF retired in separate columns. The mobility of the cavalry made them the obvious choice to cover the fall back *From Mons to the Marne*, the Greys protecting the First Corps during the punishing two weeks withdrawal. A number of actions had already been fought when, on 2 September, whilst holding a bridge over the Marne at S. Jean les Jumeaux, German cavalry rode almost into the village. Cornwallis' troop opened fire, forcing the enemy to retire.

When the BEF and French Army took the offensive and started to drive the Germans back, Cornwallis' squadron formed the advance guard, leading their brigade forward 10 miles, then acting dismounted. On 11 September Cornwallis took out an officer's patrol to ascertain the German positions, and was able to get in touch with the French, the brigade then advancing slowly on toward the Aisne. Three days later, believing the Germans were only holding the Aisne with a rear-guard, Cornwallis' squadron pushed on ahead. The enemy were however defending the line of the river in force, and in the ensuing action Cornwallis was wounded by shrapnel in the temple, arm and calf. He remembered being carried back on a limber, then enduring a three day train journey to a hospital in Angiers.

His injuries warranted a return to England to recover, but during December he re-joined the Greys at La Creche on the borders of France and Belgium.

Lieut. Stanley Cornwallis Wounded.

A telegram was received at Linton Park on Friday informing Mr. and Mrs. Cornwallis that their son, Lieut. Stanley Cornwallis, of the Royal Scots Greys, who is serving with the Expeditionary Force at the Front, had been wounded. Mrs. Cornwallis has since received a further telegram from her son, stating that he is only slightly wounded, and he is in hospital at Angers.

How the Kent Messenger *reported Stanley Cornwallis was in hospital at Angiers. Image Courtesy* Kent Messenger

As the war turned static in nature, the role of the cavalry changed, sometimes held in reserve as mounted troops, at other times acting dismounted. After training in trench warfare, including instruction in the use of trench mortars, Cornwallis spent time in the line at Ypres, and then took part in the general advance at *Neuve Chapelle* in March. He had recently been appointed Bombing Officer and, on returning to billets, took receipt of what the regiment's war diary described as two 'bomb guns', and were probably trench mortars.

Shortly after *Second Ypres* began in April, the Greys were called into the line when the Germans released gas into the Canadian Sector, causing a unit of French Territorials to give way on the left. Whilst most of the Greys returned to billets after the scare, Cornwallis remained at Verte Rue with B Echelon under Cavalry Corps command. The Greys were in the line or in support for 20 of the 28 days the battle lasted, and in the trenches north of Potijze they were lucky another release of German gas just missed their position. The heavy losses the regiment suffered at Ypres forced it into reserve for much of the remainder of the year, and during that time Cornwallis, in his capacity as 'Officer Commanding Bombs', attended a one week instruction course on Trench Mortars.

Having fallen sick, Cornwallis spent the last three months of 1915 back in England, and after returning to France the Greys were ordered into the line near Vermelles. On 13 February they exploded a mine near the German line and a number of bombers ran forward, capturing the crater and beating off determined efforts to dislodge them. Cornwallis was awarded the Military Cross, the London Gazette (*Issue 29508, 14 March 1916*) recording:

Lieutenant Wykeham Stanley Cornwallis 2nd Dragoons (Royal Scots Greys)
For conspicuous gallantry and skilful leading when a mine was exploded by us. Lieutenant Cornwallis organised his bombing arrangements most skilfully, and on the explosion of the mine immediately occupied the near edge of crater under heavy fire, and from this point gave good covering fire whilst the position was being consolidated.

Cornwallis remained in reserve with the Greys during the *Somme* offensive, waiting to exploit the breakthrough that never came. Back in winter billets he was appointed acting Captain, and when the Cavalry Division School opened on 30 December he proceeded there as an Instructor in the Grenade Course. Weeks later he returned to England where, on 30 January, he married Cecily Etha Mary Walker at St. Margaret's Church, Westminster; the page boy fittingly wearing the 18th Century uniform of the Scots Greys.

Cornwallis pictured left, with Capt Lawrence on the Western Front. From Scots DG Archives.

At the beginning of April the Greys were involved in the *First Battle of the Scarpe*, part of the *Battle of Arras*. The conditions were hard, with heavy snow falls and 20 degrees of frost, and Cornwallis spent six days of heavy fighting in charge of a working party, tasked with erecting bridges over captured trenches to ease any cavalry advance. In the early part of June, whilst acting as a dismounted battalion near Gillemont Farm, the Greys carried out a raid to take prisoners and documents for intelligence purposes. Having just spent four days in hospital, Cornwallis was not in the main raiding party, but he moved up to take command of C Squadron when Lord St. Germans was wounded, the German counter attacks that followed being beaten back with ease.

After a period out of the line, the Greys moved to the St. Pol area in October for possible use in *Third Ypres (Passchendaele),* but when no opportunities were presented for use of cavalry, the men moved south-west of Amiens. About this time Cornwallis was attached to the 5th Cavalry Brigade HQ, and so would not have been involved in operations when the regiment was deployed at Cambrai in November although little mounted action was seen. Christmas Day of 1917 was memorable for Cornwallis as he was promoted to Captain, and as the New Year dawned, rumours were rife of a planned German offensive. It was felt such an attack could easily be contained, but the ferocity of the *Kaiserschlacht* in March was a surprise to all. Cornwallis fell back with the Brigade, as the cavalry fought in rear-guard actions, and then headed north as the offensive spread.

The next months were spent reorganising and refitting, and in July Cornwallis was appointed GSO III (General Staff Officer Third Grade) at the Cavalry Corps Headquarters, a role he stayed in until June 1919. The GSO2 at the HQ was Francis Marsham who had taken up the appointment in May. Brought forward during the Amiens Offensive in August, the cavalry had to dismount for action, and during the *Battles of the Hindenburg Line* they had little to do, as the infantry and machine-guns led the way forward. As a Staff Officer, Cornwallis was more involved in the administrative duties of the Corps as the war drew to a close. He moved with the General Staff to Spa in Belgium after hostilities ended, before transferring back to his regiment. In July 1919 he received a Mention in Despatches, and the month before he had become Aide-de-Camp to Lord Haig until Haig's retirement early in 1920.

From September 1920 Cornwallis was an Instructor at Sandhurst, through to 1924 when he retired from the Army to join the reserve. Whilst ADC to Lord Haig, he was sent on a refresher course at Berkhamsted, and there he played in a charity cricket match, taking a hat-trick. Soon after, he was sent an invitation by Cloudesley Marsham, asking him to play for Kent against Sussex at Hove. Cornwallis found this amusing, obviously not rating his own ability that highly, and told Lord Haig who replied *"This is one of those things you have got to say you have done once, Cornie"* and ordered him to accept.

He took a wicket in the match, and played several more times in August. In all, Cornwallis was to play 104 matches for Kent, making 953 runs, and taking 117 wickets. He was a late starter due to his service, and his body was not trained to withstand the strain cricket put it under. The constant breaking down did not affect his leadership qualities, and during his captaincy, 1924 to 1926, the county finished fifth place twice and then third. He was capped in 1923, and his highest score for Kent was 91 against Essex at Canterbury in 1926.

His achievements in public life were many. Whilst Lord Lieutenant of Kent, he was the Queen's representative and met any royal visitors to the county. He was President of the MCC and of Kent CCC, both in 1948, was a Justice of the Peace in 1929, 2nd Baron Cornwallis of Linton when his father died in 1935, and was made KBE in 1945 and KCVO in 1968. He also held many others positions, far too many to list here.

Cecily died in 1943, and five years later Cornwallis married a second time, to Lady Esme Walker, the couple living at Ashurst Park in Tunbridge Wells. They enjoyed 26 years together before Esme died in 1969. Only a week or two before his death Cornwallis was watching I Zingari play the Duchess of Norfolk's XI at Arundel, and he passed away on 4 January 1982 aged 89.

MAJOR BARRY STEPHENSON CUMBERLEGE

Barry Stephenson Cumberlege was born in Newcastle-upon-Tyne on 5 June 1891, the sixth child of Esther Faithfull and Charles Farrington Cumberlege, a Bank Superintendent who played for Surrey and Northumberland. Attending Durham School, he was in the Cricket XI 1906-1910, as captain from 1908, and full-back in the Rugby XV 1907-1909. He received an invitation to tour South Africa with the Great Britain Rugby team which, although he declined, was an indication of his sporting prowess. He went on to Emmanuel College, Cambridge in 1910 where he was a double Blue at cricket and rugby, and received his BA in 1913. His

Cumberlege pictured four years before the war, in the Durham XI. Reproduced by the kind permission of Durham School

cricket Blue also came in 1913, and at rugby he earned the award as a Freshman in 1910, and every year to 1913, the last as captain. In 1912-13 he played for Cambridge against the Springboks and also appeared for Blackheath, Barbarians, Northumberland and England. He played Minor Counties cricket for Durham and Northumberland, and in 1913 made his first class debut for Cambridge against Sussex at Fenners. He also represented the Free Foresters against Cambridge, scoring 172, his only first class century.

Cumberlege was a schoolmaster when war broke out, and applied for a commission just five days in, being appointed 2nd Lieutenant on probation in the Army Service Corps (ASC) on 7 September. He joined No.2 Section of 414 ASC Mechanical Transport Company, attached to the supply column of the newly created 3rd Cavalry Division. The Division had two MT units, the other was 73 ASC MT, commanded by his brother Henry, who sadly died within a week of Barry's appointment. The work of the MT companies involved moving supplies of food for troops and horses, and the carriage of engineer, ordnance and other stores from railhead to forward positions. Timber and sandbags had to be moved forward for trench construction and maintenance, and also for the construction of stables for the Cavalry Division. This work brought Cumberlege within range of the German guns.

The Third Cavalry Division was sent to Belgium to help relieve the Siege of Antwerp, but on 8 October, as Cumberlege reached Bruges, Antwerp fell and the Division was redirected to *Ypres*. Cumberlege's company went about their work, keeping the Division supplied through the *Battle of Langemarck, Battle of Gheluvelt* and *Battle of Nonne Bosschen*, during which the enemy was held at bay. Both sides then settled down for the winter, engaging in regular trench warfare, allowing supply operations to form a regular pattern. Cumberlege was confirmed in his rank in February and appointed Temporary Lieutenant during March.

Cumberlege's unit provided more valuable support to the Division during *Second Ypres* and again in the autumn offensive at *Loos*, when they carried supplies forward from railhead at Aire, on the St Omer – Armentières branch line. He was confirmed in the rank of Lieutenant during February 1916, and appointed Temporary Captain in May. That December Cumberlege was granted three weeks leave from the BEF on medical grounds. Returning in January 1917 it was not long before he was employed as Adjutant at the HQ of II ANZAC ASC, MT. The Australia and New Zealand Army Corps (ANZAC) is best remembered for its role at Gallipoli, but following the evacuation had been divided into I ANZAC and II ANZAC. It was the latter that Cumberlege had joined, and at that time comprised 5th Australian Division and the New Zealand Division.

II ANZAC was the southernmost of the British forces attacking *Messines* in June 1917, which places Cumberlege at ASC MT HQ organising the Corps supply during the battle, whilst former Kent cricketer Robert O'Hara Livesay was on the Staff of the NZ Division. During the summer Cumberlege was appointed Officer Commanding No1 NZ Division

Supply Column (610 Company). In this command he took part in *Third Ypres* but, when the *Passchendaele* offensive closed in November, NZ Division left II ANZAC to join a British Corps. He became Officer Commanding the NZ Division MT Company, and was appointed Substantive Captain a week later. The Division remained in the Ypres area throughout the winter.

Cumberlege was appointed acting Major on 13 March 1918, just days before the Germans launched the *Kaiserschlacht,* and NZ Division was quickly ordered south to support Third Army. Later in the year, during *The Hundred Days Offensive* his Company had to work hard to keep the advancing troops supplied. Returning from a brief period of leave in mid-October, he joined XXII Corps Supply Column (687 Company ASC), that Corps having been created in December 1917 from what was left of II ANZAC when the NZ Division left it. From mid-October the Corps was with First Army, involved in the fighting *Beyond the Hindenburg Line* and into the *Final Push*. Cumberlege was demobilized in April 1919, and subsequently awarded the OBE for his war service and was Mentioned In Despatches. The following January he was given approval to resign his commission in the Reserve, and was granted the rank of Major.

During June 1919 Cumberlege married Louella Louisa Gillis in Kensington, and was soon back playing sport. He became full-back for Blackheath and played in that position for England between 1920 and 1922 in eight international matches, covering three Five Nations Championships, one which England won outright, and another shared. He also played for the Barbarians, and later became a referee, officiating 16 Internationals. During 1923-1924 he played for the Kent 1st XI six times. Against Warwickshire in his first match he scored 46 and 34, and against Northants at Blackheath 31 and 57 not out. He was then picked for the West Indies fixture, making 51 and 26. His three appearances in 1924 were all rain affected draws. He worked as a Deputy Underwriter at Lloyd's in London and served with the Royal Observer Corps during the 1939-45 War. Cumberlege died on 22 September 1970 in Folkestone.

DAY BROTHERS

Wine merchant Sydney Townsend Day and his wife Evelyn Ada Day had four sons, three of whom played for Kent. Sydney Ernest, born on 9 February 1884 and Arthur Percival on 10 April 1885, were the two youngest brothers and both served in the war. Their older brother Noel died whilst at Malvern, and the lack of records suggest Samuel Hulme, who was a teacher by profession, did not serve. All the boys were educated at Shirley House School in Blackheath before going on to Malvern, where Sydney and Arthur started in 1898. Sydney excelled at football, playing in the XI, although his cricket was restricted to the 2nd XI. Arthur was in the 1st XI 1901-1904, as captain in the last two seasons, and also played in the Football XI 1903-1904, and the Rackets Pairs. In 1904 Arthur topped the Malvern batting averages with 880 at 67.69 thanks to one score of 201. That same season he made 147 and GN Foster hit 153 against Uppingham, whilst CS Hurst scored 167 for the opposition.

On leaving Malvern in 1902, Sydney joined Royal Insurance Company in London, but played plenty of sport in his spare time. He was outside-right for Kent AFA and also the Old Malvernians for which club he was Secretary 1908-1910. During Arthur's last two summers at Malvern, he had played for the Kent 2nd XI, and made his first class debut for the county against MCC at Lord's in May 1905 scoring 53 not out. Awarded his Cap that season, he went on to play 143 times for Kent, piling up 6,532 runs at an average of 33.49 including 13 centuries and 33 fifties. He also took 129 wickets at 25.08 with a best performance of 8-49 against Middlesex in 1911. In 1908 he and Humphreys added 248 for the seventh wicket against Somerset at Taunton, which remains a Club record to this day, and Kent's longest standing record partnership. Arthur appeared in all four Championship winning sides, and was one of the Wisden Cricketers of the Year in 1910, the same year Douglas Carr received the accolade. In 1911 he married Ada Christine Evans at Blackheath, and was in business as a bottle agent and merchant.

LIEUTENANT ARTHUR PERCIVAL DAY

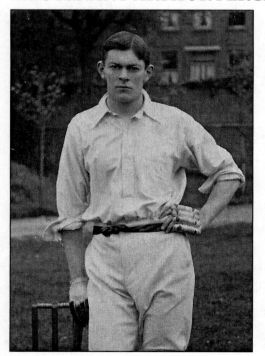

Although the exact date Day offered his services is unclear, he was attested on 29 January 1916, joining from Army Reserve B Class, which suggests he had responded to Lord Derby's call, and was not a conscript. He was returned to the reserve and to civilian life whilst awaiting his mobilization orders. A year passed before he was posted to the 2nd Battalion (Artists Rifles) OTC at Gidea Park near Romford. The Artists Rifles had been converted from an infantry battalion to a training school early in the war, and many officer candidates passed through the camp.

Arthur Day still holds the record for Kent's seventh wicket partnership with Ted Humphreys

Two months after his arrival, Day applied for admission to an Officer Cadet Unit, with a view to a temporary commission in the Territorials. His application papers reveal he suffered kidney complications having suffered scarlet fever, which left him prone to convulsions. This is no doubt the reason he was classed Medical Category B1, and although he signed an Imperial Service Obligation to serve overseas, he was to remain on home soil. Whilst waiting for his application to go through, Day scored 49 for the Artists Rifles cricket team against a Public Schools side, and a week later made 126 and took 6 for 20 in a rather one-sided match against the Inns of Court Officers Cadet Battalion (OCB) at Leyton.

On 23 May, Day was accepted for admission to a Garrison OCB, and instructed to join at Jesus College, Cambridge. Just seven weeks later he was commissioned 2nd Lieutenant in the 2/28th London Regiment (Artists Rifles), and remained at Gidea Park, assisting in the training of officer cadets for the remainder of the war. He represented the regiment at cricket again in the summer of 1918, the team now calling itself 'the Artistics'. Against a Public Schools side at Lord's in August he scored 91, then the following week 94 against the same opponents at the Oval. A third match was played at Lord's and Day did not put himself in until his side were eight wickets down, helping to pick off the last runs required for victory.

Having received a promotion to Lieutenant in January 1919, Day was demobilized in April, moving to the Reserve. In October 1920, with the pressure of business growing, he resigned his commission effective 24 November retaining the rank of Lieutenant. Working as a stockbroker and still living in Blackheath, Day resumed his cricket with Kent, but only played a few games each season up until 1925, and not at all in 1922. In his eight innings during 1921 he accumulated 555 runs at an average of 111, helped by his unbeaten 184 against Sussex at Tonbridge, 101 against Essex at Leyton and 67 and 77 not out against Surrey at the Oval. Arthur Day died on 22 January 1969 at Budleigh Salterton, Devon.

CAPTAIN SYDNEY ERNEST DAY

Sydney Day enlisted at Westminster on 15 September 1914, the same day as Lionel Troughton, and they were both posted to the 18th Battalion of the Royal Fusiliers as Privates. Ted Dillon joined them three days later. The 18th was one of several referred to as the UPS (Universities and Public Schools), raised and formed at Epsom on 11 September. The battalion was based at Woodcote Camp, Epsom, where the recruits were drilled and trained, but Day found time to play football for the Corinthians against Aldershot Command in February 1915, and was married to Faith Evelyn Pattie Winch on 13 March at Blackheath. During May the battalion moved to Clipstone Camp near Mansfield, one of many facilities built to train Kitchener's Army, and whilst there Day was appointed Lance Corporal, and then Corporal. Having applied for a commission, he was appointed temporary 2nd Lieutenant within the same battalion during the latter part of July. Six weeks later he was transferred to a reserve battalion, probably either the 27th, 28th or 29th which covered the UPS Depots.

Sydney Day, who was wounded serving with a Trench Mortar Battery, was Kent President in 1954. Reproduced by the kind permission of Kent County Cricket Club

During April 1916 Day embarked for France where he was initially attached to the 17th Battalion Royal Fusiliers in 5th Brigade, and then received some training in the use of trench mortars. Each Brigade had a Trench Mortar Battery (TMB), and Day joined the 5th Brigade's battery – the 5th TMB – from the end of July. In 1914 there had been no such thing as a trench mortar; they came into being as trench warfare developed, the TMBs working in conjunction with infantry, artillery and engineers. When Day joined, the infantry were responsible for light mortars, and he would have been using Stokes Mortars, with which an experienced crew could have up to nine rounds in flight at any one time.

Day was soon introduced to the *Somme*, the Brigade taking part in the Battle of Delville Wood on 27 July, and he remained with the 5th TMB in the same sector for the next few months as the *Somme Continued*. During the failed attack on Guillemont and Falfemont

Farm on 30 July, his unit used their mortars to deal with hostile enemy posts. A number of trench raids were undertaken during September, the TMB assisting in the preliminary bombardments, and the following month they fired on German work-parties replacing and repairing wire defences.

On 13 November the *Battle of the Ancre* was launched, the final act of the *Somme*. The plan was to attack on either side of the Ancre River, a small tributary of the Somme River which flowed through the northern part of the battlefield. Whilst the 51st Division attacked and captured Beaumont Hamel, Day joined 2nd Division advancing along Redan Ridge, their objective the German third line system of trenches and the Munich and Frankfurt trenches. The day after the attack, as the British were consolidating their positions, Day was wounded at Beaumont Hamel, hit by a rifle bullet that entered the tricep of his right arm, passing through and entering the dorsal region of his back before emerging some three inches on. He was treated at a casualty clearing station and evacuated to England.

On his arrival in England, Day was admitted to Lady Meynell's Hospital for Officers in Lennox Gardens, London, where future Prime Minister Harold Macmillan was also treated as a casualty. Day's wounds had gone septic, but healed fairly quickly, and luckily there was no damage to bone or nerves. He had however lost much weight, and needed time to recuperate. In the meantime his services were sought by the Director of the Inland Waterways and Docks section of the Royal Engineers (IWD RE). Whether Day was acquainted with anyone in the IWD is unclear, but they made a request for his transfer on the basis he had suitable qualifications for that branch of service.

By the end of January 1917 Day was found fit for Home Service and attached to the IWD RE Depot at Sandwich, being swiftly promoted to Temporary Lieutenant. The British Army had taken advantage of the extensive canal system in France and Belgium, using the waterways for transport of supplies and ammunition. An Inland Waterways section was set up and staffed by temporary RE officers, charged with purchasing barges and stores necessary for their upkeep. A base was initially established at Dover, with stores at Ashford, and it was not long before the RE Docks organization, established to handle the docks in France, was quickly associated with the Inland Waterway Transport section to form the IWD.

Several weeks later Day fell very sick with appendicitis and underwent an operation. After a period in hospital he was sent home to recuperate. Underweight and tiring easily, he spent time at Stonar Camp, Sandwich, only fit for light duties. On 1 December he was promoted to the rank of temporary Captain to fill a vacancy in the establishment of the IWD, but it was not until April, almost 11 months after his operation, that he was finally declared fit for General Service. The IWD Depot had moved to Richborough in 1916 after Dover became congested, and it was there that he saw out the War. He was demobilized in

February 1919, relinquishing his commission on completion of service, and retaining the rank of Captain.

Day played cricket for Kent between 1922 and 1925, and was considered a good batsman and a versatile fielder. Eight of his eleven appearances fell in the 1923 season, and he made his first class debut against Notts at Trent Bridge. The following season he made a crucial 45 against Worcestershire at Dudley, his highest score for the county, and one which clinched the game for Kent. Aside from his limited first class appearances, Day met much success playing club cricket for the Mote. In 1931 he was one of six players who agreed to manage the side for successive periods of the season when they had no Captain.

Active on the Kent Committee from 1946 to 1958, Day was made President in 1954. He became a Justice of the Peace, and in the late 1960's was part of the newly formed Rivermead Masonic Lodge, Deputy Provincial Grand Master to Lord Cornwallis. He and Faith celebrated their Golden Wedding Anniversary at their home in West Malling in 1965, and it was there that Day died on 7 July 1970, aged 86.

CAPTAIN EDWARD WENTWORTH DILLON

Edward Wentworth Dillon was arguably Kent's most successful Captain, leading the side to three Championships in 1909, 1910 and 1913. Born on 15 February 1881 in Penge, he was the fourth born child to shipbroker Henry Wentworth Dillon and Sarah Margaret (Hussey). His education began at Abbey School, Beckenham and he went on to Rugby where, as captain, he headed the averages in 1899 and 1900. He was described in Wisden as the best school batsman of the year and also found time to play five matches for Kent, averaging 36.50 in eight innings. At Oxford he was a cricket Blue 1901-1902 when he was Captain of the XI, often opening the batting with Cloudesley Marsham. He visited the West Indies with Bosanquet's team in 1902, although the trip was made without permission from Oxford. Dillon apparently preferred the idea of a cricket tour over attending an examination, and whilst his spirit may have benefitted his game, it also resulted in his departure from University College, and he had to migrate to one of Oxford's private halls.

Having been in the rugby team for both Rugby and Oxford, Dillon also played at international level four times from 1904-1905, and represented Blackheath, Harlequins, Barbarians and Kent. He played cricket for Kent 1900-1923 and was captain 1909-1913. Playing regularly from 1901, the season he was capped, he went on to make 223 appearances, scoring 9,415 runs, his highest score of 141 against Gloucestershire in 1905. Business as a shipbroker ultimately forced him to play less regularly, and when he led the side to the Championship in 1909 he missed the last month. He played 23 times the following year as Kent retained the title, and having guided the side to their fourth title in 1913, he went out on a high note, playing only three more times, twice in 1919 and once

in 1923. He was married to Lilian Irene Hartley in January 1908 at Westminster, and the couple lived in Hove.

Former Kent Captain Ted Dillon was wounded in Palestine whilst serving with the Royal West Kent Regiment

Dillon enlisted at Westminster on 3 September, his application stating that he had passed the Inns of Court OTC. He was posted to the 18th Battalion (1st Public Schools) Royal Fusiliers on 18 September, three days behind Sydney Day and Lionel Troughton. Within a month he was on the move having been given a commission in the Royal West Kent Regiment (RWK). Two quick promotions followed, to temporary Lieutenant in January and temporary Captain in March. Serving with the 2/4th Battalion, the company he commanded was used to form a composite battalion for the 53rd (Welsh) Division. May to July was spent in intensive training, after which Dillon joined the force selected to reinforce the MEF at Gallipoli. Their role would be to go on the offensive through the ANZAC positions.

The battalion left a quarter of their strength at Alexandria as a reserve, and sailed on to *Gallipoli*, landing at Suvla on 10 August. By now the plans for Dillon's battalion were obsolete, the attack had commenced days earlier and failed. Instead the men moved into the front line where they immediately set about deepening the shallow trenches which exposed them to Turkish snipers. The 2/4th remained in the line until relieved on 1 September, but Dillon injured his ankle the week before and returned to England. By January, when he was found fit for duty, Gallipoli had been evacuated and the 2/4th RWK were in *Egypt*.

When Dillon reported for duty, the battalion was at Fayoum Oasis, having joined the *Western Desert* campaign to defeat the Senussi. He took command of A Company, but saw no action other than making demonstrations through villages in the vicinity to deter support for an enemy that was now operating well inland, and of little threat. Temperatures in the desert reached 120 degrees in the tents and Dillon would not have been sorry to be ordered to the Suez Canal Zone. He was promoted to Captain before the move, and took over command of the battalion for a month on arrival at the Southern section of Canal Zone, where they worked on the Suez defences.

Although the battalion moved to Kantara in August when the Turks attacked Romani, the fighting was over before they arrived. Dillon took over B Company before they moved on to Moascar for two months training, and in December was made acting Major for a three month period. During December the battalion moved eastwards, ready to support the attack on El Arish, but again they missed the party, the Turks having withdrawn without putting up much of a fight. In early 1917 more moves took them to El Arish and then Sheikh Zowaid where they finally left the sand behind and gained firm ground beneath their feet. Here the battalion helped to cover the railway being constructed toward *Palestine*.

During March Dillon crossed the old frontier line into *Palestine*, where he took part in the first two attempts to take Gaza. For the first battle his battalion was chosen for a special mission on the left flank by the coast, to distract Turkish attention from the main attack. Dillon's men marched by night and laid-up by day, avoiding the quicksand as they crossed the Wadi Ghazee, only to be held up by a heavy mist. The enemy did not counter-attack, but did keep up a heavy fire throughout the night before the attack and during the next day. The mist also affected the main attack, causing delays that proved crucial and, failing to capture their objectives in daylight, the British withdrew. In mid-April when the second attempt on Gaza was made, Dillon was attached to 53rd Divisional Headquarters, as Liaison Officer, for the duration of the battle. Success eluded the attackers a second time, and the British spent six months waiting for the heat of summer to pass, and the chance to regroup.

In order to establish a regular system of reliefs, the line was divided into two sections. On 8 May the 53rd Division moved into the back area, the 52nd Division taking their place. It was during this relief, while Dillon's battalion was wending its way down a defile to a reserve area behind the Sheikh Abbas Ridge, that a German plane spotted the column and dropped bombs. One landed right in the middle of 'D' Company, causing over seventy casualties. Forty men were killed immediately or died of their wounds soon after, and Dillon was one of those injured. He was evacuated to Alexandria, and admitted to the hospital at Ras-el-Tin with wounds to the left side of his chest. Luckily the shrapnel had not penetrated the lungs, but he spent a month in hospital recovering.

Re-joining his battalion on 22 June, Dillon took command of B Company from 10 July, and at the end of the month was selected for training in Staff Duties and attached to 160th Brigade Headquarters. When Beersheba was captured that October, the 53rd covered the left flank of the attack, and then Dillon moved into the hills north of the town with 160th Brigade, the advance rapidly becoming a pursuit of the Turks northwards. He was with the Brigade when they entered Jerusalem, but on Boxing Day he was ordered to GHQ GSI 2nd Echelon, Cairo. GSI was the General Staff Intelligence Section, the second echelon being based in Cairo, as opposed to Allenby's first echelon in the field.

A system of gathering economic intelligence had been established by the British in 1914 to determine the effect of the blockade on the Central Powers, especially Germany. In 1917 the effort was extended to the Middle East, to gather economic information from military sources and also forward samples of captured equipment so it could be analysed for signs of diminished quality, which might indicate the level of the blockade's success. The Economic Section was formed in Cairo in December 1917 with only one officer and five clerks, and it was to this office that Dillon was transferred as part of the original staffing, and appointed Staff Captain in February 1918. There was an almost immediate requirement to increase the personnel numbers, and there were 35 staff by May.

Dillon remained attached to GHQ for the remainder of the War, and in September was appointed 1st Class Agent (Cl ff) Intelligence Corps. He finally departed from Cairo in February 1919, sailing from Port Said on the HT "Bermudian". In May 1919 he was disembodied to the Territorial Force, and in October 1920 he resigned his commission, retaining the rank of Captain. Dillon died on 20 April, 1941, and just two years later his son, Edward Peter Wentworth Dillon, was killed in Italy, serving as a Captain with the Royal Artillery.

GUNNER ERNEST WILLS DILNOT

Ernest Wills Dilnot was one of the new young professionals engaged by Kent for the 1914 season. He was born in Ramsgate on 14 February 1898 the second son of greengrocer John Dilnot and his wife Annie, who ran their business from premises on the High Street. Dilnot was given a trial by Kent in 1913, at the age of 15, and was described in the Kent Trials book as a right-arm bowler, and quite fast for his age. He was engaged as a Young Player at the Nursery in 1914 and took 34 wickets that season, including 4 in the two Club and Ground matches he played during August after war was declared. Too young to enlist, he worked at his father's shop until March 1917 when he attested at Canterbury. His subsequent request for the difference between his Army pay and his standard pay from the Club was initially turned down on the basis he had not volunteered. The Club did however change their stance by the end of the year, because he had been too young to volunteer until 1917.

Dilnot was appointed to 337th Brigade of the Royal Field Artillery. He was employed as a Gunner, and after initial training was posted to the RGA in October. By 5 December he was on his way to France to join the BEF. On arrival he was attached to 144 Siege Battery which handled 6 inch Howitzers and was a part of Third Army. Within two weeks he was transferred to 242 Siege Battery in 12th Brigade at St Eloi, joining them a few days before Christmas. St Eloi was in the Ypres sector, and Third Ypres had only finished the previous month, 242 Battery coming out of action to be converted into a 6 inch 26 cwt Howitzer battery. Dilnot's first action with his new unit was on New Year's Eve, firing at enemy targets from a few miles south-west of Ypres.

J. Dilnot, 60 High Street, Ramsgate.

The shop in Ramsgate High Street where Ernest Dilnot worked for his father.
Reproduced by kind permission of Phil Spain

During the early part of 1918 Dilnot's battery spent several weeks in training, but were back at Kemmel in February, engaging enemy targets and occasionally shooting at aeroplanes. Their work involved neutralizing enemy guns, contributing to concentrated fire on specific targets and generally harassing the enemy. They also regularly provided supporting fire whilst raids were made on enemy positions. Being stationed near Ypres, Dilnot's battery was not initially affected when the Germans launched their Spring Offensive, the *Kaiserschlacht*, but that changed when the second phase, Georgette, was launched on 9 April. The following day 242 Siege Battery was attached to 18th Brigade RGA.

On the opening day of the German attack the guns of 18th Brigade had been forced to pull back and Dilnot's battery was one of several moved to reinforce the area near Voormezeele. They fired a great deal on enemy positions but found communications with observation positions continually interrupted by cut lines. Whilst the other batteries of the brigade were transferred to XVII Corps, 242 remained with IX Corps and the following days were spent providing a harassing covering fire. On 20 April Dilnot re-joined 12th Brigade with his battery.

Kemmel, the place Dilnot's battery had been positioned prior to the offensive, had been captured by the Germans, but in the face of determined resistance they did not advance much further. The battery was now firing at the territory they previously occupied. They were subjected to heavy bombardments of high explosive and gas, suffering a number of casualties and several guns were put out of action. Despite the onslaught the salient the Germans now occupied was accurately shelled in return by the men who knew the terrain extremely well, and the Germans suffered thousands of casualties. During May Dilnot's battery transferred into XXII Corps, and having spent time in action north of Hazebrouck, they moved into reserve to train.

That August the battery joined Fourth Army near Amiens to assist Canadian Corps, and was soon firing in support of several Canadian attacks between Amiens and St Quentin. During the second half of the month, with the war now into the *Hundred Days Offensive*, the battery joined IX Corps, remaining with them throughout the *Battles of the Hindenburg Line* and into the final advance. They were in reserve, training, when the Battle of Epehy was fought, but at the end of the month Dilnot and his comrades were firing their guns as IX Corps fought in the Battle of St Quentin Canal. They continued to support Corps attacks during the Battle of Beaurevoir in the first week of October, then the Battle of Cambrai, and on 12 October were in action at Bohain, *Beyond the Hindenburg Line*, as the Germans were pursued to the River Selle.

The Battle of the Selle began 17 October, and the following day Dilnot was in action with his battery, firing on Wassigny Station. Two days later they were firing from Wassigny as the advance continued, and then moved to Mazinghien, which had been captured by the Americans. During the *Final Push* at the beginning of November, Dilnot's battery kept up their work, and supported the IX Corps attack during the Battle of the Sambre on 4 November. As the advance quickly pushed on, and the front narrowed, the guns of the battery were left out of range, and were still so on 11 November when hostilities ceased.

Dilnot joined his battery in cleaning up the battlefield area before entering a period of rest and training, and he was demobilized in February 1919. Although there were no 2nd XI fixtures that year, he did play for the Club and Ground and took several five wicket hauls. He was in the side at Canterbury on 23 August for a one day match against Band of Brothers, the same day the Blythe Memorial Fountain was unveiled. Days later Dilnot played for The Next XX in a match against a Kent XII at Dover. With twenty in the side, and the game a two-day affair, he did not get the chance to bat, but did catch Frank Woolley off the bowling of Godfrey Bryan. This seems to have been his last appearance for a Kent side. Dilnot died on 12 May 1948 at Sangers Hotel on the High Street, Ramsgate.

MAJOR & BREVET LT-COL ARTHUR HOUSSEMAYNE DU BOULAY

Arthur Houssemayne du Boulay was born 18 June 1880 at New Brompton, Chatham, Kent, son of Colonel Woodford George du Boulay and his wife Rose. Educated at Cheltenham, he was in the eleven from 1895 to 1897, as captain in his last year. He opted for a military career and his education continued at the "Shop", the Royal Military Academy at Woolwich (RMA). Joining the institution in January 1898, he demonstrated his sporting inclinations the following year when he shared the annual silver 'Bugle' award having won three of the annual events; the 100 Yards, Quarter Mile and Marching Order Race. He also won the 100 Yards the following year and, whilst a cadet, he headed the RMA cricket averages in 1898 and both the batting and bowling averages in 1899. Receiving the Sword of Honour, awarded to the best cadet on each course, he was commissioned to the Royal Engineers (RE) mid-term in 1899 without taking the final examination.

Du Boulay (left) wins the 100 Yards race at the RMA annual sports in 1899

During 1899 du Boulay played five matches for Kent, scored 250 runs in eight innings and was awarded his county cap. His 58 against Nottinghamshire in his second match was his highest score for Kent, and, in his fifth and final game, against Australia, he took the wicket of the legendary Victor Trumper. His cricketing success continued for the RE, representing them between 1900 and 1912. In the space of one week in July 1906 he made 204 for the School of Military Engineering (SME), 161 for RE against Oxford Harlequins and 175 against MCC. When playing for the SME in 1907 against the Royal Navy and Royal Marines at Chatham, he made 402 not out as his side made 532 for 6, and he also took eight wickets. He captained the RE side from 1906 to 1908, heading the batting averages in 1906 and 1907. Despite his army service Du Boulay did manage to fit in several first class appearances for Gloucestershire in 1908 and the MCC in 1910, and was married to Blanche Hornung in 1909.

Du Boulay (standing, right) in the Kent XI of 1899, reproduced by the kind permission of Kent County Cricket Club

Du Boulay spent a year at the SME Chatham, followed by a year at the Curragh Camp in Ireland with 56th Company. With the Boer War almost at an end he was posted to South Africa with 47th Company in March 1902, and was immediately involved in operations in Cape Colony, then in the Transvaal and Orange River Colony during April. Terms of peace were agreed between the British and the Boers in May, but du Boulay remained in the country until October 1904. He was promoted to Lieutenant in November 1902, and was awarded the Queen's South Africa Medal with 4 clasps (Cape Colony, Orange Free State, Transvaal and 1902) for his wartime service.

Back at the SME in 1905, du Boulay was appointed Assistant Instructor in Fieldworks at the Fortification School, holding that position until October 1908 when he was made 2nd Assistant Instructor and promoted to Captain. When his tenure was up at the end of 1909 he spent two months at Aldershot before heading to the capital, where he took up a new appointment as Adjutant to the 1st London Divisional Engineers, part of the TF and based at Bethnal Green. On 11 September 1914, the war a month old, du Boulay was appointed Deputy Assistant Adjutant and Quarter Master General (DAA&QMG) in the 1st London Division with the rank of Captain, his responsibilities including supply, transport, accommodation and personnel management.

It will be remembered that the 1st London was part of the TF, and the Division was gradually eroded, some parts sent to relieve the regular garrison of Malta, other battalions joining different Divisions in France. In June 1915, after the last two battalions were transferred, du Boulay was appointed to the same role in the 33rd Division, mostly made up of 'Pals' units, raised by Public Schools, sportsmen and the Church Lads Brigade. Most of these units began their training near where they were raised, and it was July 1915 before they concentrated at Clipstone Camp near Mansfield. Kent players Sydney Day and George Heslop were within the 33rd Division at that time, although both moved to other Divisions before du Boulay and the 33rd left for France.

During August 1915 du Boulay moved with the Division to Salisbury Plain for final training. Their crossing to France started in November, and within a short time the

Division had concentrated near Morbecque, 20 miles west of Armentières. Du Boulay served with the 33rd Division HQ until June 1917, during which time it took part in the fighting on the *Somme*, although not on the opening day's fighting. He was Mentioned in Despatches (MID) three times whilst serving with the Division, was appointed Brevet Major and Assistant Quarter Master General (AQMG) with the temporary rank of Lieutenant-Colonel in June 1916, and was appointed Major in November. He then served with HQ as the Division took part in the *Arras* offensive of 1917.

At the beginning of June 1917 du Boulay was raised to Corps level, being appointed Brevet Lieutenant-Colonel with V Corps, as AAQMG (Assistant Adjutant and Quartermaster General). The Corps took part in *Third Ypres* (*Passchendaele*) and du Boulay's fourth MID from Haig in November was no doubt for the role he played during the offensive. The Corps was transferred to Third Army at the start of December, to relieve IV Corps on part of the new line created by the advances of *Cambrai*. The day after du Boulay arrived, the Germans delivered their counter-attack, and he joined the forced withdrawal to the Flesquières Line.

Du Boulay was still with V Corps on the Flesquières Line when the Germans launched their Spring Offensive, the *Kaiserschlacht*, in March 1918. The Germans tried to weaken the defenders by drenching the area in mustard gas for days before they attacked. After the initial assault V Corps was ordered to retire 4,000 yards, but the extent of the withdrawal on their flanks was unknown and, in fear of being surrounded, V Corps beat a hasty retreat. By 26 March, du Boulay and V Corps had retreated across the old Somme battlefields and taken up a new line on the Ancre heights, where the German advance finally slowed to a halt. Haig's despatch from GHQ on 7 April gave du Boulay his fifth MID, and in June the London Gazette announced his being awarded the DSO.

Du Boulay moved to Army HQ level during June 1918, appointed to the Staff of the Third Army, as Assistant Quarter Master General (AQMG). The Third Army saw action during the *Hundred Days Offensive*, its Divisions fighting at *Amiens and the Second Somme* towards the end of August 1918, and then pushing forward during the *Advance to the Hindenburg Line*. Following the Battle of Havrincourt and the Battle of Epehy in September, part of *the Battles of the Hindenburg Line*, du Boulay fell victim to the influenza epidemic that was sweeping Europe. He died on 25 October, 1918 and was buried at Fillièvres British Cemetery. He left a son and two daughters. His sixth MID came posthumously, in Haig's despatch from GHQ on 8 November, and the following April the London Gazette announced he was awarded the Belgian Order of Leopold and the French Croix de Guerre.

DUTNALL BROTHERS

Pub Landlord William Dutnall, and his wife Amy, had two sons, William born on 29 August

1888 and Frank on 30 March 1895. Born and raised in Canterbury, William became a clerk at the Gas and Water Company, and Frank worked as a Coal Merchant's clerk. William played for Kent 2nd XI between 1906 and 1929, as both amateur and professional, and made a single appearance for the 1st XI. He only played fourteen times pre-war, in part because the 2nd XI had a limited fixture list until they entered the Minor Counties Championship in 1911. Typically opening the batting, he scored 153 before being run out against Surrey at the Oval in 1909, and hit 109 against the same side in 1911.

Frank followed his brother into the 2nd XI, first appearing in 1912 at the Oval, on which occasion William opened with George Collins. Having settled his nerves he struck 123 in the second innings, and became a regular feature by 1914 when he played in all ten fixtures. He scored more runs than anyone else that season, and received a special mention in the Young Players Committee Report for his performance against Surrey at Canterbury. In the last match of 1914, played against Essex at Hythe after war had been declared, he made 53 and 50 as Kent won by 5 wickets.

PRIVATE FRANK DUTNALL

Frank Dutnall started work at the Cavalry Record Office in October 1914 as a civilian clerk. In February 1915 it was found that it was difficult to maintain an adequate number of experienced clerks in the office on a civil basis, presumably as so many men were enlisting and leaving. It was therefore decided to reduce the number of civilian employees, and perhaps that was the reason behind Dutnall's own enlistment, as he attested at Canterbury in March 1915, joining the East Kent Regiment (The Buffs). With the rank of Private, Dutnall served as a 'specially enlisted clerk' in the Cavalry Record Office, doing the same job as before, but now as a serving soldier.

Frank Dutnall was employed in the Cavalry Record Office. Picture from the Burnley Express and Advertiser April 19, 1924

A record office was responsible for the administration of the regiments affiliated to it, although not for officers. In this way the Canterbury Record Office was responsible for the Dragoons and Lancers Regiments, keeping master copies of each service record that was held by the regiments, and also responsible for advising next of kin when men were missing or killed. Any articles of private property that belonged to missing soldiers were forwarded to the office, and families notified, although the personal items could not be released until approved by the War Office. In June 1916 Dutnall was advised that his services were no longer required, and he was discharged on 8 July. His military character was recorded as 'very good' and he was declared fit for service. There the trail goes cold, with no reference to his having served further. There are medal records for a Private Frank Dutnall serving with 3rd Dragoons, but whether he is the same man is, at present, impossible to say.

When cricket fixtures resumed in 1919 Dutnall made his first class debut in the County Championship against Middlesex at Mote Park, one of nine players to debut for Kent that season. He played in the first three Championship matches of 1920, but after May was restricted to the 2nd XI in seven of their eight fixtures, as the Minor Counties Championship resumed. Dutnall's relationship with Kent ended after 1921 when he was second in the 2nd XI averages with 31.66, his highest score 135 at Cambridge. He later played club cricket for Enfield and Burnley, living in Lancashire and in business as an Athletic Outfitter, but returning to Canterbury in 1925 to marry Emily Jones. Frank Dutnall was still playing for Burnley up to the 1940's, and it was in that town that he died, on 24 October 1971.

LANCE SERGEANT WILLIAM DUTNALL

On the outbreak of war William Dutnall was of age to serve, but was not attested until August 1917, the timing suggesting this was a result of the Military Service (Review of Exceptions) Act 1917. His medical papers noted that he had hammer toes on both feet and was graded C(1), fit only for Home Service, so it seems he was initially rejected on the same grounds as Frank Woolley. When he attested at Canterbury he stated a desire to serve with the RNAS, the unit both Woolley and Hardinge had joined, but was instead allocated to the Royal Field Artillery with the rank of Gunner, and transferred to Woolwich. Following his initial training Dutnall found himself at Abbey Wood with No.1 Anti-Aircraft Brigade, a mobile unit with the Royal Garrison Artillery. His conduct sheet notes he was "A very good clerk, steady, solid and reliable", suggesting he was using his pre-war skills.

On Boxing Day 1917 Dutnall was married to Edith Minnie East at St. Dunstan's, Canterbury, after obtaining approval from his Commanding Officer. He continued to serve with the AA Brigade throughout 1918, promoted to Bombardier in July and Acting Corporal in April 1919. In May he made his first class debut, opening for the Army against Cambridge University. He scored 30 before he was caught off the bowling of Con Johnstone, and was run out for 0 in the second innings. He was made Lance Sergeant that month, and was serving with No 57 AA Company when demobilized in December.

The Army was geared to assist ex-servicemen searching for work, and provided Dutnall with a good reference in 1922 when he joined the GPO in their telephones department at Canterbury. With no 2nd XI fixtures in 1919, he had to wait until the next season to resume his cricket, playing in the first second stream match of 1920, opening with his brother Frank against Essex at Tonbridge. He was a regular in the 2nd XI for several years, and played his second, and last, first class match for Kent against West Indies in August 1923. William Dutnall died at Nunnery Fields, Canterbury, where he had lived for many years, on 18 March 1960.

William Dutnall (back row, left) joined the Royal Field Artillery. Reproduced by the kind permission of Kent County Cricket Club

CAPTAIN ARTHUR CORBETT EDWARDS AND CAPTAIN GERALD DE LISLE HOUGH

Edwards and Hough played for Kent on opposite sides of the War, but their stories are intertwined by their service in the same battalion, fighting alongside each-other during the Battle of Loos. For that reason their stories are combined.

Arthur Corbett Edwards was born on 10 September, 1871 in Portsmouth, Hampshire, the son of Sir Bevan Edwards KCB KCMG, and Alice (Brocklebank). His father was a senior British Army officer who served with the Royal Engineers in the Crimean War and Indian Mutiny, and was later Commandant of the School of Military Engineering, Commander of British Troops in China and Hong Kong in 1889 and Colonel-Commandant of the Royal Engineers in 1903, as well as being elected MP for Hythe. Edwards was educated at Eton between 1885 and 1890, being in the Cricket XI against Winchester when Jack Mason was in the opposing side. After leaving school he was appointed 2nd Lieutenant with the 3rd Royal West Kent Regiment, a Militia battalion, in December 1891. He was promoted Lieutenant in December 1894, and Captain in May 1897, resigning his commission in October 1901 after almost ten years of service. He did not serve in South Africa, his battalion tasked instead with taking over the garrison on Malta whilst the regular units fought the Boers, and for that part of his service Edwards was awarded the Queen's Mediterranean Medal. In 1900 he married Lily Ethelwyn Noel Cuthbert in London, and they lived in Kensington before moving to Folkestone.

This picture of Arthur Edwards appeared in the Folkestone Express after the Battle of Loos. Image courtesy Kent County Council Libraries & Archives: Folkestone Library

Gerald Hough at Winchester in 1913, the year before he enlisted, reproduced by permission of the Warden and Scholars of Winchester College

A keen sportsman, Edwards was a shining light for Folkestone CC. He made a couple of first class appearances, one for the Europeans against the Parsees in the Bombay Presidency Match in September 1902, and for the Orange Free State against Transvaal in the Currie Cup in January 1904. His Kent appearances were restricted to the 2nd XI. In 1895 against Middlesex at the Angel Ground, Tonbridge he opened the batting, scoring 75 out of 185 and 34 out of 151. In June 1911 for Folkestone against Hythe, he and DM Radford were chasing the Hythe total. Edwards scored 169 not out, as the opening pair reached 288 without loss to win the match. He was a member of the MCC from 1909 and on the Kent committee from 1913.

Gerald de Lisle Hough was the second son of Alfred Lacy Hough and Mildred Anne, born on 14 May 1894 at Brompton in London. His father, who was born in India, worked for many years in Government service as Magistrate with the British Burma Commission, Assistant Commissioner in Karachi and later taught the Burmese language at University College, London. Gerald was educated at Winchester College, in Kingsgate House from 1907 to 1913 where he was in the Cricket XI, captain in his last year, and also made the Football XI. Despite not playing in all the 1911 fixtures he headed the batting and bowling averages, and was also in the top three of the batting and bowling averages in 1912 and 1913.

Edwards' records gives little detail of the early weeks of the war, and Hough's papers were not traced, so it is difficult to say exactly when each was attached to the 8th Battalion Royal West Kent Regiment (RWK), but we do know that Edwards was recalled to serve, whereas Hough was a volunteer. The Battalion was formed in September 1914, part of K3, Kitchener's third New Army, and it is likely Edwards was attached fairly soon after his appointment as Captain at the end of that month. Hough was appointed Temporary 2nd Lieutenant on 7 November and was probably attached to the battalion shortly after.

The recruits for the battalion had travelled from Maidstone to Shoreham in mid-September, and by October were at Oxenfield where they practised drill. In November they moved again, to Worthing, where each Company had six rifles issued for officers and NCO's to practice musketry, although they were apparently unsafe to fire! Kit and equipment were scarce for the New Armies, vital stores going to the units heading overseas. In January the battalion received scarlet battledress uniforms, but only enough for half the men, and it was not until March 1915 that they finally received khaki service dress.

By June the battalion was at Blackdown Camp near Aldershot, where service rifles were finally issued and musketry courses taken. Hough was the battalion Bombing Officer for which he would have received specialist training at some point in the preceding months, and he now held instructional courses for the men. On 12 August the Division was inspected by Kitchener, and later in the month was visited by the King and Queen during trench warfare training. These visits were a sign that they would soon be embarking for France, and sure enough on 25 August instructions were received to leave four days later. When the battalion left Blackdown for Southampton, Captain Edwards was commanding C Company, and 2nd Lieutenant Hough, Bombing Officer, was with No 15 Platoon in D Company. They disembarked at Havre on 31 August and, after a day in camp, entrained for Montreuil where they remained for three weeks. That time was spent training and, with such limited experience with their rifles, seven ranges were constructed for target firing.

On 21 September the men set off on a four night march to the front. On their first stop-over at Donnebroeucq the officers bedded down in a barn which was apparently so plentifully supplied with fleas that many wished they had bivouacked in the field with the men. The movement of men and machines required for an offensive the size of Loos resulted in heavily congested roads. The 8th RWK made slow progress, arriving at a point behind Vermelles where they rested on the roadside on the morning of 25 September. At this stage their orders for battle were constantly changing, but the idea was they would attack the next day. The *Loos* offensive had commenced that morning but the advance was held up, and Douglas Haig, commanding First Army, had requested the assistance of two Reserve Divisions in the vicinity. The 21st was one of those divisions, and of its three brigades the 73rd and 71st were otherwise engaged, leaving the 72nd, of which the 8th RWK were a part, to make the attack alone.

Edwards and Hough moved forward with the battalion that night, to a line of trenches running parallel with, and 1000 yards west of, the Lens-La Bassée road. The objective for the 8th RWK and 9th East Surreys was the German line 2000 yards away, stretching from Hulluch Village on the left, to the Bois Hugo wood on the right. The firing trench was not big enough to accommodate all the battalion and Hough and Edwards' Companies, C and D, attempted to dig a parallel trench in front, but had to abandon it and withdrew to a communication trench. Dawn arrived on the 26 September, but no order to attack, and there were a number of casualties as a result of German shelling.

Finally the Colonel received orders to attack at 11.00 but only arrived back from Brigade HQ at 10.53. The battalion quickly moved up and at 11.00 Hough went forward with the first wave of B and D companies, Edwards following in the next wave with A and C companies. The troops to their left received their orders late, and so Hulluch Village was not dealt with. The troops to their right were themselves attacked just as they were due to advance, and were pinned down in their starting positions. This left the 8th RWK and 9th E. Surreys with no protection on their flanks.

Ignorant of their vulnerability the men went forward at marching pace, apparently to conserve energy for the final charge and bayonet work. The steady pace allowed the Germans to shorten their range in time with the attacking men, and the casualties mounted. As they approached the road the German front line retired, some to Hulluch on the left, others to a sunken road near the wood on the right. From those positions they raked the flanks of the brigade with a murderous machine-gun fire as they crossed the road. Two field guns were also brought to bear upon them from Hulluch, but despite being fired upon from three sides the men marched bravely on. On reaching the German wire it was found to be totally intact, and there was no option but to drop and return fire. At this point there was barely an officer who had not been hit, effectively leaving the men leaderless.

Of the 25 officers who left the trenches an hour before, 13 were killed, including Edwards, and 11 were wounded, including Hough who was subsequently evacuated to England.

During the attack Private James Harding was standing next to Edwards, and saw him fall down, calling out to his men to go on. Harding, who was himself shot in the leg and also fell, did not think Edwards to be badly hit, but after the battle he was missing and later confirmed dead. Edwards is remembered on the Loos Memorial and his official date of death was given as on or after 25 September, most sources giving the date as 25 September. This is odd as the battalion did not go in to the attack until 26 September, and his brother officers who fell are mostly recorded as having fallen on 26 September. [After the author notified the CWGC of this anomaly they amended their website records to reflect the date as 26 September].

Without Hough's papers it is impossible to say how bad his injuries were, but having arrived back in England during October he remained in England for almost a year. On 19 July 1916 he was back in France, joining the 6th RWK at Vauchelles. The battalion was afforded a couple of days rest about this time, and it seems likely that an incident recounted in the Kent Annual 1949 occurred at this time. The story goes:

> *"In July, 1916 the 6th battalion Royal West Kent Regiment was having a few days behind the lines, and an Officers v Sergeants cricket match was arranged. The Officers bowled the Sergeants out for 9, of which 6 were byes. When the Officers went in G. de L. Hough hit the first ball – a full pitch to leg – into the mule lines. The mules started kicking and no one dared to fetch the ball except the transport sergeant, who happened to be fielding on the opposite side of the ground. There were no boundaries and the batsmen ran 11, thus winning the match with one blow. The other officer batsman was A.D. Denton (Northamptonshire)."*

Incidentally, Denton lost part of his leg during the war, and in his three appearances in 1919 and 1920 he had to bat using one of his brothers as a runner, while he fielded exclusively at point. His twin brothers, also Northants players and all team-mates of Claud Woolley, spent time as prisoners of war.

After spending time supplying digging parties and working at improving the trenches, the 6th RWK received orders to take over a recently captured position from the Buffs, to the east of Ovillers. They moved into the trenches on 4 August, and the following day the Germans sent over a heavy bombardment killing a number of men and wounding five officers, one of whom was Hough. The battalion war diary does not record that he was evacuated, but at the end of the month he attended a wedding at Tovil, wearing gold bars on his left arm denoting he had been twice wounded. The London Gazette announced his appointment as temporary Lieutenant on 1 July 1917, and then temporary Captain whilst employed as Asst. to the Assistant Provost Marshal of an Area. The Winchester School war service roll records that he was APM at Cambridge in 1918 and then Bovington in 1919. It also states he was Mentioned In Despatches but gives no date for it. Hough relinquished the appointment, and the temporary rank of Captain, on 8 April 1919, and finally relinquished his commission on 1 September 1921, retaining the rank of Captain.

Hough made his Kent debut in 1919, playing under regimental qualification. Reproduced by the kind permission of Kent County Cricket Club

Hough played his debut first class match for Lionel Robinson's XI against the Australian Imperial Forces at Old Buckenham Hall, Attleborough in May 1919. There were seven Kent players on his side, but he was unbeaten and top scorer in both innings with 30 and 87, impressing enough to be invited to appear for Kent at the start of June against Essex at Leyton. Playing under regimental qualification, he made 77 which was to be his top score for the county, and bowled two overs, taking the wicket of JG Dixon with his first ball in the county Championship. He was however handicapped by one of his war time wounds in the arm, and rarely bowled afterwards. He appeared fourteen times for Kent during the 1919 and 1920 seasons and was capped in 1920, playing his last match that July against Lancashire before taking up the position of Master at Bradfield College, where he remained for ten years.

Following the death of Lionel Troughton in December 1933 Hough was offered the role of Manager at Kent, and from 1935 combined the role with that of Secretary, holding the joint position until 1949. In 1934 he played for the 2nd XI when a last minute vacancy arose, and made 44 and 61, a performance Arrowsmith called remarkable in light of the physical handicap he had, and playing his first match outside of club cricket for fourteen years. Hough had a great sense of humour, recalling in his farewell notes in the 1950 Kent Annual the occasion at Gillingham when he devised a notice for the pavilion which read 'This balcony is unsafe. Committee only'. Leach-Lewis stood in for Hough as manager during the 1946 season when ill health prevented his carrying out those duties, and it was due to his health that he was forced to resign in 1950. In his last few years in the job one of his pet projects was to have the new gates installed at the entrance of the St Lawrence as a memorial to the players who fell in WW2. Hough died on 29 September 1959 at the Kent and Canterbury Hospital, a little over 44 years after Edwards was killed.

CAPTAIN ALFRED JOHN EVANS

Alfred John Evans was born on 1 May 1889 at Highclere, Hampshire, the eldest child of Alfred Henry Evans and Isabel Aimee Houssemayne du Boulay. His father, a master at Winchester College, founded the Horris Hill preparatory school in 1888 and Evans began his education there before going on to Winchester and Oriel College, Oxford where he graduated with a degree in History. At Winchester from 1902, he represented the school 1906-1908 at both rackets and cricket, as captain of the XI in his last year. Winning his Blue as an Oxford Freshman, he played in the fixture against Cambridge from 1909 to 1912, and was captain in 1910. Evans also found time to earn Blues at racquets in 1910 and golf in 1909, 1910 and 1912, winning each of his matches. His debut in first class cricket was for Hampshire in 1908, playing a handful of games that year and again in 1909 and 1912. Whilst representing Oxford in 1911, he played in the fixture against Kent.

On leaving University Evans was offered a teaching position at Eton, with the proviso he first spend a year in Germany. In doing so he became fluent in German which was later of use in his military service. His time at Eton was short, leaving after a year to take up a position in industry. Prior to the outbreak of war, the Intelligence Department at

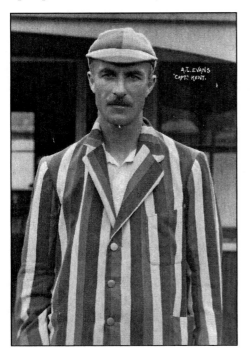

the War Office identified a number of Army Officers, Metropolitan Police officers and other civilians who would be suitable candidates for employment in raising an Intelligence Corps. Following the British declaration of war, around fifty individuals received invitations to join the new Corps, Evans among them.

Johnny Evans won the Military Cross and Bar during the War

Appointed Temporary 2nd Lieutenant on 6 August, he soon departed for France to join the mounted section of the Corps, there also being dismounted, motor-cycle and security sections. Towards the end of September whilst returning from Paris on a motorcycle, Evans was involved in a collision with a car near Soissons, injuring his knee and returning to England to recover. Prior to returning to GHQ 1st Echelon in December, he queried whether he might be considered for the motorcycle section. The request was politefully declined.

The RFC was initially used to recce and spot artillery targets, and in February 1915 Evans was attached to No.3 Squadron as an observer. The following month his new unit became the first to use aerial photography to effect, by mapping out the German lines in advance of the attack at *Neuve Chapelle*. To do this the pilots flew at 800 feet whilst observers, like Evans, leaned out to take pictures, usually under fire. This enabled a successful start to the battle, but as the enemy lines retreated they were difficult to track. In September, during *Loos*, Evans was again in the thick of things, and was awarded the Military Cross for continuing to observe whilst under attack by a German aeroplane, and was then Mentioned in Despatches for gallant and distinguished service in the field. During October he was appointed Flying Officer and became a pilot with No. 3 Squadron in early 1916.

In advance of the *Somme* offensive, Evans was occupied in spotting German artillery positions and ranging the heavy British guns as they were moved into position. From 1 July 1916 as the battle raged below, his squadron was mainly tasked with counter-battery work, directing fire onto German gun positions, and he was involved in several aerial fights. He and his observer, Lieutenant Long, were then given a special task, making a continuous series of short reconnaissances during the period the *Somme Continued*, over the lines to Bapaume and as far south as Cambrai. On 14 July they shot down an enemy plane after a manœuvering fight lasting about ten minutes. For the last twenty seconds they flew side by side with the enemy plane which Long shot down, but their own plane was riddled with bullets and they were lucky to get back. The machine was too badly damaged to be repaired and they were sent a new one from the Aviation Park. In the report of his capture two days later Evans wrote:

"On the 16th July 1916 I left the Aerodrome on a 110 Parasol Morane at about 4-0 a.m. with Lieutenant Long as my Observer. Our work was to make repeated reconnaissances of the enemy's movements for 10 or 15 miles behind his lines and to send the results by special wireless to Headquarters. On the morning in question we had been down low and thrown over some bombs which my observer carried in his lap and fired at troops in the road, and I had just climbed up to 4,000 feet when my engine suddenly cut out completely.

We were then the far side of Bapaume, 10 miles from the lines and had no possible chance of getting back. I steered towards the lines at the same time trying the few things I could to start the engine again. As we came down I had to turn to dodge fire rockets from a battery which was then just S. W. of Bapaume. I selected a large bare field where

I imagined I should have time to fire my machine and also told my Observer to have matches ready.

When we were about 50 feet from the ground, men started to shoot at us and I saw that we could not avoid landing within a 100 yards or so of a very carefully hidden German battery which I had not seen. I thought that I should probably not have time to fire my machine and decided on the spur of the moment to crash it on landing. This I did, quite successfully. It was very badly broken. Lt. Long was badly shaken and I was a bit dizzy and I was unable to set fire to the machine before the Germans came round us. I could not get at the petrol tap and could not find the Lewis Gun to fire into the tank as I think Lieut. Long threw it over board just before we landed."

Having been taken captive the two airmen were taken to Cambrai Fort where they were questioned by German Intelligence officers. All the flying officers captured on the Somme were eventually transferred to Clausthal, in the Harz Mountains. Evans' first escape from there took him to within yards of the Dutch border but he was recaptured and returned to camp. He was then sent to Ingolstadt, a series of old forts used as officer prisoner of war camps, and placed in Fort 9 with the other 'black sheep'. Here Evans was involved in many escape attempts, getting out of the fort on several occasions, but recaptured each time. In 1917 it was decided to move the Russian and English POWs to other camps, the new English camp located at Zorndorf.

Whilst the men were being transferred, Evans and another prisoner, Captain Buckley, jumped from the moving train and set off on a walk of several hundred miles to the Swiss border. It took them 18 days, walking at night and laying up in the days, but they finally made it, crossing the border at about 00.30 on 9 June 1917. Whilst in Switzerland Evans was able to visit his brother and sister in Murren. His brother was a former POW himself, having been badly wounded and captured during the Second Battle of Ypres, and had subsequently been invalided out of Germany. His sister had travelled to Switzerland to look after him.

Following his recovery Evans was keen to return to action, but new rules prevented escaped POWs serving in the same theatre of war they were captured in. He was subsequently posted to *Egypt*, arriving in Aboukir during November, and in January 1918 was sent to *Palestine* to command 142 Squadron. He was pleased with the command, although slightly disappointed it was of a bombing squadron, and not observation work. On 19 March 1918 Evans was with a flight of six single-seater aeroplanes, escorted by Bristol fighters, flying eastwards to bomb Kutrani Station on the Hedjaz Railway. He was piloting a Martinsyde and, having dropped his bombs and fired at a stationary German plane, he turned to head back. By this stage he had lost contact with the rest of the flight other than one Bristol fighter, and was close to El Karak near the Dead Sea.

"I believe I was forced to land owing to a temporary block in the petrol pipe. I had been bombing KATRANI station and had flown for about ¼ hour on the way home when the engine about stopped as if starved of petrol. I made certain by pumping that the pressure was ok. Soon after landing I was surrounded by Arabs and forced to burn the machine before I had discovered the cause of failure. Capt. Austin and Lt. Lee very gallantly landed beside me to try and pick me up but broke a wheel on a stone on landing. They were flying a Bristol fighter plane No1 Australian Squadron. We burnt both machines and all then were captured first by Arabs and soon afterwards rescued!!! By Turks."

The Australians, Captain Austin and Lieutenant Lee, had both gained the Military Cross, and made a considerable reputation for themselves on the Palestine front. The three airmen were taken to El Karak where they were entertained by Ismail Kemal Bey the Turkish commandant and military governor of El Karak. Here Evans gave his name as Everard to prevent the enemy discovering he was an escaped prisoner, which would have meant a closer guard being kept on him. Bey explained that the men were lucky to have avoided death at the hands of the Arabs, owing their lives to the reward of 50 gold pieces the Turkish Government offered for live English Officers. They also knew Bey would have hung half a dozen of them if they had murdered the airmen.

The prisoners began a journey towards Constantinople, stopping at Aman where they were questioned by a German Intelligence Officer, and then continued on to El Afule where they spent some time with German airmen who gave them a break from their Turkish guards. Soon after this Evans escaped and made for the coast, but was captured near Hedera. After several weeks in Constantinople he was sent to Psamatia where he came across the Australians, Austin and Lee, again. After a further ten days most of the prisoners there were sent to camps in the interior, Evans' destination being Afion-Kara-Hissar. When it was heard sick officers were being selected for exchange at Smyrna, Evans bribed a doctor and secured a place on the train, and once there waited for the exchange ship to arrive. He was tempted to surrender to the Turks so that he could escape 'legitimately' but, with the end of the war in sight, boarded the ship and was in Alexandria in November 1918. He was later awarded a bar to his Military Cross for his numerous escape attempts.

Evans resumed playing cricket in 1919, and was married that October to Marie Rose Galbraith. Following appearances for the Gentlemen, Hampshire (against Kent) and the MCC he made his Kent debut in 1920 against Northants, scoring a century. His performances earned him a place in the England side against Australia at Lord's but he

Evans (middle) following his capture in 1918, pictured with Austin and Lee, the two Australian airmen who landed in an attempt to rescue him. Reproduced by permission Bayerisches Hauptstaatsarchiv, Kriegsarchiv, München

was not selected again. He was to play 36 matches for the Kent 1st XI, was Captain in 1927 and was awarded his cap that same year. He made 1,303 runs at an average of 25 his highest score being 143 against Lancashire at the Mote. Between the wars he worked in the Stock Exchange and, due to his experience, was called upon to work for the government during WW2.

Employed with MI9, Evans helped craft guidelines for the escape of POWs. More than 33,000 men from British, American, and British Commonwealth forces got back to the Allied lines after being inside enemy territory, whether as escapers or as evaders. A substantial proportion of them did so with the help, known or unknown, of MI9 or of its American equivalent. He landed in Normandy in July 1944 accompanying Eisenhower's armies during the fighting in north-west Europe, helping find and release POWs. Evans passed away on 18 September 1960 in Marylebone, London. Captain Buckley, who accompanied him on his escape from Germany, once said 'he was the bravest man I ever met'.

LANCE CORPORAL WILLIAM JOHN FAIRSERVICE

William John Fairservice, better known as Bill, appeared for Kent before and after the war, and was a member of the county's first four Championship winning teams. He was born in Nunhead, Southwark in London on 16 May 1881, to William and Lucia Fairservice. At the age of ten he entered Ivydale Road School and left five years later to start work. The 1901 Census records that he was a toy store keeper, which would suggest he was working with his father, a fishing tackle and toy maker. He had trialled for Kent in 1899, but it was 1902 before he was employed as a Young Player, and by then his parents had moved from London to live in St. Mary's Road in the southern part of Tonbridge.

Bill Fairservice served in the Kent Fortress
Engineers and the Military Police

Perhaps unfortunate to be in competition with Blythe and Woolley for a place in the side, Fairservice secured his Cap in the 1903 season. His Wisden Obituary stated that he claimed the scalp of WG Grace as his first wicket in first class cricket, bowling the great man twice in the same match. That was however his third match for the county at the start of the 1903 season, by which time he had already taken a number of wickets. He had appeared twice in 1902, and although his debut was indeed against MCC, Grace did not play on that occasion. Fairservice made 4,922 runs in 301 matches for Kent, with a high score of 61 not out against Essex in 1906. He took 853 wickets at 22.59 and his best return was 7 for 44 in 1920 against Leicestershire. Although not always first choice, he took his opportunities and recorded 38 five wicket innings and 7 ten wicket matches.

Living in Tonbridge, and employed at the Nursery, Fairservice spent a lot of time with the other budding professionals. Aside from their cricket a number of the men represented the local Tonbridge football team. In a 9-1 victory over the Town Reserves in 1906, Fairservice scored twice, and Woolley five times. Weeks later against Fairhill he scored again, cancelling out a Claud Woolley own goal. Fairservice married Annie Coad in Tonbridge at the end of 1904 and was living in Goldsmid Road up until the war. He replaced an injured Blythe in the side for the last fixture in 1914 against Hampshire at Bournemouth, starting on 31 August.

Having turned 33 that year Fairservice did not enlist immediately, and was one of those written to by the Club in early 1915, asking what he was doing to support the war effort. By the time of the General Committee Meeting in March 1915, when the player's responses were read out, Fairservice was serving with the Kent Fortress Engineers. Unfortunately his papers have not survived, so accurate dates cannot be given. It is likely he was stationed with Blythe & Co at Gillingham, as he was a member of the Fortress Engineers cricket team of 1916 that included Blythe, Claud Woolley and the Jennings brothers. A newspaper report of a fixture against a Public Schools side during August reveals that he not only scored 64 runs at the Oval, but had also been promoted to Lance Corporal by that time.

When cricketers' allowances were discussed by the General Committee at Cannon Street Hotel in December 1917, it was noted that Fairservice was entitled to payment as he was one of those who volunteered. However, by May 1918 the Committee Meeting recorded that he was serving with the Military Police. The lack of records makes it impossible to determine where he was stationed, but with no medals awarded it is a safe bet that he remained in England.

Fairservice returned to playing cricket for Kent in 1919, but at the end of the 1921 season he retired from county cricket and played for Northumberland in the Minor Counties until 1926. He then held coaching positions at Tonbridge, Malvern and Lancing, and also served as an umpire in first and second class fixtures. In 1946 he began a four year stint as groundsman at Sevenoaks and also became Kent 2nd XI scorer until retiring at the age of 87. His love of cricket never waned, and even in his eighties he was to be seen bowling in the nets at King's School, Canterbury where his son, Colin, was a sports master. Bill Fairservice died at Canterbury on 26 June 1971.

2ND LIEUTENANT CHARLES LESLIE DINSDALE FAWCUS

Charles Leslie Dinsdale Fawcus was born in Bromley on 8 December 1898, the son of Charles Octavius Fawcus, a coal merchant and shipbroker, and Ethel Mary (Barrett). He attended Bradfield College from 1909-1917, was Prefect from 1916, and excelled at a number of sports. He was in the Football XI 1914-16, as captain in the last year, was Fives captain 1915-16 and was Fives Open Singles winner in 1915 and 1917. A member of the College XI from 1914 to 1916, his Wisden obituary noted that he was regarded as the best batsman ever to play for Bradfield, heading the batting averages for three years in a row. In 1916 his average was 125.25, and he was selected for the Public Schools side, scoring 24 and 65 against the Household Brigade. The following year he played for Bradfield against the RMC Sandhurst in June, and days later entered the RMA Woolwich.

Selected for the XI within a fortnight of joining, he helped crush Dulwich by scoring 153 not out and taking three wickets, and the following month made good scores in the victory over Sandhurst, as well as taking 5 wickets, including that of Bernard Howlett. Against Tonbridge School in 1918 the schoolboys included three future Kent players, Edward Solbé, John Knott and Lionel Hedges, who were treated to a fine display of batting when Fawcus struck 100 not out.

Leslie Fawcus in the Kent team 1924

As *The Hundred Days Offensive* began in August 1918, Fawcus played his last match for the RMA against the RMC at Lord's, in which future Kent player Thomas Beeching made a century for the opposition. Whilst his cricket had flourished, his studying had perhaps not done likewise – the RMA register noted he 'dipped below standard'. Fawcus left the RMA on 19 September and was commissioned 2nd Lieutenant in the Royal Garrison Artillery the following day. Just over seven weeks later the Armistice came into effect and Fawcus did not see active service overseas. He did however remain with the RGA until he resigned his commission in October 1922, by then a Lieutenant, having been promoted in March 1920.

Fawcus played cricket for the Artillery and was married to Kathleen Olive Graham Swann in September 1921 at St. Andrew's, Ferozepore, India where he was stationed for some time. In the summer of 1924, he made his first appearance for Kent 2nd XI against Surrey at the Oval, opening the batting and scoring 17, somewhat overshadowed by his partner, Jack Deed, who posted 252. Apart from his four matches for the second team, he made his first class debut, when picked for the Championship fixture against Middlesex at the Angel Ground, Tonbridge. He matched Frank Woolley's score when dismissed for a duck, and only managed 5 in the second innings as Middlesex proved too strong for Kent.

Due to the war, Fawcus had missed the usual progression from college to university, but applied to Oxford, and matriculated from Christ Church College during October 1924. The next summer he played for his college XI and also appeared several times for the University. Rumour had it that a mistake at the Oval a week before the Varsity Match, when he dropped Jack Hobbs, cost him his Blue. Hobbs went on to make 261 as he and Sandham put on 428 for the first wicket. Fawcus had his BA and MA conferred in June 1931 and took up a career as a schoolmaster, playing occasionally for Dorset in the Minor Counties. He taught at Winton House, Winchester from 1934, took over as Headmaster in 1937, and remained in charge when the school was amalgamated with Dunchurch Hall near Rugby, and became Dunchurch Winton School.

During WW2 Fawcus provided a scholarship for a Naval Cadetship as well as another to Radley, He celebrated his silver wedding anniversary in 1946, and died at Worthing, Sussex on 8 December 1967, the occasion of his 69th birthday.

LIEUTENANT GEOFFREY NORMAN FOSTER

Geoffrey Norman Foster was born on 16 October, 1884 at Malvern, Worcestershire, one of the seven sons and four daughters of Clergyman and Schoolmaster the Reverend Henry Foster and his wife Sophia. All seven brothers played cricket for Worcestershire, which at one time earned the county the soubriquet of "Fostershire", and all were educated at Malvern, where Geoffrey, a senior Chapel Prefect, was in the XI from 1901 to 1904. He also played in the Football XI in 1902 and 1903, the Rackets Pair 1902 to 1904 and the Pritchard Racket (seniors) 1902 to 1904. Going up to Oxford (Worcester College), he was awarded his cricket Blue as a Freshman in 1905, playing against Cambridge four times, his most successful performance bringing him scores of 41 and 77 in 1906. He also took part in the University Association Football matches of 1905, 1907 and 1908, being captain in the last season, and was a golf and rackets Blue.

Foster earned an amateur International Cap for England against Holland in 1907 and another against Wales in 1912. He made his debut for Worcestershire in 1903 aged 18, and although his appearances for the county were restricted by business commitments, he scored 6,551 runs in all first class fixtures for an average of 26.84 and held 151 catches. His highest score was 175 off the bowling of Leicestershire in 1913, and the Worcestershire sixth-wicket record of 195, established by him and JA Cuffe in that game, still stood when he died in 1971. Having spent time as secretary to the Jam Sahib of Nawanagar (Ranjitsinhji), including time in Nawanagar in 1909, he took up a business career in the City of London, first with Walter Judd, Ltd., and then his own firm.

Geoffrey Foster served with the East Riding Yeomanry which became a Machine-Gun Battalion. Reproduced by the kind permission of Philippa Williams

Having applied for a commission in the East Riding Yeomanry Foster was appointed 2nd Lieutenant on 10 October 1914. The 1/1st ERY went overseas in October 1915 but Foster remained in Beverley with the 2/1st ERY which came under orders of 2/1st Yorkshire Mounted Brigade, and in March 1915 he was made temporary Lieutenant. The brigade was actually converted into a cyclist unit in July, and by November was in the Bridlington area. Foster was appointed Adjutant during January 1917, responsible for regimental administration, and subsequently confirmed Lieutenant in August, and acting Captain whilst in command of a company in December.

Unfortunately Foster's papers remain elusive so exact dates are unknown, but around the end of 1917 he was posted to *Egypt* to bolster the 1/1st ERY's numbers before their transfer to France. The battalion had been active in *Palestine*, and this gave Foster the opportunity to visit Junction Station and Jerusalem, whilst he was stationed at the Yeomanry Base Camp at Sidi Bishr. During April the order was given for the battalion to merge with the 1/1st Lincolnshire Yeomanry to form a Machine Gun Battalion. As an officer, Foster was seconded to the new battalion whilst still attached to the ERY, whereas the ranks were officially transferred. Instruction in machine gunnery began mid-April after which the men sailed for France, landing at Marseille on the first day of June, then moving across France to Etaples by train. Several weeks later Foster's new unit was formally designated D Battalion Machine Gun Corps (MGC).

As the men underwent more intensive training and attended courses at Camiers Camp, the MGC base depot in France, Foster and the others had plenty to do. Small groups of officers and men were then attached to front line units for instruction, and to ease them into their new role. The Battalion's official title changed from D Battalion to 102nd (Lincs and East Riding Yeomanry) Battalion MGC on 17 August, and a few days later their Instructors returned to their own base camp, their work done. The 102nd Battalion MGC were ready for the front line.

The *Hundred Days Offensive* was underway as Foster joined the 102nd MGC's march to Gauchin Legal near Arras at the end of August. The battalion was split into four companies, A, B, C and D, although which Foster was attached to is unknown. The companies were often used in slightly different areas, and occasionally at the disposal of different Divisions, the machine guns being deployed where required. Each company had about 16 guns and they were moved around in their lorries which carried the boxes of machine gun belts, spare parts for the guns, the guns themselves and of course the men. Unlike the typical infantryman, the machine gunner could not carry enough ammunition to last for long, and transport was of the utmost importance.

During the *Battles of the Hindenburg Line*, Foster was in the Arras area, his company in and out the line at the disposal of 56th Division and 11th Division. The battalion took part in the operations that opened the Battle of Cambrai-St Quentin at the end of September, providing covering fire for the infantry advance and firing a barrage on German positions, as the enemy was pushed back. *Beyond the Hindenburg Line* Foster joined the push forward, his battalion taking up positions which would cover the crossing of the Selle. Although the Germans were on the back foot, they were not giving up easily, and the 102nd MGC experienced several gas attacks during this period. Undeterred, the line of the Selle was attacked as Foster's unit sent a barrage of thousands of rounds towards the enemy positions, and also those areas German reservists were likely to be sent from. In the next days they were also involved in beating back several German counter-attacks.

On 1 November, as the *Final Push* began, Foster's battalion was used in support of the attack towards Valenciennes, and after hard fighting the town fell the following day. On 8 November the battalion was partially in France and partially in Belgium, with companies in Sebourg, Angreau and Roisin. They joined the advancing infantry, marching 12 miles across country, manhandling their guns, ammunition and equipment as there was no transport available. On 11 November a telegram was received, ordering hostilities to cease at 11.00. The fighting was over. Foster moved to Calais during the early part of 1919 and was then demobilized. On 23 June 1920 he was officially restored to the establishment of the ERY, and relinquished his commission the following year.

Qualifying by residence at Blackheath since 1914, Foster turned out occasionally for Kent between 1921 and 1922. His highest score for the county was 71 against Essex at Leyton in 1921, and he opened the batting on several occasions. In May 1921 he was one of three Kent players appearing at Lord's for the MCC against Australia, the others being Hubble and Evans, and in August 1921 he and George Wood were in an England XI playing the Australians at Eastbourne. The year 1921 also marked the launch of the Cricketer magazine, in which Foster was instrumental.

A tireless man, Foster also played football for the Corinthians, of which club he was honorary secretary from 1919-1924, was Secretary of the Oxford and Cambridge Golfing Society and Treasurer of the Tennis and Racquets Association at Queen's. His son, Peter Foster, played for Kent and served in WW2, as did his son-in-law the Kent Captain Gerry Chalk, and his brother-in-law Harold Prest is referenced elsewhere within this book. Geoffrey Foster died on 11 August 1971 at Westminster.

MAJOR-GENERAL LOVICK BRANSBY FRIEND

Lovick Bransby Friend made six first class appearances in total, three of those for Kent, and would no doubt have played more but for his military career. He was born on 25 April 1856 at Bexley in Kent, the fourth son of merchant Frederick Friend and his wife Fanny. Having spent his early life at Woollett Hall, the family home in North Cray, he attended Cheltenham from 1868-1872 but did not make the 1st XI. At the age of 16 he entered the Royal Military Academy (RMA) at Woolwich, where he won a prize for Artillery and did make the XI, present in the side that beat Sandhurst in 1873. He was commissioned into the Royal Engineers (RE) as a Temporary Lieutenant in 1874, the appointment made permanent in 1876.

Friend spent some time stationed at the Curragh Camp in Ireland, but was back in England to play in goal for the RE in the 1878 FA Cup Final, under the captaincy of Walter Hedley's brother. He was then posted to Hong Kong (not because Wanderers won the Cup) where he was tasked with starting submarine mining defences. In 1881 he returned to England and was appointed Fortifications Instructor at Sandhurst in September 1883. During his year in that role the cadets passing through his company included Haig, Rawlinson and Maude who were all to play major roles in the Great War. A promotion to Captain followed in 1885.

Lovick Friend, commander of the forces in Ireland during the Easter Rising 1916. Courtesy of the National Library of Ireland

Friend played cricket for the RE from 1874, as an upper order batsman wicket-keeper. In 1885 he made 198 against a Band of Brothers team that included Arthur Fulcher and Lord Harris, the latter also scoring a century. Perhaps that performance was the reason he was invited to play for Kent the following season, when he made his first class debut under Harris at Hove. He played twice more for Kent, both games in 1886, once against an MCC side that included WG Grace, and also against Lancashire at the Bat and Ball, Gravesend. Friend played for the Gentlemen of England on two occasions, and his final first class appearance was for the MCC against Kent in 1891, the occasion of Gerry Weigall's first class debut. He continued to play for the RE and also represented Northumberland, Free Foresters, Southern District and United Services.

Having spent two more years overseas, raising and training the West Indies Fortress Company, Friend was promoted to Major on his return to England in 1893, remaining in the country until posted to Egypt in 1897. When the Nile Expedition arrived to avenge the death of Gordon at Khartoum, he served as Staff Officer at Aswan in 1898, organizing the supply system. In advance of the Battle of Omdurman Friend was attached to the Intelligence Department as Provost Marshall, and during the battle was galloper to the Commander-in-Chief, Kitchener. Winston Churchill later wrote how, as he was passing the Intelligence mess not long before the battle began, Major Friend kindly offered him some luncheon, which he gratefully accepted. Friend was subsequently Mentioned in Despatches, and awarded the Khedive's Sudan Medal with a clasp for Khartoum, and the Queen's Sudan Medal in silver. The following year he was awarded the Order of the Osmanieh, fourth class, in recognition of his services in Egypt and the Sudan.

In the years that led up to the Great War, Friend was promoted to Lieutenant-Colonel in 1900, Brevet Colonel in 1904, Colonel in 1906, temporary Brigadier-General in 1908 and Major-General in 1912. From 1900-1904 he was Director of Works and Stores with the Egyptian Army, CRE Egypt in 1904, Director of Egyptian Public Works in 1905, Assistant-Director at the War Office 1906, and Commander of Coast Defences in Scotland 1908-1912. For his services in Egypt he was awarded the Medjidieh, third class in 1902, and the Order of the Osmanieh, third class in 1904. In January 1913 he was appointed General Officer in Charge of Administration in Ireland.

When the BEF mobilized in August 1914, Friend succeeded to the command of the forces in Ireland. He complained in November 1914 that in the event of civil trouble the force available to Irish Command amounted to 400 cavalry and 2,000 infantry, although the level of troops available from England was dramatically increased during the war. He was responsible for the formation and training of three new Divisions by early 1916, when he was sworn in as a member of the Privy Council in Ireland. At that time British Intelligence decoded German messages, discovering details of an arms shipment, designed to support an uprising of the Irish Volunteers. Friend attended meetings with the Police and Intelligence to examine ways of thwarting the plans, but when the arms ship, the *Aud*, was captured on 21 April, and Roger Casement was arrested, the authorities were satisfied that the danger had passed.

Friend immediately departed for London on leave, which turned out to be unfortunate timing, as the Easter Rising began on Monday 24 April. He arranged for the transfer to Ireland of approximately 10,000 troops from a camp at St Albans, and quickly returned to Dublin to set up his HQ in Trinity College. He opted to construct an inner cordon around the GPO to cut off the head of the Rebel force. This was achieved by the Thursday afternoon, and the *RE Journal* recorded that Friend received the surrender of the rebel leaders on the Saturday. The handling of the Rising is well documented, and officially it was said Friend had handled the situation firmly, and order was restored by the time Sir John Maxwell arrived in Ireland. The fact Friend had been in England when the trouble started was however seen by his superiors as an error of judgement, and he was replaced by Maxwell.

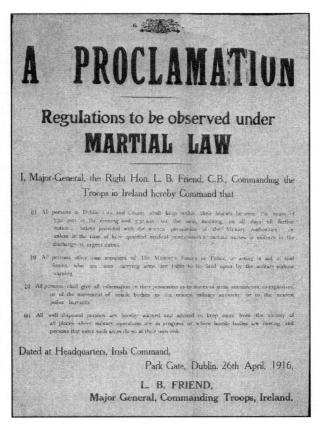

A proclamation of Martial Law, issued on 26 April 1916 by Lovick Friend, the Major General Commanding Troops, Ireland at the time of the Easter Rising. Courtesy of the National Library of Ireland

A week after his recall to England, Friend was given a special appointment as President of the Claims Commission to the BEF, and his new role took him to GHQ France. The remit of the commission did not cover '*faits de guerre*' like shell fire; such losses were instead registered with a French commission to be dealt with post-war. The role of the British Commission was to investigate and settle claims for damage caused by the passage of British troops, or by their occupation of French territory. This might include soldiers helping themselves to the occasional chicken or bottle of wine, but most claims related to the sort of damage which was inevitable with large armies being transported over agricultural land, or large camps and billets established on farms and meadows. Thousands of such claims were settled, though most were small. The Commission also organized a scheme whereby troops being brought into a village occupied the same area vacated by the troops leaving.

During his time with the Commission, Friend was awarded the Belgian Ordre de Léopold, the French Croix de Commandeur of the Légion d'Honneur and the Croix de Guerre. In 1919 he was made Knight of the British Empire (KBE) and was mentioned in despatches for a fourth time in Haig's Despatch in March, by which time he was Director of Hirings and Requisitions. Haig stated that 'our business relations with the French, the obtaining of sites and buildings, called for the establishment of a Directorate of Hirings and Requisitions', and Friend's organizational skills brought him to the fore.

On the last day of June 1920, Friend was placed on retired pay and relinquished his appointment, after 47 years of military service, although he remained in France until March 1921, as Chairman of the French Committee of the Disposal Board. He was given full authority to settle all small claims immediately and the total of such payments was in excess of two million pounds. A long retirement followed during which Friend spent time in South Africa and South America. He died in a nursing home in London on 19 November 1944, aged 88.

FULCHER FAMILY

The Fulcher family is the only instance in this book of two generations of a family serving, although it was certainly not unheard of, and John le Fleming and Tufton had sons in the army. Arthur Fulcher was 59 years old on the outbreak of war, but played his part, as did his sons, Eric and Edward.

TEMPORARY CAPTAIN ARTHUR WILLIAM FULCHER

Arthur William Fulcher was born on 7 May 1855 in Pau, France the son of Captain Edward William Johnson Fulcher of the Royal Irish Fusiliers, and Caroline Frances Green. In January of 1868 he entered Grant's House at Westminster School in London, where he was in the XI 1871-1872. In the following years Fulcher played a fair amount of club cricket for Hadlow, Sevenoaks Vine and the MCC amongst others. His Kent debut was made on 3 June 1878 at the Old County Ground, Town Malling when Kent took on Nottinghamshire. Kent were bowled out for 36 in their first innings and Fulcher top scored with just 13 runs, the only player to reach double figures. After Notts posted 134, Kent were bowled out for 50 to lose by an innings, Fulcher being one of four Kent players to make a duck. He played twice more that season, making an undefeated 44 against Hampshire at Tunbridge Wells, which was to be his highest score for the county.

In business as a wine merchant, Fulcher was married to Gertrude Elizabeth Coope on 16 February 1882, and the following year was commissioned Lieutenant in the West Kent Yeomanry. He resumed his association with Kent in 1886, in the team against Derbyshire at Mote Park, and played three more times the following summer. An appearance for Mote Park in 1888 seems to have seen the end of his cricketing career. Having transferred to the Suffolk Yeomanry in 1890 he was appointed Captain, and thereafter concentrated on his passion for sailing, becoming a member of the Royal Yacht Squadron in 1891. Eric had been born the previous year, and the family were living at Milgate House near Bearsted in Kent. In addition to his sailing activities, Fulcher was still with the Suffolk Yeomanry, but in 1897 was granted the honorary rank of Major, and then resigned his commission.

From 1898 Fulcher took part in a great number of sailing events with the Royal Yacht Squadron, annually racing at Cowes Week and winning a number of trophies with a variety of yachts. He also served as a Justice of the Peace in Kent from 1899 and in Hampshire from 1911. When war broke out in 1914, he was soon able to put his sailing skills to good use. He joined the Royal Naval Reserve in November 1914 and was appointed temporary Lieutenant Commander. Given command of the yacht *Hersilia*, Fulcher was soon patrolling the Hebrides, helping to enforce the naval blockade. The *Hersilia* would have been used to police neutral shipping, which was stopped and searched to ensure vital war supplies were not reaching Germany.

In early 1915 Fulcher resigned his commission to take up the position of Assistant Provost Marshal, South Irish Command, with the rank of temporary Captain (Honorary Major). There was a sizeable British force stationed in Ireland, and Fulcher joined the Provosts that were used to police them in places like Fort Carlisle, Queenstown in County Cork, where there was also a naval base. His appointment lasted only until the end of 1915, when he reached the age of 60. For his service, Fulcher was awarded the British War and Victory medals. In 1918 he was again acting as a JP in Kent, and died in London on 17 May 1932 after contracting pneumonia.

FULCHER BROTHERS

Edward Arthur and Eric Jesser were the first and third sons of Arthur and Gertrude. Both boys were born in Kent, Edward at Ospringe on 15 October 1884 and Eric at Bearsted, on 12 March 1890. From 1898 to 1901 Edward was educated at Chaterhouse where he was a member of the Rifle Corps, and on leaving became an engineer, living in Andover. He made his debut in the Minor Counties Championship in 1905 for Devon, opening the batting for them a number of occasions that season. The following year he matriculated from Hertford College, Oxford but did not earn a degree. Although he was living in the West Country on the outbreak of war, he did at some point return to Kent, as he played for the 2nd XI on two occasions in 1909, opening the batting against Middlesex at Lord's and Surrey at the Oval. During 1913 and 1914 he was back playing for Devon, scoring a century in the match against Cornwall that ended on the day war was declared.

Eric was educated at Castlemount College in Dover, and then went on to Radley in 1904, where he was in the XI 1906-1907. On leaving school he moved to Attleborough, Norfolk, acquiring farming experience and studying land agency. He represented the Norfolk XI from 1910 to 1914 and was selected for Lord Hawke's MCC team visiting Argentina 1911-12, along with Eric Hatfeild and Lionel Troughton, his first class debut in Buenos Aires bringing scores of 51 and 39. He as good as assured himself a place in the Norfolk side in his third match at Trent Bridge against the Notts 2nd XI. In just over thirty minutes he scored 83 out of 108, a dazzling display of fierce hitting, and although he made higher scores on subsequent occasions, he regarded it to be one of his best knocks. When the Minor Counties Championship was decided by a challenge match in 1913, Fulcher helped Norfolk to the title with a shining performance.

Eric Fulcher in the 1913 Norfolk XI, reproduced by the kind permission of David Armstrong

LIEUTENANT EDWARD ARTHUR FULCHER

On the outbreak of war Edward Fulcher joined the 2nd King Edward's Horse, a reserve cavalry regiment, as a Trooper at Langley Park, Slough. He then applied for a commission and was appointed 2nd Lieutenant in the 12th Reserve Regiment Cavalry on 6 October. An ailment prevented him from doing little duty or training, and his CO recommended he resign his commission, but by February 1915 he was found fit for duty. On the last day of August 1915 Fulcher was appointed 2nd Lieutenant on probation with the 11th Hussars, but at the end of the year was deemed supplementary to establishment (surplus to requirement), and joined a reserve unit.

He was made temporary Lieutenant from June 1916 but relinquished the appointment in September when he finally embarked for France to join the 11th Hussars in the field. When he reported for duty the regiment was in bivouac near Daours, and he was duly attached to 'A' Squadron. The *Somme* offensive was still in progress and, with all five Cavalry Divisions recently assembled in that area, it was obvious that a major attack was planned. Two days after Fulcher's arrival, all of the officers in the Brigade were summoned to a meeting where the Divisional Commander explained the plans. The idea was much the same as that on 1 July, and Fulcher's Brigade were tasked with leading the Division. Once Morval and Les Boeufs had been captured, they were to head for Roquigny. Tanks were to be used and it was hoped a rapid advance would deliver the cavalry an opportunity to exploit any breakthrough.

The Battle of *Flers-Courcelette* opened on 15 September, Fulcher's regiment having made their way to the Carnoy Valley the night before, where they waited with anticipation. About an hour after the attack began, the Hussars moved up the cavalry track toward Leuze Wood. They waited there all day, but were eventually stood down and returned to bivouacs at Daours. The attack had succeeded to the north, but the trench-works in front of Ginchy, close to where Ken Hutchings had been killed just weeks earlier, prevented any advance for the cavalry to exploit. Fulcher left the Somme on 25 September as the Division departed for the Third Army area, and spent a month in training west of Amiens. During October the Hussars returned to the Somme, where an attack on Achiet le Grand was planned for 25 October – Balaklava Day. Poor weather resulted in that attack being cancelled, and Fulcher joined the move west into winter billets.

His Squadron spent the winter at Maresville in training, and remained there when the Germans began withdrawing to the Hindenburg Line as part of *Operation Alberich*. They were not called upon until April, when they moved forward to within a few miles of *Arras*, where the first offensive of 1917 was to be launched. Fulcher spent many days in the poor weather with the Hussars, yet again waiting for a breakthrough that never came, despite infantry successes. *Third Ypres* brought no opportunities for the Hussars either, and during August, about the time he was promoted to Lieutenant, Fulcher was admitted to 7th Stationary Hospital at Boulogne with a 'fistulae in arm', and returned to England where he was struck off the strength of the regiment at the end of October.

Having recovered, Fulcher joined the 3rd Reserve Regiment of the Hussars in January 1918 and returned to France in April, reporting to the British Cavalry Base Depot at Rouen. The Depot records show he was posted to the 19th Hussars on 2 June, but reported at the Cavalry Corps Reinforcement Camp, and did not actually join his regiment until 25 July. Oddly the war diary states he returned to Base the next day, and the next reference to him is when he was admitted to No.2 Stationary Hospital (Abbeville) with influenza during October. So it would seem he either joined the Hussars a second time or he did not return to Base at all.

Without that detail it is impossible to be clear on what actions he might have taken part in between the end of July and September. It is also unclear when he left hospital, and whether he took part in any actions in the last weeks of the war. For the record, the 19th Hussars took part in *Amiens* in August, Cambrai as part of the *Battles of the Hindenburg Line* in October, just before Fulcher was admitted to hospital, and were active with Fifth Army during the *Final Push*.

On 27 December Fulcher was cross-posted to the 11th Hussars. That day the regiment crossed the Rhine, and were part of the Army of Occupation until March 1919. Before they left for England, Fulcher was attached to the Indian Royal Artillery Base Depot at Rouen, but was admitted to 8 General Hospital with appendicitis on 1 April. He did not return to the Indian RA until 16 June, and remained there until September when he joined 83rd Labour Group in the Somme area. It was November 1919 when Fulcher was finally demobilized, a year to the day after the Armistice. He resigned his commission in April 1920, retaining the rank of Lieutenant.

Although Devon resumed playing cricket in the Minor Counties Championship in 1920, Fulcher did not feature in the side again until 1922, and then played regularly through to 1930. Thomas Jennings, who joined the Kent Fortress Engineers with the Kent contingent in 1914 was in the Devon side from 1926, and both men played in several fixtures against the Kent 2nd XI. On the outbreak of WW2 Fulcher enrolled in the Officers Emergency Reserve, and attained the age limit in October 1944 when he was removed from the list. He died on 2 February 1946, survived by his wife Olive who he had married in 1924.

CAPTAIN ERIC JESSER FULCHER

Eric Fulcher applied for a commission on 18 August 1914, and the next day played in the match against Cambridgeshire at Fenners, his last of the season. He was attested as a Private in the 10th Royal Fusiliers on 29 August, serving for several months with 3 Platoon in Colchester, and was then appointed 2nd Lieutenant on probation with the 3rd Royal West Kent Regiment (RWK) toward the end of November. Having undergone basic training he embarked for France on 13 May to join the 1st RWK. Fulcher's new battalion had been involved in the attack at Hill 60, in which Cecil Tuff, brother of Frank, was killed leading D Company. One of many drafts sent to bring the battalion back to strength, he spent his first weeks in the line at St. Eloi during *Second Ypres*. That June Fulcher was confirmed in his rank but, just like his brother Edward, his health was to suffer throughout the war, the first occasion in July when he spent a week at a rest station recovering from tonsillitis.

During August the 1st RWK departed the Ypres sector for Ribemont, south-west of Albert on the Somme, a quieter area where they even had a cow to supply Fulcher and the other officers with milk, something of a luxury. Here he suffered a recurrence of his illness, and spent a week recovering at a Base Hospital. The battalion underwent a great deal of training for the latter part of the year, and Fulcher went on a number of courses in the back areas, and took his turn at passing through the poison gas chamber, used to prepare men for gas attacks. The 1st RWK also prepared for an attack from Carnoy during *Loos*, but that was cancelled when the offensive faltered.

As the year was closing Fulcher was appointed temporary Lieutenant and, following a harsh winter, he and the 1st RWK arrived in Arras at the start of March, where they remained for four months. They were pleasantly surprised to find very deep dug-outs with electricity, something of a novelty. One German bombardment in May landed around 700 shells on D Company, but the dug-outs proved their worth, and not a single man was hurt. The men enjoyed a Divisional Horse Show the next month, and although the records do not show if Fulcher was in the cricket side (highly likely), they do reveal he rode another officer's charger to win a prize in the riding events.

Fulcher's battalion was earmarked for a role in the *Somme* offensive, and although that failed to materialise the 1st RWK were heavily involved as the *Somme Continued*. They moved into the line for an attack near High Wood on 23 July, but the German guns in the wood had not been silenced by another Division as planned. Their flank exposed, nearly all the officers were hit at once and, with over 400 casualties, the task proved impossible. Shelling during the next days left the battalion reduced from 1,100 men to 350 in the space of a fortnight. The Division was withdrawn to reorganise, and shortly afterwards Fulcher fell ill with tonsillitis and influenza. He spent several weeks recovering in England, and the war diary entry that recorded his return on 10 September refers to him as Regimental Transport Officer, but it is not clear when that was effective.

Having suffered heavily at Guillemont, the battalion was down to 270 men and were used to form a composite Brigade. They were moved to Leuze Wood in anticipation of an attack, and although that was cancelled they suffered 68 casualties from shelling. Withdrawn from the line on 26 September, Fulcher's battalion had more than played their role in the Somme offensive, losing 31 officers and 900 men in ten weeks. During October, whilst in the support line, Fulcher received a promotion to Lieutenant, and had a reasonably quiet end to the year. At Gorre in November, he was in the battalion football team that defeated 13th Machine Gun Company 4-2, but he was soon suffering from the winter conditions. He fell sick with pneumonia in January and was ordered to England again.

Fulcher did not re-join the 1st RWK until August, delayed by a bout of measles whilst in England. The battalion was concentrated west of Hazebrouck as *The Hundred Days Offensive* began, and he was given command of 'A' Company and appointed Captain within days. He led his Company to Gommecourt Wood as the battalion moved to support Fifth Division, attacking the village of Irles as part of *Second Somme*. Taking up the high ground beyond the village, the New Zealand Division passed through to continue the advance. The two Divisions continued to leap-frog each other as the Germans were forced back. After the NZ Division passed through Bapaume, the RWK were instructed to push out patrols and, meeting strong opposition, a lively action ensued.

It was during the day's action that Fulcher won his Military Cross. *"INVICTA" (Molony, 1923: 308)* records that Fulcher:

> *Whilst in command of a support company near Bapaume on 29th August 1918, finding that all the officers of an attacking company had become casualties, and that the attack was wavering, pushed up a platoon of fresh troops and urged the line up to the objective, which, by his action, was successfully gained and consolidated. His initiative and energy restored a very ticklish situation, and secured the flank for a further advance which took place, and was successful mainly through his action.*

The battalion remained in reserve until mid-September when they took over the trenches near Havrincourt Wood. Two tough actions were fought for 'African Trench' during the *Battles of the Hindenburg Line*, and after a period out of the line Fulcher and the 1st RWK joined the *Final Push*. They advanced through the Mormal Forest and Fulcher crossed the Sambre on 8 November, the battalion taking up an outpost line where they remained until news of the Armistice arrived. Christmas was spent in Belgium, after which Fulcher returned to England on leave and was demobilized on 17 February. He briefly joined the 4th Battalion Norfolk Regiment as a Captain, but resigned his commission on 16 December 1920.

During May 1919 Fulcher played for Lionel Robinson's XI against the Australian Imperial Forces, alongside several more of Kent's ex-servicemen, including Hough and Jack Bryan who were making their first class debuts. Whilst he scored 19 and 31, his lack of bowling practice was evident, conceding four wides in his two overs. At the end of the following month he made his Kent debut against Lancashire at Old Trafford, his 32 in the first innings remaining his highest score in his four appearances for the county. He was out to a catch by Marriott, who was yet to play for Kent, and then he and Hough opened the second innings, each scoring 2 to seal the victory.

Back in Norfolk, Fulcher joined the directorate of Norwich City Football Club and settled into playing Minor Counties cricket, on several occasions meeting the Kent 2nd XI. He played for MCC in 1921, but by 1922 was farming in Monmouthshire, playing cricket for Chepstow and also represented North Wales against South Wales at Cardiff Arms Park during August. This turned out to be his last match. Fulcher died on 14 February 1923, *The Times* reporting:

> *Captain E.J. Fulcher of Pilston Court farm, Llandogo, Monmouthshire, was found dead in a wood near the farm on Wednesday evening. He had been shooting rabbits. The trigger of the gun caught in a twig and he received fatal wounds in the head.*

SERGEANT MAJOR HAROLD THOMAS WALTER HARDINGE

'Wally' Hardinge was born on 25 February 1886 in Greenwich, at that time still a part of Kent, his father William, a Master Mariner, having settled in the county before marrying Ellen. Hardinge first attended the Tonbridge Nursery in July 1899 at the age of 13, and was working as an apprentice cricket ball maker when he played his first match in 1901. He was a promising bowler, taking over 100 wickets in 1902 and 1903, but that took a back seat as his batting developed. He made his debut against Lancashire at the Angel in June 1902, aged 16, taking two wickets as Kent lost by an innings. In 1906 he made 1,265 runs at an average of 74, and played four times in the Championship as Kent won it for the first time. From this season onwards Hardinge secured a regular place in the side.

Awarded his cap in 1907, Hardinge made his first century against Sussex at Hove, and the following season made 1,000 runs for the first time, something he did 18 times in his career. He was a key player in Kent's Championship successes of 1909, 1910 and 1913, scoring over 2,000 runs in the latter season, a feat he repeated four more times after the war. During his formative years he also displayed a talent for football. Having played for several amateur clubs he signed for Newcastle United in May 1905 but, after only nine league games in three years, he was sold to Sheffield United where he scored almost fifty goals in 150 appearances, and was picked to play for England in the Home Championship against Scotland at Hampden Park in 1910. Married to Daisy in August 1908 at Deptford, Hardinge spent his winters boarding close to whichever club he was with, but in 1913 was able to settle in the south, when he transferred to Woolwich Arsenal. He played in their

Wally Hardinge, footballer and cricketer

first ever game at Highbury Stadium in September 1913, fresh from celebrating Kent's Championship. His football commitments did however prevent him touring Australia or South Africa.

Although the Cricket Championship was suspended in 1915, Hardinge won the accolade of being one of Wisden's Cricketers of the Year, based on his previous performances. He also received something from Kent, although perhaps not as welcome. When the Club wrote to those employees who were not serving at the start of the year, Hardinge was one of the professionals who received a letter. He replied that he was the sole support of his parents, and his married brother was ill, but despite all this he had offered to serve as a Special Constable. Hardinge subsequently joined the Royal Naval Air Service (RNAS), his service reckoning from 27 April.

The RNAS was part of the Navy, and Hardinge joined with the rank of Petty Officer Mechanic and was, according to his papers, 'Cyclist – Armoured Car Division'. For a time the RNAS possessed the country's only mechanised land force, made up of Rolls-Royce Armoured Cars. These had been used in Belgium and France early in the war to make raids, and were also used to pick up aircrew that had been forced to land in enemy territory. The unit was effectively disbanded in August 1915, but one squadron was retained in England.

Hardinge was promoted to CPO3 (Chief Petty Officer Mechanic third class) in 1915 and CPO2 (second class) in January 1918. In March 1918 he moved to Blandford which was being used as an 'intake camp' for the RFC as it merged with the RNAS, and on 1 April he officially became a member of the RAF. During June Hardinge was attached to the Cadet Brigade HQ at Hastings, now carrying the rank of Sergeant Major. Whilst stationed there he was selected to play for England against the Dominions at Lord's and again in August before a crowd of 10,000. During October he was sent to the Armament School where he remained until January 1919 when he was demobilized and attached to the RAF 3 Reserve.

Hardinge served in the RNAS. Reproduced by the kind permission of Shaun Caveney

In February 1919 Hardinge was selected for the England side against Scotland in an RAF International football match, showing he hadn't lost his touch with two goals in the first half and a further three in the second. Perhaps the seventy wartime appearances he made for Woolwich Arsenal FC had helped keep him sharp. He was finally discharged at the end of April 1920, by which time he was living in Tonbridge with Daisy. He resumed his cricket with Kent that summer, and also returned to Arsenal to play for one last season before dropping to the reserve side and retiring in 1921. His cricket career lasted somewhat longer, playing for Kent until 1933. By that time he had scored 1,000 runs in a season 18 times, 2,000 in a season five times, hit 75 centuries and four double tons. His best bowling was 7-64 against MCC at Lord's in 1932, his match figures being 11-128.

He played a single Test against Australia at Headingley in 1921 when Hobbs fell sick with appendicitis, scoring 25 and 5 and was not selected again. His highest score for Kent came in 1928 when he struck 263 at Gloucester. After he retired Hardinge spent time working on the staff of Wisden, and for the Cement Marketing Board. He also returned to football in the 1930's as coach to Tottenham's reserve side, and was caretaker manager to the first team when Percy Smith quickly departed following the team's relegation in 1935. Sadly he lost all his sporting trophies during WW2 when his house suffered a direct hit in a German bombing raid. Wally Hardinge died on 8 May 1965 in Cambridge after a long illness.

BREVET LIEUTENANT- COLONEL HERBERT HENRY HARINGTON

Herbert Henry Harington was born on 14 August 1868 at Oaklands, Chichester in Sussex, his parents both born overseas. His mother Isabella Jane (née Crowdy) was a British subject, though born in France, and his father Emanuel Thomas Harington was born at sea, off the coast of Mauritius. Curiously his father was born Emanuel Poe, not Harington, and was an East India Merchant and former Indigo Planter. Harington first went to school in Worthing, and entered Cheltenham College in September 1892 as a member of Leconfield, the same house in which Lovick Friend had boarded. He did not make the XI, and left the College early, during Easter 1884, due to ill health.

Harington's military career began when he was appointed Lieutenant in the 4th Battalion East Surrey Regiment, a militia battalion, in February 1886. Towards the end of the following year he transferred to the regular forces, as 2nd Lieutenant in the 2nd Battalion Lincolnshire Regiment. Within months Harington sailed for the East

Herbert Harington served as DAAG at the War Office

Indies where the battalion had been stationed since 1882, and he remained there for the next four years. During that time he undertook an Army Signalling course and was promoted to Lieutenant in 1890.

The first record found of Harington playing cricket was after his return to England in 1892. He appeared several times for Incogniti, scoring 192 against Hounslow Garrison, including a third wicket stand of 240 in 100 minutes. For Kensington Park he made 101 against the Ne'er-do-wells, who lived up to their name, but somehow held on for a draw. Harington's return to England was short lived. In December his battalion sailed for the Straits Settlements in Ceylon, modern-day Sri Lanka, where he is recorded as having played several times for the Straits Settlements side in October 1893. After returning to England in March 1895, Harington resided at the Cambridge Barracks, Woolwich. His two appearances for Kent were made in May, firstly in the county's opening fixture against Lord Hawke's MCC side. A week later he played at the Mote against Gloucestershire, caught by WG Grace in the first innings for 4.

Harington was posted to Sheffield in September 1897, not returning south to Aldershot until just before Christmas 1899. Orders had been received to embark for South Africa, where he saw action and was part of the advance guard that marched into Pretoria. Mentioned in Despatches by Lord Roberts, he was also awarded the Queen's Medal with three clasps, for Paardeberg, Johannesburg and Cape Colony, and the King's Medal with 1901 and 1902 clasps. Harington remained in South Africa, stationed in East Transvaal, until the battalion returned home in March 1904, and retired from the Army at the end of the year to join the Reserve of Officers. He played for the MCC each summer from 1904 to 1907, and played regularly for Royal Eastbourne Golf Club from 1908 onwards.

On the outbreak of war Harington was mobilized and in December was appointed Staff Captain at the War Office. His Medal records reference that he was Adjutant at HQ No.5 General Base Depot, base for the Cavalry and Royal Army Medical Corps at Rouen, but also shows that he was deleted from the 1914 Star Medal Roll and marked as having had no overseas service. It is possible that he initially accompanied the BEF to France to assist at the depot, but did not qualify for the 1914 Star as he was not close enough to the front.

During June 1916 Harington was appointed Brevet Major and in July became Deputy Assistant Adjutant General (DAAG) at the War Office. The rank came with the position, and in this role the responsibilities would have been personnel related; promotions, appointments, medals, pay and medical matters. The Adjutant General's office had many responsibilities, covering mobilization, drafts and reliefs, medals, Prisoners of War and the Graves Registration Commission. Other branches and sections were created to move with the times, administering the Machine Gun Corps, Tank Corps and Women's Auxiliary Corps as each rose to the fore during the war years.

Precisely what Harington was responsible for is not clear, but the records of Cheltenham College record that he was Mentioned in Despatches three times. He remained with the War Office until hostilities ceased, and on 1 January 1919 was appointed Brevet Lieutenant-Colonel, one of the New Year Honours bestowed by the King for services in the war. Harington remained with the Reserve of Officers, but on attaining the age limit in January 1922 he was retired. Herbert Henry Harington died at Tunbridge Wells on New Year's Day 1948. No obituary appeared in Wisden.

COLONEL AND COUNTY COMMANDANT GEORGE ROBERT CANNING HARRIS

George Robert Canning Harris, better known as Lord Harris, was born at St. Anne's, Trinidad on 3 February 1851, where his father was Governor. His mother, Sarah Cummins, was the daughter of the island's archdeacon, but Harris never grew to know her as she died in 1853 whilst he was still an infant. After some years in India, when his father was Governor of Madras, he returned to the family home at Faversham and spent two years in London before entering Eton. He was at the school from 1864-1870 and in the XI from 1867, as captain in his last year. In 1870, at the age of 19, he joined the Kent Committee which was established to manage the new Kent County Cricket Club formed that year. His father was the first President.

Lord Harris in levee dress of the REKMR, wearing
the Grand Cross of the Star of India and the Grand Cross of the Indian Empire.
Reproduced by permission Kent & Sharpshooters Yeomanry Museum

Having made his first class debut for Kent against MCC at Canterbury in August, he went up to Oxford to study at Christ Church College, entering as the Honourable George Harris, and leaving as Lord Harris, having succeeded to the title in November 1872. He was in the XI 1871-1874, playing in the fixtures against Cambridge in all years except 1873 when nursing an injury. During July of 1874 Harris was married to the Hon. Lucy Ada Jervis at Godmersham. He had missed several terms at Oxford, and having failed to obtain an honours degree in Classics, he returned that winter to study further, finally leaving in 1875 with a pass degree in Arts. During his time at Oxford Harris made several appearances for Kent, and was appointed Captain in 1875, a position he held until 1889.

Awarded his cap in 1882, Harris went on to score 7,842 runs for the county at an average of 30.04, including ten centuries and a top score of 176 against Sussex in 1882. He was also President in 1875 and Secretary from 1875-1880, working tirelessly for the Club and the game in general. He became the second captain of the England team, visiting Australia for a single Test at Melbourne in early January 1879, and was captain for three more Tests, all against Australia. His involvement in the efforts to stamp out unfair bowling led to the cancellation of a fixture with Lancashire, and also to Walter Hedley's engagement with the county being cut short.

Harris was MCC President in 1895, and his last match at Lord's was played in 1929 against an Indian side, when he was aged 78. Aside from his involvement in the game, he had a busy political career. He was made Deputy Lieutenant of the County of Kent in 1884, Under-Secretary of State for India in 1885, and Under-Secretary for War 1886 to 1890. He left for India in 1890 to take up the position of Governor of Bombay, where he worked for five years, active in encouraging the development of cricket there, and was appointed Knight Grand Commander of the Order of the Indian Empire (GCIE). When he returned to England in 1895 he was appointed to the Order of the Star of India Knight Grand Commander (GCSI) and became Lord in Waiting to the Queen for the next five years.

Harris attended the weddings of Queen Victoria's daughter, Princess Louise in 1871, and her son Leopold in 1882, and two years later was a pall bearer at the Leopold's funeral. At Queen Victoria's Diamond Jubilee celebrations in 1898 he was in attendance on Empress Frederic, and later that year attended Gladstone's funeral. At the Coronation of Edward VII in 1902 Harris had the honour of carrying the sceptre with the cross, and he became Aide-de-Camp to the new King in 1908. In 1910 he attended Edward's funeral and became Aide-de-Camp to King George V.

Harris' association with the military began in 1873 when he was appointed Captain in the East Kent Yeomanry Cavalry. He was granted the Honorary rank of Major in 1888, promoted to Major in 1895, and to Lieutenant Colonel in 1897. Keen as he was to join the British forces fighting the Boers in 1899, the Secretary of State for War appointed him to chair a committee reviewing the future of the Yeomanry Force. He was then granted the honorary rank of Colonel and appointed Assistant Adjutant General for the Imperial Yeomanry, but the fighting was mostly over when he sailed for the Cape in 1901, with the temporary rank of Colonel in the Army. As the Haldane Reforms reshaped the armed forces in 1908, Harris was made Honorary Colonel of the 4th Battalion Buffs Regiment and appointed to the Territorial Force as a Military Member.

When war broke out in 1914 Harris was soon involved in the affairs of the county, commissioned a Vice-Lieutenant of Kent effective 31 August. He found himself charged with organizing the Kent contingent of the VTC when that body was divided into County Regiments and made subject to the supervision of the Lord Lieutenants. The VTC rapidly expanded – by March 1915 there were 48 units and thousands of men to administer, and Harris was quick to appoint trusted men under his command. A conference was held in February at which he presented his plans to representatives of each local corps, and he soon organised the volunteers into three regiments, one each for East, Mid and West Kent, broken down into battalions and companies. The chain of command Harris designed meant each regiment had a Chief of Staff responsible for reporting into him.

Following the introduction of conscription under the Military Services Act in early 1916, the administration of the Volunteer Training Corps was taken over by the War Office, so taking some responsibility from Harris. He was however kept busy with an appointment to the East Kent Appeal Tribunal, also a consequence of conscription, sitting to hear appeals from those who sought not to serve for a variety of reasons. Also serving on the panel with Harris was Frank Tuff's father, Charles Tuff, who had by that time lost two sons to the war. Harris' own son was serving in France and would be wounded by the end of the year. Whatever their own personal experiences might have been, the tribunals dealt with their cases even-handedly.

At the hearings in March 1917, a Broadstairs widow appealing for her 18 year old son informed the Tribunal that four other sons had joined the Army. Two had been killed and a third, recovered from wounds, was dying from consumption. Harris told the mother the tribunal felt it justified to allow the son to stay at home. In a case the following month, a farmer from Rainham was appealing for his 27 year old son, and it was learned he had already obtained exemption for two other sons to work on his farm. Harris expressed his displeasure none of the sons was serving, and told the man he preferred his own business to that of the nation. The farmer eventually agreed his second son should join up.

Harris attended the House of Lords throughout the War, where he championed county connections for the Volunteer units and fought for soldiers' allowances. Outside of the House he raised funds for Kentish prisoners of war and arranged sports events. In 1917 he was patron of a baseball game between the Canadians and Americans held at Lord's, organised to raise funds for Canadian war widows and orphans. He also played there himself the following year for Pelham Warner's XI against a Public Schools side, some fifty years after his first appearance at the home of cricket. As ADC to the King he attended the monarch when he made troop inspections, and did not relinquish his commission until 1920, and his position as ADC until he attained the age limit.

Harris was present when Lord George Hamilton unveiled the memorial fountain at

Canterbury, commemorating Colin Blythe and the other members of the Kent elevens who fell during the war. He and Fiennes Cornwallis were trustees of the Kent War Memorial Fund which raised money to erect a war memorial for the county at Canterbury. Many more memorials were raised across the county and Harris unveiled several of them, including those at Margate and Birchington, and the East Kent Yeomanry Memorial at Canterbury. Lord Harris, who did so much for the county and its cricket club, died at Belmont two years after his wife, on 24 March 1932.

HATFEILD BROTHERS

Charles Eric and Herbert Seymour were born almost exactly a year apart on 11 March, 1887 and 14 March 1888 at Hartsdown, near Margate. Their parents, Captain Charles Taddy Hatfeild, Kings Dragoon Guards and Justice of the Peace and his wife, Maud Harriet Sinclair of Maxstoke County Warwick, were one of the prominent landowning families in the Margate area. The boys were schooled at Wellington House, Westgate-on-Sea, and went on to Eton, where Eric was in the XI 1903-1906, and Herbert 1905-1907, both captaining the side in their final year. Eric played each year against Harrow, and in the first of those matches in 1903 he showed great promise of becoming a successful slow bowler. He took 5 wickets in the first innings and 7 in the second to finish with 12 for 91, helping Eton to their first win in this fixture since 1893. In 1905 Herbert opened the batting against Harrow, and in 1906 when Eric opened against Winchester, Herbert scored 84 and 57 whilst batting at number seven. On leaving Eton, Eric went to university whilst Herbert chose a military career, commissioned 2nd Lieutenant in the 2nd Bucks (Eton College) Volunteer Rifle Corps in November 1906.

CAPTAIN CHARLES ERIC HATFEILD

Hatfeild played for Geoffrey Foster's XI in the 1907 Oxford Freshman's Trial Match, and for the University that summer against Worcestershire. In 1908 he had success with the bat, and it was for this reason he gained his Blue. He played only a few matches in 1909, one of those against Kent, but was left out of the Cambridge fixture. During 1910 and 1911 he attended Wye Agricultural College, afterwards touring Argentina with an MCC team captained by Lord Hawke over the winter of 1911-1912. He took 52 wickets at an average of 12.59, and was also lead wicket taker on an Incogniti tour of the USA in 1913. In 1910 he appeared for Kent twice and thereafter more regularly until the War, although less so when the side was at full strength. Although Kent chose Troughton to succeed Dillon as captain, Hatfeild was also considered, and like Troughton he was unlikely to feature regularly on ability alone. He was on the Committee, having been elected in 1913, and his last county game prior to the declaration of war was against Essex at Tunbridge Wells in mid-July.

The single 'pip' on the uniform points to the photograph being taken between Eric Hatfeild's commission in February 1913 and his promotion to Lieutenant in April 1915. Reproduced by kind permission of Jonathan Tapp

Hatfeild was one of the pre-war members of the Royal East Kent (The Duke of Connaught's Own) (Mounted Rifles) (REKMR), commissioned 2nd Lieutenant in February 1913. Upon mobilization he was ordered to Canterbury with the Kent Yeomanry Regiments to assist with coastal defences, and was made temporary Lieutenant in April 1915. Several months passed before the Yeomanry were earmarked for service at *Gallipoli*. On 23 September 1915 Hatfeild was made temporary Captain, and the following day his brigade sailed from Liverpool for Gallipoli, where they served for the last three months of the campaign as dis-mounted infantry under the orders of the 42nd Division. As with the other Kent players in the South East Mounted Brigade (SEMB), Hatfeild arrived at a time when the fate of the campaign had effectively been decided. The REKMR dug in at Helles, remaining there throughout the remainder of the year in difficult conditions; shell fire, sickness and the harsh winter contributing to a high casualty rate. Hatfeild was evacuated to Mudros with the REKMR on 31 December.

In early February the REKMR moved to *Egypt* to serve on the Suez Canal defences, and joined the Western Frontier Force during July, to help tackle the Senussi uprising west of Suez, as part of the *Western Desert* campaign. The enemy were however operating well inland by this stage, so little action was seen, and the men spent time training at Sollum. During August Hatfeild was appointed Captain and shortly afterwards is recorded as being President of a Court of Enquiry, such courts generally being held to determine punishments for misdemeanours and maintain discipline. In February 1917, whilst in Sollum, the East Kent and West Kent Yeomanry Regiments were amalgamated. The merged unit became the 10th Battalion, the Buffs, attached to 74th Division, and Hatfeild was given command of 'A' Company. The lack of available horses had given reason to use the men as infantry, and the new Buffs battalion underwent intensive infantry training before leaving Sollum on 23 March 1917, travelling to Alexandria by sea and then on to Sidi Bishr.

In early April 1917 Hatfeild moved with the battalion to the vicinity of Gaza in *Palestine* where the 74th Division was placed in Reserve for the *Second Battle of Gaza*. After the battle was lost General Archibald Murray was replaced by General Edmund Allenby, and Hatfeild was mentioned in Murray's last despatch in June 1917. For the next six months the Buffs were employed digging trench systems and training, then in September the order came to prepare for an attack on *Beersheba*. At the end of October Hatfeild's battalion marched for four consecutive nights to reach their positions, and acquitted themselves well in the fighting that captured Beersheba.

Several days later the Buffs were in an outpost position when the British attacked and took Sheria, and then had to wait 38 hours for a supply of water. Keeping men and beasts watered was a constant problem and the troops were trained to consume as little as possible. At the end of November Hatfeild joined the march east towards Jerusalem, past the recently captured Junction Station and into the Hills of Judea. Here the roads ceased to exist and they were forced to build new ones to support their move forward. On occasion the rain was so bad that the camels and mules could barely stand, but the advance continued. On 7 December Hatfeild brought his men to a spot below the village of Beit Surik, moving quietly to their positions beneath the Turkish trenches. He led A Company uphill, reaching half way before dawn broke and they were spotted, drawing heavy shell fire. Luckily the brigade to their right advanced quickly and, seeing their flank threatened, the Turks withdrew. Pressing on a little further Hatfeild and his fellow Buffs saw the spires of Jerusalem for the first time. That night the Turks fell back and the City fell. Hatfeild led his Company into the attack on many more occasions before the order came for the 74th Division to depart for France.

Most units transferring to France from other theatres were used in a relief capacity, and the 10th Battalion Buffs were no different. After landing at Marseilles on the 7 May the battalion started training for the different type of warfare the Western Front demanded. It was not until early August that Hatfeild moved into the line near St. Floris, the 74th Division now forming part of Fifth Army. During the *Advance to the Hindenburg Line*, life for the Buffs became irregular, having to eat, sleep and wash where they could, advancing as and when their own arrangements and the Germans allowed. They were frequently shelled with a mixture of gas, high explosive and shrapnel before they reached the Faustine Quarries on 16 September.

The Battle of Epehy, part of the *Battles of the Hindenburg Line*, began on 18 September, with Hatfeild's battalion attacking the German outposts. After taking the Quarries at Templeux-le-Guérard, the Buffs moved on to Hargicourt, where they captured their objectives despite difficult terrain and fierce opposition. Hatfeild's bravery during this action earned him the Military Cross, which the London Gazette (*Issue 31480, 29 July 1919*) reported thus:

"For conspicuous gallantry in leading his company during the advance at Templeux Gerard towards the Hindenburg Line on September 18th 1918. In spite of the fire of hostile machine guns which repeatedly held up the advance, he got his men forward, exposing himself fearlessly. It was largely due to this officer's splendid example that the advance during the day was carried out so rapidly."

The next advance was on the 21 September, the objective uphill towards Quennemont Farm, across open ground towards enemy positions protected with wire and machine guns. After the usual early artillery barrage Hatfeild's brigade moved forward, forced to halt at the wire, unable to get through. Under an intense fire the men took shelter in shell holes and waited until dark to return to safety. The Buffs had suffered heavily, and Eric Hatfeild was amongst those who were killed, just seven weeks before the Armistice. He was buried at Hargicourt Communal Cemetery Extension.

CAPTAIN HERBERT SEYMOUR HATFEILD

We left Herbert when he joined the 2nd Bucks in 1906, and this turned out to be a short term arrangement. In 1907 he transferred to the 1st (King's) Dragoon Guards (KDG), the regiment his father had served with. Just three months later the KDG sailed for India, where Hatfeild remained for the next seven years. That time was broken up with manoeuvres, training and inspections, although there were also several special events to provide some relief from routine garrison soldiering. During December 1908 the regiment celebrated the Diamond Reigning Jubilee of the Emperor of Austria, who was the Colonel-in-Chief of the King's Dragoons, and Hatfeild was one of the officers to be decorated with the Austrian Commemorative Medal in Silver. Two years later, during October, the regiment marched to Patrala to take part in the ceremony marking the installation of the new Viceroy, for whom they carried out escort duty. During 1911 a large assembly was held at Coronation Park in Delhi to mark the Coronation of King George V. The Durbar was held three times during the height of the British Empire, in 1877, 1903 and 1911, the latter being the only one attended by the sovereign. Hatfeild attended with his regiment, and Lord Harris was also present, having travelled to India for the occasion with his wife and son.

Hatfeild did enjoy some periods of leave to England, during which he appeared for the Kent 2nd XI in 1911 and 1913. His debut was against Buckinghamshire at Stoke Poges in August 1911, and two years later he played in the matches against Glamorgan and Staffordshire, the latter being his one appearance at the St. Lawrence. Confirmed in the rank of 2nd Lieutenant in August 1909, Hatfeild had to wait until June 1914 before he was promoted to Lieutenant. By that time the regiment had relocated from Ambala to Lucknow and it was whilst stationed there that mobilization orders were received on the last day of August 1914. The regiment and its horses moved to Bombay by train and sailed for France aboard two ships, Hatfeild with D Squadron on the HT 'Chilka'. Two other squadrons left on the HT 'Franz Ferdinand', and that vessels name may have caused some consternation among its passengers, especially when it developed engine problems and had to fall out the convoy heading to Europe.

After a long voyage Hatfeild reached Marseilles on 10 November, and moved on to Orleans. After spending the end of the year at Lisbourg, the regiment moved by bus to Bethune during January. Hatfeild's Squadron was in reserve in the village of Festubert, tasked with holding the reserve trenches and five men were hit going into the line, the battalion's first casualties. During the first day water rose above the men's waists and the following morning, when Hatfeild took his turn in the trenches, the water was up to the men's arm-pits. Orders soon came to retire to the support line and the Germans made no attempt to occupy the British positions, being far too busy baling out their own. The regiment returned to Lisbourg, having suffered casualties of 1 dead, 6 wounded and 82 evacuated sick, almost entirely with frost-bitten feet.

On 11 March the KDG marched to a position of readiness at Bois des Dames near Lapugnoy. The battle of *Neuve Chapelle* had commenced the day before and the cavalry were readied to exploit any breakthrough, although the attack was ultimately called off and they returned to billets. During *Second Ypres* they were occasionally put in a state of readiness, but saw no action. About this time it was decided in London that the Emperor Franz Josef of Austria could no longer be colonel in chief of the regiment, due to the small matter of Britain being at war with that country. Their cap badge was also altered from the Austrian double headed eagle, which the KDG had worn since 1897.

At the end of May the regiment was ordered to the front line trench held by the 3rd Dragoon Guards near Hooge in the Ypres area, to attack and hold Chateau Hooge. Finding the chateau empty, they quickly occupied the buildings and stables. During the reliefs of 2 June, Hatfeild's Squadron was withdrawn to Zouave Wood and remained there whilst the Germans shelled the Chateau positions for seven hours, the garrison sheltering in the cellars. When the shelling stopped, Hatfeild's Squadron moved up in support, but the Germans recommenced their bombardment an hour later and then launched an attack. Numerous assaults were repelled and after much heavy fighting the Lincolnshire Regiment arrived to relieve the KDGs who had held their position with great tenacity whilst suffering heavy casualties. Chateau Hooge was the scene of fierce fighting throughout the War, changing hands many times.

The KDG stood to during the Battle of *Loos* in September 1915, and again during the *Somme* Offensive, but each time the cavalry were denied being sent into action as the infantry attacks faltered. During March 1917 Hatfeild was engaged in operations south of Amiens as the Germans carried out *Operation Alberich*, retiring to the Hindenburg Line. He was undoubtedly pleased to finally spend some time in mounted operations,

tasked with keeping touch with the enemy. After eight days in action the regiment became Divisional Cavalry to the 7th Division, taking up posts opposite the new German positions. The weather was notably severe during this week, and by the time they were relieved many horses had died from exposure. The men's horses suffered as much as the men in many ways, and were sensibly issued with their own gas masks. In the trenches near Epehy in August a German bombardment resulted in 66 gas shells falling around the KDG but luckily the wind drove the gas away. On the last day of that month Hatfeild was promoted to the rank of Captain, although his days in France were numbered. One month later orders were received to return to India.

Herbert Hatfeild joined the BEF from India in 1914.
Reproduced by kind permission of Jonathan Tapp

On his arrival Hatfeild was stationed at Meerut, and from August 1918 at Risalpur, life returning to the pre-war routine from three years before. The peace was interrupted in May 1919 when the Afghan Army crossed the border and occupied some wells inside India, so starting the *Third Afghan War*. Hatfeild's regiment was mobilised on 6 May, marching to Peshawar, where local police had discovered the postmaster was organising a rising to assist the invasion of India by Afghans. The KDG seized control of all sixteen gates of the city, placed machine-gun posts at each, and carried out mounted patrols to cover the walls between gates. One man trying to escape was captured 'at lance-point', and Hatfeild's regiment remained in control of the city for three days while agitators were arrested.

The KDG were then ordered to march to the frontier, and on reaching Loe Dakka, a village in Afghan territory north-west of the Khyber Pass, they found it deserted. Hatfeild was commanding A Squadron, and remained with them at camp whilst the other three squadrons went out as part of a force to reconnoitre towards Basawal, protecting the infantry units clearing the Khyber Pass. As the 15th Sikhs secured the hills a large number of Afghans appeared, threatening the British flank and forcing them to withdraw to camp. A large Afghan force chased them across the plain and, on seeing the situation, A Squadron immediately saddled up, and Hatfeild led them to protect the retreating force. During the fighting the next day, Hatfeild and the KDG were kept in reserve in a nullah to protect the horses from shrapnel and bullets. The camp held off the Afghans long enough for a relieving force to arrive, after which the heights were stormed and the enemy driven off. On 8 August 1919 a peace treaty with Afghanistan was officially signed to end the Third Anglo-Afghan War, but when Hatfeild was on patrol the next day his Squadron was fired upon and one man wounded. Later in the month the KDG left Dakka for their station at Risalpur.

Hatfeild remained with the KDG and spent time stationed in Iraq in 1920, Edinburgh 1921-23, Germany 1923-26, Aldershot 1927-1929 and finally Tidworth from 1929 before his retirement from the Army on 31 March 1931. During his posting in Germany he played for the Rhine Army against Cambridge University Crusaders in a 12-a-side game at Cologne, top scoring for his side in the first innings with 34 out of 125. After leaving the Army he played a few times for Band of Brothers in 1933 and 1934, still able to make useful scores. He was made Deputy Lieutenant of Kent in March 1936 and married Ebie Fowler at Kensington in 1940, spending ten years a married man, living at Rushett Norton, Faversham.

Elected to the Kent General Committee in 1936, Hatfeild was also President from 1939 to 1945. The 1951 Club Annual recalled that he bore the brunt of keeping the county and the St. Lawrence Ground going through WW2 and was a tower of strength in assisting Gerald Hough and others in getting county cricket going again after the war. He also served as Chairman of the Managing Committee and as a Trustee from 1945 until his death on 18 April 1950 at the Royal Masonic Hospital, Hammersmith after three months illness. His funeral service was held at Norton Church, the address given by the Bishop of Dover, and the service attended by Lord Cornwallis.

ACTING CORPORAL ARCHIE CHARLES HAYWOOD

Archie Haywood was born on 20 November 1897 at Eltham, Kent, the second son of Robert John Haywood and Elizabeth (formerly Allnutt). His father made a single first class appearance for Kent in 1878 and his older brother, Robert Allnutt Haywood, had a lengthy career with Northamptonshire, playing alongside Claud Woolley. Haywood was engaged at the Tonbridge Nursery in 1913 and whilst he appeared for Club and Ground he did not break into the 2nd XI pre-war. His eighteenth birthday fell at the end of 1915 and he was among a number of young players who enlisted once they were of age. Unfortunately his service papers no longer exist, but it is possible to determine where he served.

The Kent AGM minutes of March 1916 reveal that Haywood was serving with the Kent Cyclists. The 1/1st Kent Cyclists were posted to India around February 1916, but once there they were renamed the 1/1st Kent Battalion and used as non-cycling infantry. The battalion joined the 9th (Secunderabad) Division of the Indian Army and, after training on the plains of southern India for several months, were ordered to move north. For Haywood this meant a six day journey of 2,222 miles, to the colder mountainous region near Burhan, north of Rawalpindi, not far from the Khyber Pass. Although this was not a battle front, Haywood served through a number of disturbances on the Frontier, caused in part by German efforts to undermine and destabilize Britain's position in the region.

During March 1917 Divisional manoeuvres were cancelled abruptly owing to an outbreak of violence by Mahsud tribesmen. Travelling by train and then on foot, Haywood accompanied his battalion to the frontier fort at Jatta. They arrived to find the Mahsud had already been dispersed, and with little likelihood of further violence they returned to their base. It was, however, not long before the Mahsud caused more problems. Toward the end of May Haywood's battalion, now officially part of Waziristan Field Force, headed to the frontier fort at Miran Shah in the heart of Waziristan. The Mahsud sent a force to attack them en route, but troops were sent out from other posts to intercept the tribesmen, and their arrival was made unhindered.

The three month stay at Miran Shah was unpleasant, with many men falling sick and a number dying as a result. The battalion finally returned to Dalhousie during August when Waziristan Force was dispersed. Garrison duties were the order of the day for Haywood until March 1918 when the Kents were ordered to Barkhan in Baluchistan, further south from the prior troubles. This time they were to confront the Marri and Khetran tribes who had burnt and looted Government buildings, and whilst half of the battalion joined a strike force, the remainder worked on communications. When the tribal chiefs surrendered, it was Haywood's battalion that guarded them until certain conditions were met. A long march back to Ferozepore followed, where the Kents spent the rest of the year, and were as badly affected by influenza as the armies in Europe.

When the Armistice was celebrated in November, and the ramparts of the fort at Ferozepore were illuminated at night with large letters proclaiming 'PEACE WITH VICTORY', the thoughts of Haywood and his comrades probably turned to demobilization and home. Trouble was, however, brewing elsewhere. Civilian protests in the Punjab during April 1919 led to the declaration of Martial Law and the mobilization of the army. Haywood's battalion formed part of a column and were despatched from Ferozepore, marching to Amritsar, and declaring martial law in each village en route.

The following month, yet more trouble came Haywood's way. Incursions into British territory near the Khyber Pass gave the Indian Government cause to declare war on

Afghanistan on 6 May, so starting the *Third Afghan War*. Haywood and the Kent battalion left for Peshawar on 19 May, journeying to the remote Frontier fort Suhban Khwar near the Khyber Pass. On the day of their arrival the enemy attacked, burning down some unoccupied blockhouses. Temperatures reached 115 degrees whilst Haywood was there and 26 men were evacuated to Peshawar Hospital with heat related illness. Luckily it was not long before the local tribes surrendered, and the Amir of Afghanistan sought an Armistice.

By July the men of the 1/1st Kent were being demobilized, and as one of those who served in India and fought in the Afghan campaign, Haywood earned, in addition to his Victory and British medals, an Indian General Service Medal with 'Afghanistan NWF 1919' bar. The battalion returned to England during December, and Haywood went through the dispersal unit at Crystal Palace. He had kept his hand in by playing for the battalion during the war years, being a key player in their numerous victories, and soon returned to playing cricket for Kent. There had been no 2nd XI fixtures in 1919, but there were eight fixtures in 1920 and Haywood featured in two matches during August. In 1921 there were ten fixtures, but Haywood again only played in two. His busiest season was in fact his last, playing nine times out of ten in 1922, and finishing on a winning note against Surrey at Hythe.

Haywood, far right, cricket coach at Taunton School and former member of the Kent Cyclist Battalion. Reproduced by kind permission of Taunton School Archive

In the summer of 1922 Haywood was married to Alice Victoria Hurdridge in Lewisham, and moved to Somerset where he was Head Groundsman and Cricket Coach at Taunton School from 1923 until his untimely death in 1938. He was renowned at the school for his desire to teach the boys to play in the correct way, and he shared his knowledge tactfully. His work on the playing fields was also admired, and those who played on the pitches did so with satisfaction. On 6 June 1938 he umpired a game between the school and the Old Boys, and was said to have headed home in good spirits. That night Dr LP Marshall, who had played for the Old Boys that day, was called to see Haywood at his home, but when he arrived the cricketer had already passed away.

COLONEL WALTER COOTE HEDLEY

Walter Coote Hedley played against Kent more often than he did for the county, spending the majority of his first class career with Somerset. He was born on 12 December 1865 at Monkton Heathfield, a village near Taunton, the son of Catherine (née Coote) and Robert Hedley, a Poor Law Inspector and former Army Captain. Hedley entered Marlborough College during May 1878, was awarded a scholarship to the Modern School in his first term, and within two years was top boy of the School. He was appointed a College Prefect, but did not get the opportunity to represent the cricket XI.

In March 1883 Hedley entered the Royal Military Academy (RMA) at Woolwich. Whilst there he represented the cricket team in a number of matches, and was commissioned into the Royal Engineers (RE) as a Lieutenant just days before his nineteenth birthday. His first posting was to the School of Military Engineering at Chatham in 1885 to take various courses, and he then moved to Shorncliffe with 38th (Field) Company. In 1890 he was posted to Gibraltar where he served with 6th (Fortress Company) as Adjutant and later as Officer Commanding 20th (Fortress) Company. Promotion to Captain came in in January 1894, and the following month was married to Anna Susan Fellowes at the Cathedral on Gibraltar. His father-in-law was Major James Fellowes of the RE, who himself played for Kent from 1873-1881.

Hedley made his first class debut in 1888 for Gentlemen of England, and played three times for Kent that same season. There were some doubts over his delivery after he took 8 for 31 and 6 for 78 against Middlesex, and Lord Harris had him independently watched. Unfortunately the verdict meant he did not play for Kent again. Hedley was however undeterred – that same season he represented I Zingari against the Gentlemen of England and played in the same fixture in the next two seasons. He appeared for MCC several times in 1890 and then turned to Somerset. He had actually played for the county of his birth in 1886, before they gained first class status, and secured himself a regular place in the side from 1892. Only the Boer War prevented him playing as much as he might have otherwise done, but he still scored 2,395 runs in all for Somerset, took 254 wickets, including 3 ten wicket hauls, and held 55 catches.

Hedley (right) pictured with his father-in-law James Fellowes in the RE team that played the Royal Artillery in 1890. Reproduced by permission of the Institution of Royal Engineers

On his return from Gibraltar in 1895, Hedley joined the Ordnance Survey, working at York and then Southampton. In 1899 he briefly moved to 19th Survey Company, but on the outbreak of the Boer War he joined 17th Field Company in South Africa. One of the major problems the British encountered was a lack of suitable maps, and his surveying experience proved valuable. Hedley took part in various actions on the Tugela River, and was present when Ladysmith was relieved. His records show he was invalided in 1901, presumably by illness, and was subsequently awarded the Queen's Medal with 6 clasps, having received two Mentions in Despatches (1900 and 1901), and a brevet promotion to Major. He returned to England at the end of 1901 and was promoted to substantive Major in January 1902.

Hedley played three Minor County matches for Devon during August 1902, resumed playing for Somerset from 1903 to 1904 and appeared three times for Hampshire in 1905. He headed overseas again when he was made as an advisor to the Survey of India in 1906, tasked with modernising the production of maps. Despite meeting some resistance he did make successful reforms, and returned to England in 1908 to start work on new colour printing techniques with the Ordnance Survey. A promotion to Lieutenant-Colonel followed in 1910 and the next year he was appointed General Staff Officer Class I (GSO1) at the War Office, one of a number of RE officers serving on the HQ Staff.

His new role gave him command of the Geographical Section, also known as MO4, the MO standing for 'Military Operations'. Hedley's contribution to the 1914-1918 War began as head of MO4, before hostilities even started. Under his direction large numbers of maps, suitable for a possible campaign in France and Flanders, were packed and stored, ready to be issued with mobilization equipment. Survey work was also carried out in Northern Sinai, Palestine, Turkey in Asia and the Balkans. Under Hedley's leadership a small mobile printing section was equipped with hand presses, and included in the War Establishments,

for mobilization with the Expeditionary Force created by Haldane. This was the result of the lesson learnt by Hedley during the Boer War – that the ability to print maps locally was vital. In 1913 whilst he was carrying out this work, he was promoted to Colonel.

Walter Hedley worked tirelessly in the Geographical Section of the War Office. Reproduced by permission of the Institution of Royal Engineers

In August 1914 the Geographical Section consisted of six officers and 43 others, including clerks, lithographers, draughtsmen and photographers. Almost immediately all five assisting officers and twelve others were taken from the Section, and one new officer joined. The two remaining officers only managed to meet the demands from so many theatres of war due to the assistance of the Ordnance Survey and the Geographical Society. Hedley's foresight in producing maps before the war was also proved a good decision. Under his leadership the section was responsible for producing all maps required by British forces worldwide, their greatest work undoubtedly on the constantly changing front line in France and Flanders.

In 1915 the Section was labelled 'Intelligence' instead of 'Operations' and became MI4. Survey personnel in the field increased to 5,000 but Hedley remained the single technical adviser and manager at the War Office. On a daily basis it was not uncommon for 8 tons of maps to be sent to the Western Front, in addition to the maps and diagrams required by the Cabinet and the War Office, a testament to his efforts. In 1915 there was talk of 'sound ranging', a method of surveying hostile guns which was eventually used at Cambrai in 1917. Unlike the French the British were slow to react to the idea, but Hedley had seen the progress made in Paris when in France at the start of 1915, and he directly intervened to have the British investigate.

Hedley's influence was far-ranging and co-ordinated, and he ensured experience gained on one front was shared with another. He was appointed a Companion of the Order of the Bath (CB) in 1915, made a Companion of the Order of St Michael and St George (CMG) in 1917, and Knight Commander of the Military Division of the Order of the British Empire (KBE) in 1919. Hedley also received three foreign awards: the Croix d'Officiers of the

Légion d'Honneur from France, and the Ordre de Léopold and Officier of the Ordre de la Couronne from Belgium.

Before the war ended, Hedley was convinced the post war peace conference would need small scale maps to allow easy comparison across the continent. At Hedley's suggestion a geography commission was set up at the start of the Peace Conference in Paris in 1919 to review and decide which maps were most suitable. The Geographical Society's 1:1 million scale map was ultimately approved and used. Hedley was also known for his ability to recognise ability and potential in a man. It was he who found a position in his Department for TE Lawrence (of Arabia) when he failed to secure admittance to an OTC at Oxford, and also recommended Lawrence for service in Egypt when Turkey entered the war.

Hedley retired from the Army in December 1920, having reached the age limit. He was a Fellow of the Royal Geographical Society, and served on the society's council. On 27 December 1937 Walter Coote Hedley died at his home, The Cottage, Sunningdale, Berkshire.

CAPTAIN GEORGE HENRY HESLOP

George Henry Heslop's appearances for Kent came between the declaration of War and the commencement of hostilities at the end of August 1914. He was born on 10 April 1895, the son of George Henry Heslop senior and Gertrude Mary, his father the Headmaster of Sevenoaks School. He was a pupil at Sevenoaks for six years before going on to Lancing College from 1910 to 1914, and was in the Cricket XI 1911 to 1914, as Captain in the last two years. He gained a military grounding in the College Officer Training Corps, earning a Certificate 'A', and was a fine cricketer. He topped the College averages every year, and finished the 1914 season with 981 runs at an average of 89. He was also capable of bowling, as he proved when taking 9 for 14 against Eastbourne College in July 1913, only denied the chance of a clean sweep when the last Eastbourne wicket fell to a run out.

During the summer of 1913 he shared an opening stand of 238 with GE Palmer, making 148 himself, and in 1914 scored 223 against Steyning, 158 not out against MCC, 157 against Eton Ramblers and 151 against St Bostock's XI. Not content with excelling at one sport, Heslop was in the Football XI 1911 to 1914, Captain in the last three of those years, won sports colours 1912 to 1913 and was 'Victor Ludonum' (winner of the games) in his last year, winning the Hundred, the Quarter and the Throw. His Wisden obituary noted that *"He was perhaps the most promising young all-round cricketer who had yet to appear in a first-class match."*

Returning from college to the family home in Kent in the summer of 1914, Heslop was selected to play for the Rest against Lord's Schools on 3 August, Charles Capes on his side, and George Whitehead and Jack Bryan playing for their opponents. He then made his debut for the Kent 2nd XI on 10 August, six days after the declaration of war, against Monmouthshire at Newport. He opened the batting, scoring 23 in each innings, and took two catches. Of the first five in the Kent line up for that game, four lost their lives in the War: Heslop, Jennings, Wycherley and Whitehead. He next played for the 2nd XI against Essex at Hythe on 14 August and rounded off his brief time with the county playing for Club and Ground against Merion CC Philadelphia at Tonbridge, opening the batting with Jack Bryan. Heslop had been accepted to enter Trinity College, Cambridge, but in September he chose to join the army and serve his country.

George Heslop in uniform with Captain's pips, the photograph probably taken before he departed for France in November 1915. Reproduced by kind permission of the Lancing College War Memorial

Heslop enlisted with the Middlesex Regiment as a Private on 11 September, and was commissioned 2nd Lieutenant in the 16th (Service) Battalion (Public Schools) Middlesex Regiment on 29 September. The Battalion was formed in London, setting up camp at Kempton Race Course until December, then moving to Warlingham, Surrey to train. Heslop was promoted to Lieutenant on 25 January, and then to Captain on 17 May 1915. In July the Battalion travelled to Clipstone Camp near Mansfield, joining 33rd Division until August, when they moved again, this time to Perham Down on Salisbury Plain to finalise their training. The Battalion departed for France in two parties on 16-17 November, landing at Havre and Boulogne, then moving on to Le Hamel in the Somme Valley. Platoons were immediately put in the line with the 1st Middlesex Battalion to gain experience of trench warfare.

The battalion was holding a reserve line at Bethune when the line was heavily shelled by the enemy on 28 January. As Heslop was leading a group of men through the trenches, a barrage fell on them, wounding him and killing or wounding nineteen others. Heslop's name appeared in the casualty lists as 'Hyslop', giving his father cause to write to the War Office to have the mistake corrected. The matter of his surname rectified, and his wounds healed, Heslop returned to his unit. During the following months the 16th Middlesex remained in the Somme area, training and taking part in a number of raids on enemy positions, and in the summer of 1916 the battalion was moved to the 29th Division as part of the preparations for the *Somme* offensive.

Heslop's chaplain wrote of his attendance at Holy Eucharist shortly before the attack which began in the early hours of 1 July 1916, as the seven day bombardment of the enemy positions finished. The battalion moved up from Auchonvillers to their assembly positions, arriving at 03.00 and remaining in the trenches until zero hour, which was 07.30. Their brigade was to attack the German line from Beaumont Hamel to a position just west of the Hawthorn Redoubt, where a large mine was to be exploded ten minutes before they over the top. Heslop was leading D Company on the left of the battalion's front, the 16th Middlesex in support to the 1st Lancashire Fusiliers. The Lancashire men attacked at 07.30 and the Middlesex followed at 07.55. Heslop's Company formed into ranks which were later described as "parade ground straight", and moved forward. As was the case along much of the line, the German machine-gunners strafed the British lines and thousands fell, the survivors scrabbling to find shelter in shell holes. The battalion suffered heavily with 338 killed or wounded and 186 missing, and Heslop was shot and killed whilst leading his men forward. Several days later his father received a telegram from the War Office:

"Deeply regret to inform you that Captain G.H. Heslop Middlesex Regiment was reported missing believed killed on 1st July. The Army Council expresses their sympathy."

Missing believed killed. For the family this phrase held uncertainty and hope. The aftermath of the Somme offensive was an administrative nightmare for the authorities, and with so many casualties the process of interviewing survivors and establishing losses was a slow process. The Army was however thorough, and the wounded were interviewed to try to establish the fate of the missing. Heslop's papers, held at Kew, contain details of a number of interviews with members of his battalion, all of them recovering in hospitals from wounds received that day. They include:

"I started out with the Colonel, but got separated from him and found myself with Capt. Heslop who was in charge of the Pioneers. By his order, we lay down by the wire and advanced about 100 yards. Then we saw him drop down. At first we thought he was giving the signal to halt, but as he lay still, we concluded that he was dead and continued on, leaving him there. Later we retired and reported to the Colonel. Search parties were sent out, but could find no trace of him." Sergeant Valentine, No 11 General Hospital, Camiers.

The family were notified of the statements and by March 1917 the War Office wrote to

Heslop's father to advise that for official purposes, in view of the lapse of time, death was now accepted as having occurred in action on 1 July 1916. In August Heslop senior received another communication that a report from Base stated "killed in action 1.7.16 Burial reported by GOC", suggesting Heslop's body had been recovered. In March 1918 the Office of the Director of Graves Registration and Enquiries at the War Office wrote advising his son was buried in Hawthorn Ridge No.1 British Cemetery, Beaumont Hamel, North of Albert. The grave, as with all others at the time, was marked with a durable wooden cross with an inscription bearing full particulars. In time the grave was given a white Portland Stone headstone by the Commonwealth War Grave Commission. Heslop's name was not recorded on the Blythe Memorial.

ACTING LIEUTENANT CHARLES VICTOR LISLE HOOMAN

Charles Hooman was a talented all-round sportsman who appeared for Kent in the 1910 season when they carried off the championship for the third time. He was born in Ditton on 3 October 1887, the only son of former shipbroker Thomas Charles Hooman, and Louisa (née Holt). As a young boy Hooman was actually a neighbour of Ted Humphreys whose father was landlord of the Walnut Tree in the village. The two boys were however destined to take rather different paths through life, Hooman through the public school system. He entered Girdlestoneites House at Charterhouse in 1901, where he was known to his friends as 'Chubby', and soon showed his talent for sports.

A member of the Cricket XI from 1903-06, Hooman was captain in the last year, when he averaged 85.71 and also won the Rackets Pairs at the Public Schools Championships. The school records reveal he played as wicket-keeper in 1905 when there was no one else available, and in one match scored 83 as well as taking four catches behind the stumps without letting a single bye. He only lost one match as captain, and it was noted that he undoubtedly inherited some of his sporting talent from his father who played football for Wanderers when they became first winners of the FA Cup.

Hooman served in the RNR during the war

In 1906 Hooman entered Brasenose College, Oxford and continued his sporting exploits. He represented the University at Rackets in 1907, Golf 1907-1910, as Captain in 1909 and President of the Club in 1910, and was in the Cricket XI 1909-1910. He played Golf as an amateur for England against Scotland in 1910, and played for Devon in the Minor Counties from 1906-1909. In 1907 he received his Blue for Golf, and in 1910 for Cricket, as well as playing for the Gentlemen v Players at Lord's in which match he scored a pair. He appeared for Oxford against Kent in 1909, and the following season made his debut for the county against Derbyshire at Gravesend, top-scoring in both Kent's innings. The summer was exceptionally wet and Hooman, who made 1,070 runs in all matches, showed he was a capable player. He received his Kent cap, but was not destined to play for the county again. He went on to study law, and married Adelaide Florence Caroline Porcelli-Cust in 1912 at Newton Abbot in Devon.

As a married man in August 1914, Hooman was outside the volunteering criteria, but nevertheless joined the Royal Naval Reserve (RNR) in February 1915, and was appointed temporary Assistant Paymaster on the *SS Stephen Furness* in the mercantile fleet auxiliary. The *Stephen Furness* was used to stop, board and examine shipping to enforce the blockade against Germany. Such 'boarding steamers' typically worked with Cruiser Squadrons, taking on the risky role of stopping whilst neutral ships were inspected, something the Cruisers were reluctant to do as they would present good targets for U-Boats. This suggests that Hooman had a fairly risky role whilst his vessel operated in the Lough Larne patrol area on the coast of the North Channel in the Irish Sea.

In 1916 Hooman was attached to the *Thalia*, an ex-troopship acting as a shore base at the mouth of Cromarty Firth in Scotland. This was perhaps a lucky move for him, as the *Stephen Furness* was sunk by a U-Boat in 1917. It was in January 1917 that Hooman moved again, to be Assistant Paymaster on the yacht *Eileen* and remained attached to that vessel for the remainder of the war. *Eileen* belonged to South African financier Solomon Joel, and had been lent to the Navy for war service. In April of 1917 she was at Bermuda, to join the patrols in that area. Hooman was, by 1919, the Paymaster Sub Lieutenant, acting Lieutenant in the RNR, and was awarded the Victory and British Medals for his services during the war.

In 1922 he represented England in the Walker Cup. Hooman and his opponent found themselves all-square after thirty-six holes and, with no instructions on how to proceed, decided between themselves to play one more hole which Hooman won with a birdie. Having already given up his cricket due to lack of time to spare, he was ultimately forced to stop playing golf due to trouble with his legs. In 1925 his wife died, and he married again five years later to Evelyn Margaret Ryder. In 1940 Hooman again answered the call to the colours, joining the RAF Volunteer Reserve as a Pilot Officer. He was subsequently promoted to Flight Lieutenant and Squadron Leader, and resigned his commission in November 1944 at the age of 57. Hooman's second wife died in 1947 and he married a third time to Alice Victoria Jarrett. The couple were living in Palm Beach, Florida when Hooman died in a nursing home on 20 November 1969.

LIEUTENANT BERNARD HOWLETT

Bernard Howlett was born in Stoke Newington, London on 18 December 1898, the son of Gertrude Emily and Thomas Edwin Howlett, a clerk in Holy Orders. Thomas Howlett baptised his son but died when Bernard was only five years old. Educated at St. Edmund's School, Canterbury, Howlett made the XI and, with the country at War, entered the Royal Military College at Sandhurst, where he made the XI in 1917.

Howlett (back, right) with the 1st RWK at Agra, India a year after the war ended. Courtesy of The Queen's Own Royal West Kent Regimental Museum

Howlett was commissioned 2nd Lieutenant in the Royal West Kent Regiment (RWK) on 24 April 1918. He was posted to France and joined the 7th RWK near Warloy in the Somme region on 28 August where *Second Somme* was being fought. At this time static trench warfare was a thing of the past, and Howlett's experience of fast moving mobile warfare perhaps lay the foundations for his exploits in WW2. He did not have to wait long to see action. The battalion was attached to 55th Brigade on 1 September to assist 38th Division, and captured Sailly-Saillisel within three hours, beating off a counter-attack the following day. During the *Battles of the Hindenburg Line* the 7th RWK took their objective on the outskirts of Rossnoy and pushed on to contest the area around Sart Farm until relieved several days later.

On 23 October as the British pressed on *Beyond the Hindenburg Line*, Howlett's battalion crossed the Richemont River south of Le Cateau with the assistance of light wooden bridges they carried with them. During the crossing they were constantly in danger from German mortars, but carried the attack and captured Gardemill, Ervillers Wood Farm and Corbeau where they went in to billets, south east of Cambrai. This last attack took the Germans by surprise and netted 400 prisoners. The 7th RWK were on the edge of the Mormal Forest when, on 4 November, Howlett joined the *Final Push* as the battalion pressed forward, advancing behind three tanks. The machines were put out of action during hard fighting, but one crew used their machine-gun to good effect and the enemy finally fled. Howlett spent the last days of the war in billets at Le Cateau as German resistance collapsed.

Following the cessation of hostilities Howlett fell sick and returned to England on 23 November. He did not join the many thousands being demobilized, instead remaining with his regiment, and was promoted to Lieutenant in October of 1919. Based at the RWK Depot at Maidstone he did not have to look far for a cricket club, and appeared for the Mote 1921 to 1924, taking a number of five wicket hauls. His debut for Kent came in May 1922 against Worcestershire at the Bat and Ball, Gravesend, when he took two wickets and was treated to a masterful display of bowling by Frank Woolley. He went on to appear 26 times for the county as well as a handful of 2nd XI fixtures, taking 39 wickets including 3 for 62 against Yorkshire in 1928 at the Crabble, Dover. In 1923 he appeared in a Lord Harris XI against West Indies, and took three wickets in each innings.

Howlett with the 4th RWK at Aldershot 1932 (left) Courtesy of The Queen's Own Royal West Kent Regimental Museum and a member of the 1928 Kent team (right)

The gap in his English appearances up to the 1928 season was due to a posting in India, although he did still manage to play a little whilst there. Back in England in 1928, and now a Captain, he played for Kent from May to September, but was posted to Bangalore in December, where he married Helena Beatrice Joan Whitby on 2 April. From 1930 he spent four years as Adjutant to the 4th RWK (Territorial Army) based at Tonbridge, leaving to become Staff Captain of the 40th (West Riding) Division. More promotions followed, to Major in August 1938, and Brigade Major of the 132nd Infantry Brigade in April 1939.

Howlett's brigade departed for France in April 1940, and was part of the forces withdrawn to Dunkirk. He was Mentioned in Despatches on 20 December and was also unsuccessfully recommended for an award by his commanding officer. In July 1940 he was given command of 6th RWK in 36th Brigade, and made temporary Lieutenant-Colonel in October. The Brigade then moved to Scotland to train as part of Amphibious Force 110. Finally in 1942 an offensive was planned for North Africa, and Force 110 became First Army, in which 36th Brigade joined the new 78th 'Battleaxe' Division.

Howlett led his battalion in the Algiers Landings and throughout the bloody advance to Tunis, during which he took command of 36th Brigade as acting Brigadier. Bryan Valentine served under him, and it was Howlett who recommended Valentine for the Military Cross when the anti-tank guns he commanded disabled eleven tanks as they approached their positions. On 27 April Howlett was told he had been awarded the DSO for his Brigade's success, and he celebrated in the mess of old battalion, the 6th RWK, that evening. His Division was then called upon to help Montgomery in Sicily when the Eighth Army was held up. Their capture of Centuripe was the decisive blow of the Sicilian campaign, earning Howlett a bar to his DSO, which Montgomery said was 'well earned'.

In September Howlett joined the invasion of Italy, leading the 36th Brigade to fight with the forces north of the Appenines. There were a series of laterally running rivers to cross, each defended well by the enemy. After several successive victories the Germans were pushed back to a line behind the River Sangro during November, and Montgomery planned the crossing toward the end of the month. Howlett's Brigade was tasked with capturing German positions on the lower ridge opposite. He was promoted from Major to Lieutenant-Colonel on 24 November, still acting-Brigadier, but was probably too occupied with preparations for the main offensive to spare time to celebrate. During the fighting that followed, 'Swifty' Howlett was killed whilst visiting his forward troops near Santa Maria Imbaro. A fellow officer recalled that he had gone forward on horseback, and the shell which killed him also injured his Brigade Intelligence Officer.

At the time of his death, Howlett was due to be promoted to Major-General to command a Division in the Normandy landings. For many years the 'In Memoriam' section of *The Times* carried the following piece, on the anniversary of his death: "*In proud and perfect memory of SWIFTY, BRIGADIER BERNARD HOWLETT D.S.O. The Queen's Own Royal West Kent Regiment who fell in action on the Sangro, Nov 29, 1943".* Howlett was mentioned in despatches posthumously and is buried in the Sangro River War Cemetery.

ABLE SEAMAN EDWARD HUMPHREYS

Ted Humphreys was born in Ditton on 24 August 1881, the ninth son of Henry and Kate Humphreys. At the age of 9 he was living with the family at the Walnut Inn where his father was landlord, and was neighbour to three year old Charles Hooman whose father was a local manufacturer of Portland Cement. Humphreys was one of the first hopefuls to enter the Tonbridge Nursery in its inaugural year, having trialled with Kent in 1897 at the age of 16. He started out as a slow left arm bowler, making his 1st XI debut at the Oval in 1899, but soon showed promise with the bat. He was awarded his Cap in 1901, and earned a regular place in the team by 1904.

Ted Humphreys took part in raid on Ostend

The Kent side was brimming with talent, and Humphreys' worth is testified by the fact he retained a regular place throughout the successful years of 1906 to 1913. He was often used as a change bowler to Blythe and Woolley and in 1906 he took 7 Middlesex wickets for 33 runs. His skill with the bat was however his main asset, and when Kent won the

Championship in 1909 he shared in 21 first wicket partnerships of over 100 runs. That year he made his highest score of 208 against Gloucestershire at Catford, following it up the next year with 200 not out against Lancashire at Tunbridge Wells. In fact 1908 was a good season for Humphreys; he and AP Day put on 248 at Taunton, which is still a Kent record for the seventh wicket, and he scored 1,000 runs each season from that year to 1914. For several winters he coached in New Zealand and Jamaica and toured the West Indies with the MCC in 1912/13.

Humphreys did not immediately volunteer his services when war broke out, and was one of the players the Club wrote to early in 1915. He replied that he was responsible for his 70 year old father and the widow of his brother Albert who had been a stoker on *HMS Hogue*, when it was torpedoed by a U-Boat seven weeks into the war. Humphreys subsequently joined the RNVR, training cadets, and then followed his brother's footsteps into the Royal Navy in 1917. He was posted Ordinary Seaman Humphreys in February, attached to *HMS Thames* in March and *HMS Arrogant* in May, the latter a depot ship for submarines and motor launches. Promoted to Able Seaman in November, Humphreys was soon serving on the Coastal Motor Boats (CMBs) that formed part of Dover Patrol.

The CMBs also had a base across the Channel at Dunkirk, from which they patrolled the coast up to Belgium. The majority of these vessels were forty feet long with a maximum speed of 34 knots, were able to carry either a single torpedo or depth charges, and were fitted with Lewis guns on swivel mountings for use against enemy aircraft. Chlor-sulphonic acid was used in the exhaust when the boats were required to lay a smokescreen, and this versatility ensured the CMBs were used in the Raid on Zeebrugge in April 1918.

Operation ZO was a two pronged attack on the harbours of Zeebrugge and Ostend, waterways leading from both places to Bruges, where the German submarine fleet sheltered. The plan was to sink vessels filled with concrete, 'blocking ships', at the harbour entrances to seal the submarines pathways. The operation generally became known as the Raid on Zeebrugge because the Ostend raid was a failure. Humphreys was stationed at Dunkirk at the time of the raid, and he was therefore was not a volunteer as such. Unlike the main attacking fleet that sailed from Dover, which was a volunteer force, the six CMBs from Dunkirk that were involved were simply enrolled in the venture. All were used for the Ostend Raid, and it was therefore that part of the operation that Humphreys took part in.

After two aborted attempts due to bad weather, the raid finally took place on St Georges Day, the task force divided in two. In advance of the arrival of the blockships *Brilliant* and *Sirius*, Humphreys was with the CMBs as they entered the approaches at Ostend, marking navigational buoys with calcium floats and laying a smokescreen. Unfortunately the enemy, perhaps anticipating a raid, had repositioned the Stroom Bank Buoy by over a mile, and the blockships were fooled into foundering on a sandbank away from the canal.

It was dark, the smokescreen obscured the view and the situation for Humphreys and his crew was confusing. One CMB helped the crew of the *Sirius*, whilst the others performed their work under heavy fire, and they fled the scene quickly.

For the remainder of the war Humphreys continued to patrol the coast, avoiding minefields, and constantly at risk from the German shore batteries that were attracted by the noise the CMBs made. The small boats had open cockpits and were vulnerable to attack by German aircraft, a good many crew being wounded in this way, and night operations were preferable. Humphreys managed to play a little cricket when he was picked for an England XI against Dominions in June 1918, but was out of practice and was bowled for a duck. He left the Navy in February 1919 and took up the position of cricket coach at Uppingham School which meant he could only appear for Kent from August.

Retiring from the game in 1921, Humphreys concentrated on his coaching role, with Percy Chapman and Gerry Chalk among his pupils. Lord Harris rated his ability so highly he persuaded him to leave Uppingham to take up the position of coach at Kent in 1929. He remained in this role until 1948, and also umpired a little, including a number of Kent 2nd XI fixtures through to 1947. He died at Maidstone on 6 November 1949.

HUTCHINGS BROTHERS

Three of the four sons of surgeon Edward John Hutchings and Catherine Lotherington (née Colebrooke) played for Kent. All were born in Southborough, William Edward Colebrooke on 31 May 1879, Frederick Vaughan 3 June 1880 and Kenneth Lotherington 7 December 1882. They, and their third born brother John Stewart, were educated at Tonbridge School, where all four represented the XI, and on occasion there were three of them in the side. The school publication *The Tonbridgian*, recorded their exploits. William was noted to be a useful bat, with an average of 35.9 in 1897 and when Captain in his last year, 1898, he made 184 not out, carrying his bat in the match between 'Past and Present'.

Frederick scored 108 not out against the Oxford Authentics in June 1897, 'amid loud cheers', and he finished the season top of the averages with 35.9. In 1898 Ken became the third brother in the side, posting 40 not out against Oxford Authentics after William and Frederick had opened with 72 and 29, the brothers securing most of the school's 207 total. Ken was the team Captain in his last two years, 1901 and 1902, was in the Racquets Pair in 1901 and won the Dale Cup in his last three years, with averages of 57.15, 47.45 and 63.30. William and Frederick both represented the school at Racquets (Queen's Club) in 1898.

2ND LIEUTENANT FREDERICK VAUGHAN HUTCHINGS

Frederick Hutchings left Tonbridge School in the summer of 1899, and started work as a Stockbroker's Clerk. He made a single appearance for the Kent 2nd XI in July, opening the batting with James Mason, another Old Tonbridgian, against Sussex at the Nevill. His first class debut for Kent was against MCC at Lord's in 1901, on which occasion he made a respectable 31 in each innings. Days later he played for the county against the South African tourists at Beckenham, the home side winning by seven wickets. Hutchings' next, and last, outing for Kent was against MCC after a gap of four years, and he scored 18 but missed the second innings, absent hurt. His final first class game was for the MCC against Yorkshire in August and, as with his first game, he made the same score in both innings, although this time only 4.

Frederick Hutchings, injured in a motor accident whilst serving with the ASC. Reproduced by kind permission of the owner of the photograph

After marrying Maud Ethel Margaret Spens at Trinity Church, Chelsea in May 1907, the couple lived in Woking. The wedding banns show Hutchings was working at the Stock Exchange in 1907, the Census of 1911 lists him as living on private means and, by the time he enlisted, his former occupation is shown as Golf Club Secretary. When Hutchings volunteered in September 1915, a little before the Derby Scheme was introduced, he was 35. He was found fit for service and was commissioned on 4 October, serving as Temporary 2nd Lieutenant with the Army Service Corps. His first posting was to the Mechanical Transport Reserve Depot at Grove Park, where his brother William was serving, and within two weeks both men were attached to the Holt Caterpillar Section at Aldershot. Whilst William then returned to Grove Park, Frederick was sent to the Avonmouth Tractor Depot.

According to Ken Hutching's obituary in *Tonbridge School and the Great War (Tonbridge School, 1923: 173-175)*, Frederick was seriously injured in an ASC motor accident near Aldershot the following year, in which the driver was killed, and he himself injured his leg and spine and suffered internal injuries. A Medical Board in November 1916 found him unfit for General Service and he was attached to the MT Depot at Bulford whilst sick. By January 1917 he was considered fit for light duties and stationed at Larkhill on Salisbury Plain. Two months later however, he suffered an attack of haematuria, something he had suffered from a few years previously. He was admitted to hospital and, following an examination and another Medical Board, was found permanently unfit for General Service.

The London Gazette of 25 April 1917 announced Hutching's retirement on account of ill-health. He was granted the honorary rank of 2nd Lieutenant and subsequently awarded the Silver War Badge. By 1918 he was employed under the Admiralty, working in the Cash Office at the Naval Ordnance Depot, Woolwich Arsenal. He wrote to the War Office during May, seeking reappointment to a commission, but on the basis of his medical history this was turned down. When Hutchings died suddenly in Hamburg on 6 August 1934, he was aged 54.

LIEUTENANT KENNETH LOTHERINGTON HUTCHINGS

Ken Hutchings started playing for Kent in 1902 and had secured a regular place in the 1st XI by 1906 which was to prove his most successful year. He was renowned for his hard hitting and strength of forearms and wrists, which also made him a safe pair of hands in the field and well able to throw the ball over great distances with little apparent effort. A heavy hitter, he broke three bats whilst accumulating 131 against Yorkshire at Sheffield in 1906 and then a further three against Lancashire at Canterbury when making his career-best 176. His best bowling figures also came in 1906 when he took 4 for 73 against the West Indies at Catford.

In 1906 Hutchings scored 1,454 runs for Kent at an average of 60.58, then exceeded 900 runs in 1907, 1908 and 1911, and over 1,000 runs in 1909 and 1910. In total he made 9,003 at a very respectable average of 34.94. He was the first Kent player to score a Test century when he made 126 at Melbourne on the MCC tour in 1908, and appeared for England when Australia toured in 1909. He was selected for the Gentlemen against the Players on seven occasions, and was Wisden Cricketer of the Year in 1907. In 1906 he was top scorer in England and second in the averages in 1910.

After retiring from first-class cricket at the end of 1912, Hutchings worked in business in Liverpool. He played cricket for Formby and it was there he volunteered within a few weeks of war breaking out. He was declared fit at his medical at Seaforth on 4 September, and was commissioned into the 4th Battalion The King's (Liverpool Regiment) three weeks later. Hutchings was posted to France in April 1915 and attached to the 2nd Battalion Royal Welsh Fusiliers. He reported his arrival at Gris Pot on 2 May where the battalion was in billets, moving into the trenches to relieve the Cameronians near Bois Grenier three days later. Throughout May 1915 Hutchings and his battalion alternated between the trenches and their billets, the line being regularly shelled by both sides.

In *The Kent & Sussex Courier* of 4 June 1915 Hutchings wrote:

"I have been near to death two or three times already, but it is very hard to realise how near one has been to it when you look round and see your surroundings. In the first

place, we discovered an enemy patrol the other evening right up in our barbed wire, cutting them, so we got our machine gun ready and about 20 men on the parapets. We then sent up a flare and spied them about 100 yards away, and let them have it.

I was on the parapet directing the fire of my small squad of men, and keeping my head only just above the top, just enough to be able to see in front. All of a sudden I felt a loud crack (a bullet near you makes a crack like the snapping of a branch) just by my right ear. I thought it must have been pretty close, and then discovered that the bullet had actually hit and ripped away the top of the sandbag on which I was resting my head.

The other shaves were even closer, and I and three officers with me cannot make out why we were not hit – it is simply miraculous. We were talking about being wounded, when all of a sudden I thought I heard a shell coming. I shouted, "Look out!" Before we had time to throw ourselves down on the ground the shell burst clean over our very heads; in fact, when we found we were not hit we looked up, and there was the smoke of the burst shell not twenty feet above our heads.....

We had not got twenty yards before I heard the bang of another gun. We listened for a second, heard the thing coming along, and threw ourselves into a ditch, which, luckily, was pretty deep, but had a lot of water in it. This time the shell burst ten yards to our left, but we then had managed to get practically under cover, and once again we got off.

Our trenches and dug-outs are wonderful, with flowers, roses, pansies, ferns etc., which we have grown all along our lines."

Ken Hutchings was killed near Ginchy in 1916. Permission to use this image has been granted by Tonbridge School

From June to August Hutchings was in the line south-west of Armentières, frequently moving position. On taking over the trenches at Givenchy on 14 September, his battalion was greeted by the Germans exploding a mine nearby, followed by a period of shelling that left five dead and fifteen wounded on the first day of the tour. Another mine was exploded three days later, only damaging a stretch of parapet, but the men were no doubt thankful to be relieved that night.

The preliminary bombardment for the *Loos* Offensive began on 21 September, the war diary of Hutchings' battalion recording the daily shelling near Bethune in the days before. On 25 September, the day the attack was launched, Hutchings joined the Welsh Fusiliers moving into their assembly trenches opposite Cambrin, in support to the Middlesex Regiment who went over the top at 06.30. The Middlesex men were cut down by machine-gun fire, and several platoons of the Welsh Fusiliers pushed forward to assist, also suffering heavily. A second attempt along the brigade front was ordered for 09.30, and the artillery opened fire until that time. Due to the casualties, and the realisation that reorganizing for a second attempt would simply take too long, the order to attack was cancelled.

Hutchings had an operation during October and, once able to travel, returned to England to convalesce, during which time he was attached to the 3rd (Reserve) battalion. His promotion to Lieutenant became effective just days after he departed, perhaps giving some cause for cheer. Upon leaving a nursing home in January 1916 he moved between Tunbridge Wells and South View, Lancashire, undergoing monthly medical boards until declared fit for service again. When he returned to the front in July, Hutchings was attached to 12th Battalion the King's (Liverpool Regiment), joining them in the trenches opposite Messines on the Ypres front. He was soon on the move as the Division headed south to the *Somme* area where the summer offensive was still in progress.

Ken Hutchings is named on the cross erected by members of his battalion at Ginchy Dressing Station in 1916. Reproduced by the kind permission of the Vicar of St. Peter's in Formby, the Rev. Paul Ormrod

On the last day of August the battalion moved into the support line facing *Guillemont*, where an attack was planned. After several delays they moved into their assembly trenches east of Bernafay Wood on 3 September. The battalion was held in reserve whilst 20th Division went into the attack, Lionel Troughton taking part with the Rifle Brigade. After Guillemont was captured the British flank was threatened by the enemy at nearby Ginchy, which another Division had failed to capture. The 12th Kings were ordered to move forward through Trones Wood to help protect the north of Guillemont from a possible German counter-attack.

Two companies of the battalion passed through Guillemont to face Ginchy, along with other units of the 47th Brigade. When the situation became critical, the 12th Kings moved forward to dig in on a defensive line facing Ginchy village, one platoon advancing further ahead to Ginchy Wood. The King's line was held bravely against determined German attacks that evening, and during the fighting Kenneth Hutchings was killed. A brother officer wrote *"I knew him before the war at Formby, and had a great admiration for him. Out here you get to know a man very intimately, and every-one thought what a fine fellow he was."*

CAPTAIN WILLIAM EDWARD COLEBROOKE HUTCHINGS

William Hutchings appeared for Kent 1st XI twice in 1899, at Blackheath against a Gloucestershire side that included WG Grace, and then at Catford against Nottinghamshire in a rain affected match. He scored 31 runs in his two innings but was not destined to play for Kent again. Several appearances for Berkshire followed in 1901 but he dropped out of first class cricket until 1905 when he played for Worcestershire, chalking up 22 appearances for them. His high score for Worcester was the 85 he made against Kent at the Nevill Ground in 1905, guiding them to 203 for 9 at the close, and narrowly avoiding defeat. In 1906 at the County Ground he scored 17 and 30, caught behind off his brother Kenneth's bowling in the second innings. Hutchings worked for United Brewery in Abingdon, Berkshire, and then in the same line of business in Shropshire around the time his association with Worcestershire began. He was married to Winifred Daisy (Fitzsimmons) on 25 November 1909 in Dudley, and their first child was born in 1910.

Hutchings did not volunteer until August 1915. On the outbreak of war he was married, 36 years of age, and his wife was expecting their second child, so he was not likely to have been in a rush. His application form to join the Army Service Corps (ASC) shows his occupation as that of chauffeur, and reveals that he had previously been an Army Driver, serving five years with the Royal Engineer Volunteers. By this time he was living in North Wales and signed his papers in Wrexham. He joined the ASC Mechanical Transport as a Private, but did not have to wait long for a commission. He was appointed Temporary 2nd Lieutenant on 27 September, stationed at the Motor Transport (MT) Depot at Grove Park, and in October spent time at Aldershot as Road Officer in 52 Holt Caterpillar Section. The War Office had ordered a Holt Tractor when hostilities broke out, and put it through trials at Aldershot, being suitably impressed and choosing to use it as a gun tractor. The Holt Tractor was extensively used throughout the war, mainly to haul medium size guns.

Hutchings subsequently returned to Grove Park as Road Officer 602 MT Company, 36th Brigade of the Royal Garrison Artillery (RGA) before being posted to *Egypt*. He arrived there on 20 January 1916 as part of the Expeditionary Force, 602 MT Company now attached to 48th Siege Battery, RGA. Siege Batteries of the RGA were equipped with heavy howitzers, firing large calibre high explosive shells, designed to destroy enemy artillery, and wreak havoc behind the lines. Hutchings spent some time stationed at Port Said and Suez, and whilst there he had to sell his business, unable to maintain it whilst serving.

Several months later Hutchings was transferred to France, landing at Marseilles during April. He was appointed Temporary Lieutenant on 1 May and went on leave, re-joining his unit just prior to the opening of the *Somme*. He was stationed at Albert as the guns opened fire at 06.25 on 1 July, and remained in that area for some weeks, moving the guns to new positions as required. At the start of August Hutchings was exposed to the noise of heavy gun fire and, on returning to his quarters, discovered he was bleeding from both ears. He did not report sick, but perhaps should have done so, the damage causing him some deafness before the war was over. During that month his unit took up a new position north-west of Fricourt, which had been captured on the second day of the Somme, and in February 1917 he was appointed Adjutant at Headquarters II Corps ASC MT.

When the Battle of *Arras* opened, Hutchings moved to Camblain-l'Abbé, north-west of Arras, to act as Senior Mechanical Transport Officer (SMTO) First Army Dumps. The following month HQ moved to Steenvoorde, not far west of Poperinghe, but just over the border in France. The unit war diary references the capture of *Messines* Ridge on 7 June, and their involvement in organising Siege Parks for the numerous vehicles in the area that were used in the operations. Although not on the front line, Hutchings was still within range of the German guns, and some men at the Ammunition Park were wounded and gassed at this time. Moving to Hoograaf at the end of June, his unit did valuable work as *Third Ypres (Passchendaele)* was fought, and he was appointed acting Captain in August and Temporary Captain in December.

On 28 January 1918, whilst still based at Lovie, Hutchings was in the SMTO's office at II Corps HQ when there was an air raid and the lights were put out. Rushing to answer a phone in the dark, he collided with a table corner injuring his groin quite badly. He was already recovering from bronchitis, influenza and trench fever, but carried on for a couple of days before seeing a doctor. He was invalided back to England, unfit for General Service, and although he received awards and pension payments for his injuries, the process in making such claims was slow. With a wife and children to support, his business sold, and an opportunity of promotion to Major missed, Hutchings had to write to the War Office regularly to ensure the claims were dealt with. These processes lasted into 1919, and in July he relinquished his commission on completion of service, retaining the rank of Captain. He died on the 8 March 1948 at the Mount, Prees, near Whitchurch, Shropshire, England.

2ND CORPORAL DAVID WILLIAM JENNINGS

David William Jennings played for the Kent 1st XI between 1909 and 1914, which covered three Championship winning seasons. He was a fine right hand batsman, but struggled to secure a regular place in a side brimming with talent. Born in Kentish Town on 4 June 1889 he was the son of Isabella and David James Jennings, who played for Devonshire from 1892 to 1914. His father also umpired minor county matches, was groundsman at Exeter, and for many years was coach and head groundsman at Marlborough College. Jennings junior occasionally played as twelfth man for Exeter Cricket Club when his father worked there, but was resident in Maidstone and playing club cricket for the Mote when

trialled by Kent. His 2nd XI debut was against Middlesex at Lords in May 1908, and he scored 48 in a match they won by an innings. The following season he made his first class debut in the nine wicket victory over Surrey at the Oval, his only appearance that season. In fact he played just twice in 1910 when Kent retained the title, but was playing more regularly for Mote and the 2nd XI.

Jennings died from the effects of gas poisoning in 1918

His struggle for a first team place continued, and in 1911 he only played three matches, but was awarded his cap. Against Somerset at Tunbridge Wells he was in century partnerships in both innings with Frank Woolley, and top scored with 104 not out in 115 minutes, finishing the season on top of the batting averages with 75.33. He played six Championship matches in 1912 and in the drawn match against Australia he was unbeaten on 4 when the Kent innings was declared early. Another eleven appearances followed in 1913, with a top score of 72 in the innings victory over Warwickshire at

Edgbaston when he was missed early on at the wicket, a costly mistake as he stayed for an hour and twenty minutes scoring at a good rate, including eight boundaries. In 1914 he made his career best 106 in 135 minutes, including 15 fours, against Essex at the Neville ground. Jennings was also a fine fielder, holding 28 catches in his 35 matches for Kent, and he had a promising future ahead of him.

Shortly after war was declared, Jennings joined the Kent Fortress Engineers in Tonbridge with his brother Thomas, Colin Blythe, Henry Preston and Claud Woolley. Embodied into No1 Company on 10 October, 1914, the cricketers were soon transferred to the Woodlands Depot. He was appointed Acting 2nd Corporal in February 1915 and 2nd Corporal the following month. Having settled into his training, Jennings suffered a hernia in October, and spent a month in hospital at Marlborough, close to his family home. Once he recovered he was able to play cricket as well as performing his other duties, appearing alongside Blythe in the Fortress Engineers cricket side from May 1916. He scored 26 for the Army against the Australian Imperial Forces in July 1917 at Lord's, and also opened the batting with Wally Hardinge for Army and Navy against the Australians and South Africans the following month. He made 11 before falling victim to McCartney who, in that same match, became Colin Blythe's last ever victim.

In May 1917 Jennings was attached to the 489th Field Company, but was not posted overseas until 1918. On his arrival in France he went to the Royal Engineers Base Depot, and from there was attached to the 206th Field Company at the beginning of February. His time at the front was brief but dangerous. The 206th was at Yser Canal Bank in the Ypres sector when Jennings arrived, employed on back area work, building bath houses and incinerators. His unit moved to Paratonnarres Farm to perform similar duties, and then returned to Yser Canal Bank where they were tasked with improving the billets, the bath houses, and then a pill box for the Commanding Officer at Welsh Farm. Later that month the 206th took over the Corps Line and forward posts, and then moved to Dykes Camp.

The German *Kaiserschlacht*, the Spring Offensive, was by now underway, and the front was very lively. Whilst the Engineers continued their duties they were harassed by German artillery bombardments of gas and high explosive shells. On 9 April Jennings was ordered to move to Bienvillers, south-west of Arras, arriving late in the day. During their first day's work in this area a number of gas shells were fired over by the Germans, wounding nineteen men of 206th Company, including David Jennings. He was evacuated to England, and admitted to Newport Section, 3rd Western General Hospital on 17 April, where it was found his eyes, throat and chest were affected. He spent two months recovering in hospital, but just two weeks after his release he was admitted to St. Mark's VAD Hospital, Tunbridge Wells, showing signs of pleurisy. The hospital administered vaccines for five weeks, but his condition gradually deteriorated. David William Jennings died at 03.35 on 5 August, 1918 aged just 29. His body was conveyed on a gun carriage, covered by the Union Jack, to the railway station and taken to his family's home town of Marlborough, where he was buried in the Old Cemetery.

LIEUTENANT CONRAD POWELL JOHNSTONE

Conrad Powell Johnstone was born in Sydenham on 19 August 1895, the eldest son of William Yuile Johnstone, a Gentleman of independent means, and Katherine Johnstone, formerly Thompson. After attending Hartford House for five years he entered Rugby School in 1910, where he was in the XI 1912-1913, as captain in 1913 when he was also in the Racquet Pairs. After a year of private tutoring, Johnstone was admitted to Pembroke College, Cambridge in February 1914. He passed a University examination in the last term and was due to go into residence there in October. During July he appeared for the Kent 2nd XI on three occasions, and weeks later came the news that Britain was at war.

Johnstone at Rugby School in 1913, reproduced
by kind permission of the Rugby School Archives

On the last day of August 1914, whilst living at Kingston Hill, Surrey, Con Johnstone enlisted as a Private in the 1/15th (County of London) Battalion (Prince of Wales Own Civil Service Rifles). His time with the Territorial Force was brief, twenty-six days to be precise. Having applied for a commission he was appointed temporary 2nd Lieutenant on probation, with the Highland Light Infantry (HLI). Initially attached to the 13th Battalion in error, he was officially transferred to the 3rd Battalion, in which his uncle, Captain WA Malcolm, was serving. The 3rd HLI was a Depot in Portsmouth and it was there Johnstone received his initial training before being appointed temporary Lieutenant in February 1915.

Posted to France at the end of March, Johnstone was attached to the 1st HLI, part of the Sirhind Brigade in the 3rd (Lahore) Division, which had just come out of the line at *Neuve Chapelle*. It was not a quiet time in reserve – amidst a heavy bombardment, one shell landed near the billets of D Company, killing and wounding 30 men. Johnstone had his first experience of life in the trenches when the battalion moved into the line near Vielle Chapelle on 30 March and, as *Second Ypres* began, the Lahore Division moved to that sector and took up positions in the fields south of St. Jean, soon attracting steady shell fire. When the Division attacked on 26 April, Johnstone started in reserve with the HLI, and then pushed up in support. For several days they were constantly shelled, unable to press on or retreat without exposing their flank, as the French on the left struggled to make ground. On 1 May Johnstone was wounded, hit by a bullet in the root of the neck whilst in the trenches.

Johnstone passed through a typical chain of medical facilities. He was initially treated at a First Aid Post, then a Field Ambulance, followed by a week in a Casualty Clearing Station (CCS). The bullet had grazed his face and struck the right side of his chest, and he was in a lot of pain and unable to breathe properly. During the operation to remove the bullet from his back, doctors found it had fractured two ribs and punctured his lung. He was sent back to England, where his recovery was slow, and he followed the 3rd HLI to Scotland as they relocated in Leith where he continued his convalescence. It was August 1916 before he was passed fit for General Service, fifteen months after being wounded.

Having been accepted for a permanent commission in the Regular Army, Johnstone embarked for France on 19 November. On arrival he was attached to the 17th Battalion Lancashire Fusiliers (LF) at Arras. Later records state that he was the Transport Officer, but when he was appointed to that position is not clear. The 17th LF had a quiet end of year, and moved to the Somme region in February. When the Germans withdrew to the Hindenburg Line as part of *Operation Alberich*, Johnstone's battalion moved to St. Quentin where they remained until September when they marched to Proven to take part in *Third Ypres (Passchendaele)*.

The 17th LF carried out an attack on 22 October, taking their objectives easily, but having to concede ground due to a lack of progress on their flank. When darkness fell Johnstone organised a special party of men at headquarters, leading them over extremely difficult ground with supplies of water, rations and, most important of all for the men who had lain in water filled holes all day, rum rations. A week later a bomb was dropped on the Transport Lines, injuring Johnstone and another man. He had been hit by a shell fragment which lodged in the chest wall. The shrapnel was removed at a Field Ambulance and Johnstone was then transferred to No47 CCS at Lozinghem, where Ernest Simpson had been treated four weeks earlier. After a few days at a Red Cross Hospital in Rouen, he returned to England to begin his second period of convalescence.

Apart from some limitation in moving his right arm, his wounds healed and he was deemed fit for Home Service, taking up duties as an Instructor with No.6 OCB at Oxford. Johnstone seems to have seen out the remainder of the war at Oxford, and in May 1919 resigned his commission and joined the Reserve so he could resume his studies at Cambridge. He returned to Pembroke College and was awarded his BA in 1920 after being credited four terms and excused the examination in military subjects. He played in the Cambridge XI 1919-1920, and was awarded his Blue whilst playing with George Wood, Charles Marriott and Percy Chapman. He also led the University Golf Team to an unexpected victory over Oxford, and squeezed in his Kent debut in 1919 against Hampshire, although his studies restricted his ability to play.

Johnstone then took up work with a liquor manufacturer in Calcutta, and became involved with the development of cricket in India. In 1925 he returned to England and played for Kent twelve times, earning his cap and scoring a century against Gloucestershire. As the season ended he married his fiancée of three years, Kitty Read Birchall, at St. James Church, New Brighton. Johnstone played for Kent again in 1929, passing 2,500 first class runs in the match against MCC, but apart from several 2nd XI appearances in 1937, his cricket was mainly played in India up to WW2. He received the CBE for his involvement with the game in Madras.

Keith Miller was once about the best catch he was out to. "You will never guess it" he said, "It was some fellow in Madras called Johnstone, at slip". This was of course Con Johnstone, playing for South Zone against Australian Services in December 1945, at the age of 50. Johnstone served with the Reserve of Officers up until 1937, and was for many years on the Kent Committee, involved in the development of young players. He was elected President in 1967, the year Kent won the Gillette Cup for the first time, and died at his Eastry home on 23 June 1974, aged 78.

CAPTAIN FREDERICK HAMMETT KNOTT

Frederick Hammett Knott was born on 30 October 1891, the eldest of the four sons of Alice Annie and the Reverend Frederick George Knott, the first Headmaster of Skinners' School, Tunbridge Wells. His younger brother Charles Harold, better known as John, played for Kent after the War. Freddie was educated at Rosehill, Banstead and then Tonbridge School 1905-1910 where he was in the XI 1908-1910, Captain in his last year. He was second

in the averages in 1908 and 1909, and topped them in 1910 when he averaged 80.43, scoring an incredible 1,126 runs including six centuries. Rewarded by selection for the Public Schools side playing the MCC, he hit 155 in his second innings. Not content with cricketing excellence, he represented the school Football XV in 1908-1909, Racquets at Queen's Club 1909-1910 and Gymnastics at Aldershot in 1910.

Freddie Knott was wounded in Salonika and won the MC. Photograph courtesy The Roger Mann Collection

On leaving Tonbridge School, and just a week after playing for the Public Schools side, Knott went straight into the Kent first team against Somerset at Taunton. His third match was his home debut, against Worcestershire at the Crabble, and he marked the occasion with a fine 114 in 135 minutes. He earned his Kent Cap that summer, and then went up to Brasenose College, Oxford. Although he failed to get Blue as a Freshman, he did so in 1912-1914, as captain in the last year. He was also a Rugby Blue, in the XV 1910-1913, and played for The Rest v England in the Final Rugby Union trial in January 1911, *The Times* reporting that he scored 'a beautiful try'. Despite turning out for England in the corresponding match in 1912, he did not win an England cap. During his time at Oxford he played a handful of matches for Kent during the summer months, and also played for the University against the county. During August 1914, having gained his BA, he took up the position of Assistant Master at Marlborough College.

Having barely arrived at Marlborough, Knott enlisted and was commissioned temporary 2nd Lieutenant on 3 December 1914. Located in the West Country, he joined the 7th Battalion Duke of Edinburgh's Wiltshire Regiment which had been raised in Devizes that September as part of Kitchener's Third New Army, or 'K3', and was part of 26th Division. The battalion spent winter in billets at Marlborough and moved to Sutton Veny for final training in the spring. That summer Knott was appointed temporary Lieutenant, and in September he departed for France. The 26th was one of many New Army Divisions put in the field around that time, with the hope they would bolster the planned *Loos* Offensive. As it happened Knott's Division were not called into action, and the following month they were ordered to Salonika.

Knott arrived at *Salonika* on 21 November, his battalion's first task being to assist in the construction of defences against a potential Bulgarian attack. This work took up most of the winter months, during which time they moved to the mouth of the Derbend Pass. Knott's first sight of the enemy was on New Year's Eve, when Austrian aeroplanes flew overhead dropping bombs. The British force were required to dig trench-works for months, earning themselves the nickname 'the Gardeners of Salonika', and most succumbed to one illness or another. A constant flow of men were hospitalised with malaria and dysentery, the worse cases evacuated to Malta. Knott was himself in hospital during May, although his ailment was not recorded.

That July Knott's battalion took over the trenches near Kalinova from the French. The line proved quite lively, and on 22 August the Bulgarians attacked the forward positions. Knott was with C Company on the left of the battalion line as the fighting continued all day, but the enemy were held off, the 7th Wilts suffering 20 casualties in the process. Having moved to Cidemli, Knott was promoted to temporary Captain toward the end of September, and the following month moved again, to the area facing Doiran. He remained in the sector into the next year, as the battalion transformed the shallow trenches into a sound line of defence. The line was very close to the enemy, and constantly shelled by mountain guns, both sides using patrols and observation balloons to gain intelligence about what the other was up to.

Knott fell ill in January, the cause again unrecorded, but severe enough to keep him absent for five weeks. Spirits were raised in March, with the news Baghdad had been occupied, and Knott's battalion was soon training for their own attack at Doiran. During this time gas shells were dropped on another Division and the 26th quickly added 'attendance at gas school' to the training schedule. The artillery bombardment in advance of the attack began on 21 April, and the enemy responded in kind. Unfortunately for the 7th Wilts, the wire was still intact in places when they attacked the Bulgarians on the night of 24/25 April.

When the assault began, the uncut wire prevented 'D' Company providing support to Knott's Company, and the enemy made several determined counter-attacks. With mounting casualties, a lack of ammunition and the inability of reserves to get forward, the survivors were eventually forced to withdraw. All the Company Officers and eight senior NCOs were killed or wounded, and the Company Sergeant Major was left commanding the battalion, overseeing the withdrawal. Having gone into battle with around 500 officers and men, the battalion suffered casualties of 14 out of 15 officers, and 318 men. Stretcher parties, led by the Medical Officer, went out during the night and day to bring the wounded in, and the enemy did not interfere.

Knott was one of the wounded, shot in the left arm and suffering radial nerve damage that would affect his cricket in later years. He was evacuated to England to recover and from April 1918 was Regimental Bombing Officer attached to the 3rd Wilts, a depot unit based at Sittingbourne. The New Year's Honours of 1918 brought Knott the Military Cross, and the battalion war diary records he was also Mentioned In Despatches. After the Armistice Knott was seconded for duty as Brigade Bombing Officer, but in April 1919 he relinquished his commission on account of ill-health caused by his wounds, and he left the Army with the rank of Captain.

Knott returned to teaching though not at Marlborough, becoming a Preparatory School Master at Eastbourne from 1920-26, at Haywards Heath, Sussex from 1926-29 and Little Common, Bexhill-on-Sea from 1929-32. Thereafter he was Secretary to Worplesdon Golf Club and later of NZ Golf Club, and was a scratch player himself. His wounds perhaps prevented him excelling at cricket, with no sign of his former brilliance, but he did play a handful of first class matches, turning out for HDG Leveson-Gower's XI in 1921, 1924 and 1926 and making a single appearance for Sussex in 1926 against Cambridge. He also played once for the Kent 2nd XI in 1921.

Knott lived in Surrey between the wars, and by 1939 was working for a company distributing Morris and MG cars. He applied for a commission in the Army Reserve during November and, on appointment to Captain with the RASC, was posted to the Training Centre at Aldershot. During WW2 he rose to Temporary Major and held various positions as an Instructor, whilst commanding HQ Companies. Post war Knott lived a quiet life with Joan (Pike) who he had married in 1922, and finally relinquished his commission in 1954. On 10 February 1972, after a short illness, Freddie Knott died, leaving his wife of fifty years, and two sons.

LIEUTENANT-COLONEL HERVEY MAJOR LAWRENCE

Hervey Major Lawrence was born on 24 March 1881 at Hadlow in Kent, the first child of Emily Alice and Doctor Henry Major Lawrence. After a private education he made his debut for the Kent 2nd XI against Sussex in August 1898 at the Angel, where he made 30 not out. His first class debut came the following season against Somerset, again at the Angel, but his fast-medium bowling bore no fruit until his third outing for the first team, the away fixture against Somerset. The three wicket haul at Bath proved to be his only first class victims whilst playing for Kent, his last appearance at the Oval proving wicket-less. His club cricket was far more successful – in all matches that year he took 209 wickets and made 1,953 runs. Lawrence turned out for the 2nd XI twice in 1906, once in 1907 and once in 1908. Thereafter he appeared for the Army and Navy in 1910 and 1911 and for Suffolk five times in 1913, whilst serving with the Suffolk Regiment. He also played for the Army in June 1914 against the Navy.

Hervey Lawrence of the Cameronians served at Gallipoli, in Egypt, Palestine and France and commanded the 1/5th Suffolk, the 1/7th Cheshire and 1/1st Herefordshire

Lawrence was commissioned 2nd Lieutenant on 21 March 1900 in the 3rd Cameronians (Scottish Rifles), a Militia battalion. Both of the Cameronian Militia battalions volunteered for service in South Africa, and Lawrence joined them. He was promoted to Lieutenant in November, and eleven months later received a commission into the 1st Cameronians, a regular battalion, reverting back to the rank of 2nd Lieutenant. After the war ended in 1902 he was awarded the Queen's Medal with three clasps (for Cape Colony, Orange Free State and a 1901 date clasp), and was posted to India. In January 1905 he was promoted to Lieutenant and later that year the regiment returned to England. As mentioned, Lawrence made two appearances for the Kent 2nd XI in the summer of 1906, but a dislocated knee prevented his playing more. He had however recovered sufficiently to go ahead with his marriage to Dorothy Lawrence in Penshurst during November.

In May 1911 Lawrence took up the position of Adjutant to the 5th Battalion of the Suffolk Regiment, which had become part of the Territorial Force under Haldane's Reforms in 1908. Their annual camp in July 1914 was at Holkham Park, and just as the event finished, war was declared. On the night of 4 August 1914 Lawrence, as Adjutant, had the job of telegraphing the word 'Mobilize' to each detachment commander. Concentrating at Colchester the territorials were asked to volunteer for overseas service and, although they had only contemplated home service, 72% volunteered and became the 1/5th Suffolk. Those who chose not to volunteer became the 2/5th Suffolk. Training continued into 1915 and during July the 1/1st departed for *Gallipoli*.

Lawrence and his battalion suffered from start to finish during their time on the Peninsula. Two days after their arrival the 163rd Brigade was given thirty minutes' notice to make an advance, which they performed with no artillery cover and under a murderous fire. Lawrence and his men reached their objective and dug in, but had lost 11 officers and 178 other ranks, including the Commanding Officer, with many more hospitalised. The battalion war diary suggests they had been shelled by their own side, and when dysentery was added to the mix the battalion fell to half strength within nine days. On 1 September Lawrence was appointed Major as the battalion moved to South Wales Borderers Gully, where they joined the NZ Mounted Rifle Brigade at Hill 60. This was an important strategic position that had been captured only days before at the cost of 1,000 Allied and 5,000 Turkish lives. In many places the parapets were made up of corpses covered in dirt, and the stench remained for months, as did the flies.

November saw the harsh and the light sides of war. When a mine was exploded on 15 November near Lawrence's position, the men were bizarrely not granted permission to take cover and, as a result, one was killed, eight wounded, and others so shaken they were taken out of the line. This left Lawrence as one of only four of the original officers remaining. The light hearted moment came when it was spotted the Turks had knife rests on the edge of the crater, and the Suffolks put a bomb on the end of a rope, throwing it at the rests to try and snare them. The Turks grabbed the end of the rope, and a tug-of-war ensued between the two trenches, laughter and shouts coming from both sides. Eventually as the Suffolks pulled hard they fell back in a heap on the ground. The Turks had cut the rope.

The terrible weather that hit everyone at Gallipoli in November was particularly troublesome for Lawrence's battalion. They had received orders to prepare to return to Mudros on 27 November to rest, and accordingly packed up, sending their baggage ahead. Lawrence, like all the other officers, had no blankets when the bad weather came, and hasty bivouacs were constructed as the gales, rain and blizzards hit the area. It was 6 December before Lawrence was evacuated to Lemnos and, to give some idea of the men's condition, fifty had to fall out of the four mile march to camp despite a slow pace being kept. Having been transferred to Egypt for a well-earned rest, the CO left on account of ill-health, and Lawrence was appointed temporary Lieutenant-Colonel and given command of the Battalion. After six months in command he took up the position of CO of the 1/7th Cheshire Regiment, which was working on Canal defences with 53rd Division. That December he led the battalion to Romani where they spent winter, then moved to El Arish toward the end of January 1917.

The advance into *Palestine* soon began, and when the First Battle of Gaza started on 26 March, the Cheshires were initially kept in reserve. It was 15:30 before Lawrence received orders to advance to the attack, the 53rd Division having ground to a halt. The objective was pointed out and Lawrence led the battalion some 4,500 yards without a halt, and established his HQ at the Citadel in Ali El Muntar. The 7th Welsh Fusiliers had pierced the Turkish Line minutes before and it was an opportune moment for the Cheshires to arrive and help consolidate. Lawrence organised the various units present into a temporary garrison, and placed the Citadel in a state of defence.

After spending the night in this position, Lawrence was ordered to withdraw because the mounted troops had to leave their positions to water their horses, so exposing the infantry. He was awarded the DSO for his part in the fighting, and was also involved in the return match, the Second Battle of Gaza, on 19 April. On that occasion he again led his battalion into action, but although they took their own objectives the city was not taken. The Allies withdrew to discuss what to do next, and the men dug in their positions where they remained for the following months. The line was divided in two to establish a regular system of reliefs and it was during one such relief that Ted Dillon, also serving with 53rd Division, was injured by an aircraft bomb.

That summer Allenby took over command of the EEF from Murray, and chose to attack Beersheba to catch the Turks unaware. Lawrence's Division was used to guard the left flank of the attack on 31 October, having no trouble from the enemy in that position. Beersheba was carried and Lawrence joined the advance into the hills, where the Division's presence threatened the enemy in Gaza, which soon fell. On 5 December the Cheshires formed the advance guard, leading the 53rd Division to Jerusalem. Lawrence was instructed not to stop to reconnoitre, but to go full steam ahead until shot at. Eventually the battalion encountered strong enemy resistance, having unknowingly come up against the main enemy positions defending the city. The following day the Jerusalem fell and Lawrence led his men into the city, posting guards on the various gates in the ancient walls. They were among the first troops to enter Jerusalem, two days before Allenby arrived.

Toward the end of the month Lawrence was given command of 1/1st Battalion Herefordshire Regiment, also within the 53rd Division, and, having received orders for France, left Palestine. On arrival at Proven his battalion was attached to 34th Division. The Germans launched the last part of their spring offensive, the *Kaiserschlacht*, on 15 July with the Second Battle of the Marne. They failed to break through and an Allied counter-offensive three days later overwhelmed the German right flank. Lawrence led his battalion into the attack near Bois de Reugny on 23 July, immediately coming under heavy machine-gun fire, and further held up by the failure of units on either flank to advance. Despite the difficult situation and heavy casualties, Lawrence's battalion maintained the high ground until they were relieved, experiencing their first gas attack during that time. Lawrence was awarded the bar to his DSO, the London Gazette (*Issue 30997, 5 November 1918*) announcing:

> "*Lawrence, Hervey Major DSO., Major (Acting Lieut-Col), Scottish Rifles. He set a magnificent example of leadership and courage in an attack. When both his flanks were held up and he was suffering from wounds in the side and arm, he led his battalion forward in the face of heavy rifle and machine-gun fire and advanced the line 1,000 yards. He held the captured position against great odds. His personal influence had the most inspiring effect on officers and men.*"

He led the battalion into the attack again in the first days of August, south of Soissons in support of the French advance, for which he awarded the Légion D'Honour Croix de Chevalier. Lawrence returned to England on leave on 9 August, not returning until the end of the month. A little over a week later he was admitted to hospital, and although the reason for this is unclear, it was presumably fairly serious, as he was struck off the strength of the battalion at the end of the month. Here the trail goes cold, and it is possible this was the end of his war, in which he was Mentioned in Despatches four times and awarded the OBE in 1919. He retired from the Scottish Rifles in May, and found time to relax with a little post-war cricket, turning out for I Zingari that summer against Tonbridge School.

Lawrence was married a second time in 1921 to Kathleen Galbraith, and continued to serve with the Reserve of Officers, playing for Suffolk Regiment against the Colchester Garrison during 1928. In 1936 he reached the age limit of liability to recall, and lived a long retirement. When he died at Ely on 17 September 1975, Wisden recorded he was the last known survivor of those who played first class county cricket before 1900.

LE FLEMING BROTHERS
John and Lawrence Julius le Fleming were both born in Tonbridge, almost fourteen years apart. John was the eldest son of John and Harriette Mary le Fleming born on 23 October 1865, and Lawrence was the sixth and youngest son, born on 3 June 1879. Their father was an Army Tutor at Tonbridge School, and the family often had students boarding with them. All the brothers attended the school, John from 1878 to 1884 and Lawrence 1892 to 1896, John staying through sixth form, but Lawrence leaving from the Army Class. Whilst a sixth-former John was in the Cricket XI, as Captain in his final year, when he accompanied the team on a tour of Holland, and was also in the Rugby XV 1882-83. A fine athlete, he won the Athletics Points Cup in 1883 and 1884 and was awarded both the Smythe and Lampard Exhibitions on leaving to go up to Cambridge. Lawrence was in the Cricket XI in his last year, scoring over 400 runs and heading the averages, which won him the Dale Cup, opening on at least one occasion with William Hutchings, against the Marlborough Blues.

John studied at Clare College, and was conferred his BA in 1887 and MA in 1902. His sporting achievements continued whilst he was at University and, although he did not achieve Blue at Cricket, he was in the Rugby XV 1884-86 and played against Oxford three times. He ran in the hurdle race in the inter-University sports in 1886-88, winning on the last two occasions and in 1887 won the amateur hurdle championship as well as competing in the Hammer. Not content with all this, he was also playing rugby for Blackheath and was selected to play for the England XV against Wales in 1887. He appeared for Gentlemen of Kent versus Gentlemen of Philadelphia in July 1889, batting alongside Lord Harris, and a week later made his first class debut for the county against Surrey at the Rectory

Field. That same year he also played for the Tonbridge Club, making one score of 228 against Southborough. By 1891 he was employed as a Military Tutor at Tonbridge School, following in his father's footsteps, and was married to Ethel Agnes Hall at Tonbridge Parish Church.

John still found plenty of time for sports, scoring his only first class century against Sussex at Hove in 1892, and received his county cap the following season. An excellent skater, he also won the Davos Challenge Bowl and Shield awarded by the Davos Platz Club for figure competitions in 1893. His last appearance for Kent 1st XI was against Essex at Leyton in July 1899, making 44 and 51, and passing 1,000 runs in county championship matches in the process. Lawrence, meanwhile, made his debut for the Kent 2nd XI against Sussex at the Angel Ground in August 1897. His score of 97 earned him an appearance for the 1st XI in the last Championship game of the year against Middlesex at Lords in which he made 40 and 2. He went on to play eight times the following season, and three times in 1899, although his top score remained the 40 he made in his first game.

BREVET MAJOR JOHN LE FLEMING

On the outbreak of the war John le Fleming served as a platoon commander with the Volunteer Training Corps and, although 49 years of age, he volunteered to join the Territorials in March 1915. The TF Association approved his commission into the 3/1st Kent Cyclist Battalion which was formed that year as a training/depot unit, and he was gazetted 2nd Lieutenant and Temporary Captain on 15 May. During August he organised a military sports day on the school grounds at Tonbridge, at which several of his brothers were judges, including Lawrence who was recovering from his second Blighty wound. He was given command of the battalion and appointed Temporary Major in October. His appointment seems to have ruffled some feathers, and several letters were written naming officers of the 1/1st and 2/1st battalions who could have taken the command. In the meantime le Fleming was appointed Temporary Lieutenant-Colonel and continued in his duties, ably assisted by Captain Gerry Weigall.

John le Fleming served with the Kent Cyclist Battalion, the West Kent Yeomanry and the

Royal West Kent Regiment. Reproduced by permission of the Institution of Royal Engineers
At the end of the year a letter from le Fleming was published in *The Kent & Sussex Courier*, appealing for 1,000 volunteers for the Kent Cyclists. The recruitment drive presumably failed, as by June 1916 it was apparent that the 3/1st Kent Cyclists were to be disbanded. Le Fleming wrote to the Officer Commanding the 3/1st West Kent Yeomanry (WKY) asking if he could be considered for a transfer. By July the 3/1st Kent Cyclists had been reduced to cadre strength under Gerry Weigall, and the following month le Fleming took up an appointment with the 3/1st WKY as 2nd Lieutenant and Temporary Captain. He reported for duty at Crowborough a few days later, now under the Home Counties Division. The battalion was a training unit, and le Fleming was no doubt able to use his experience as an Army Tutor to good effect. The battalion moved to Tunbridge Wells in November, but in early 1917 le Fleming found for a second time his unit was to be disbanded. Some men transferred to the 2/1st battalion, but le Fleming joined a number of others in transferring to the 4th (Reserve) Battalion of the Royal West Kent Regiment. His new battalion was also based at Tunbridge Wells, and he joined them as 2nd Lieutenant.

Le Fleming relinquished his acting rank of Captain in May 1917, but just two months later was promoted to Lieutenant and acting Captain. During August he was appointed acting Major whilst attached to the battalion Headquarters, and saw out the remainder of the war in that position, occasionally playing cricket for the regiment. He remained in the Territorial Force after the Armistice, and in January 1919 was made Brevet Major on his promotion to Captain. In June Le Fleming relinquished the acting rank, but in November, now in the Territorial Reserve, was promoted Lieutenant-Colonel. He retired from his position as Army Tutor in 1925 at the age of 60, but retained links with the Kent Cyclists through the Old Comrades Association, of which he was Vice president, in 1935. An old dinner menu shows he ultimately attained the rank of Colonel in the TF. On 9 October 1942 John le Fleming died at Montreux, Switzerland, where he was staying at the Beau Rivage with his wife, and his widow died there the following year.

MAJOR & BREVET LIEUT-COLONEL LAWRENCE JULIUS LE FLEMING

Lawrence le Fleming joined the 4th Battalion East Surrey Regiment as 2nd Lieutenant on 2 March 1898 and was appointed Lieutenant the following February. Serving with a Militia battalion, he attended drills and training camps but otherwise continued in his normal work. On 11 October 1899, the day war was declared on the Boers, he transferred to the regulars, joining the 2nd Battalion East Surrey Regiment as a 2nd Lieutenant. After reporting to his battalion in South Africa, he was present during the Battle of Tugela Heights which forced the Boers to lift the siege of Ladysmith. His medal awards were the Queen's Medal with five clasps and the King's medal with two clasps, the bars to his medals showing he took part in the Battles of Colenso and Spion Kop, and the later operations in the Transvaal, Orange River Colony and Cape Colony. He was invalided from 1 July 1900, presumably a result of illness as no wounds were recorded, and re-joined in March 1901. About the time he returned he was promoted to Lieutenant.

The regiment was posted to India in 1902, based at Lucknow and Mhow and, whilst still there in 1905, le Fleming was promoted to Captain. He was recalled to England in 1909 to take up the Adjutancy of the Territorial Battalion at Wimbledon, a position he held for three years, after which he re-joined 2nd Battalion in Burma. A year later he was on the move again, this time to take up the post of Instructor at the Royal Military College, Sandhurst. Le Fleming played cricket when he was able, including for the Army, Free Foresters and the Band of Brothers, and he was also competent with a golf club or hockey stick. In 1914 he played for Kent 2nd XI again, against Staffordshire at the Bat and Ball ground, Gravesend, just a week before war was declared. His 85 in Kent's second innings was the highest individual score in the match.

On 4 August 1914 le Fleming was still engaged at Sandhurst, but he relinquished the appointment to join his Regiment with the BEF in France. The retreat from *Mons to the Marne*, and subsequent advance to the Aisne had led to both the British and German Armies digging in. As both sides now tried to outflank each other, the *Race to the Sea* began. Following their arrival in France, and after several engagements with the enemy, 1st East Surrey Regiment found itself in a position south of Richebourg L'Avoué. Le Fleming reported for duty on 25 October, the next few days seeing the East Surrey's trenches suffer heavy shelling. On 28 October, just three days after joining the battalion, le Fleming was wounded along with 4 other ranks, when he was shot in the face. He returned to England to recover, and whilst there was married at the Parish Church, Tonbridge on 5 December 1914 to Frances Loulo Frend.

On his return to the front on 3 March 1915 le Fleming was appointed Temporary Major and given command of the 2nd Battalion East Surrey Regiment. The following day he led his men to the trenches north of Wulvergham, establishing his HQ at Scotch Farm. This was the period between *Ypres* and *Second Ypres*, but was nonetheless still a lively part of the front. On the morning of 6 March, Scotch Farm was shelled and the men were left with no choice but to leave the buildings and take cover in ditches by the roadside. Initially the wounded remained in the farm-house cellars but, when the shelling set the buildings on fire, le Fleming and other officers and men went back and took the wounded from the cellars to safety.

On 10 April the Battalion moved to trenches close to Zonnebeke. The following afternoon it was reported the Germans were mining the trenches in two places, and

Lawrence le Fleming, wounded twice before he was killed on the opening day of the German Spring Offensive 1918. Reproduced by permission of Surrey History Centre and Copyright of Surrey History Centre

getting uncomfortably close. Le Fleming started round the trenches to give instructions on how to deal with the mines and, whilst passing from one company to another, he was hit by sniper fire in the foot. For a second time he returned to England to recover, and was Mentioned in Despatches (MID) by General Haig in June 1915. Recovering sufficiently from his wound he was recalled to Sandhurst and, despite applying to return to the Front, he remained there as GSO in command of a company of Gentlemen Cadets from October 1915 until April 1917 when permission was finally granted for him to return to active service. *Tonbridge School and the Great War (Tonbridge School, 1923: 200-202)* records that *"The fine work he did at Sandhurst brought a mention in the Secretary of State for War's List of February 2nd 1917, and promotion to Brevet Lieutenant-Colonel, both "for services rendered in connection with the war"."*

In the summer of 1917 le Fleming went to the Front a third time. Almost immediately he received news his wife was ill, but arriving back in England he found she had already passed away. Still mourning his loss he was back in France to take command of the 9th Battalion East Surreys on 8 August, gazetted Acting Lieutenant-Colonel the following week, and spending a week in hospital before he could finally get to grips with his new command. The battalion spent the end of the year east of Hargicourt.

During March 1918 le Fleming was based near St Quentin. The enemy artillery had been unusually quiet for a few days, and intelligence suggested the Germans were planning some form of attack, so on the night of 20 March le Fleming and his men slept with their gas masks in reach. About 04.30 what is now known as the Battle of St. Quentin, part of the German *Kaiserschlacht*, began with an intense bombardment. It was a very misty morning, and B Company, when manning their reserve trench, had to join hands and be led up to their positions by an officer. They suffered many losses from the shelling but held the line until, with their ammunition running short, they were rushed by the Germans who captured around twenty men. The remaining thirty survivors managed to escape and re-join the battalion.

At 10.00 le Fleming received orders to move his men forward to occupy the high ground east of Villecholes. Typically he went to reconnoitre the ground ahead himself and, when satisfied all was in order, he called the battalion forward. As they moved up they met several artillerymen heading in the opposite direction, carrying their breech blocks, reporting that the enemy were advancing not far behind them. On reaching Villecholes le Fleming positioned most of the battalion on the high ground to the east. Neighbouring units were consulted but the exact whereabouts of the enemy remained a mystery. Le Fleming went forward with another officer to make a personal reconnaissance and, on walking over the crest of a rise, heavy machine-gun fire was opened on them. Le Fleming fell, shot through the head. A volunteer brought his body in the next day, but as the line was subsequently overrun during the rapid German advances that followed, his last resting place remains unknown. His name is recorded on the Pozieres Memorial.

MAJOR ALLAN FRANCIS LEACH-LEWIS

Allan Francis Leach-Lewis was born on 11 March 1883, son of Anna Jane and William Leach-Lewis, JP. His father was a County Councillor, Principal of Margate College and several times Mayor of Margate. When their parents retired, Allan and his siblings took over the running of the College. As a boy he first went to boarding school in Guilford and then on to Aldenham School where he was House Captain 1899, in the XI 1898-1901, captain in 1901, and in the Football XI 1897-1901, captain 1900-1901. In 1901 he made a score of 68 against Mill Hill that matched the opposition's total. He also represented the school in the Long Jump, 100 Yards and Swimming at the Public Schools' Athletics Championships.

Going up to Cambridge to study Law, he was at Pembroke College from 1901-1904, but did not make the Cricket XI. He was perhaps concentrating on his football for which he was a Blue 1904-1905 and by all accounts a fine player. He represented the University against the likes of Millwall and Clapton, regularly appeared for Corinthians, and he made two appearances for Tottenham Hotspur as an amateur against Luton and Portsmouth. His cricket was restricted to the Kent 2nd XI between 1911 and 1922, coming in eighth man on his debut and top scoring with 53. As a wicket-keeper the 1st XI was perhaps always out of reach, bearing in mind the talent at Kent's disposal.

Leach-Lewis of the East Kent Yeomanry was Kent President in 1953. Reproduced by the kind permission of Kent County Cricket Club

Between 1901 and 1904 Leach-Lewis was in the Cambridge University Rifle Volunteers, progressing from Private to Colour Sergeant. On leaving University he joined the Royal East Kent Mounted Rifles (REKMR) in September 1904 as 2nd Lieutenant and was promoted to Lieutenant in April 1908, then to Captain in May 1912. Being part of the Territorials he attended annual camps and regular drills, but otherwise spent his civilian life as Headmaster at Margate College. When the REKMR was mobilized in August 1914, Leach-Lewis joined them in Canterbury where they set about contributing to coastal defences whilst training. He was promoted to Major in February 1915, and in September joined the South East Mounted Brigade (SEMB), as it travelled to Liverpool and then sailed for *Gallipoli.*

The SEMB had missed any major offensive at Gallipoli and were destined to remain at Helles, in uncomfortable circumstances, for several months. Not long after their arrival the winter weather set in and during November Leach-Lewis and his Brigade endured the region's worst blizzard in forty years. He was in command of 3rd Squadron, spending time either in the front line, support line or in reserve. The ANZAC and Suvla areas were the first to be evacuated in December, but those at Helles, the SEMB included, were among the last to leave in the early hours of New Year's Eve.

After some reorganisation at Mudros, Leach-Lewis joined the move to Egypt where the REKMR was absorbed into the 3rd Dismounted Brigade, formed by the Eastern and South Eastern Mounted Brigades. The new formation served on Canal defences between Suez and Geneifa until July 1916 when it joined the Western Frontier Force. Leach-Lewis now found himself a part of the force sent to tackle the Senussi uprising, although by this time there was little threat and time was spent training. He had left Egypt for a month of leave during July and by the time he returned at the end of August the Brigade was in Sollum, where one of his responsibilities was to oversee courts-martial. At the beginning of October 1916 he was attached to the Western Force Headquarters.

The East and West Kent Yeomanry Regiments were amalgamated during February 1917, becoming the 10th Battalion, the Buffs, and were attached to 74th Division. The men returned to Egypt to concentrate in advance of the offensive into *Palestine.* The first two battles of Gaza were lost by end of April, and General Archibald Murray was relieved and replaced by General Edmund Allenby in the summer. During June of 1917, as the command structure was changed, Leach-Lewis was appointed Deputy Assistant Adjutant General (DAAG) serving GHQ (General Headquarters) of the EEF, and he was to remain in this position throughout the remainder of the war. On 2 November, several days after the Armistice with Turkey took effect, he was in England on leave, marrying Dorothy Russell at Milton near Gravesend. In March 1919 he returned to England for good, and joined the Territorial Reserve as a Major in 1920. For his service in Egypt, he was awarded the Order of the Nile, 4th Class.

Leach-Lewis was playing for Band of Brothers against Club and Ground on the day the Blythe Memorial was unveiled, and the following season he turned out for the 2nd XI when their fixtures resumed. He played until 1922, scoring 90 against Surrey in his last game, and appeared for Lord Harris's XI against the West Indies the following year. Leach-Lewis remained closely involved with Kent, as a Member of the Committee at various points between 1919 and 1957, Chairman of the Young Players 1951 to 1953, General Manager in 1945 and President in 1953. When Royal East Kent Yeomanry reunions were held in their tent at Canterbury Week, he was sure to attend. He was appointed a Justice of the Peace for Kent in 1930, and was Land Tax Commissioner for the Thanet District. In 1939 aged 56 he applied to enrol on the Officers Emergency Reserve but his application was declined, presumably on grounds of age. Not a man to stand idly by he became regional officer for the Midland civil defence region from 1940 to 1945. Leach-Lewis died at York House Nursing Home, Broadstairs on 7 July 1963 at the age of 80.

RED CROSS SEARCHER, FREDERICK BARCHAM LENEY

Frederick Barcham Leney was born in Maidstone on 29 November 1876, the eldest child of Augustus and Kate Leney. Educated at Bradfield College between 1887 and 1894, he was in the Football XI in 1893 and the Cricket XI in 1894, showing his potential when taking 9 wickets in the match against Sherborne. Leaving school he entered the family brewery business, his father having established the Phoenix Brewery at Wateringbury in 1843. By 1911 he was a Director of the Company.

Leney's debut for the Kent 2nd XI was in June of 1903 at Town Malling when he took ten wickets against Surrey. In the 1904 fixture against the same team he bowled Bill Sarel, and in the two matches against Sussex made scores of 53 not out and 94 not out. He made scores of 30 and 9 and took a single wicket in his only appearance for the Kent 1st XI against Oxford during May 1905, and the following year an FB Leney XI, which included Ted Humphreys, beat Gravesend by six wickets. In club cricket he was Captain of the newly formed Wateringbury CC in 1905, and also played for the Mote, taking 58 wickets in 1907, and scoring 143 out of 272 against an MCC side that included Sir Arthur Conan Doyle in 1908, finishing that season with an average of 47. Between 1908 and 1911 Leney represented the MCC on seven occasions.

Aged 37 on the outbreak of war, Leney chose to serve with the British Red Cross and became a Searcher. The Red Cross attracted thousands of volunteers who worked alongside the professional staff, providing services which were paid for by extensive fundraising. Aside from Transport, Hospitals and Work Parties, the Red Cross also set up centres to record and trace the wounded and missing in France. Searchers visited local hospitals and villages where fighting had taken place, seeking out wounded men and taking statements.

Information was then passed on to the authorities and relatives, and this work marked the beginning of the tracing and messaging service that remains a part of the work of the Red Cross to this day.

Leney arrived in France on 3 January 1915 and carried out his work there until September. He then transferred to *Egypt* where casualties from *Gallipoli* were often hospitalised or convalescing. Working at Alexandria, Cairo and at Mudros on the Island of Lemnos, he may well have encountered the novelist EM Forster, who was a Red Cross searcher in the same region. In October 1915 Leney made a report from Montazah regarding a Private O'Shea of the Australian Imperial Force, giving a small insight into the work he undertook:

> *"Witness reports that the O'Shea he means came out with the 6th Reinforcements, and was hit in the head in an advance on Aug:6th and was left on the ground behind the front taken and consolidated. Witness was himself wounded later on. (Evidence seemed good.). F.B. Leney 13.10.15"*

Similar statements are to be found in the files of those Kent players who died, and were used by the authorities to establish whether a missing man had been killed, in order to give some idea of that man's fate to his family.

The History of the Mote Cricket Club (Osborn, 1990: 72) details a letter that appeared in the press in April 1916, telling of a dinner attended by former members of the Club:

> *"Sir,*
>
> **Mote Cricket Club**
>
> *I think it may interest many who have taken an interest in the Mote Club to hear that even in war the old club is remembered in distant climes. I have just had a menu sent to me of a Mote Club dinner from 'somewhere abroad'. The autographs on the menu were CHB Marsham, DW Carr, RW Mitchell, HRN Ellison, FB Leney, E Cleveland-Stevens, WH Samuel, and a guest, A Leach-Lewis, who had often played at the Mote. Not a bad nucleus for a side! A very pleasant evening was spent. The following toasts were drunk – 'The Mote Cricket Club', 'Sir Marcus and Lady Samuel' and 'The Secretary of the Club'."*

Around the time in question, Marsham and Leach-Lewis were in the Alexandria area following evacuation from Gallipoli and Carr was there with the Army Ordnance Department. The brief, but extremely useful, records held by the Red Cross suggest Leney was discharged in December 1916. His father had died in a hunting accident in 1915 and perhaps it was a good time to return to the family business. He was aged 40, and although the upper age of conscription had by now been established at 41, there does not seem to be a record of him having served in any further capacity. During 1917 Lloyd George introduced measures to halve the volume of beer brewed, and at the end of the year Frederick Leney & Sons was fined £100 for brewing an excess of 247 barrels! On 25 July 1921 Leney was at the Railway Hotel in Galway, Ireland when he died suddenly. He was brought back to England and his funeral held at Wateringbury on Friday, 29 July 1921.

COLONEL (HON. BRIGADIER-GENERAL) ROBERT O'HARA LIVESAY

Robert O'Hara Livesay was the only son of Rose and Robert Algernon Livesay, born on 27 June 1876 in Old Brompton, Gillingham, where his father, a Colonel of the RE, was stationed. He attended Wellington College from 1890 and was in the Cricket XI 1892-94, and also the Rugby XV. In 1894 he played for the Kent 2nd XI at the end of July at Lord's, making 78 in the second innings, and then entered Sandhurst. He made his mark in the XI, scoring 169 against Woolwich in 1895 and 128 the following year, and also made the Rugby XV. The year 1895 also marked Livesay's first class debut for Kent against Surrey, in which he made two ducks. Although in his defence it should be noted he was one of six who failed to score a run in the first innings. He was used as an opener for several games, before dropping down the order where his scoring began to improve. His highest score for the county was 78 against the South Africans at Canterbury in 1904.

Livesay (right) a Lieutenant with the 2nd Royal West Surrey Regiment in 1899

Livesay left Sandhurst in 1896 and was commissioned 2nd Lieutenant in the Royal West Surrey Regiment. Having received his Kent Cap in 1897, he represented England Rugby team against Wales in the Home Nations Championship in 1898, and earned his second cap against the same side in 1899. Between those two fixtures he was promoted to Lieutenant, and in 1900 he accompanied the 2nd West Surreys to South Africa, where he served part of the time with 26th and 10th Mounted Infantry, units of his regiment. He was awarded the Queen's Medal with five clasps, the King's Medal with two clasps, received a Mention in Despatches, and was awarded the DSO in 1902. Promoted to Captain he returned to England to be seconded to the Staff, and was employed as an Instructor at Sandhurst from 1904 until 1908. He squeezed in an appearance for MCC against Dorset and was then appointed Adjutant of the OTC. In January 1914, after almost 18 years' service, Livesay joined the Reserve.

His retirement did not last long. When the BEF sailed for France in August, the Territorial Force and the Special Reserve of Officers (SRO) took on responsibility for Home Defence, assembling 'Central Force'. Livesay was recalled on 5 August as a Captain in the SRO, employed as General Staff Officer 2nd Class (GSO2), serving with 48th Division in Central Force. The 48th was ultimately posted overseas, and by mid-April 1915 Livesay was with the Division near Cassel. In July, after a series of appointments and promotions, he was GSO1 with the New Zealand Division as Brevet Major and Temporary Lieutenant-Colonel, the officer responsible to the Divisional Commander for planning, directing training, and the conduct of operations.

Livesay remained with the New Zealand Division for 16 months, and their success during the Battles of the Somme owed much to his outstanding work – his careful planning preceded the successful capture of 'Switch Line' during *Battle of Flers-Courcelette* in September. The following May he was awarded the Chevalier of the Legion of Honour by the French Republic, and during *Messines* in June he was again deeply involved in plotting the Division's success when they captured Messines Ridge. Livesay was granted leave in July, returning to England to marry Margaret Amelia Pretyman at Torre Church, Torquay, but back with the Division for their part in the First Battle of Passchendaele in October, part of *Third Ypres*. Livesay again received recognition from his seniors for his role in operational planning.

During October Livesay was appointed GSO1 at the American Staff School in France, where he served until March 1918 and was then appointed GSO1 to the 61st Division, as Brevet Colonel. The *Kaiserschlacht* was launched days later, and the Division fought a successful retreat over the Somme. They moved north to a quieter sector on the La Bassée Canal near Bethune, which was unfortunately in the German's sights when they opened the next phase of their offensive. The 61st suffered badly and was withdrawn to rebuild, during which time Livesay was appointed Brevet Colonel. He was transferred during *The Hundred Days Offensive*, appointed Temporary Brigadier General commanding the 24th Infantry Brigade. The brigade joined the advance on the Rouvroy-Fresnes Line a week into October, and on *Beyond the Hindenburg Line* toward the St Quentin Canal.

Livesay gave the 1st Worcester's the first attempt at crossing the Canal, but they were unable to penetrate the defences. The delay was a short one, but only because the Germans retired, the Canal having become a salient that they could not afford to defend. By 17 October Livesay was reporting that the enemy were withdrawing on his Brigade's front and he put out patrols which crossed the Canal, entering and capturing Douai. On 26 October, with the Divisional front narrowing to the extent that only the 24th Brigade was at the front, Livesay and his men were relieved. They moved forward again on 8 November and were holding the Corps front when hostilities ceased.

From April 1919 Livesay took command of the 10th Royal West Surreys, stationed at Lindlar in Germany as part of the Army of Occupation. He was awarded the CMG on 3 June 1919 and, on his return to England in July, was appointed temporary Brigadier-General whilst commanding 1st Infantry Brigade at Aldershot. That same month Livesay was also awarded the American Distinguished Service Medal from the President of the USA for his services at the American Staff School, and was also appointed Vice President of the Army Rugby Union. He relinquished his temporary rank in November 1920, and retired on 17 September 1921 with the honorary rank of Brigadier General. He died at home at Magham Down, Manor House, Sussex on 23 March 1946.

LANCE SERGEANT FRED STANLEY LOWE

Fred Stanley Lowe was born at St Stephens, Canterbury, Kent in the summer of 1888. His father Tucker Lowe and mother Clara lived in Hackington near Canterbury, running the Tyler Hill village Post Office. His father was a former tile and brick maker, as was his father before him. His grandfather's birth was registered using the surname 'Low', although he was using the version 'Lowe' by 1861. Fred Stanley Lowe had five brothers, Thomas, Albert, Edward, Tucker and William. He married Helen, known as Ellen, on 8 April 1912 in Dublin and they were to have two sons, born in 1913 and 1914. When he enlisted he gave his occupation as that of gardener.

The first record found of Lowe playing cricket was in 1911 for Stanley Cochrane's club, Woodbrook Park Club and Ground in Wicklow, Ireland, against Hampshire, at which time he was a Corporal with the Buffs. By the time he played for the Kent 2nd XI in 1914 he had joined the Reserve to see out his service. Wisden recorded that he was a promising fast bowler, and he appears to have been a useful lower order bat as well. In the match against Staffordshire at the end of July he top scored in Kent's first innings with 35 out of 113 whilst batting ninth. His time with Kent was brief, his last match being a two day affair against Essex at Leyton, finishing on 4 August. That same day the orders to mobilise reached the 1st Battalion the Buffs (East Kent Regiment) at Fermoy.

Lowe had first served with the 1st Volunteer Battalion of the Buffs, part of the Militia, although the date he joined is unclear. In April 1906 he was attested to join the 7th Dragoons at their Depot in Canterbury, but he bought himself out for £10 after just 44 days service. Why he left is a mystery, but the following year he had a change of heart and joined the regulars again, this time enlisting with the Buffs (East Kent Regiment) Depot at

Canterbury on 4 March as a Private. After a promotion to Lance Corporal he was posted to the 1st Battalion, reverting to the rank of Private, but promoted to Lance Corporal in June 1908 and Corporal in September 1910.

When he was transferred to the Reserve on 20 July 1912, Lowe's papers noted he was trained in regimental transport duties, and was planning to reside in Bray, Ireland, having married in Dublin just three months prior. His conduct sheet shows he was somewhat high spirited, being reprimanded five times. There were some minor infringements, one for "smoking whilst on duty in South Great Georges Street" in Dublin, but the worst was saved for 24 April 1912, just a couple of weeks after his wedding. He broke out of barracks after Tattoo Roll Call remaining absent for 11 hours. Perhaps he was missing his newly wed wife, but whatever the reason he was docked a day's pay.

When the Army mobilized, Lowe was one of 554 reservists recalled to the 1st Buffs. The battalion was attached to 16th Brigade in 6th Division, and left Ireland for Cambridge on 12 August, arriving a week later. With so many reservists in the ranks, a period of training was required to sharpen the men's skills, after which Lowe sailed with his unit on 7 September from Southampton to St Nazaire to join the BEF. Trains then carried the men through Nantes, Angers, Tours, Verdun, Paris and Mortcerf, a journey lasting 26 hours, which was followed by an eight day march. Overnight stops were made in temporary billets as they crossed France, once in a cowshed, and often with Belgian refugees for company.

Lowe reached the line on 21 September as the Buffs relieved the Royal Fusiliers at Vailly on the Aisne. Following the Retreat from Mons, the British had pushed the Germans back to the river, and the *First Battle of the Aisne* had been in progress since 13 September. The Germans soon took a chance on attacking what they rightly suspected were fresh troops in the field, but the Buffs repulsed them. They remained in these trenches until 12 October, by which time most of their Division had moved further north. Both sides were continuously trying to outflank each other, and the *Race to the Sea* carried the line ever northwards.

The Buffs were relieved on 12 October and headed for Cassel, rejoining their Division the next day. On Sunday 18 October a reconnaissance was ordered in force, and the Buffs pushed towards La Vallee and Bacquart. Lowe joined the advance from Grand Flamengrie Farm to seize the line of the Hameau de Bas to La Vallee Road. Before reaching that line the Buffs captured the village of Radinghem, near Armentières, without much opposition. Advancing across a small plateau some 300 yards wide, they came towards woods in which the Chateau de Flandres stood. It was here that Lowe and his comrades came under a heavy cross fire followed by a German attack and fierce hand to hand fighting. The Buffs were pushed back to the wood at the side of the plateau later in the day.

A French postcard depicts the Buffs assault on Chateau de Flandres in which Lowe was killed

It was during this fighting that Fred Lowe was killed, the first Kent cricketer to fall in the war. Although he died in France, he is remembered on the Ploegsteert Memorial in Belgium, which was raised to those men who died in the region whose bodies were not found or marked with a grave.

LIEUTENANT CHARLES STOWELL MARRIOTT

Charles Stowell Marriott was born at Heaton Moor, Lancashire on 14 September 1895, the son of solicitor Joshua Hyde Marriott and Gertrude (née Stowell). He was sent to Ireland for his education, apparently for the benefit of his health, and attended Monkston Park School, Dublin 1904-1909, Royal School Armagh 1909-1912, making the XI in 1911, and St. Colomba's College in Dublin 1912-1913, where he was in the XI both years. He served in the St. Colomba's College Officer Training Corps (OTC) from 1912-1913, attaining the rank of Corporal and, having entered Dublin University, he joined the University OTC in March 1914.

During September 1915 Marriott applied for a commission in Stockport, his mother signing his application as his legal guardian. The following month he was appointed

temporary 2nd Lieutenant in the 21st (Reserve) Battalion Lancashire Fusiliers. He was posted to France in March 1916, joining the 16th (Service) Battalion Lancashire Fusiliers, more commonly known to its members as the 2nd Salford Pals, in recognition of its roots. The 2nd Pals had been in the *Somme* area, at Albert, for several months, and plans for the summer offensive were well underway. The battalion belonged to 32nd Division which was earmarked for an assault up the slopes approaching Thiepval, to capture the village and open the way for British control of the Pozieres-Bazentin Ridge. Marriott spent much of June in training for the assault in which his battalion would be in support to the attacking units, ready to push through when the first objectives were reached, and protect those gains against counter-attack.

Marriott at Albert, April 1916. Reproduced by the kind permission of The Fusilier Museum, Bury

The offensive was preceded by a massive artillery bombardment lasting a week, but at Thiepval the Germans were able to shelter in a number of cellars at the Chateau. The attack was delayed by poor weather, and finally set for 1 July. Marriott moved forward to the support line trenches the night before, the 2nd Pals suffering their first casualties to German shells in the process. The next day gas was released toward the enemy lines, and at 07.30 the lead units went over the top. The German gun positions were relatively undamaged from the bombardment, and men were immediately scythed down by machine-gun fire. The survivors of the lead battalions were pinned down in shell holes, communication virtually broken down. The 16th Northumberlands had been decimated and, it being clear they could not man their own line, Marriott was ordered to take his men into the front line trench. He later recalled:

"I sent a message to A Coy on our left to say what I was doing, and started to lead up a communication trench between us called Hamilton Avenue – or rather what was left of it. Gerry was plastering the whole sector with H.E., and already it was less a trench than shellholes and hummocks. Our scrambles over these were speeded by the German machine-gunners above, who weren't missing much that morning. After all these years I still clearly see certain gruesome sights, burnt into the memory, as we struggled up to the front line. Hands, feet and shin bones were protruding from the raw earth stinking

of high explosive. A smallish soldier sitting in a shellhole, elbows on knees, a sandbag over his shoulders. I lifted it to see if he were alive, and he had no head. Further on, a corporal lying doubled up and bloody; just in case anything could be done for him I bent down to raise him a little, and his head was only attached by a bit of skin. The front trench was so blown up and gouged by H.E. that only bits of it remained, and it took some time to deploy out along it.

Meanwhile I was told that a badly-wounded officer was lying in it about twenty yards along. I got to him over a great blown-in block, bullets whizzing like wasps, and found a tall young Northumberland Fusilier Lieutenant, shot through both knees, one wrist and one shoulder: the moment he got up onto the parapet the impact of the bullets had flung him backwards into the trench. I tried to bandage him up a bit (his courage was so superb I think I was weeping as I did so, which wasn't really much help) and sent an urgent call for stretcher-bearers. But there was too much to see to, I had to leave him, and never knew what happened to him. We found others like him shot straight back off the parapet, one, a sergeant, drilled through the forehead, his brains spread like hair over the back of his neck. At last we were ready, and I was bracing myself for the hideous decision to go over the top when we were saved from further massacre in the nick of time by a sweating runner with a message from the C.O. to stay put. My God, what a moment! No Man's Land, covered with bodies, was a sight I can never forget: the whole of the 16/N.F. seemed to be lying out there."

Marriott and C Company, together with A Company, manned the Northumberland line, suffering casualties all day. Meanwhile, B and D Companies were sent over the top to assist the 1st Pals, and were also cut down by the German machine-gunners, a small force managing to advance just fifty yards. The British soon realised the German machine guns had not been dislodged by the bombardment. Marriott wrote:

"Most of their machine-guns were in steel rail and concrete nests, proof against anything less than a direct hit by a 12-in., cunningly camouflaged in No Man's land, and superbly sited for crossfire."

There was no peace for Marriott that night. His Company was ordered to hold part of the line whilst the remainder of the Pals were relieved.

"At dark a few survivors and slightly wounded came in, but the dead were everywhere. We spent the night searching for the badly wounded and bringing in all we could. One of my chaps, Corporal Chidgey, carried in seven on his own back."

The following day, in addition to repairing the shell-damaged trenches, Marriott and his comrades cleared the dismembered bodies and discarded equipment of their fallen pals from the trenches, a difficult task, but one that had to be done. They were finally relieved on 3 July, but were back in the line at Ovillers within a fortnight. At the end of July Marriott left the Somme area, the entire Brigade moving north, beyond Arras, into the trenches facing Bethune, Cambrin, Cuinchy and La Bassée.

The men of 11 Platoon of the 2ⁿᵈ Pals, who survived the first day of the Somme. Marriott is seated centre. Pictured on Minden Day 1916 the men sport roses on their caps. Reproduced by the kind permission of The Fusilier Museum, Bury

At the end of August a party of four from C Company went to reconnoitre the German wire in front of the 1ˢᵗ Pals trenches, Marriott approaching the German positions with Lieutenant Smith and two NCOs. Unfortunately the Germans heard the men close to the wire, sent up a flare and opened fire. One NCO was hit and the other three men started to carry him back, when the second NCO was also hit. The two officers quickly pulled the injured men into a shell hole, where they attempted to stop the bleeding. Smith set out to crawl back and muster help, whilst Marriott tended to the wounded men and guarded their position, only fifty yards from the German trenches, a precarious position. The 1ˢᵗ Pals came to their assistance, but one of the wounded men died before they got to safety and the other before they could get him to a dressing station.

A week later a planned raid was foiled when the German wire was found intact despite shelling, and another attempt was made on the night of the 10-11 September. At 02.30 the artillery fired a short burst at the German lines, and then fired a box barrage around a party of 71 raiders under Marriott and two other officers, Smith and Foss. Two Bangalore Torpedoes were carried up and detonated to blast the wire, whilst a diversionary attack took place on their right, and a Lewis Gun team covered the left. Marriott examined the front line as far as the right communication trench, and found no one, the two dug outs in the area being empty. Several prisoners were taken on the left, but no Germans were found in the main trenches. When the recall signal was given, Marriott ensured everyone had left the enemy trenches safely before leaving himself, and the raiders made their way back through three avenues prepared through their own wire. Whereas Smith and Foss were awarded the Military Cross for the events of the past days, Marriott was perhaps unlucky not to be recognised in the same manner, only being recommended for special leave.

After a brief return to the Somme at the end of November, the Pals were withdrawn from the line and the same day Marriott was made Temporary Lieutenant. He was then appointed acting Captain whilst commanding a Company, from early December to early January, as the most severe winter to date on the Western Front settled in. When he moved to Beaumont Hamel in February, the temperatures were persisting below zero. The ground was so solid that no new trenches could be dug, and some communication trenches were too icy for use. In these conditions Marriott slipped on an ice covered board injuring his elbow, and was sent to England for treatment. Luckily there was no break and he was back in France during April.

At that time the enemy was conducting *Operation Alberich*, giving Marriott's battalion their first experience of mobile warfare as they engaged the enemy rear-guard at Savy Wood. They then moved to hold the extreme right of the British line, in outposts near the railway of St. Quentin, where Marriott was appointed acting Captain again. He led his Company as the Pals moved towards Ypres during June, but they were not destined for the main front, posted instead on the extreme north of the Western Front, on the Belgian coastline at Nieuport. Here the Allies were building troop numbers as part of the planned *Operation Hush*. It was envisaged that a landing on the Belgian coast, combined with a breakout from Nieuport and Yser, could capture the Belgian coast as far as the Dutch border. Unfortunately the Germans detected the British activity, and made a pre-emptive strike.

The 2nd Pals were at Nieuport on 22 July when a party of 120 men came under gas shelling, some showing signs of being affected. The symptoms continued after their return to camp, disclosing the presence of a new gas, generally described as smelling like mustard but not unpleasant. Men's eyes were mostly affected, but later also their mouths, throats and chests, the symptoms lasting longer in some than others. As a result of the gassing one officer and 12 men were sent to hospital. Marriott was that officer. He was sent back to England on sick leave, and returned to Dublin. His doctor wrote to the War

Office explaining Marriott was *"suffering from intense photophobia, and he will not be fit to proceed over-seas"*. In November he was noted to be suffering neurasthenia, palpitations of the heart, his hands slightly tremulous, all signs of shell shock.

Although he joined the 3rd Battalion Lancashire Fusiliers, a reserve battalion based near Withernsea, in early 1918, Marriott was not fit for overseas service. That July he was appointed to a temporary commission as Lieutenant with the RAF, and having appeared for FS Jackson's XI at Lord's, he joined the Cadet Wing in Hastings in September where he remained for the duration of the War. He was still only fit for guard duties in January 1919, and his service came to an end that April. Following his release he chose to continue his studies, and went up to Peterhouse College, Cambridge. He was a Blue in 1920 and 1921, and very successful in the University matches. Being 25 years old when he arrived at the University, he picked up the affectionate nickname of 'Father', which stuck thereafter.

Marriott's debut in county cricket was for Lancashire against Essex at Leyton, and it was incredibly the first county cricket match he had ever seen. In all he played 12 matches for the county of his birth up to 1921, but having taken up the post of Master in Modern Languages at Dulwich College, he was approached by Lord Harris to play for Kent. He initially declined but, luckily for Kent, he changed his mind and went on to play in 101 matches between 1924 and 1937, awarded his county cap in his first season. As a schoolmaster, Marriott's appearances were mostly limited to August each season, but he made a remarkable impact on the side. In his first season he topped the averages, his best performances including 10 for 110 against Hampshire and 11 for 79 against Lancashire at Dover. His personal highlight of the year though, was undoubtedly his marriage to Phyllis Madeleine Taylor in Kensington.

Marriott in the Kent XI of 1929

Marriott was able to bowl the googly, but did not use it often, and being an exponent of leg-break bowling he was inspired to write a book called "The Complete Leg-Break Bowler". He had only completed part of the book when he died, but it was published, with Ian Peebles and Richie Benaud adding contributions. Marriott played for the Gentlemen in 1921, 1931 and 1933, toured South Africa in 1924/25 with SB Joel's XI, India in 1933/34 with the MCC, and appeared in one Test Match against the West Indies in 1933 when he took 11 for 96. For Kent he took 429 wickets at an average of 20.16.

Under his guidance as master in charge of cricket at Dulwich from 1921-1926, he produced a number of first class players, and instilled a love of the game into many more boys, who affectionately knew him as 'Doggie'. During the Second World War he served as an anti-aircraft gunner in the Home Guard, answering the call to arms a second time, and turned out for the London Home Guard and Lord's cricket teams at Lord's in 1944 at the age of 47. Marriott was well known at Dulwich for his love of literature, taking on the various roles in plays that were being read, and also for his enthusiastic playing of the trombone in the school orchestra. He retired three years early from Dulwich due to ill health in 1953, and died in a nursing home in Dollis Hill 13 October 1966.

The quotes in Marriott's entry are from his unpublished account of the first day of the Somme.

MARSHAM BROTHERS

Cloudesley Henry Bullock Marsham was born on 10 February 1879 and his brother Francis William Bullock Marsham was born 14 July 1883, both at Stoke-Lyne. They were the first sons of Frances Penelope and the Reverend Cloudesley Dewar Bullock Marsham. Their father played for Oxford, MCC and England, and their uncle George Marsham, played for Kent. The family took up residence at the Rectory, Harrietsham before Cloudesley was sent to Eton in 1892. He made his first appearance at Lord's against Harrow in 1897, and in the following season's fixture he scored 53 and 31. Francis went to Eton in 1896, and was in the XI in 1901 when he scored 27 against Winchester and 61 against Harrow at Lord's, heading both the batting and bowling averages.

Apparently generations of Marshams at Eton were affectionately known as 'Slug', and the name stuck to both brothers throughout their lives. On leaving school Cloudesley went up to Christ Church College in 1898, where he was in the XI and a Blue 1900-1902, captain in the last year. Against Cambridge in 1901 he scored 100 not out, salvaging a draw, and had his BA conferred in 1903. Francis left Eton in 1901, opting for a military career rather than university, having reached the rank of Serjeant in the Eton Rifle Corps.

CAPTAIN (ACTING-MAJOR) CLOUDESLEY HENRY BULLOCK MARSHAM

Marsham made his debut for both the Kent elevens in 1900, was capped in 1902 and succeeded Burnup as captain in 1904, leading the county to the Championship in 1906. His first class career was fairly short and his last season of note was 1908, although he played in three Championship winning seasons in total, appearing several times 1909-

1910. Statistically 1908 was his best season, bringing 963 runs at an average of 26.75, and in 1908 he became the first Kent player appointed as a Test selector. Working as a Land Agent, Marsham joined the West Kent Yeomanry (WKY) as 2nd Lieutenant in August of 1902, and was promoted to Lieutenant seven years later. In 1911 he was married to Algitha Parker at Malpas in Cheshire, and Francis was best man.

Cloudesley Marsham served at Gallipoli, in Egypt and Palestine

The WKY concentrated in Canterbury days after mobilization, and moved to Westbere in November. Marsham spent those months in training, his Brigade (SEMB) agreeing to serve dismounted if it meant getting the overseas posting they craved. Orders were finally received in September, and at the end of the month the yeomen left Canterbury by train and sailed from Liverpool for *Gallipoli*. Their ship first docked at Mudros on the Isle of Lemnos, and Marsham initially stayed there with the Yeomanry Base Depot as the main force went on ahead. He joined his regiment on 14 October, twelve days after they had landed at Cape Helles, and was hospitalised ten days later although the reason why is unknown. Not long after he returned to unit, at the end of October, a terrific storm hit the area, turning from rain to sleet to snow, claiming many lives.

The SEMB came under 42nd Division which helped them settle into trench life, and within weeks Marsham joined the WKY at Fusilier Bluff. The newcomers were soon sending out patrols and harassing the Turks, as well as learning to tunnel for mining operations. One such mine dug by A Company in November ran straight into a Turk counter-mine resulting in a frantic action. When Suvla and Anzac were evacuated during December, Helles was briefly retained on the basis the British might want to resume the offensive. Marsham and the other men at Helles continued offensive operations to assist in covering the evacuation process, and were themselves evacuated from Gully Beach on 27 December.

After hot baths and some rest at Mudros, Marsham's regiment, now part of the 3rd Dismounted Brigade, departed for Egypt, where they were soon engaged on Canal defences. At the end of March, 'B' Squadron and the Machine Gun Section took over No 4 Ghurkha Post, with Marsham in command, and remained in the area until mid-April when they moved south to Suez, and later to El Shatt and El Ferdan. When the general advance on El Arish began, the regiment was transferred to Alexandria, but instead of the expected move east, the WKY sailed 125 miles west to Marsa Matruh to join the campaign against the Senussi in the *Western Desert*.

The Senussi had been driven from the coast and were by now operating well inland, but troops were sent to Matruh and Sollum, where wire defences and forts were established. Marsham stayed there for the remainder of the year, and in December began intensive infantry training as the WKY had their cavalry status removed. The changes did not stop there. A further message revealed that the WKY were to amalgamate with the Royal East Kent Mounted Rifles to form the new 10th Battalion of the Buffs. The WKY made up the new C and D Companies, Marsham within the latter.

Marsham, third from left without a cap, pictured on the Kantara Railway en route to Deir el Belah, April 1917. Reproduced by permission Kent & Sharpshooters Yeomanry Museum

The Senussi surrendered in February 1917, and Marsham was soon on his way back to Sidi Bishr, where the 10th Buffs were attached to 74th Division. On the last day of March he was granted the rank of Acting Major in advance of the Division's move into *Palestine*, the Buffs travelling to Deir el Belah on the Kantara railway.

During the First Battle of Gaza, Marsham was with the Buffs in reserve where the Division was tasked with digging a system of trenches. As the battle closed he left his unit suffering from mastoid disease and, following treatment in Egypt, returned to England during July. It was April 1918 before he was deemed fit for service, but Marsham did not return overseas and was instead attached to the RAF that October. He served with No.1 RAF Cadet Brigade at St Leonards on Sea for administration duties, was attached to Irish Command HQ in March 1919, and was disembodied the following month, transferring to the TF Reserve Depot.

In September 1921 Marsham relinquished his commission retaining the rank of Captain. He played a little cricket after the war, including one match for Kent against Nottinghamshire in 1922 in which he captained the county one last time, standing in for Troughton. He played club cricket for the Mote and remained living in Kent until his death at Wrotham on 18 July 1928 at the age of 49. His wife outlived him by some considerable time, passing away in 1972 aged 91.

MAJOR FRANCIS WILLIAM BULLOCK-MARSHAM

After leaving Eton in 1901, Francis Marsham was commissioned 2nd Lieutenant in the 7th Kings Royal Rifle Corps, a militia battalion, and was promoted to Lieutenant in July the following year. He made a single appearance for the Kent 2nd XI against Sussex at Hove in 1904, the year his brother took over the Kent captaincy, and the following season made his

first class debut for the 1st XI against Oxford at the Christ Church ground. The latter appearance was originally accredited to Cloudesley in *The History of Kent County Cricket (Harris, 1907: 404),* but it was actually Francis that played, and he likely captained the side too. He had a second shot at the University side when both he and Cloudesley appeared for MCC a few weeks later, and made 3 and 6. So ended Marsham's first-class career, although he did continue to play cricket whilst in the Army.

Francis Marsham served with the Cavalry on the Western Front 1914-1918. ©National Portrait Gallery, London

At the end of 1905 Marsham joined the regular cavalry as 2nd Lieutenant on probation with the 19th Hussars, and two years passed before he was confirmed in that rank. He was promoted to Lieutenant in May 1910 and two months later took up the position of Adjutant which he held until July 1913. With war looming, he received his promotion to Captain on 25 June 1914.

Marsham's whereabouts in the early part of the war are unclear. The Squadrons of the 19th Hussars were split up and attached to different Divisions, and he does not seem to have been with any of them. His papers reveal he landed in France on 11 September, after the majority of his regiment, and it seems most likely he served with one of the Cavalry Brigades. He had missed the retreat from Mons, arriving just in time for the Battle of the Aisne. Marsham can be pinned down from 14 April 1915, the day the 9th Cavalry Brigade was formed at St Sylvestre Cappel, as he was appointed the Staff Captain. The Brigade, which included his old regiment, was ordered to Elverdinghe on 23 April, the day after *Second Ypres* began.

In the role of Staff Captain, Marsham liaised with Divisional HQ to organise billeting as the Brigade moved around the Ypres line, digging new trench-works and holding them as and when required. The brigade took part in the Battle of Frezenburg Ridge, and on 24 May was ordered to defend the line between the Lille and Menin gates when the Germans released a gas cloud on a 7km front. The line around Ypres was generally withdrawn after counter-attacks failed to regain lost ground. Marsham signed the war diary that month as acting Brigade-Major, but had reverted to Staff Captain by 12 June when he greeted the Bedfordshire Yeomanry as the brigade's third battalion.

Having spent several months supplying digging parties and practising schemes, Marsham was able to organise the route marches that took the brigade to a position close to *Loos* on the eve of the battle, 24 September. The next day, as information came in confirming a successful attack, the brigade moved into a position of readiness at Bois des Dames. There was, however, no success for cavalry to exploit and after several days waiting, watching prisoners and the wounded pass through, they were withdrawn. On 19 October orders were received to proceed to winter billets, and Marsham received a Mention in Despatches, announced in the Gazette on 1 January 1916. He received a second MID later in the war.

On 5 February 1916 Marsham took up the position of Brigade Major with 1st Cavalry Brigade, having held the same position on a temporary basis with 1st Dismounted Brigade during the previous months. In his new role Marsham would execute his CO's orders by planning the Brigade's operations, and had frequent contact with the men in the trenches, key in keeping morale high. He was awarded the Military Cross in the King's Birthday Honours during June, and soon joined the masses gathering in the *Somme* region for the summer offensive.

Despite hopes that the cavalry would push through and seize the Bapaume road, Marsham found his Brigade in the same position as all the cavalry units in the first week of July – waiting around with little to do. The horses were in fact seen as a strain on water supply and the railways, which found transporting bulky forage an unnecessary burden. On 4 July Marsham's brigade was sent back to the Abbeville region. When the offensive was resumed by Fourth Army on 14 July, the cavalry were still included in the plans. 1st Cavalry Division was to attack Leuze Wood, but Marsham's brigade was able to do little more than send patrols out. As the *Somme Continued* the story was always the same – no opportunities for the cavalry, and the *Battle of Flers-Courcelette* in September proved no different.

After spending winter in coastal billets Marsham's brigade moved to the front to take part in the *Arras* offensive on 9 April, but determined German resistance and the snow put paid to hopes of cavalry action. Two months later Marsham was appointed GSO2 with the 2nd Cavalry Division, and remained out of the line from July until mid-October which gave him time to get to grips with his new position.

The Division was involved in the offensive at *Cambrai* which started on 20 November, when the first day's success was not sufficiently exploited by the cavalry, and was also involved in the operations to capture Bourlon Wood days later. When the Germans delivered their counter-attack on 30 November, Marsham helped organise operations as the cavalry assembled in readiness to support the Guards Division holding Bourlon Wood, but they were eventually ordered back. His role throughout the offensive included issuing Divisional Orders to the individual brigades, and he had a busy time of it. As the line settled again, the cavalry went into winter billets.

Marsham was appointed temporary Major in February and joined the Division's move to Quesmy, just south-west of St Quentin, in mid-March. This left him perfectly positioned for the German bombardment that marked the opening of the German *Kaiserschlacht* on 21 March. The following day he was temporarily appointed GSO1 as the Battle of St Quentin was fought. Dismounted brigades were sent to help where they could, but several days later they were 'mounted' again, to hold bridges and drive back hostile patrols, under orders not to engage in an infantry battle. As the front was pushed back, the Division joined the French in holding the line near Montdidier before returning to Fifth Army, when Marsham reverted to GSO2.

The fighting carried on into April at considerable loss to the Division, in both men and horses. The war diary reveals another of Marsham's duties was opening an advanced report centre when the Division was in action, collecting news to report back to HQ and higher. He went higher himself during May, when he was appointed GSO2 Cavalry Corps, joining that HQ on 9 May. *The Diary of a World War I Cavalry Officer (Home, 1985: 171)* includes the entry by Home that "*Slug Marsham joined today and is taking place of Babe Nicholson*". On 3 June the Gazette announced Marsham had also been awarded the DSO.

Operation Blücher-Yorck, part of the *Kaiserschlacht*, was launched against the Allied lines at the end of May, but was held up at Belleau Wood by some of the first US troops to fight in the French part of the line. One of Marsham's first jobs was to visit the French GHQ and he brought back the welcome news that the attack had been stalled and many Germans killed. That month the flu epidemic hit both sides of the line, and Marsham fell sick for a while, as did most of the Corps HQ. Luckily the German advance was generally coming to a standstill.

As the tide turned, and the *Hundred Days Offensive* began with *Amiens* on 8 August, Cavalry Corps was with Fourth Army, ordered to gain possession of the old Amiens line and push on forward. The extent of what the cavalry could do was still limited, and they had to take on a support role more often than not. Marsham carried out his duties during the Battle of Albert and then the Battle of the Scarpe as the Corps was used to disrupt enemy communications. They then pressed on during the *Advance to the Hindenburg Line* and *Battles of the Hindenburg Line*, playing a part in the Battle of Drocourt-Queant, and the Battle of St Quentin Canal which was crossed at the beginning of October.

After fighting up to the Selle, Marsham's Corps was withdrawn. Although they had captured 500 prisoners, 10 guns and 16 machine-guns, they had suffered heavily, and the supply of ammunition and rations took precedence over forage for horses. The Corps moved back into the fray on 12 October, and joined the advance *Beyond the Hindenburg Line*. During the *Final Push* Cavalry Corps was attached to Fifth Army, and the Divisions of the Corps were all active on 11 November. On receiving news of the Armistice at 07.00 Marsham was probably involved in sending despatch riders to order them to stand fast. Luckily they were all informed in time.

Marsham took up an appointment at the War Office in February 1919, as Deputy Assistant Adjutant General, helping out with all the administration that the end of the War brought with it. The position came with the temporary rank of Major which was made substantive six months later when he became a GSO2. In November 1921 Marsham joined the 3rd Dragoon Guards and six months later was appointed to the Staff College. Just several weeks earlier, on 19 April, he had married Finovala Marianne Eleanor Maclean in Elham. In October the 3rd Dragoon Guards was amalgamated with the 6th Dragoon Guards (Carabiniers) to become the 3/6th, and Marsham became a Major of the new unit. He left the Staff College in January 1925 and six months later he was made Brevet Lieutenant-Colonel, which was followed by promotion to Lieutenant-Colonel in July 1927 when he was given command of the 3rd Carabiniers, which was a restyled 3/6th regiment.

Memorials were still being erected in the memory of those who died in the War, and during November 1928 one was unveiled at La-Ferte-sous-Jouarre by the Imperial War Graves Commission to commemorate BEF operations between August and October 1914. A Guard of Honour of about 110 officers and men was present, representing all regiments and corps that participated in the fighting, and Marsham attended as the representative for the cavalry. In October 1931 he was promoted to Colonel and given command of the 5th Cavalry Brigade (TA) and six months later was appointed temporary Brigadier to command the 1st Cavalry Brigade, retaining that position until 1936. In 1935 he was made ADC to King George V which was a short lived role as the King died the following spring. Marsham attended the funeral and the Coronation the following year and continued as ADC to the new monarch until 1938.

From 1939–1940 Marsham was Chief Umpire to the 1st Armoured Division, and in 1940 joined the Home Guard as a Staff Officer GSO1. Having been re-granted the temporary rank of Brigadier he was County Commandant of the Berkshire Cadets from 1942 through to 1946. He lived to the grand old age of 88 and died at Maidstone three days before Christmas 1971.

MASON BROTHERS

Ann and Richard Smith Mason, a solicitor, had six sons of whom three played first class cricket. The two who played for Kent were John Richard, better known as Jack, who was born 26 March 1874 and James Ernest born on 29 October 1876. Their older brother Charles played for MCC, and all three brothers represented Blackheath. Jack and James were both educated at Abbey School, Beckenham, Jack going on to Winchester in 1887 whilst James went to Tonbridge School in 1892. Jack was in the Winchester XI from 1890-1893, as captain in his final year. Against Eton in 1892 he led by example, scoring 141 and 71, taking 8 wickets and holding three catches. In his last year he also played rackets in the Princes' Pair. James showed great promise as a batsman at Tonbridge, but did not share the success his older brother had. When he left the school he immediately began studying for a legal career.

Jack also became a solicitor, but had great success as a cricketer. He made his Kent debut the summer he left Winchester, received his Cap later in the year and went on to make 300 appearances. In 1895 he made over 1,000 runs, a feat he repeated the following six seasons. He toured Australia with Stoddart 1897/98, playing in all five Tests, but never appeared in a home Test. One of Wisden's Cricketers of the year in 1898, he was appointed Kent Captain and the following season became the first Kent player to score 100 runs and take 10 wickets in a match, something he achieved four times. He was also the first Kent player to perform the double in all matches, with 1,561 runs and 118 wickets in 1901. He gave up the captaincy in 1901 to concentrate on his work.

James was still playing cricket, but mainly with his brothers for Blackheath. He made his first appearance for Kent 2nd XI in 1897, playing five times over three years, coincidentally against Sussex on each occasion. His only 1st XI match was in 1900 against Yorkshire at Headingley, when he scored a single on his only trip to the wicket.

LIEUTENANT-COLONEL JAMES ERNEST MASON

Admitted as a solicitor in April 1899, Mason was in practice at Maidenhead and Bourne End for some years before joining Messrs Amery Parkes & Co in London during 1912. He was 38 years old when war was declared but offered his services straight away; joining the RNVR in October for the duration of hostilities and, with the rank of Able Seaman, was posted to an Anti-Aircraft unit. Several of his brothers were serving with the Army Service Corps (ASC) and, keen to join them, Mason asked permission to leave. He was discharged on 31 March 1915 and, after arranging to leave his practice, he applied to the War Office for a commission in the ASC, and was appointed temporary Lieutenant from 4 June 1915. He commenced duties with the Farmers Committee in London, and the Forage Committee which was responsible for organizing feed for men serving abroad as well as the thousands of horses used by the Army.

His Colonel put him forward for promotion in September on account of his important duties and responsibilities as Chief Accountant of the whole area. Whilst that was being considered Mason applied for permission to give up his position, with a view to serving abroad, even asking for leave to obtain the necessary clothes. He was told to report on 1 January 1916 and be prepared for immediate embarkation for France, but his Colonel was not prepared to lose him and persuaded him to stay, making him Assistant Area Administrator. He also pushed for Mason's promotion which was granted, and he became temporary Captain, backdated to December 1915.

In January Mason moved to Reading when the Accounts Branch of the Central Southern Area Forage Committee relocated, and continued his work from there. His position involved keeping the accounts for the purchasing of feedstock such as hay for animals, and farm produce like potatoes for the Army. There were hundreds of thousands of troops to be fed, and a huge amount of animals. The Forage Committee was represented by both farmers and the War Office in an attempt to co-ordinate supply, and the Army purchased the forage at negotiated prices, and imported the difference in what was required. Three years into the war, Britain alone had purchased 591,000 horses.

Mason contracted influenza in April, and spent some time at the Queen's Hotel recovering, but was soon back to work. He was still harbouring a desire to serve at the front and made another application for an overseas posting during June 1916. This time his Colonel decided to grant him his wish. He forwarded the application on, along with a glowing reference. It was, however, decided that a man of Mason's ability was too valuable to lose, and he was again talked out of leaving. In continuing his work he earned a further promotion to the rank of acting Major in June 1917, and that was substantiated in May 1918. In September he took over as Area Administrative Officer of Eastern section, Forage Branch of the ASC, and was appointed acting Lieutenant-Colonel for the remainder of the war.

In March 1919 Mason was given a week of leave to make arrangements to return to civilian work, and relinquished his commission the following month. During June he received the news that he was being awarded the OBE for services rendered during the War, and *The Register of Tonbridge School (Furley, 1951: 211)* notes that he was also Mentioned in Despatches. Having spent the previous four years in a senior administrative role, his return to civilian work was perhaps not so hard a change as for some, and he was soon back working with Amery Parkes & Co in London. In 1934 he was married to Violet Goodman Armsden, but died just four years later at the age of 61 at South Beddington, Wallington. In May 1944, his son Major John Ernest Mason was killed in action at Anzio.

LIEUTENANT JOHN RICHARD MASON

We left Jack Mason as he gave up the Kent captaincy, although he still played when he could. He toured the USA with Kent in 1903, topping the batting averages, and played a number of times during each of the Championship winning years of 1906, 1909, 1910 and 1913. When Dillon or Marsham were unavailable, Mason often stood in as Captain,

and in 1909 he headed the national batting averages, his 783 runs at average 65 greatly contributing to the title win. He played his final game for Kent in July 1914 against Gloucestershire at the Mote.

Jack Mason was involved in the war on U-Boats whilst serving with the RNVR

At forty years old, Mason was outside the age limits for volunteers in August 1914, and it was not until 1917 that he joined the RNVR, appointed temporary Sub Lieutenant and posted to Tarlair. HMS Tarlair was the base of the Hydrophone Service, hidden away in the fishing village of Aberdour in Fife, and in commission from Spring 1917. The hydrophone was a listening device, using a type of microphone to pick up the sounds beneath the surface of the sea. Men were trained to listen to the sounds by use of gramophone records, study the graphs produced, and pinpoint German submarines. Drifters, a type of ship, had sets attached to them, the microphones relaying sounds through cables to the vessels where 'listeners' examined the results. There were also shore stations dotted around the coast and several in the Mediterranean, from which cables were run from between two and ten miles out to sea, fanning out to cover a wide area.

Mason, like all the men joining the service from spring 1917, received his initial training at Tarlair. This would have commenced with the theory behind the invention, followed by practical training which included listening both on land and at sea. This could be hit and miss. Some men found that the U-Boat they had identified was in fact a sperm whale, but there were successes, and submarines were identified and destroyed as a result. It was highly important work, especially with the increase in German submarine activity about the time Mason joined the service. Once trained, he was posted to Freshwater on the Isle of Wight, one of the shore stations. The cables from his post went out into the Channel, playing their part in the sea defences.

On 7 June 1918 Mason was appointed temporary Lieutenant, but the following month he applied to join the RAF. It is likely he was drawn to the newly created service by the recruitment campaign, but he was informed he could not be spared for transfer. The fight against German submarine tactics was still not won, and the Hydrophone Service, like the RAF, was expanding. During 1918 ten new shore stations were authorized and by the end of the war there were 120 officers attached to Tarlair, of which number Mason was one, and they were in charge of some 650 ratings. Approximately 1,500 ships were supplied with hydrophones and almost 4,000 officers and ratings had attended the hydrophone training establishment at Hawkcraig. Once the war was over, Mason returned to Scotland to be demobilized, the Officers' Mess near Tarlair being used for that purpose.

Mason officially left the service on 26 January 1919, and that May was playing for Lionel Robinson's XI against the Australian Imperial Forces at Attleborough. The match was 12 a side, and seven of his team mates are also subjects of this book. Both Jack Bryan and Gerald Hough made their first class debuts that day, as Mason bowed out of first class cricket. There were subsequent appearances for Band of Brothers and Lord Harris' XI, and his association with Kent was far from over. He was appointed to the Committee in 1919, serving through the 1920s and 1930s, and he was President in 1938. Twenty years later, on 15 October 1958, Jack Mason died at his home in Sussex at the age of 84.

CAPTAIN WALTER TURNER MONCKTON

Walter Turner Monckton was born in Kent on 17 January, 1891 at Plaxtol, Wrotham where his parents, Frank William Monckton and Dora Constance (formerly Golding), ran a paper manufacturing business. Monckton's education began as a boarder at Knoll School,

Aspley Heath, where he became head boy. He then attended Harrow 1904-1910, and was a member of the XI, keeping wicket against Eton in 'Fowler's Match' in 1910. Having played fairly regularly for Harrow that summer, Monckton played twice for the Kent 2nd XI during August, in the home and away fixtures against Essex. He won an exhibition to Hertford College at Oxford, but chose to enter Balliol College as a commoner instead, and during his time there he became good friends with the Prince of Wales.

A young Walter Monckton, picture courtesy The Roger Mann Collection

At Oxford from 1910 to 1913, Monckton became President of the Oxford Union in his last year and, although not a Blue, he did play cricket for Kent 2nd XI again during the summer holidays of 1911 and 1913, and for a combined Oxford and Cambridge XI against Army and Navy. His BA and MA were not conferred until 1918 when he was actually serving in France. He was married in July 1914 to Mary Adelaide Somes at Igtham, weeks before the declaration of war. Whatever plans the couple had were about to be rudely interrupted.

Although specific dates are not available, it is known that Monckton volunteered not long after the declaration of war, but was rejected by the army, navy and RFC on account of defective vision in one eye. On the advice of a medical officer of the Royal West Kent Regiment (RWK) he read the eye tests with his good eye, memorized the letters to repeat for his bad eye, and passed his medical at Gravesend in May 1915. He would later wear a monocle in the trenches. Monckton was commissioned 2nd Lieutenant and directed to the 3/4th battalion, signing his agreement to serve overseas. The battalion was however destined to remain in the UK until mid-1917, as its members anxiously awaited a posting.

During his time in England Monckton held temporary appointments as Lieutenant and Captain, was made Adjutant in February 1917 and promoted to Lieutenant in May, with precedence from the previous June. The 67th Division was broken up in May and, whereas some battalions were disbanded, the 3/4th finally received its orders for France. In the position of Adjutant, Monckton would have been involved in organising the move from Canterbury on the last day of the month, as the battalion embarked from Southampton to Le Havre. The 3/4th were temporarily attached to the 9th Division in the Arras area, and Monckton was among the first to be trained in the line. The first weeks were reasonably quiet, although the battalion suffered its first casualties, and Monckton was admitted to hospital from 29 June to 7 July for reasons unknown.

During July the 3/4th was attached to 17th Division as a Pioneer battalion and began work on improving communication trenches with No1 NZ Tunnelling Company. Monckton was appointed Acting-Captain in August when the battalion ceased their pioneer role, and days later they went into the line as an infantry unit for the first time. Whilst the men got several trench-tours under their belts, Monckton was based at Cadiz Trench with HQ. The organizational skills that he displayed throughout his life were of great use in arranging the battalion's affairs. Orders for reliefs were made with great precision, and he also used his talents as defending officer in courts martial.

Monckton organized the battalion's move to Ypres during October, whilst *Third Ypres (Passchendaele)* was moving into its third and final phase. Positioned north-east of Langemarck the 3/4th was detailed for work under RE supervision, constructing roads between Pilckem Ridge and Langemarck Church. The men were still within range of the enemy, and twenty casualties were suffered in twelve days as a result of shelling. On 9 November the 3/4th was moved into the front line where a further thirty casualties were suffered in the space of four days through shelling and sniping. Monckton assumed temporary command of the battalion whilst the CO was on leave, and during his watch the 3/4th captured their first German prisoner.

On 14 November Monckton relinquished both the position of Adjutant and the acting rank of Captain. This was perhaps due to nervous exhaustion which he suffered from about this time, something that would afflict him throughout his life, and which on this occasion was seemingly caused by the stresses of war. He was Mentioned in Despatches in December, at which time the 3/4th moved to Flesquières a few miles south-west of *Cambrai*, where the line was settling after the German counter-attack. During January the battalion received the news it was to be disbanded, and the majority of the men were dispersed to other battalions of the RWK. Monckton however was attached to the 9th West Riding Regiment at the beginning of April, as second in command.

Monckton's new appointment coincided with the German spring offensive, the *Kaiserschlacht*, and his new brigade had suffered badly during the initial German advances. They were situated in the Ancre Valley, and Monckton took temporary command of the battalion whilst the CO did likewise with the brigade, as reinforcements arrived and the units were reorganised. The battalion went into the line on the high ground overlooking Beaumont Hamel on 15 April, and with concerns the Germans might be planning a further advance, Monckton joined parties of officers reconnoitring the front line. At the end of the month the battalion went into reserve and groups of Americans were attached to gain practical experience of British methods.

Back in the line during May, the battalion war diary entries made by Monckton make reference to the persistent heavy shelling and use of gas by the enemy. Just two weeks later he was transferred to the 17th Division HQ where he was made Education Officer, and remained in that role for the remainder of the war. He was demobilized in February 1919 and awarded the Military Cross in June as part of the King's Birthday Honours. In September 1920 Monckton was officially transferred to the Territorial Force Reserve, back with 4th Battalion RWK, and promoted to Major during October.

During the last months of 1914 when he been unable to enlist, Monckton had taken the preliminary law exams, and he was called to the bar at the Inner Temple in 1919. He soon acquired a large practice, took silk in 1930, and was appointed Attorney-General to the Duchy of Cornwall in 1932. The Prince of Wales became King Edward VIII early in 1936, and he and Monckton were good friends, having been contemporaries at University. Monckton was the first person Edward knighted when he became King, almost slicing his ear off with the sword when dubbing him. He is said to have quipped "Well Walter. We did not manage that very well, but neither of us had done it before."

As the year progressed the nation was gripped by the abdication crisis, and Monckton wrote the abdication speech the King read to the nation. He was also on the guest list when Edward married Wallis Simpson in France the next summer. During WW2 he worked in various roles for Chamberlain and then Churchill, travelling to the Soviet Union on a propaganda mission, working in Egypt, and attending the Potsdam Conference as the British delegate on the Reparations Commission. He was elected MP for Bristol West in 1951 and appointed Minister of Labour in Churchill's government. Eden wanted Monckton to be his Minister of Defence in 1955, but Monckton disagreed with the policy on Suez and was instead made Paymaster General. He was created Viscount Monckton of Brenchley in 1957, was President of the MCC in 1956-1957 and held many other public positions. Monckton died on 9 January 1965 at his home in Sussex, having been ill for some time.

AIRCRAFT MECHANIC 1ST CLASS – PERCIVAL ERNEST MORFEE

Percival Ernest Morfee, known as 'Pat', was born in Ashford on 2 May 1886, the son of George Walter and Catherine Ann Morfee. His mother was a dressmaker and his father had been a pub landlord but not long after he was born, Morfee senior was working for the South Eastern Railway Company (SER). When Morfee left school two of his brothers were also working for the SER, and he followed suit, taking up employment as a coach maker. The railway works at Ashford had grown in size over the preceding years, building locomotives and carriages, and the New Town area that housed the workforce was fairly self-sufficient.

Pat Morfee served with the RFC in France

Morfee was employed as a Young Player at the Tonbridge Nursery in 1907 and made his debut for the 2nd XI that year, taking five wickets in the Sussex first innings and four in the second. The second stream fixture list was limited until 1911 when Kent first participated in the Minor Counties Championship, giving him the opportunity to play more often. His first class debut came against Middlesex at Lord's in May 1910 and he marked the occasion by bowling Pelham Warner for 0 in both innings. In the first innings he and Blythe bowled unchanged, and he took 4 for 71 as Kent won by an innings. He played in ten Championship games in total, across the 1910 and 1911 seasons, and in 1912 appeared against the South African tourists. A move north saw him playing for Dunfermline, and also in the Scotland side that played Northants in August 1913, when he claimed four wickets including that of Claud Woolley.

On the outbreak of war Morfee was 30 years old and he did not join up until February 1916 as conscription was introduced. He enlisted in the RFC on the last day of the month as an Air Mechanic 2nd Class, and his papers show his civilian occupation as 'Driver'. Many of the cricketers' service papers throw up a question or two and Morfee's are no different. There is one reference that he served in France from March 1917, but another that he was admitted to hospital in Etaples in January 1917 some two months earlier suffering from a fever. The next reference to him is at the end of June 1917 when he was admitted to a convalescent hospital in Etaples, and within a week transferred to another at Bayeux. In August 1917 Morfee was discharged to his unit at St. Omer, which was No.1 Aircraft Depot (AD).

The two ADs at St Omer and Candas were fixed supply and repair depots. Due to erosion rates a large amount of new aircraft were required in France each month to keep the number in use at a steady level. The Depots maintained the operational effectiveness of the RFC during the Somme and then *Third Ypres* whilst Morfee was employed at St Omer. During September, the month after Morfee returned from hospital, 930 new aircraft were issued and over 200 reconstructed and erected. The men worked day and night to achieve this and by October new Aeroplane Supply Depots (ASDs) were created next to each AD, responsible for receipt of new aircraft, and repairs.

Morfee was promoted to Air Mechanic 2nd Class from 1 November and on 1 April 1918 became a member of the RAF when it was created by the amalgamation of the RFC and RNAS. There were already plans to move the Depots nearer to the Channel Ports, and the German Spring Offensive, the *Kaiserschlacht*, gave those plans a little more urgency. During April the operations at St Omer were transferred to Guines, and it is about this time that Morfee's papers suggest he left France. This is perhaps a red herring as he was transferred from 2 ASD to 1 Aerial Range in December 1918, and 2 ASD was obviously still in France. So it seems perhaps that Morfee was in France before 1917 through to the end of the War, although his whereabouts cannot be established for the whole period he was there.

In January 1919 Morfee was back in the UK and was married to Ann March Miller in Dunfermline. He was transferred to the RAF Reserve the following month, and in April 1920 was deemed discharged from service. He played no first class cricket after the War, but had spells as the professional at Nelson, Todmorden and Accrington in the Lancashire League between 1919 and 1931. In 1937, at the age of 51, he was the club professional for Darlington CC, and it was in Darlington that Percy Morfee died on 12 February 1945.

ACTING LIEUTENANT-COLONEL FRANK PENN

Frank Penn Jr was born at Owsden in Suffolk on 18 August 1884, son of Frank Penn, who played for Kent 1875 to 1881 and was Club President in 1905. His mother, Grace E Penn, died in 1900, two years before he embarked on a military career. He initially joined the Militia as 2nd Lieutenant with the 7th Battalion Royal Fusiliers (City of London) Regiment on 8 May 1902, perhaps encouraged by the national support for the war in South Africa. At this time his father was living at Burlingham Hall, Norwich, but later moved to Bifrons, Canterbury, and in November Frank Jr transferred to be 2nd Lieutenant in the Royal East Kent (Duke of Connaught's Own) Mounted Rifles, part of the Imperial Yeomanry.

Penn made his Kent 2nd XI debut in July 1903 and failed to score a run in either innings at Leyton. The following month he was in the MCC side playing Norfolk at Lakenham, and was bowled by his cousin, Eric Penn, who was killed in France in 1915. His 1st XI debut was made at the Mote in 1904 against Worcester, his only other first class appearance that season being against Notts at Trent Bridge. He played three more times in 1905, against MCC, Oxford and Lancashire, and made 43 against the University, his highest score for Kent. The following year he scored a century in each innings, 101 and 123, for Household Brigade against the Royal Artillery at Chelsea. Penn transferred to the Household Cavalry in January 1905, joining the 2nd Life Guards Regiment, part of the regular army. Promoted to Lieutenant a year later, he served as Assistant Adjutant from 1907-1909, was promoted to Captain in 1910, and served as Adjutant from that year to 1913.

Frank Penn served on the Western Front 1914 to 1918

When the BEF was mobilised in August 1914, memories of riots during the strikes of 1911 and 1912 gave rise to concerns of potential unrest in London. For this reason the 1st and 2nd Life Guards and Royal Horse Guards were stationed in the London district, and did not form part of the BEF. Instead, each of the three regiments contributed one squadron towards a Household Composite Regiment, which served with the 4th Cavalry Brigade. Penn was in the squadron contributed by the 2nd Life Guards, and arrived in France on 16 August, serving with the Composite Regiment until November, when it was broken up. He was to see much action in that short space of time.

The Regiment reached Saultain on 23 August, but had to evacuate two days later under pressure from the enemy. Caught up in the retreat from *Mons to the Marne*, they were briefly involved in the Battle of Le Cateau. The British withdrew from this action just in time, and Penn's regiment helped to protect General Snow's Fourth Division all night, as the retreat continued. A nasty rear-guard action was fought at Vendhuile, and Penn then passed through Cressy and Montepilloy, reaching Lognes at the outskirts of Paris on 3 September. As the French counter-attacked at the Battle of the Marne, the Germans were forced back, and the BEF turned to advance.

Penn crossed the Marne at Azy on 9 September, and the British pushed on for five days before meeting stiff resistance at Pargnan. The Germans had dug in, and the British did likewise, the battle line spreading northwards in the *Race to the Sea*. From 10 October the regiment became part of 2nd Cavalry Division, and within a week moved north to Messines where the Division was concentrating. The following day, 19 October, marked the opening of the first battle of *Ypres*, and the cavalry men soon found themselves being used as infantry to help resist enemy attacks. On the last day of the month the Germans shelled the trenches east of Wytschaete and Penn's Regiment joined the British counter-attack. The following day they were forced to fall back, digging in on the ridge to the west. Penn remained in the line in this sector, constantly being shelled, until orders were received for the men to return to their own units.

Penn's true regiment, the 2nd Life Guards, had arrived at the front in October, and seen some action during *Ypres*. When he re-joined them on 11 November they were being used as a mobile reserve, but were put in the trenches on the Zillebeke Ridge a week later. As *Ypres* came to a close, the Life Guards returned to Eecke to refit and reorganize – winter was approaching, and shelter had to be arranged for the horses. The men were kept busy training, with the occasional order to 'stand to', though nothing came of it. Penn was back in the trenches of Zillebeke for a while during February, working to improve the works in knee deep water, whilst avoiding snipers. A letter appeared in the *Evening Telegraph* toward the end of the month, written by "a well-known county cricketer" at the front. It included the following:

> In the 2d Life Guards Frank Penn, who has played for Kent, and who is a prolific scorer for the Household Brigade, is going strong. He had his trench blown up the other day, and was unconscious for nearly an hour, and had to be carried back. But his men went on fighting, and when he came to he got on with it again, and at night retook his trench, and never went to hospital for a minute. He is as silent and determined as ever he was when he was waiting for the right ball to spank past cover.

The Life Guards were trained to act as dismounted troops as trench warfare took a grip, and during *Second Ypres* were used to dig trenches near the front. The battle had seen the use of chlorine gas, and the men soon received instruction in the use of gas masks. Another German gas attack during the Battle of Frezenburg Ridge in May, forced a gap in the line, and the Life Guards were part of the reinforcements rushed forward to the trenches at Hooge to steady the situation. Several attacks were repelled but Penn and his regiment were eventually forced to withdraw to the support trenches, before being relieved. Penn was in the trenches at Sanctuary Wood in June when the regiment's trenches came under heavy shell fire, but the greater part of the remainder of the year was spent in training and providing working parties.

The year 1916 began with a Mention in Despatches (MID) for Penn, and he spent some time in command of a dismounted company in the line ten miles north of Loos. He received a second MID in June, but the year was a fairly quiet one for his regiment, and they took part in no major engagements. At the end of June he joined the officers as they went to view the British bombardment prior to the *Somme* offensive, but subsequent events gave no opportunity for the cavalry to exploit. To keep the horses exercised and the men's cavalry skills sharp, a number of events were organised in September. Penn, by now the only officer of the regiment who had been out through the entire campaign, came third in an officers jumping event and was also a judge at the Divisional Competitions. He was promoted to Major in November whilst the regiment was preparing winter quarters, and took command whilst the CO was on leave. On Christmas Eve he was allowed special leave to return to England himself, owing to the serious illness of his father. Frank Penn Senior died at Canterbury on Boxing Day aged 65.

Penn was awarded the Military Cross in the New Year Honours, and returned to France on 13 January 1917. He resumed command of the Regiment and, several days later, was called upon to preside over a Field General Court Martial. Life was quiet until April when the Life Guards were brought forward during the Battle of *Arras*. They saw no specific action, but did spend four consecutive nights in the open in freezing temperatures, the conditions so bad that at least thirty horses died. The next months were spent training in the Somme area, and in August Penn was chosen for the Officers Jumping category of that year's Divisional Competition. He went on to represent the Division at the Corps Show and won the open class at the Divisional Jumping competition.

The Life Guards went into winter billets at St Gratien, but an outbreak of the contagious disease '*Epizootic Lymphangitis*' led to some of the horses being destroyed. At the end of December all the regiment's horses were isolated at No. 1 Veterinary Hospital near Beauvais. Three officers and 170 other ranks duly moved to Beauvais by train on 2 January under Penn's command, and a major exercise of disinfection took place. He remained there until April when he returned to England. Over the next two months a new Guards Machine Gun Regiment was formed. It contained four battalions, three of which were made by converting the 1st and 2nd Life Guards and the Royal Horse Guards into machine-gun units, and the fourth was made up of the existing machine-gun companies of those regiments. Penn became a Major of the new regiment, but did not return to France until August.

When he joined the 4th (Foot Guards) Battalion MG Regiment at St Leger at the start of September, it was to replace the wounded second-in-command. *The Hundred Days Offensive* was underway and the battalion moved to Lagnicourt as part of the *Advance to the Hindenburg Line*, the Allies pushing to take the bank of the Canal du Nord. The companies of Penn's battalion were allocated to different brigades of the Guards Division, depending on which had need of them. They assisted in the attack on Havrincourt, part of the *Battles of the Hindenburg Line* and, during fighting around the Canal du Nord on 27 September, they provided barrage fire on the Hindenburg and Hindenburg Support Lines. The day after the Battle of Cambrai was launched the Guards Division went into the attack and Penn's battalion was employed in providing covering fire.

As the fighting continued *Beyond the Hindenburg Line* Penn crossed the River Selle and then the battalion was withdrawn from the line and moved to Boussieres where they spent the rest of the month. Moving to Villers Pol they were back in action on 4 November as the Battle of the Sambre began, doing good work in silencing German MGs although they suffered a good many casualties themselves. The advance continued daily but the enemy refused to give up easily, and just three days before the Armistice they shelled les Mottes heavily. The OC was wounded in the right wrist, and Penn was given command of the battalion and appointed acting Lieutenant-Colonel.

The battalion war diary entry for 11 November simply reads "hostilities ceased at 11.00 hours". In the days that followed Penn led the battalion through France and Belgium, finally settling in Germany at Christmas. Demobilization started in the New Year, and those that remained with the battalion returned to England on 16 March, Penn relinquishing command the following day. When the Guards marched through London the following week, as part of the victory celebrations, he rode alongside the new CO. Resuming service with the 2nd Life Guards, Penn received a third MID for his services during hostilities. The following January he was married to Audrey Lees in Northamptonshire, and retired from the Army in 1922 whilst Major and Brevet Lieutenant-Colonel.

Penn remained in the Reserve of Officers until August 1939 when he reached the age limit of liability to recall. When he died at Bawdsey Hall, Woodbridge, Suffolk on 23 April 1961 he was survived by his wife.

2ND CORPORAL ARTHUR POVEY

Arthur Povey was born in West Bromwich on 16 May 1886, the fifth child of Alfred and Sarah Ann Povey. His father was a Sad Iron Polisher, a trade that at least two of his older brothers followed their father into but, by the age of 14, Arthur was a house

painter. He took up residence at Dartford in the summer of 1908, and four years later Fred Huish, the Kent wicketkeeper, recommended Povey for employment at the Tonbridge Nursery. As there was no vacancy, and he was not Kent-born, the matter was referred to the Management Committee who decided against an appointment. Something changed, as on 27 May 1912 he played for the 2nd XI against Surrey at the Oval. In 1914 one of his six appearances was again at the Oval, when he made four stumpings and took two catches.

Arthur Povey (centre, back row) served in France with the Royal Engineers. Reproduced by the kind permission of Kent County Cricket Club

Povey was actually a recruit of Corporal Colin Blythe, applying to join the Kent Fortress Engineers in January 1915. His skills as a painter could not be tested at the Military Workshop and Blythe confirmed he should be tested by a civilian tradesman, which was duly done in Tonbridge. His application approved, Povey signed an agreement to serve overseas and was embodied as a Sapper in No.6 Company, a works company based at Southborough. Several promotions followed, to Lance Corporal at the end of January and acting 2nd Corporal within another week. Later in the year Povey married Agnes Paice in Basingstoke and on return to his unit was appointed Acting Corporal within 546th (1/6th Kent Fortress) Field Company.

The Field Company was attached to 73rd Division for Home Services from about the time Povey joined until March 1918. During September 1917 he was appointed Acting Sergeant, and in March 1918, when the 73rd Division was disbanded, he transferred to the Royal Engineer Training Depot at Chatham. On 4 April he was transferred again, this time to the BEF as 2nd Corporal, and he embarked for France. The RE Base Depot in France allotted Povey to 9 Field Company at the beginning of May and he joined his new unit in the field. This was during the *Kaiserschlacht* and so there was plenty to be done on the 4th Division front, a few miles north of Bethune. His papers show he was wounded on 10 June but as he stayed on duty it was presumably not serious. The following month he caused himself more damage when he came off his bicycle whilst on a pass to visit a local village. He spent two weeks in a Field Ambulance.

As the War entered *The Hundred Days Offensive*, Povey and 9 Field Company were involved in the *Battle of Scarpe* at the end of August, and the *Battle of Drocourt-Queant* at the start of September. As the Allies pressed on east of Amiens, the engineers began repairing rail lines and roads to ensure supply lines ran as needed. During the *Battles of the Hindenburg Line,* Povey's company had a hand in the successful crossing of Canal du Nord, as the Canadian Corps breached the enemy defences and pressed on to take Bourlon Wood and Cambrai in October. *Beyond the Hindenburg Line* the Germans fell back to the River Selle, and Povey's company helped to bridge the river during the Battle of the Selle. The Germans now fell back to the Sambre, and when the Battle of Valenciennes was fought, 9 Field Company were again involved.

Povey remained at Valenciennes after the Armistice, and returned to England in February. When the Minor Counties Championship resumed in 1920, Povey played in all of Kent's eight matches, and regularly through to 1924. His highest score of 90 was made against Bedfordshire at Tonbridge in 1921, and against Wiltshire at Swindon in 1924 he top scored for Kent in the first innings with 14 not out, two more than a young Les Ames. The first of his five 1st XI appearances was at Northampton in 1921 against a side that included former Fortress Engineer Claud Woolley. He played three more games that season and one the next, keeping wicket on several occasions, but retained as a lower order bat when Hubble was available.

Povey spent 20 years as the Cricket Professional at Tonbridge School, popular with masters and boys alike. An article appearing in the school magazine, *The Tonbridgian*, after his death recalled how he enjoyed having stories told about himself, such as:

> *The incident occurred in an away match – not against a school – early in the War. Arthur was umpiring as usual: the School XI were batting somewhat doubtfully against accurate bowling. A loud appeal for a catch at the wicket against the one batsman who had seemed likely to make runs was duly negative by Arthur. When the batsman arrived at the other end, next over, Arthur whispered "Did you hit that one Mr------?" "Yes, Arthur," was the reply. "I thought so," said Arthur with his inimitable chuckle.*

The article goes on to say that Povey was due to retire the following December, at the age of 60, and that this brought on an attack of depression, which undoubtedly contributed to his untimely death. Arthur Povey took his own life on 13 February 1946. A Memorial Service was held at the Tonbridge School Chapel ten days later.

2ND LIEUTENANT LEONARD MAURICE POWELL

Leonard Maurice Powell was born in Chiselhurst, Kent on 24 August, 1894, where his parents, Robert Leonard Powell, a hide and leather merchant and JP for the County of London, and Bessie Constance resided. Educated at Loretto School in Scotland between 1908 and 1913, he was a House Prefect and in the Cricket XI from 1911. In his last year he made 460 runs at an average of 27.05, and took 23 wickets at 9.91. Having passed his matriculation exam for Cambridge University, Powell entered Caius College and played in the Fresher and Senior trial matches. In 1914 he appeared for the Kent 2nd XI on four occasions, batting at third or fourth. He scored 76 runs in 8 innings, and his last appearance was at Leyton against Essex on 3-4 August 1914. Extremely keen on cricket, he was also a member of the MCC.

Powell was killed near Ypres in 1915. Reproduced by kind permission of Loretto School

Powell had some military experience, having been a Sergeant in the Loretto School's Officer Training Corps, and days after war was declared he joined the Public Schools Battalion. Having applied for a commission in the 3rd Battalion Gordon Highlanders in October 1914, the Medical Officer of the Army Recruiting Office in Bromley examined and declared Powell fit for service at the end of the month. Hugh K. Anderson, Master at Cambridge, confirmed his good moral character for the past year, his mother signed the forms as his guardian, and by 10 November he had been seen in Aberdeen and recommended for a commission. He was commissioned 2nd Lieutenant in the 3rd Battalion Gordon Highlanders on 18 November 1914.

After a winter spent training at Aberdeen, Powell was posted to the front to be attached to the 1st Gordon Highlanders, joining them in Flanders as part of 3rd Division on 20 May 1915 near Hooge on the Ypres front. The battalion diary recorded that the month of May had begun quietly but, a week before Powell reported for duty, they had relieved the South Lancs and found many corpses, rifles and equipment left by the West Riding Regiment in the wake of a German gas attack. *Second Ypres* was in progress, and was the first occasion the enemy used gas on a large scale. The trenches were under an almost constant bombardment, the parapets regularly blown in, and there was little peace to be had. The Highlanders made the best of the situation, sending out patrols at Hill 60 until 20 May when they were relieved by the Dorsets, marching back to billets at La Clytte where Powell and any other new arrivals were waiting to join them.

Four days after his arrival Powell joined the march to a mile west of Ypres, from where they were ordered into the line on the 26 May. The part of the line they took over was from Hooge heading southward, and the men spent much time trying to improve the state of the trench-works in spite of the German shelling. Heavy casualties were suffered on 2 June, when the battalion lost 22 men killed and 46 wounded, but it did quieten down again and the Highlanders were relieved on 7 June. The Battalion marched to bivouacs at Brandhoek, between Poperinghe and Vlamertinghe, where some men were trained for gas attacks, finding their new smoke helmets combined with respirators an efficient defence.

On 13 June Powell moved back to the town of Ypres, where the battalion was billeted. Two days later a British attack saw the German first line trenches captured, and 150 or so prisoners were brought in, the battalion war diary recording that they were of "very poor physique, dirty and undersized". Later in the day they moved forward to relieve the troops who had captured the German trenches, experiencing their first gas attack on the way, their new respirators proving to be very effective. The positions the British had won were heavily shelled throughout 17 June, the Gordon Highlanders suffering about 80 casualties. One of those casualties was Leonard Powell, killed by a shell, not a month after arriving in Flanders. His parents received a telegram on 20 June, simply saying:

"2-Lt LM Powell Gordon Highlanders was killed in action on 18ᵗʰ inst. Lord Kitchener expresses his sympathy".

Later records show he was killed on the 17ᵗʰ and not the 18ᵗʰ as stated in the telegram. Powell Senior wrote to the War Office thanking them for the telegram and a subsequent telephone call regarding his son's death:- *"the blow was a terrible one but it is shared by thousands of my fellow countrymen who are sacrificing the lives of their sons for King and Country, the greatest cause for which they are fighting".* He went on to ask if it *"is possible to find out under what circumstances he fell".* It must have been a question thousands of other parents asked. In July 1919 Lord and Lady Powell wrote to thank the King and Queen for the "beautifully worded" seal sent in memory of their son.

MAJOR HAROLD EDWARD WESTRAY PREST

Harold Edward Westray Prest was born at Beckenham on 9 January 1890, the fourth son of Emily Charlotte and Stanley Faber Prest, a Civil Engineer. His education began at Abbey School, Beckenham, where he was in the Cricket XI from 1901-1904, as Captain in the

last two years. Moving on to Malvern he was a School Prefect and in the Cricket XI 1906-08 and the Football XI 1905-07, playing alongside Frank Noel Tuff in both teams. Whilst at Malvern he was in Foster House from 1904-1908, Foster being the Rev. Henry Foster, father of the cricketing Foster brothers. One of the brothers was Geoffrey Norman Foster who was to marry Prest's younger sister, Vera.

Harold Prest, awarded the Croix de Guerre for leading his men against a German attack. Reproduced by kind permission of Hedley Prest

Proceeding to Cambridge in 1908, he joined Pembroke College and made 53 in the Freshman's match. His first class debut was for HDG Leveson-Gower's XI against Cambridge in June 1909, and a few weeks later he changed allegiance, appearing for the University in the return match and scoring 38 in each innings. The year 1909 was a memorable one for Prest, in which he gained his Cricket and Football Blues, made his Kent debut against Derbyshire at the Nevill, and was awarded his Kent Cap. He played cricket against Oxford again in 1911, and also added a Golf Blue to his collection. Against Somerset in August 1911 he scored 133, passing 1,000 first class runs in the process, and was in the side against the Australian tourists at Canterbury in 1912. Although not a bowler, he did actually send down five balls for Kent in 1911, claiming the wicket of George Leach at the tail end of the Sussex order, giving him an impressive bowling average of 4.00!

Prest joined the Royal Berkshire Regiment at Reading on 4 September 1914, and was posted to the 3rd Battalion four days later. He was quickly promoted to Lance Corporal and on 21 November was commissioned 2nd Lieutenant on probation within the same battalion. Based at Portsmouth, Prest attended a Machine Gun course at nearby Hayling Island during November, where he was instructed on the old Maxim guns. During 1915 he attended another course, this time on the new Vickers guns at the Machine Gun School at Grantham in Lincolnshire. He was confirmed in his rank during December 1915 and promoted to Lieutenant effective 1 January 1916. In due course Prest was posted to France, joining the 2nd Royal Berkshire on 16 May at Albert. He then attended two more courses, one on bombing followed by a month at the 4th Army Infantry School.

The 2nd Royal Berkshire remained in the Somme area in the build-up to the summer offensive, having been chosen to take part in the offensive. Battalions typically left a number of men and officers with the Transport during an attack, so that in the event of a disaster the remaining core could rebuild the unit. On 1 July 1916 when the *Somme* offensive was launched, Prest was one of those with the Transport, which would suggest he did not go over the top. The 2nd Berkshire's objective was Ovillers, just north of the Albert to Bapaume road, and they attacked at 07.30. The battalion diary recorded an *"intense rifle and machine gun fire which prevented any of their waves reaching the enemy's lines"*. That day the 8th Division lost 218 out of 300 officers, and 5,274 out of 8,000 men. They were withdrawn from the campaign, and Prest moved into billets at Allouagne, where the battalion took in drafts and began rebuilding.

After several weeks the 2nd Berkshire moved to the line near the old Loos battlefield which, although quieter, was still littered with corpses from 1915. Prest remained there until October when the Division was ordered to return to the Somme sector. His battalion had been chosen to make an attack on the strongly defended German positions centred round Zenith Trench. The first attack on 23 October failed, as did a second attempt the following day, and the battalion was taken out of the line. With 5 officers killed and 7 wounded, Prest was given a company command and appointed acting Captain. The Division was given a new commander, and he planned an attack to give the battalion back its confidence. Training was so well-rehearsed that each man knew his role backwards. The scheme took place on 4 March 1917, the objective a hill overlooking Bouchavesnes. Success would give the British a valuable vantage point.

To achieve the element of surprise, there was no preliminary bombardment, but machine-gun cover was enhanced instead. Prest joined the attack as it began at 05.15 and the first objective, Pallas Trench, was taken with little loss, the men passing on to Fritz Trench. Here they consolidated, expecting a German counter-attack. At 06.30 a message came back that all objectives were gained, and at 08.00 a second message that it was believed the line could be held. Soon after this the telephone lines were cut. A little later a runner came back with a message from Lieutenant Prest, commanding C Company in Fritz Trench, advising:

> *"Am in Fritz Trench and consolidating. Enemy have been seen moving into Bremen Trench and going up Moislains Avenue and also moving up to the left. The enemy Artillery are active – try and get support on Bremen Trench."*

A bombardment was sent over, scattering the enemy, and reinforcements were sent forward to help hold the position. During the night the Germans attacked in strength, capturing one section of trench, and advancing along it. Prest, on his own initiative, launched a counter-attack with bombs down Fritz Trench, supported by Captain Cahill with rifle grenades, Lewis-gun fire and bombs. All lost ground was recovered. Two weeks after the attack Prest was again appointed acting Captain, and was 'Mentioned in Dispatches'. He was also awarded the Croix de Guerre by the French, the accompanying letter referencing his distinguished action that night.

Having enjoyed a fortnight of leave in early April, Prest was seconded for duty as Chief Instructor at the XV Corps Lewis Gun School and was appointed acting Captain. In the autumn he was given command of the School for about six months up until March 1918, and in May transferred to the Lewis Gun and Light Mortar School at Quesques where he became an Instructor in the Lewis Gun Branch, with the acting rank of Major. Granted leave at the end of September, to attend to urgent private affairs in England, Prest did not return to France, and was demobilized in February 1919, relinquishing his commission the next year and retaining the rank of Major.

Prest played his last two matches for Kent in June 1922 against Worcestershire and Yorkshire, and also played for the Old Malvernians and Yellowhammers. A keen golfer, he represented the Seaford Club, the Oxford and Cambridge Society, and the Royal Worlington and Newmarket Club amongst others. During the Second World War he again answered the call to colours, serving with the Royal Norfolk Regiment from 1940 to 1941 as a Lieutenant. He joined the 8th (Home Defence) Battalion at Tottington and was posted to the regimental Infantry Training Centre at Norwich in July 1941. Illness however put a stop to his service, and he relinquished his commission at the end of October. In November 1944 he was married to Alice Lauriston in Surrey, and lived in the county until his death on 5 January, 1955 at Chinthurst, Shalford.

2ND CORPORAL HENRY JOHN BERRIDGE PRESTON

Henry John Berridge Preston was born on 25 October, 1883 in Bareilly, India, although some sources refer to his birthplace as Maidstone. He was the first-born child of John Stephen and Mary Preston, and his father was serving with the Artillery in India when he entered the world. A right-handed slow to medium pace bowler, he was engaged at the Tonbridge Nursery in 1903, played in the 2nd XI from 1904, and had his chance in the 1st XI in 1907 against Essex at Leyton when he took three wickets. He had made only 19 appearances by the end of 1913, most of his cricket being for the second team, but he did have the satisfaction of playing in the Championship winning sides of 1909, 1910 and 1913. Capped in 1910, his best return was 5-23 against Northants in 1912. Preston retired from first class cricket in 1914 and joined Nelson in the Lancashire League, his enlistment papers showing that club as his employer. He also played football, and at the end of the 1906 season he headed to Newcastle United with Wally Hardinge, but presumably did not make the grade.

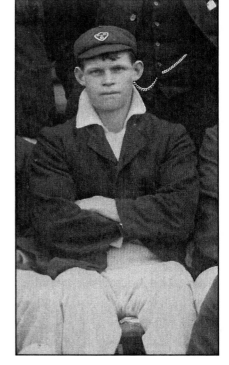

Henry Preston served at Gallipoli and in Egypt, the Western Desert and Palestine

Preston returned to Tonbridge at the end of the 1914 season and joined Blythe, Claud Woolley and the Jennings brothers as the group enlisted with the Kent Fortress Engineers on 9 October. After initial training the men were posted to Gillingham, and whereas the majority did not sign to serve overseas, Preston did. He was appointed Acting Corporal in September 1915 just days before he sailed for *Gallipoli* with 1/1st Kent Field Company. Accompanying him was Charles Woolley, brother of Claud and Frank, who had joined the KFE days after the cricketers enlisted. They landed at Suvla on 7 October, where the main engineer tasks included water supplies, roads and tracks, shelter and maintenance of the piers. Tools were in short supply, and the men had to make the best of a bad situation. Engineer projects to improve water supply were regularly shelled by the Turks who had control of the heights. Charles Woolley became the 1/1st Field Company's first casualty, badly wounded a week after their arrival when a shell burst in front of him.

The engineers were continually repairing the damage caused by the bad winter weather until Suvla was evacuated on 12 December. Whilst the infantry stopped off at Mudros, Preston changed ships and sailed for Alexandria with his Field Company. Once in *Egypt* the 1/1st became part of the Western Frontier Force and was sent to Mersa Matruh to help the *Western Desert* operations against the Senussi. Preston's company was tasked with organising water supplies for the coastal advance and, once Sollum was recaptured on 14 March, worked on defences, roads and a new pier. The company headed east in June, to join the 54th Division as part of the Egyptian Expeditionary Force (EEF), and were employed on Canal Defences. This was initially at El Kubri, the southernmost section, and then from November at Serapeum, the middle section. The engineer's work included bridge construction, clearing trench-works that were constantly filled with drifting sand, and repairing hutting which was continually damaged by high winds.

The beginning of 1917 saw plans for a large force to move into Palestine, and at this time the 1/1st Kent Field Company was retitled the 495th Field Company, still within 54th Division. Preston moved with them to El Arish, where they were engaged on water supply and defence work prior to the first attempt on Gaza. When that operation was underway on 26 March, Preston was to the east of Deir el Balah, working under intermittent artillery fire. Amidst the general withdrawal a day later, the 495th had to abandon their water gear but recovered it two days later. Water supply was again the focus of Preston's company in advance of the second attempt on Gaza, and roads also needed to be improved, and crossings made over the Wadi Ghazee. On 19 April as the attack faltered, they moved eastwards, under fire, to Sheikh Abbas, and the attack was ultimately abandoned.

Throughout the summer Preston worked on road improvements, water supply, and defence works. The 495th was transferred to the 75th Division, and in July Preston was promoted to 2nd Corporal and acting Corporal. Shortly before the autumn offensive began he fell ill and was admitted to hospital, and then joined the General Base Depot at Alexandria. He did not re-join his unit until July 1918, missing the action at Beersheba and Jerusalem. The 495th was by then in the Judean Hills with 54th Division whose proposed move to France had been cancelled. The company was working on the track running to Lydda, converting it into a drained, metalled road, some 19 feet wide. Several thousand men were employed on the project and the road was opened on 19 August. The work for Preston continued to be primarily water and roads as the offensive continued on into Syria, and Damascus was taken.

Hostilities ceased on 30 October, and a week later Preston spent a fortnight in hospital. He remained in Syria and Palestine for some time, appointed acting Corporal again in January 1919, and was not demobilized until June. The medical carried out when he was transferred into the Reserve revealed that he had suffered from varicose veins since 1916, caused by marching and wearing of puttees, and his condition had resulted in periods of non-duty and time spent at field ambulances. This was perhaps behind his two hospital admissions.

Following the war Preston spent time as a player and cricket coach in Scotland and, whilst playing for a Scotland XI against Australia in 1930, took the wickets of Woodfull and Hornibrook. He subsequently returned south and became groundsman at the Angel, Tonbridge, and when that closed he took on the same role at the Central Cricket Ground, Hastings. He also apparently played for Priory CC when over the age of sixty, but retired when he lost his right hand in an accident with a mowing machine. Henry Preston died suddenly, whilst watching television, on St George's Day 1964 aged 77.

LIEUTENANT CHARLES EDWARD SIGISMUND RUCKER

Charles Edward Sigismund Rücker was born 4 September 1894, at Chislehurst, Kent, the second son of sugar and coffee broker Edward Augustus Rücker and Mary Emmeline (née Farmer). He was in Girdlestoneites House at Charterhouse from 1908 and made the cricket XI for three years from 1911, as captain in the last. Primarily a fast bowler, his batting also flourished, as his 71 against Westminster in 1912 demonstrated, followed the next year with 103 against the same opposition. During 1913 he represented 'the Rest' against a Lord's Schools side and also a Public Schools side against the MCC, taking 5-93 in his 20 overs.

Rucker pictured in the Charterhouse XI in 1913. Reproduced by kind permission of the Headmaster and Governors of Charterhouse School

Rücker matriculated from University College, Oxford at the end of the year, and was awarded his Blue in 1914, also appearing for the Kent 2nd XI that same season. Against Surrey at the St. Lawrence in July he made a duck but took two wickets in his 14 overs. Earlier in the season he had played his debut first class match, for Oxford against Kent at the Parks. Last man in, he made 26 not out and then took 2 wickets whilst Kent were compiling a 571 total. It will be remembered that this game also saw the career high scores of Troughton and Sarel with whom he was to serve.

Rucker was quick to volunteer, enlisting on 29 August 1914 as a Private in the 10th Battalion Royal Fusiliers, which was raised as part of Kitchener's second New Army – K2. He was still 'Rücker' on his 1913 matriculation form, but plain 'Rucker' on his Army application forms, the umlaut presumably dropped as a consequence of anti-German sentiments at the time. References to him in the Kent Blue Book of 1915 also refer to him as Rucker, and the umlaut did not reappear after the war. He was based at Colchester in early October when he applied for a commission, and was appointed temporary 2nd Lieutenant with the Rifle Brigade. Just four weeks later he was appointed temporary Lieutenant with the 15th Battalion, a reserve unit.

It is not clear precisely when Rucker was attached to the 1st Dublin Fusiliers as some parts of that unit's war diary are missing, and the first reference to him is on the day he was wounded at Cape Helles, *Gallipoli*. The battalion was part of the initial landings at V Beach on 25 April 1915, and they suffered heavily. Having dug in, the men settled into the harsh trench life experienced by all who served there. On 28 June an attack was made on Turkish positions, and the Dublin Fusiliers were called forward to repel an enemy counter-attack. The position they were ordered to hold at all costs was found to be in Turkish hands and, whilst digging in where they could, they were attacked. In the following action 9 officers and 45 men were killed, and 1 officer and 138 men wounded. Three of the officers killed were attached from the Rifle Brigade, and Rucker was the one wounded officer, shot in the left arm.

Many casualties from Gallipoli were treated on Malta, and that was where Rucker was evacuated to, before heading back to England to a hospital in Plymouth. The bullet wound was noted to have only affected the 'soft parts' but he was also suffering from dysentery. When a Medical Board passed him fit for duty during October, they recommended he not be posted to a tropical or semi-tropical climate where dysentery prevailed. So it was that Rucker found himself posted to France during November, reporting to the 10th Battalion with a draft of 14 men in the Armentières area.

A trench raid was planned for the night of 15 December, and with the attacking party split in two parts, Rucker was given command of that on the left. He led the wire-cutting team out to a suitable point for them to make a way through, and was looking for a second access point when four Germans passed within a few yards of him and went into a listening post. Rucker withdrew his party a short distance and had them watch the post whilst he reported back. A decision had just been made to 'make do' with the one entry through the wire, when the sound of bombing and firing was heard further along the front.

With flares in the sky and the enemy disturbed by the action in the distance, the raid was put on hold. Instead Rucker led a party of bombers to attack the listening post, which he successfully accomplished, throwing 8 bombs from a few yards away. It is likely the men in the post were killed, but having drawn fire from the parapets he did not stick around to find out. All parties were withdrawn to safety without a single casualty, and Rucker was awarded the Military Cross for his bravery, the London Gazette (*Issue 29447, 21 January 1916*) recording:

> **Temporary Lieutenant Charles Edward Sigismund Rucker, 10ᵗʰ Battalion, The Rifle Brigade (The Prince Consort's Own).**
> *For conspicuous gallantry on the night of 15ᵗʰ-16ᵗʰ December, 1915, at Cordonnerie.*
> *He took out two parties to cut wire before a raid, and commenced work, but, being interrupted by an enemy listening post, he returned to report. The enemy being aroused, the raid was abandoned, but Lieutenant Rucker took out a bombing party and destroyed the listening post under a heavy fire. This post was inside the German wire and close to the enemy's parapet. He volunteered for both these duties.*

The winter was harsh that year, and trench conditions were appalling at Ypres where the battalion moved during February. On the evening of 21 March the enemy machine guns were active, and Rucker was wounded – hit by shrapnel and also by a machine-gun bullet which struck his left femur, breaking it in several places. He was evacuated to a Casualty Clearing Station behind Poperinghe, where he remained for ten days, and was then evacuated to Duchess of Westminster's Hospital, where his leg was amputated above the knee because of gangrene. He was gravely ill, suffering septicaemia, a secondary haemorrhage from the stump, and an abscess in his right shoulder.

After a second operation Rucker was transferred to Lady Carnarvon's Hospital in London where doctors noted that the abscess had caused limited movement in his right shoulder. By November he was referred to a specialist to have an artificial limb fitted, but more problems required another operation. Remarkably he was deemed fit for light duty by January 1917, and was officially attached to 5ᵗʰ Battalion Rifle Brigade. The orders to join the battalion were cancelled in September 1917, and at the same time his services were requested by the RFC for light duties. By the end of the month Rucker was appointed Officer in Charge of Messing at the School of Aerial Gunnery, New Romney, but he found standing too painful to carry out his duties.

Another medical board found him unfit for further military service and he wrote to the War Office requesting he be discharged as he was *"anxious to start work in the firm of I.A. Rucker & Bencrof"*, a produce broker of which he was a partner. Rucker was struck off the strength of the RFC from 25 October, and on 1 January 1918 he relinquished his commission on account of his wounds, receiving the honorary rank of Lieutenant. He had several more dealings with the War Office. His request for additional pension payments on account of his right shoulder was denied in February, and in April he was awarded the Silver War Badge. Rucker returned to Oxford to continue his education, the Tutorial List for 1919-20 showing that he was reading Modern Languages and Economics, and his BA was conferred in April 1919.

Rucker (right) pictured with his brother Patrick, in the University College XI in 1919. Image courtesy The Master and Fellows of University College, Oxford.

Although his cricket career was effectively ended by his injuries, Rucker did not let that stop his enjoyment of the game. He appeared for Oxford Authentics at the start of the summer in twelve-aside matches against Rugby and Harrow, scoring 36 not out in the latter. The image of him with his brother Patrick, is from a photograph of the University College Cricket XI of 1919, and he appears to have played for them as well. Rucker also took up the post of Secretary of Oxford University Cricket Club, whilst his brother was in the XI. He was married to Nancy Winnifred Hodgson at Tonbridge in September 1925 and later lived in Chislehurst, and then Ashmore near Salisbury. Charles Rucker died on 24 November 1965 at Blandford Hospital.

MAJOR WILLIAM GODFREY MOLYNEUX SAREL

William Godfrey Molyneux Sarel was born in Dover on 15 December, 1875 the son of Lieutenant General Henry Andrew Sarel CB and Margaret Jane Phyllis (née Molyneux). He was educated at Stubbington House, Fareham, a boy's preparatory school where he was in the XI 1889-1890, and then attended Oxford Military College and Loudwater, Westgate-on-Sea before following his father into the military. Commissioned 2nd Lieutenant in the 3rd Battalion Queen's Royal West Surrey Regiment, a Militia unit, in April 1900, not many weeks passed before he embarked for South Africa. During June 1901 he was promoted to Lieutenant, and at the end of August he transferred to the Regular Army, as 2nd Lieutenant in the 2nd Battalion Northumberland Fusiliers. He remained in South Africa until February 1903 and was awarded the Queen's South Africa Medal with 2 clasps (Cape Colony and Orange Free State) and King's South Africa Medal with 2 clasps (for 1901 and 1902).

William Sarel was recalled from the Reserve in 1914 and served with Lionel Troughton in the 10th Rifle Brigade on the Western Front

Following his promotion to Lieutenant in May 1904, Sarel appeared for the Surrey 1st XI several times over the summer, and was then seconded for service on the Staff, as Aide-de-Camp to the Governor and C-in-C Trinidad. During his posting he represented both Trinidad and West Indies before returning to England in June 1906. He married Ellen Margaret Heysham at Biggleswade that summer and the following year was posted to Peshawar, as part of the NW Frontier Expedition, which earned him the India General Service Medal. Back in England in 1909, as the Haldane Reforms were put in place, Sarel resigned his commission and joined the 5th Battalion Rifle Brigade in the Special Reserve. He made the first of his appearances for Kent 2nd XI in 1911, his first XI debut the following season against Somerset, and went on to play for the county ten times before the war. His highest score was 93 against Oxford University at the Parks in May 1914 when he stood in for Eric Hatfeild who was busy with the East Kent Yeomanry. Playing for the Mote in 1912 he was undefeated on 238 against Band of Brothers, and he also toured America with the Incogniti team in 1913, heading the batting averages.

Sarel was still with 5th Battalion Rifle Brigade when they were mobilized, but during October he transferred to be a Major in the 10th Rifle Brigade at the request of the Officer Commanding that battalion, one Colonel Cleveland Edmund Greenway. Sarel was personally known to Greenway, having not only served under him for six years in the 5th

Battalion, but also when Greenway captained the Incogniti team in America. When the London Gazette reported Sarel's appointment, it stated he was serving with the 3rd Rifle Brigade, however that battalion had already been posted to France, and it was to be a further nine months before the 10th Battalion followed. In the intervening months the men trained for war, and Sarel became a father when his first daughter was born in early 1915.

As the battalion left Salisbury Plain that July, Sarel led half of it to Folkestone where they sailed for Boulogne. Concentrating near Laventie, they were eased into the line under the tuition of the front line troops. Although the battalion was not involved in the main thrust of *Loos* that September, they were employed in firing on the German lines to prevent them from transferring reserves. The remainder of the year was spent in the Armentières area, where Sarel would have found modern trench warfare vastly different to his experiences during the Boer War and in India. Constant shelling and sniping took their toll and he fell sick, suffering from nervous exhaustion. He left his unit in December and was sent home to recover.

On arrival in England Sarel was transferred to a reserve battalion but problems with his knee cartilages set back his return to duty, and it was not until January 1917 that he was presented with the opportunity of employment in the war effort, working in the Military Secretary's office. The effects of the nervous exhaustion resurfaced several times, and Sarel was forced to spend some time in an Officers Hospital whilst recovering, but he was not a man to sit still. In September 1918 he was appointed Staff Officer 3rd Grade (SO3) at the Air Ministry in the Directorate of Air Organisation, granted a temporary commission as a Major in the RAF. When the war ended and all the services started the process of demobilization and reduction of staffing, Sarel was not alone in finding himself excess to requirements. He left the RAF and returned to the 5th Rifle Brigade.

In April 1920, with his ten year obligation to the Special Reserve completed some months previously, Sarel resigned his commission and was granted the rank of Major. He had been appointed Secretary of Sussex CCC in 1919 and played for them up until 1921 despite having no qualification to assist the side. When he played against Kent his former 2nd XI team-mate Tich Freeman took him in both innings, and he managed to score only 5 runs. He resigned his position at Sussex in 1921 and went on to become the golf club secretary at Beaconsfield and Berkshire. Sarel was also a renowned green-keeper, and patented several devices to improve the condition of lawns. Bill Sarel died on 5 April 1950 at Whitechapel in London.

2ND LIEUTENANT ERNEST HERBERT SIMPSON

Ernest Herbert Simpson was a promising cricketer who played for Kent on seven occasions in 1896, but gave up the county game to concentrate on business. He was born on 17 December 1875 in Clapham, the second-born son of Frederick Henry and Rose Simpson, and both he and his elder brother followed their father in working at the Stock Exchange. He went to boarding school at Littlehampton until aged 15 when, in the Second Term of 1891, he entered Malvern. A member of School House until 1895, Simpson was a school prefect, played in the Football 2nd XI and rose to the rank of Lieutenant in the Cadet Corps. In the Cricket XI from 1893 to 1895, he played alongside Pinky Burnup and Tip Foster, succeeding Burnup to the captaincy in his last year, when he made 72 not out against Repton, as Malvern won by ten wickets. The year ended sadly for Simpson however, when his mother died on 1 December.

Ernest Simpson was fatally wounded whilst serving with an Anti-Aircraft Battery during Passchendaele. Image from the Stock Exchange Roll of Honour

The Kent fixture against Gloucestershire in May 1896 saw the debuts of both Simpson and Burnup, and a week later against Lancashire at Old Trafford Simpson made 94 out of 254, his highest score for the county. In front of a 15,000 strong crowd he made a less than confident start to his innings, offering a return catch when on 11. Once settled he gave a good account of himself, striking twelve fours during his three hours at the crease. In 1900 he became a member of the Stock Exchange, and subsequently dealt in the American market and as a 'stock jobber'. In April 1913 he was married to Violet Amy Bishop at Holy Trinity Church, Sloane Square.

On the outbreak of War the call for volunteers was for men aged up to 30, raised to 35 in September. Simpson was approaching his 39th birthday and over the age limit. As the war progressed, and the debate over conscription raged, Lord Derby's Scheme came into effect in the latter part of 1915. It was then that Simpson became a 'Derby Man', enlisting at Hove on 7 December just weeks short of his 40th birthday. He was taken on as a Private in the Army Reserve and went home, to await his call-up. On 30 May 1916 he applied to join an Officer Cadet Unit with a view to obtaining a temporary commission, stating a preference to serve with the Royal Garrison Artillery (RGA) Anti-Aircraft section. On 14 June he was accepted as an Officer Cadet, joining "B" Reserve Brigade, Royal Horse Artillery at St. John's Wood for the RGA Anti-Aircraft Course. Two months later he was commissioned from the unit, and made temporary Lieutenant on probation with the RGA.

Simpson left Southampton for Havre with the 201ˢᵗ Anti-Aircraft (AA) Section of the RGA in the middle of October 1916, and during December he joined 29ᵗʰ AA Section in the field. Anti-Aircraft organisation was developed throughout the war, as the use of aircraft increased. The Germans had made their first major night-time air attack in June 1916, targeting the British ammunition dump at Andruicq, north-west of Omer, inflicting major damage. Night attacks followed during the Somme, and in November 1916, not long after Simpson arrived in France, the first 3 inch 20 cwt transportable guns arrived. An AA Artillery Group HQ was established at each Army HQ, and one for the Line of Command. Each Group was commanded by a Lieutenant-Colonel and new 'lettered' batteries were formed, made up of varying numbers of sections.

By the end of 1916 there were 91 AA Sections, of which ten had the new 3 inch gun, and 22 AA Searchlight Sections of the Royal Engineers. Simpson's Section would typically have consisted of 43 men of all ranks, including 2 officers (of which he was one), 2 detachments of 12 men each, ASC drivers, telephonists, linesmen, a height finder, a setter, a lookout man, a cook and an orderly. Air defence required the co-operation of the AA Artillery, machine guns, searchlights and aircraft.

Simpson served with 29 AA Section until August, apart from ten days leave to England during March, and was then attached to 'G' AA Battery, one of the new 'lettered' sections previously mentioned. 'G' Battery was part of Second Army, which was positioned around the Ypres front for most of the war, and Simpson was with the unit as *Third Ypres (Passchendaele)* took place. On 27 September, near Vlamertinghe, a German aircraft bomb exploded at around 22.00 wounding Simpson in the back, the shrapnel penetrating his chest wall. He was evacuated to an advanced dressing station, and then moved to No.4 Casualty Clearing Station (CCS), accompanied by his servant, Gnr. George Ryan. From the CCS, which was based at Lozinghem, Simpson was moved to 7 General Hospital at St. Omer where the Officer Commanding sent a telegram notifying the War Office he was dangerously ill. The War Office in turn telegraphed Simpson's wife, Violet. The following day a second telegram was sent:

"Deeply regret to inform you No 7 General Hospital Saint Omer reports 2/Lt EH Simpson RGA attached ANZAC Corps died of wounds October second the Army Council expresses their sympathy."

Violet Simpson later received a communication from the Director of Graves Registration, notifying her that her husband was *"buried in Longuenesse (St. Omer) Souvenir Cemetery. The grave has been registered in this office and is marked by a durable wooden cross with an inscription bearing full particulars."*

2ND LIEUTENANT GERARD AMYATT SIMPSON

Gerard Amyatt Simpson was born on 30 March 1886 at Trinity, Edinburgh, the son of Beatrice Caroline Amyatt and George Gregory Simpson, a Colonel in the Royal Field Artillery. He was educated at Wellington from 1899 to 1903 but does not appear to have made the XI. In fact the first we see of him playing cricket is in Argentina in 1907, when he opened the batting for North versus South at the Hurlingham Club Ground, Buenos Aires. He played in the same fixture the following year and was living in Argentina up until the War, working as a rancher, breeding cattle and horses. When the MCC toured Argentina in 1912 Simpson played against them three times, for Combined Camps, Argentina and the North. Kent players Troughton and Eric Hatfeild were in Lord Hawke's side, as was Eric Fulcher who was still to play for the county. Simpson played in the North v South fixtures again in 1913 and 1914.

Simpson (back row, left) returned from Argentina to join the Artillery. Reproduced by the kind permission of Kent County Cricket Club

With the war just a few months old, Simpson returned from Argentina on the "Arlanza", landing at Liverpool on 10 January. He applied for a commission in his father's old unit, the Royal Field Artillery and, having been found fit for service, was appointed temporary 2nd Lieutenant RFA just six days after setting foot on British soil. Within two months he was in France where he was attached to the RHA, as part of the Divisional Ammunition Column of the 2nd Indian Cavalry Division. He was soon on the French-Belgian border near Houtkerque, but spent most of the summer further back behind the line in billets at Flechin. It was August before Simpson moved up to the line, as the RHA batteries took up positions near Martinsart in the Somme area.

Setting up the guns to get ranging and telephone communication correct took several days, and even then the cavalry needed to check the points at which artillery support would best assist them. The 4th Squadron of the RFC also established a wireless installation to allow co-operation between their observers and the artillery. Just two weeks later however, the RHA was ordered back to billets and marched to Yzeux. Time was spent at various billets during October, and in November Simpson was at Ramburelles, well west of Amiens. His war then came to a sudden end.

On 18 November a fire broke out in his billets and, whilst climbing a ladder to help put it out, he fell and twisted his right knee. He returned to England at the end of the month and was operated on to have cartilage removed, before convalescing at home in London. Although the wound healed, the tender scar and synovitis left Simpson unable to ride, and subsequent Medical Boards noted he also had a very bad stammer and an old injury to his left ankle that was playing up. In March 1916 he reported for duty with 2 'B' Reserve Brigade RFA at Brighton, but subsequent Medical Boards found him permanently unfit for service.

Simpson requested he be allowed to resign his commission, which was accepted, the resignation effective 11 October 1916, and he was later awarded the Silver War Badge. He made plans to return to Argentina, and departed Liverpool for Buenos Aires at the start of November to resume ranching. In 1919 he was married to Annie Katherine O'Brien in Buenos Aires and he remained there as manager of a factory throughout most of the 1920s. He also returned to playing cricket for North, Argentina and Rosario, and in 1926 appeared for an Anglo-Argentine XI that played the MCC at Lord's. The MCC side included Bill Sarel and Gerald Hough, the latter having Simpson caught in his second innings.

Simpson returned to live in England and in 1929 made his Kent debut in the County Championship against Yorkshire, and then played in the fixture against Lancashire at Old Trafford. He played once more for the 1st XI in 1931 against Lancashire at Tonbridge, but in 1930 had taken over as captain of the 2nd XI and played regularly for them until 1939 and again after WW2 up until 1949. He also captained the Club & Ground until 1949 and played his club cricket for St. Lawrence. During WW2 he was a County / Local Army Welfare Officer and when he reached the age limit and retired in 1949, he retained his honorary rank of Captain. Simpson was living at Nonington, Kent when he died on 22 February 1957 at St Augustine's Hospital, Chartham.

PRIVATE ARTHUR OWEN SNOWDEN

Born on 7 May 1885 at St. Peters, Broadstairs, Arthur Owen Snowden was the first born son of Augusta Louisa and the Reverend Harcourt Charles Vaux Snowden. He lived at Hildersham House where his father ran a private school and it seems likely he was taught there himself, as the school fed into Rugby and that is where Arthur headed at the age of 13. He was a member of the Cricket XI from 1901 to 1903, as captain in his last year when he topped the bowling averages with 41 at 16.31 and scored 299 runs at an average of 20. The school magazine *The Meteor* noted in October 1903 that Snowden was a good left hand slow bowler and a free bat with a powerful off drive, and had been most successful at Lord's. This last comment was a reference to the matches against Marlborough in which he had particular success with the ball.

Snowden in the Cricket XI at Rugby, reproduced by kind permission of the Rugby School Archives

Snowden matriculated to Trinity College, Oxford in October 1903 and his BA was conferred three years later, followed by his Masters in April 1910. Whilst at Oxford he did not gain a Blue, but did appear in the XI three times in 1905 following a solid 95 in the Seniors' Match. His first appearance for the University was against a Gentleman of England side that included WG Grace and Gerry Weigall, and he helped Oxford to a 50 run win with scores of 54 and 6. Snowden first appeared for the Kent 2nd XI against Sussex at Town Malling in 1908, when he took 3 for 26 in his 7 overs. He played a handful of times for the 2nd XI and in 1911 made his single 1st XI appearance against India at Catford, the match also marking the last time Lord Harris played first class cricket. Snowden's last match for the 2nd XI started the day after war was declared, with Kent convincingly beaten by Staffordshire.

Arthur and his brother Harcourt were both assistant school masters at Hildersham House. His work restricted his availability to play, but he did manage several appearances for the MCC and Kent 2nd XI. In January of 1913 he was married to Molly Woodman at St. Barnabas, Pimlico, and the couple lived in Broadstairs, where they started a family. He took on the role of Headmaster after his brother was killed in France in January 1915 whilst serving with the Hertfordshire Regiment.

Snowden was one of Kent's cricketers who enlisted during the Derby Scheme experiment. He attested at Broadstairs in December 1915, was appointed a Private and moved into the Army Reserve. In December 1916 he attended a medical at Canterbury, and was deemed fit for service, but was still not posted. In fact it was not until May 1918 that he was provisionally accepted for enlistment in the OTC. He underwent a second medical, this time at Leamington, and was posted as a Private in the Inns of Court OTC on 12 June.

The Inns of Court OTC operated at Berkhamsted and Catterick. Officer candidates received their basic training at the former and then went on to No.14 OCB (Officer Cadet Battalion) at the latter, for officer training. The surrounding countryside of Berkhamsted offered good terrain for soldiers to train, and full scale battalion exercises were held weekly, with thousands of yards of trenches dug in the area. During the few months Snowden was at Berkhamsted, the OTC organised battle exercise, rifle meetings and sports events in addition to the usual training. In August the camp was hit by an outbreak of Spanish

Influenza, and a further outbreak in October caused 14 deaths. Snowden was with the OTC for five months before the Armistice came into effect, after which training gave way to education, sports and games.

Having been demobilized in February 1919, Snowden returned to Hilderhsam House. Interestingly, there were a series of caves and tunnels below the school which were used as an air raid shelter for up to 400 people during the Great War. Snowden did play cricket on occasion for Free Foresters, Band of Brothers and Old Rugbeians, and maintained ties with Kent as their librarian in his later years. In 1958 he attended the Memorial Service for Jack Mason, held at St. Margaret's Westminster, along with a number of other former Kent players. Snowden died at home, The Oast, Old Dover Road, Canterbury, on 22 May 1964.

PRIVATE HORACE JAMES TAYLOR

Horace James Taylor was born in Sevenoaks on Boxing Day 1895, the son of Emily and Alfred Taylor a shopkeeper and harness manufacturer. He was schooled at Sevenoaks, and started work as a bank clerk not long before the war began, being just 19 years old when he enlisted in the West Kent Yeomanry (WKY). He signed his papers at Maidstone on 27 August 1914, witnessed by Major Fiennes Cornwallis, a Major in the 2/1st WKY and the father of Stanley Cornwallis, and was certified fit for service by CGB Marsham, the cousin of Kent's Cloudesley Marsham. Within days of the outbreak of war the men of the regiment had been asked whether they would agree to serve overseas, and those who

did formed the 1/1st West Kent Yeomanry, whilst the remainder formed the 2/1st. Taylor signed his agreement to serve outside of the UK on the day he enlisted and was accordingly embodied in the 1/1st WKY. Although the regimental depot was in Maidstone, the men had by now moved to Canterbury and Taylor headed there once he had received his initial training.

Horace Taylor served with the West Kent Yeomanry at Gallipoli, in Egypt and in Palestine

The Kent Yeomanry regiments remained in the country until the end of September when they received their orders to embark at Liverpool. Their destination was *Gallipoli*, and Taylor joined the other Kent cricketers on the peninsula for what

292

turned out to be a very uncomfortable few months. Although he was still to play for Kent, Taylor was presumably not deterred by the fact that former Kent Captain Cloudesley Marsham awarded him seven days guard duty for being late on guard duty parade at Geoghan's Bluff during November. Like all the men in the line, Taylor would have taken his turn in the trenches and in reserve, sheltering from Turkish sniper fire, and then from the winter storms. He joined the evacuation of Helles on 27 December and sailed for Mudros where the regiment regrouped.

In early 1916 the regiment, now part of 3rd Dismounted Brigade, sailed to *Egypt* and were put to work on the Suez Canal defences. Taylor was still serving in B Squadron under Marsham, and that unit took over No.4 Gurkha Post during March, and the following month moved south for employment on other canal sections. During July, with events to the east creating some excitement, the regiment moved from El Ferdan to Sidi Bishr. But instead of the anticipated move toward El Arish, Taylor and his comrades were ordered west to Matruh for operations in the *Western Desert*. Arriving on the 6 August, the regiment was to remain there and at Sollum for some months, as part of the force sent to defeat the Senussi uprising. When Taylor arrived the Senussi had already been driven well inland and he was to see little of them, spending a great deal of time in training.

During December Taylor was officially transferred into the 10th Buffs, the battalion created by the amalgamation of the West and East Kent Yeomanry regiments, and attached to 74th Division. On 1 March, shortly after the surrender of the Senussi, he and Marsham were posted to D Company, and moved to Sidi Bishr, from which place the Division began its advance into *Palestine*. The 74th was in reserve during the second battle of Gaza, and Taylor would have been engaged in digging defensive trenches throughout. When the battle ended in failure, and British policy turned to establishing a defensive line until autumn, Taylor had a summer of training to look forward to. The war diary for that period seems to be an endless list of men proceeding to hospital, the heat proving detrimental to their health. Finally, during October, the battalion received orders to prepare for operations at Beersheba.

Taylor's company was in reserve for the attack on 31 October, but was moved forward to fill a gap in the line as the attacking companies came under heavy shrapnel fire. When the line went forward as one man, the wire was breached, the objectives taken and Beersheba soon fell. Moving on to Wadi Saba, Taylor's company had to deal with an attack by an enemy patrol and soon received orders for an attack on Sheria. They were again in reserve for the main attack after which they took over the line. The push toward Jerusalem now began in earnest, but as the 53rd Division became held up it was given use of the transport of 74th Division. This meant Taylor had to make a long march in a sand-storm, back to Deir el Balah to wait until their transport was made available.

Eventually the Buffs headed back toward Jerusalem, again marching the entire way, and once in the Hills of Judea they had to help build roads to facilitate the advance, naming their efforts the New Kent Road. After assisting in the capture of several of the peaks, Taylor and the Buffs saw Jerusalem fall into the hands of the Allies, and pressed on to capture Ram Allah. The battalion then went into rest, which was enjoyed to the maximum by employment in more road-making, but most of the men did manage to go sight-seeing in Jerusalem. After a further period in the line, the Buffs received their orders for France, and started the journey back to Alexandria from where they would sail. During March Taylor was promoted to acting Lance Corporal, and at the end of April he set sail for Marseilles, arriving there on 7 May.

Whilst the men started to train for a different type of warfare, Taylor left the unit for England. He had been accepted for entry to an Officer Cadet Course in order to obtain a commission. After a period of leave, he was attached to No.2 Reception Battalion at Larkhill to begin his training. Before he finished his course the war ended, and on 22 November 1918 he was posted as a Private to No.8 OCB at Lichfield where he remained for three months whilst awaiting dispersal. He was duly demobilized during February 1919 and transferred to the reserve.

Taylor first played for Kent in 1922, scoring 143 for the 2nd XI against Bedfordshire, and days later he made his 1st XI debut against Warwickshire at Edgbaston, making a respectable 30. In all he played a dozen times for the first team between 1922 and 1925, with a top score of 33 against Sussex. His 2nd XI appearances spanned from 1922 to 1928 after which his work as a civil servant took him to Kenya. He is recorded as playing for cricket in Africa up until 1938, and appears to have returned there after WW2 at which time he was an Inspector of Produce. In 1935 he married Doris Austin at Sevenoaks, and she died in 1952 in Maidstone. Horace Taylor died in Tunbridge Wells on 13 October 1961.

LIEUTENANT COLONEL LIONEL HOLMES WOOD TROUGHTON

Lionel Holmes Wood Troughton was born at Seaford, Sussex on 17 May 1879, second child of Kate Wood and William Henry Troughton, a Brewer, Wine and Spirit Merchant, and later Solicitor, of Gravesend. He was educated at Dulwich College and was in the XI in 1897, the XV 1897-98, and also played Fives. Having left college in 1898 he became an articled clerk in his father's office and qualified as a solicitor in 1907. He played club cricket for Gravesend after leaving school, as captain for several seasons, and in 1903 he scored 203 against Cobham. His first appearance for Kent 2nd XI was in 1900, and his 1st XI debut followed against Essex at Leyton in 1907. He went on to make 164 first team appearances, scoring almost 3,500 runs with a high score of 104 against Oxford University in 1914.

He toured Argentina with MacLaren's side in 1911-12, making 112 not out against the Combined Camps at Buenos Aires, and in 1914 was awarded his Kent cap as well as the captaincy, which he retained until 1923.

Lionel Troughton won the Military Cross at Guillemont in 1916 and was taken prisoner the following year during the German counter-attack at Cambrai

Troughton joined the Royal Fusiliers on the same day as Sydney Day, the two Privates posted to the 18th (Service) Battalion on 15 September 1914. It was also referred to as the 1st Public Schools battalion, being one of four the regiment raised that month. He served in that role for five months and was then commissioned as temporary 2nd Lieutenant in the 10th Battalion Rifle Brigade with good references. William Sarel, former Kent team-mate and a Major in the battalion, certified his moral character, and Lord Harris certified his good standard of education. On completion of training, Troughton departed Salisbury Plain and arrived in France with the battalion on 22 July. The following month they moved into the line near Laventie to undergo instruction in trench warfare.

When the *Loos* offensive opened in September Troughton was not directly involved, the 10th Rifle Brigade instead providing covering fire on their own part of the line to keep the enemy from moving troops as reinforcements. The remainder of the year was spent in the Armentières area. Whilst undergoing instruction on bombing at the beginning of October, Troughton was slightly injured by shrapnel but remained at duty and was appointed temporary Lieutenant nine days later. During the winter months the battalion carried out the trench raid that is described in Charles Rucker's entry, and in February 1916 was moved to the *Ypres* sector to join Lord Cavan's newly formed XIV Corps.

Troughton remained on the Ypres front until the summer, as the battalion battled against the weather to keep the trenches usable, although the continuous shelling had left the line a series of isolated posts rather than a continuous line. He was promoted to temporary Captain in March (backdated to October 1915) and the next few months were spent in training as the *Somme* offensive loomed. In June, still on the Ypres front, Troughton took over command of B Company. The battalion war diary entry for 21 June recorded:

Captain Troughton observed a German Officer inspecting new work on the German front line. The Adjutant and he communicated with Forward Observation Officer, A/93

Battery and a direct hit was made with the third shot. At 9.30 p.m. enemy aeroplane dropped two bombs near our lines. No damage was done.

Troughton did not leave Ypres until mid-July, the battalion taking over the line south of Hebuterne on 27 July as the *Somme Continued*. Just two days later the war diary states:

Captain Troughton going out with 5 men to site a new trench, encountered enemy of about 25. They at once collected and began to withdraw. Capt. Troughton fired his revolver, hitting one man.

During August the battalion was moved to Meaulte, south of Albert, where they learnt they would be part of an attack on Guillemont. Days before the attack Troughton moved into the line south of Guillemont, where the trenches were full of British dead from recent fighting. The regimental history recalled that "*to visit the trenches of the Tenth Battalion was, in sober seriousness, like a descent to the ante-rooms of Hell. Few Brigades ever prepared for a great enterprise in less auspicious surroundings and circumstances*". The attack was eventually set for 3 September, and Troughton led his men into the trenches and dugouts at the Craters of Carnoy in preparation. Zero hour was at noon, and the attackers first had to overcome a sunken road, in which 150 German dead were counted after the battle.

Moving on to their second objective, they encountered a communication trench which was not on the maps. A machine-gun in the trench was pinning Troughton's men down, and he was seen to run towards the enemy, firing his rifle, and his men were encouraged to follow him and take the position. They then reached their third objective but could not progress further as the Divisions to their flanks had been held up. Later, when German reinforcements were seen heading to Leuze Wood, Troughton led his men in directing rifle fire on them, inflicting many casualties. The attack was a success but costly – 220 casualties, and Troughton was one of only two officers unscathed. He was subsequently awarded the Military Cross which was reported in the London Gazette (*Issue 29824, 14 November 1916*):

Temp. Capt. Lionel Holmes Wood Troughton, Rif. Bde
For conspicuous gallantry in action. He led his men with great determination, reforming at each objective and then leading on. Between the first and second objective he took a rifle and rushed forward, firing into the enemy's trench, quickly followed by his men. Finally he found himself in command of the battalion and consolidated the final objective under heavy fire.

Troughton spent the remainder of the year in the Somme area, where much time was given to training the drafts that arrived to bring the battalion back to something near full strength. During this period, and into January and February 1917, he spent several periods in command, being appointed temporary Major in January and temporary Lieutenant-Colonel when given permanent command in March. *Operation Alberich* was by now in progress, the Germans withdrawing to the Hindenburg Line, but not on the line faced by the 20th Division. Under Troughton's command the battalion attacked Metzen Couture successfully despite the enemy being strongly entrenched, and around the same time the French decorated him with the Croix d'Officiers of the Légion d'Honneur.

In August, as part of *Third Ypres (Passchendaele)* the 20th Division was tasked with capturing Langemarck, and a preliminary operation was designed to seize command of the Steenbeck Valley. Once the line of Steenbeck was taken, the attack to cross it began on 14 August. Troughton was given command of the operation and had his own battalion and two companies of the 11th Rifle Brigade to work with. During the preparations the Germans shelled their positions with gas and despite being affected by it, Troughton stayed on duty and in command of the impending attack. Although troubled by heavy fire, and finding their pre-prepared bridges were too short, the attack was a success, and a counter-attack was repelled.

When the attack on Langemarck took place in September, both of the tanks brought up to help broke down, one either side of the Langemarck Road. This also placed them each side of Troughton's HQ, which was frequently hit by shells aimed at the failing machines. The month that followed was spent opposite the Hindenburg Line, but in November the battalion took part in the attack at *Cambrai*. The 20th Division broke through and advanced to capture a bridge at Masnieres that crossed the St Quentin Canal. Tanks caused problems for Troughton's battalion yet again; one crossing the bridge caused it to partially collapse. Although the first day of Cambrai was highly successful, the Germans rallied well enough that the advance ground to a halt in the following days, and the British dug in. The following is Troughton's own account of the events at the end of November:

"My Battalion from reserve relieved a Battalion of the KRRC by Crevecour on the 30th November 1917 at 3 A.M. in the morning shortly before the German counter attack on the CAMBRAI salient. I was supporting Battalion to the 10th and 11th KRRC who were in the front line. At dawn SOS came through from BANTOUX well on my right. I rung up my Brigade but they could give me no information as to what was happening. I did not see or receive any SOS from my own force. I stood to with my Battalion. Almost immediately after this I saw the Germans had broken through the 12th Division on my right. I tried to form a flank on my right near the CAMBRAI-MASNIERS road and to hold my own front, but it was quite impossible to stop the many German lines which

had by this time also broken through the 10th and 11th KRRC and was also attacking us strongly from the right flank. I tried to inform my Brigade by telephone of the situation but I found they had been previously attacked and had left their Head Quarters. I thought this most important task must be attempted at all costs and also that it was my duty as a Senior Officer to stay and try to pull things together. Within a minute of this very heavy machine gun and rifle fire was concentrated on to where I was at close range – we were surrounded – we fought but were bombed out and I was taken prisoner with the small party of seven who were left with me, all the others having been killed or wounded."

Troughton's file contains a notification from a Prisoner of War Camp with his details on, thus confirming his status as prisoner to the British authorities. Officer Kriegsgefangenlager Karlsruhe, the Officer's POW Camp at Karlsruhe, was possibly a central camp to which officers were sent to be interviewed before they were sent on to other camps. Other sources refer to his spending time in two different camps during his captivity, but neither is named. Troughton was repatriated on 30 December 1918, unsurprisingly reporting unfit, and was given two months leave. A subsequent medical found him unfit for general service and he relinquished his commission in April 1919, retaining the rank of Lieutenant-Colonel.

Troughton resumed his cricket with Kent during 1919, and his most successful post-war season was 1921 when he scored 761 runs. He retained the captaincy until 1923 when he handed the mantle to Cornwallis, and took over as Kent's business manager following Tom Pawley's death. He was by all accounts a better golfer than a cricketer, and was three times a member of the winning fours in the Sussex County Golf Championship. He had succeeded his father as secretary of the Gravesend and Milton Gas Light Co., in 1912 and held that post until 1921 when he became a director of both the Gravesend and Milton Gas Light and Water Companies. In 1927 Troughton married Gwendolen Maude Henderson, but just six years later, at the age of 54 he died on 31 August after pleurisy set in following an operation at Guys Hospital. There was some suggestion this was a result of his having been gassed during the war.

2ND LIEUTENANT FRANK NOEL TUFF

Frank Noel Tuff played infrequently for the Kent 2nd XI between 1911 and 1914, and his first class cricket was predominantly for Oxford University. He was born in Rochester, Kent on 26 November 1889, the fourth son of Marian and Charles Tuff, JP, of Westfield, Singlewell, Gravesend. Tuff's father was the Member of Parliament for Rochester from 1903 to 1906 and was also Mayor of Rochester. Tuff shared much of his education with another future Kent player, Harold Prest. They were born within two months of each other; both attended

Abbey School, Beckenham; went to Malvern between 1904-1908 where each was a prefect and both played in the Cricket XI and Football XI. The similarity ended when University beckoned. Tuff went up to Brasenose College in October 1908 to study Law whilst Prest went to Cambridge, and although the pair both earned their Blues they did not feature in the same Oxford v Cambridge fixture.

Frank Tuff before the war (left) and a 2nd Lieutenant with the Royal East Kent Mounted Rifles (right). Photographs courtesy The Roger Mann Collection

At Malvern Tuff played in the football and cricket elevens for several seasons. In the cricket eleven he and Prest played together in the Repton and Clifton fixtures several times between 1906 and 1908, and Tuff headed the bowling averages in 1907 and 1908. He was a Football Blue 1909-1911, and at cricket he scored 29 not out and 36 and then took three wickets in the Freshmen's match of 1909, and received his Blue the following season. In 1910 he took 5-28 in the Gentlemen of England's first innings, including the wicket of Lionel Troughton for a duck, then had Troughton caught for 3 in the second innings. He also played football for the Corinthians and cricket for the Free Foresters and Band of Brothers.

Having played for Oxford against Kent in May 1911, Tuff was invited to play for the 2nd XI later that season and appeared in a handful of games up to 1914. Against Wiltshire in 1911 he would have struggled to take wickets with an on-form Preston taking 15-96, and against Cornwall he top scored in the Kent second innings with a respectable 42 out of 102. In his last recorded match before War was declared he played alongside future Kent legend Tich Freeman against Lincolnshire at Town Malling. The Kent team also included Leonard Powell who like Tuff was killed in 1915. Tuff was married at St. Michaels, Chester Square, Pimlico on 11 December 1912 to Muriel Mary Smith, and the couple moved into Uplands, Singlewell Road in Gravesend, Kent. Having left University, Tuff commenced working as an Articled Law Clerk for Arnold, Day and Tuff in Rochester.

Tuff received his commission into the Royal East Kent Mounted Rifles (REKMR) on 1 June, 1915 as a 2nd Lieutenant, and within days was posted to 1/1st Regiment 'Additional'. By this time the 1/1st was based at Canterbury and it was there that Tuff headed. In September the regiment received their orders, and journeyed by train to Liverpool, where they embarked on the "Olympic". The ship was a vessel of the White Star Line and a sister of the Titanic, employed as a troopship during the war, and she carried the yeomanry to Lemnos via Alexandria. Three days after arriving at Lemnos Tuff's regiment trans-shipped to Gallipoli, landing at Cape Helles on 7 October and proceeding to bivouacs at Gully Ravine.

The East Kent Yeomanry was gradually integrated into the trenches, and were in action continuously until evacuated in January 1916. Tuff and three other officers of the REKMR were wounded through the explosion of a cricket ball bomb at Helles on 23 October, just sixteen days after landing. He was evacuated to Cottonera Hospital on Malta, the island at that time known as the 'Nurse of the Mediterranean'. The hospitals located there dealt with more than 2,500 officers and 55,400 troops from the Gallipoli campaign and more than that again during the Salonika campaign in 1917. Having arrived at Malta on a hospital ship, it is likely Tuff first passed through Valetta Military Hospital, a sorting station for new arrivals, and then transferred to Cottonera, one of 30 hospitals and camps dealing with casualties on the island.

On 5 November, 1915 at 16.30, Frank Noel Tuff died of his wounds at Cottonera. He was buried at Pieta Cemetery the following day. The Tuff family were hard hit by the War, Frank's oldest brother Bertram served with the RNVR during the war, and his next eldest sibling, Cecil Thomas, gave his life at Hill 60 in 1915 whilst serving with the Royal West Kent's. It was said their father never recovered the loss of his two sons.

MAJOR JOHN SACKVILLE RICHARD TUFTON

John Sackville Richard Tufton was born at Hothfield Place in Ashford on 8 November, 1873, the eldest son of Alice Harriot Argyll Clitherow and Henry James Tufton, the first

Baron Hothfield. His father was President of Kent CCC in 1877, and the family had a strong cricketing tradition. Tufton did not make the XI whilst at Eton 1887-1892, and on leaving was commissioned 2nd Lieutenant in the 3rd Battalion of the Royal Sussex Regiment, a Militia unit. After a promotion to Lieutenant in 1893, Tufton applied to join the regulars, and was commissioned into the 1st Battalion Life Guards in June 1894, reverting to 2nd Lieutenant. He was appointed Deputy Lieutenant of the County of Westmorland six months later, and resigned his army commission in May 1896. A few weeks later he was married to Lady Ierne Hastings, daughter of the late Earl of Huntingdon, at St. Anselm's Church in London.

John Tufton pictured on 26 February 1915, the day before he embarked for France
©National Portrait Gallery, London

All of Tufton's first class cricket appearances took place in the three years following his departure from the Army, after which he returned to the military to serve in South Africa during the Boer War. His first class debut was for MCC against Leicestershire at Lord's in May 1897, and his Kent debut in June, against Yorkshire at Halifax. The next month he made his highest score for the county, 25 against the Gentlemen of Philadelphia at Mote Park, and altogether played for the county eight times, plus several 2nd XI appearances. He re-joined the 3rd Royal Sussex Regiment in March 1900 to join the fighting in South Africa, and was promoted to Captain in August.

The Boer War was the first time that Volunteer Units served overseas, and the 3rd Sussex, still a Militia unit, volunteered as a whole. They performed good service on lines of communication, security and guard duties, and after peace was declared Tufton moved with them to St Helena to guard Boer prisoners of war. He returned to England in August 1902, and was awarded the Queen's Medal with 5 clasps, including those for service in the Transvaal and Orange River Colony. In June 1908, as part of the Haldane Reforms, the 3rd became a reserve battalion of the regiment, and Tufton was appointed Honorary Major. He was back in his cricket whites that same month, playing for Free Foresters against Oxford University, after which he made sporadic appearances for I Zingari and Band of Brothers.

Promotion to Major came in June 1913 and the next year he joined the first I Zingari team to tour outside the British Isles as they sailed for Egypt.

Tufton had served on the Kent Committee from 1894 to 1914, but he disagreed with Lord Harris' position on the continuation of cricket after war was declared in August 1914, and soon resigned his position. Having immediately volunteered for active service, he moved with his battalion to Dover, and remained there until he was ordered to France in February 1915. Once at the front he was appointed Assistant Provost Marshal (APM) attached to 6th Division Headquarters. Each Infantry Division had an APM, and Tufton was responsible for organising the police under his command, receiving orders from the Divisional Assistant Adjutant General (DAAG). As the line was hardening after *Second Ypres*, the Division moved from Armentières to Ypres in June 1915 and the sector became home for the next year. During that time they were involved in the retaking of Hooge, and Tufton received the news his son had been wounded and evacuated to England.

The New Year Honours of 1916 brought Tufton a DSO, and his file references he was also MID. During August, the 6th Division moved south as the *Somme Continued* and joined in the tail end of the offensive, before moving north to the La Bassée sector in November. Remaining in this middle ground between Ypres and the Somme, the Division spent time in the line near Loos in March 1917, and followed up on the retreating Germans after the Canadian success at Vimy Ridge during the *Arras* offensive. Tufton moved to the Riencourt area as the Division joined Third Army for the operation that became the *Battle of Cambrai* that autumn Following the German counter-attack the Divisional HQ was shelled out three times in the space of nine days.

During March 1918 the Belgians decorated Tufton with the Ordre de Léopold, Chevalier Class, shortly before the German *Kaiserschlacht* was launched. On the opening day the 6th Division was driven back sharply, digging in on a new line before being relieved. The Division had taken a mauling and was sent to Ypres to reorganise. That front was, however, now held by tired troops in understrength units, reinforced by men with no fighting experience. It was against this sector that the Germans launched the next phase of their offensive, and although the 6th Division area was without major incident, the Salient was reduced twice in April by organized withdrawal.

When the *100 Days Offensive* began, Tufton was not far from St Quentin, the 6th Division having moved south in the preceding months. The Division took part in the attack at St Quentin during the *Battles of the Hindenburg Line* and advanced into territory that had not seen fighting since 1914. Buildings were still standing but the Germans had laid time delayed mines, and one exploded close to HQ showering the staff cars with debris. *Beyond the Hindenburg Line,* as the enemy made a stand on the high ground east of the River Selle, 6th Division pushed through to the Sambre Canal. They were establishing a bridgehead at the end of October when they were relieved, and saw no more action.

Following the Armistice the Division became part of the Army of Occupation in Germany, and Tufton joined Divisional HQ at Bruhl in time for Christmas Dinner. Demobilization started in the New Year and he relinquished his appointment as APM in April, and was MID in July. Tufton and the Military Police did not have it all easy, as might be thought. They often had to control traffic at crossroads which were favoured targets for the German heavy gunners, in particular during an action, and several awards were given to the Military Police for conduct under these conditions. In addition to his DSO, two MIDs and Ordre de Léopold, Tufton was awarded the French Order of Agricultural Merit.

During the Emergency of 1921 Tufton served briefly with the Depot of the Royal Sussex Regiment, but the National Strike was soon called off and he was back playing cricket for I Zingari during the summer. In 1925, having exceeded the age limit of 50 for retention in the Militia, he relinquished his commission retaining the rank of Major. The following year he succeeded his father, becoming the Second Baron Hothfield, and became one of the better lawn tennis players in the House of Lords. He farmed extensively in Yorkshire and Westmorland, and was elected Mayor of Appleby in 1937-38. His wife, Ierne, died in January 1935 and he was married a second time on New Year's Eve of that year to Sybil Augusta Sant. Sybil died in 1950, and two years later on 21 December 1952 Tufton passed away at his London home.

CAPTAIN JAMES RICHARD TYLDEN

James Richard Tylden was born on 26 April 1889 at the family home, Milstead Manor, Sittingbourne in Kent. His father Richard James was a gentleman farmer and JP, married to Edith Marion (Jones). Tylden was educated at Rugby from 1903 to 1907, where he joined the Rifle Corps and was a member of the XI, playing and winning against Marlborough at Lord's in 1906 and 1907. He went on to study at St John's College, Oxford, and though not destined to obtain a Blue (or a degree) he did play in the Seniors' match of 1909 in CVL Hooman's side, scoring 85. He was injured for the 1908 Freshmen's match in which he was to have played in CS Hurst's team.

Tylden in the XI at Rugby, reproduced by kind permission of the Rugby School Archives

In February 1908 the Lord Lieutenant of Kent signed a commission for Tylden to be Deputy Lieutenant, and in November 1909 he was appointed 2nd Lieutenant in the Royal East Kent Mounted Rifles (REKMR). By 1912 he commanded the Shorncliffe and Sheppey Troop, a position his father had held some years previously, and at the summer camp at Somerhill he won the officer's race on 'Bill Dree'. During June 1913 he was married to Mary Estelle Clayton Swan in London, and was made Lieutenant at the end of August 1914, just as his wife gave birth to their daughter. It was quite a hectic time for him as his regiment was concentrating at Canterbury following mobilization, and he spent the rest of the year training and working on coastal defences. Tylden sailed from Liverpool in September 1915 when the REKMR was posted to *Gallipoli*, initially remaining at Mudros with base details. He joined the regiment at Helles on 14 October, by which time there was no realistic chance of a breakout, but plenty of hardships ahead. The blizzard of November would remain etched in the memories of all who survived it.

The REKMR came under the command of 42nd Division whilst at Gallipoli, and at the time of the evacuation in December Tylden was appointed Aide-de-Camp (ADC) to Major-General William Douglas the Divisional Commander. He was seconded to 42nd Division Headquarters, and struck off the strength of the REKMR. The Division left Mudros for *Egypt* mid-January 1916, sailing to Alexandria and setting up camp near Shalluffa where the men were employed on Canal Defences. In June Tylden returned to England for business reasons, and attended a Gas course at Tadworth before returning to Egypt. The Division was part of VIII Corps which was transformed into a Mobile Column for desert operations, and in August made a very long march to take part in the Battle of Romani. After the battle the Division HQ was based at Pelusium and Tylden remained there until the push toward El Arish later in the year.

Tylden returned to the Canal at Moascar in February 1917 as the Division concentrated to prepare to move to France. On arrival the Divisional HQ was set up at Peronne, as the men underwent training for a new type of warfare, and they soon moved into the line near Epehy. After some time at Ytres and then in reserve near Albert, the Division moved to Ypres at the end of August, where the officers and men took turns attached to the 15th Division to learn the geography of the area. In October the Division moved out of the mud and desolation of Ypres and headed to Nieuport where Tylden was with HQ at La Panne, a seaside village. This was the extreme left of the line, and although quiet in comparison to Ypres, it was constantly shelled, often with gas.

During October Tylden became ADC to Major-General Solly-Flood, who assumed command of the Division, and in November they moved to Givenchy on the La Bassée Canal near Bethune. Here Tylden relinquished his appointment and was seconded to 6th Division during February 1918 as Camp Commandant and ADC to Major-General T.O.

Marden. From this point until the end of the war Tylden's experiences were much the same as JSR Tufton, the Division's APM. During the *Kaiserschlacht* the Division was pushed back by the initial onslaught, and after a period of hard fighting Tylden was back in the Ypres sector. During May the Division moved southwards, and in August had the American 27th Division attached for instruction. By September Tylden was with HQ near St Quentin.

As the *100 Days Offensive* began the 6th Division was involved in the *Battles of the Hindenburg Line*, taking part in the attack to take the high ground overlooking St Quentin. When the German line was breached the Division pushed on *Beyond the Hindenburg Line*, across the Selle and on to the Sambre which was crossed with the support of American tanks. The Division was relieved at the end of October, so Tylden was not in the line during the *Final Push*, but he did join the Army of Occupation in Germany following the Armistice. In April 1919 he relinquished his commission on account of ill health contracted on active service, retaining the rank of Captain. That same month his wife gave birth to his second daughter.

Back in England Tylden became a JP for the County of Kent in 1920, made his debut for the 2nd XI, and was also elected to the Kent Committee. He appeared sporadically up to 1923 when he was asked to captain the side, and although he played only a handful of times he did make his single 1st XI appearance that year against Oxford. He played a lot of club cricket, turning out regularly for the Band of Brothers 1921-1929, and also appeared for I Zingari 1925-1929, the Mote 1923-1929 and for a Lord Harris XI against the West Indies in 1923. He also fielded his own side, Captain JR Tylden's Team, against The Loyal Regiment in 1928 at the County Ground, Gravesend, but unfortunately failed to score. Having all but given up playing, he was re-elected to the Kent Committee, a role he served in until the end of 1932. He was also Master of the Tickham Hunt.

In 1931 Tylden was married a second time, to Margaret Lilian Forbes at St Ethelburga's Bishopsgate, and they spent many years farming at Milstead. During WW2 he served again, appointed Captain and Adjutant to the 2nd London Battalion in the Home Guard during 1940. After two years' service he resigned his commission aged 53. *The Times* reported that he died from the effects of an accident on 24 February 1949.

CAPTAIN GERALD JOHN VILLIERS WEIGALL

Gerry Weigall was associated with Kent cricket for many years, as both player and coach. Born in Wimbledon, Surrey on 19 October 1870, he was the third son of Henry Weigall and Lady Rose Sophia Mary Weigall, daughter of the eleventh Earl of Westmorland. His father was a renowned artist of the Victorian era, and was also a Justice of the Peace for Kent and the Cinque Ports. Living at Marylebone, Weigall's education began at Wimbledon before entering Wellington College where he was a member of Hardinge Dormitory from

1884-1888. It was there he learned his cricket, and was in the XI from 1886 to 1888. He matriculated at Easter 1889, and was at Emmanuel College, Cambridge until 1892, a Blue in his last two years. He made 63 not out in the 1892 University match, and for Emmanuel College against Peterhouse in 1891 he made his career-highest score of 265. In addition to cricket, he was passionate about squash rackets, and played in the doubles against Oxford in 1892.

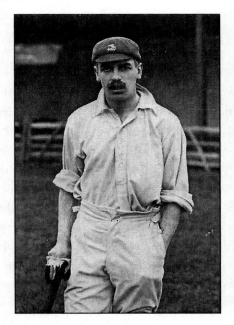 

Weigall, pictured in his playing days (left) was Coach at the Tonbridge Nursery in 1914 and was commissioned into the Kent Cyclists (right)

Weigall made his debut for Kent against Warwickshire in 1891 in a non-first class fixture, and made his first class debut against MCC, scoring 61 in the second innings. All this before he was awarded his Blue. He went on to play 130 times for the county between 1891 and 1903, received his cap in 1892, and travelled to America with the Kent team in 1903. He played for the Gentlemen against Players in 1900, and also made numerous appearances for Gentlemen of England and the MCC. During these years he was as a member of the Stock Exchange and in September 1897 was married to Josephine Harrison. On the retirement of Capt. McCanlis, Weigall was appointed cricket Coach at the Tonbridge Nursery in 1912, and he played for the 2nd XI on occasion up to August 1914.

Weigall was not slow to volunteer, and having undergone his medical at the end of November, he enlisted with the Inns Of Court Officer Training Corps (OTC) three days later. He was embodied as a Private in the TF, signing to serve for 4 years, but actually only serving for one month. Just days after his embodiment, Weigall was submitting his application for a commission and on 28 December was appointed Temporary Captain with the Kent Cyclists. He joined the 1st (Reserve) Battalion, which was carrying out coastal defence duties at Swale and Rye.

During March 1915 orders were issued for all TF units to form a second reserve unit, and Weigall, with the Reserve battalion, now became a member of the 2/1st. When John le Fleming took command of the 3/1st battalion in October 1915, Weigall was transferred to join him. About this time Weigall was, perhaps embarrassingly for a member of the Cyclists, fined in court for riding his cycle without the correct lights. Whilst the 1/1st Kent Cyclists had their cycles taken away and were posted to India, Weigall and le Fleming's battalion became a recruiting and training unit, mainly seeking volunteers in Tonbridge and Cambridge, and passing drafts on to the 2/1st at Canterbury.

By summer of 1916 the battalion was reduced to a cadre under Weigall and, although his papers are not particularly enlightening, it seems that as the 3/1st was run down he was posted overseas, attached to the Bedfordshire Regiment, to serve in Burma and India 1916-1920 on garrison duties. Whilst in the East he found ample opportunities to play cricket. In December 1917 he, and his brother Louis, represented the Europeans and Parsees versus the Hindus and Muslims in the Bombay Quadrangular Tournament. Aside from playing in the tournament annually, he was in an England side playing India at Bombay just ten days after the Armistice. Whilst Weigall was in India, Lord Harris wrote to the War Office on his behalf, seeking an appointment for him as a Physical Training Instructor. Unfortunately for Weigall such positions were being filled by Regular Officers only, and as a Territorial he was ruled out.

Back in England Weigall was demobilized and retired from the service with the rank of Captain in 1921, having attained the age limit. He resumed his position as coach at Tonbridge Nursery, playing for and captaining the 2nd XI until 1929. During that time he also toured Argentina with the MCC 1926-1927, and visited Jamaica with Tennyson's XI in 1928. The Kent Committee moved the Nursery from Tonbridge to Canterbury in 1927, and by 1929 persuaded Weigall to resign his position. He rarely missed a Kent match and continued to play club cricket and squash up to the outbreak of WW2, during which he suffered poor health. He died in a Dublin hospital on 17 May 1944, and was buried at Mount Jerome Cemetery.

WHITEHEAD BROTHERS

George William Edendale and James Hugh Edendale Whitehead were the sons of Lord George Hugh Whitehead, a stock broker and Justice of the Peace, and Lady Gertrude

Grace Whitehead, of Wilmington Hall, Dartford. Both boys were born in Bromley, James on 8 July 1890 and George on 27 August 1895. James was educated at the Old Ride, Branksome Park at Bournemouth before attending Clifton College, Bristol. There he played cricket and was also one of the school's best Fives (or hand-tennis) players. In 1908 against Malvern he scored 42 out of 195 and then 17 not out as Clifton reached the 78 required for victory. His batting average in 1909 was 28.27, including scores of 70 and 58 against Rugby, and 63 in the drawn match against Cheltenham.

James and George Whitehead, the picture taken when James was at Clifton and George at Cordwalles. Copyright Clifton College

George attended Cordwalles preparatory school in Maidenhead from 1904 to 1909, playing in the Cricket XI 1907-1909, as captain in the last two of those three years. In 1909 he scored 457 runs in nine innings, thus averaging 50 per innings, the next highest being 13.5. He followed James to Clifton College in 1909 where he held two scholarships, represented the school at Fives, was in the Football XV for two years, and the Cricket XI for four years, as Captain in 1913 and 1914.

James left Clifton for Trinity College, Cambridge, where he was Captain of the college XI and scored 57 and 17 in the Freshmen's match. He was awarded his Blue for athletics, and represented Oxford in the hurdles in 1912. George meanwhile was still making his mark at Clifton, breaking the school record when he made 259 not out against Liverpool in 1912. The following year his aggregate was 701, including three centuries, at an average of 46.73, and in 1914 he scored over 400 runs at an average of 40.41. Both brothers played for Kent in the 2nd XI between 1912 and 1914, and whilst George made two appearances for the 1st XI in 1914, James had made his first class debut against the county when selected for the MCC at Lord's two years previously. The last time James played for Kent was at the Oval in 1914 where he hit 61 in the first innings. His last match before war broke out was in August 1914 for MCC against the Public Schools for whom his brother was playing.

George Whitehead on the occasion of his Kent debut at Gravesend in August 1914, shortly after the declaration of war. Copyright Clifton College

George made his Kent debut against Warwickshire at Gravesend on 24 August, by which time the BEF had been despatched to France. Just days short of his nineteenth birthday, he opened with Ted Humphreys and, although unsuccessful with the bat, he was on the winning side. He held two catches to dismiss Frank Field in both innings, once off the bowling of Woolley and once off Freeman. A few days later, on 27 August, he was at Lords for the match against Middlesex. Again the runs did not flow off his bat, but he did catch Patsy Hendren off Blythe's bowling in the first innings. He was a very promising player, and who knows what he might have achieved but for the War. George was entered at Trinity College, Oxford, to take honours in the Classical School and would no doubt have earned a Blue. Instead he, and James, chose to serve their country.

LIEUTENANT GEORGE WILLIAM EDENDALE WHITEHEAD

Whilst at Clifton, George Whitehead had been a sapper in the College Engineer Corps, and he applied to take the entrance exam for the Royal Military Academy (RMA) at Woolwich at the start of October 1914. He passed with flying colours and studied at the RMA from December to July, the wartime courses being much shorter in duration than those in peacetime. The London Gazette listed him amongst the "*Gentleman Cadets from the Royal Military Academy, to be Second Lieutenants. Dated 28th July, 1915*" as he was commissioned into the Royal Horse and Royal Field Artillery (RFA). Some five weeks later he was on his way to the Front.

Reaching France not long before the Battle of *Loos*, which opened on 25 September, Whitehead joined 75th Brigade RFA and took part in the four-day preliminary bombardment that was designed to cut the wire defences and soften up the enemy. He wrote several letters to his family on the eve of, and during, the offensive, and in the lead up to the attack he penned the following [*Clifton College: Foundation to Evacuation*, ed. C S Knighton (Bristol Record Society 65, 2012), p. 372]:

There is something of a show on. I think we are to bombard the Germans and their line of approach for about four days – then the advance begins. Several batteries have been moved up for it like ourselves.

The general bombardment begins at daylight and goes on until dusk. Our show begins at 6.00 p.m. and goes on until 7.00 a.m. We have to keep a couple of guns firing one on each of two roads at the rate of six rounds an hour per gun with irregular intervals between rounds. In between our five machine-guns play on the road. These roads are two targets that should have been registered by aeroplane. We had to measure them off the map and lay by the compass. I hope we shall hit something but it doesn't seem likely to me.

Four days into the battle he wrote that there was no more ammunition for them and they were not able to fire their guns. This and his question as to whether they were actually hitting their targets sum up the situation. The initial bombardment had been weak through lack of ammunition and the initial attack and capture of Loos was in reality through advantage in numbers. The fact the wire was not broken in some parts of the line, saw the attack falter, and British gains were not consolidated. The following days' renewed attempts to advance failed. Three days after the battle began the British were, in some places, back in their original positions with more than 20,000 casualties.

Watching the wounded return, Whitehead wrote of the '*poor devils*', and revealed an admiration for their nerve:

Fancy knowing twelve hours beforehand when you are going to charge. Do you remember what I was like before the Rugby match last year and that was only a game?

Whitehead took his turn as a Forward Observation Officer during the offensive. On one occasion, in the middle of a German counter-attack, he struggled to tap into the British wire and spent the night creeping up and down, trying to report in without success. Subsequent German attacks failed, as did a last attempt by the British on 13 October. On that day Whitehead wrote:

I've got an awful mope on. War makes one awfully angry. Poor devils getting blown to bits, houses and villages and towns destroyed and thousands of people, innocent civilians getting ruined and turned out of their homes.

There were a lot of dead men lying about unburied – by the Buffs H.Q. – the other day. They must have been there for several days as they were between our old front trenches and the Germans and they had been killed in the attack. I don't know whose job it was to have buried them. It was disgraceful that they should be left like that…

They were mostly Scotchmen, and there were a few Germans as well. I don't mind bullets or shells or dead men particularly, but the whole show makes me angry and mopy.

Following the failure of *Loos*, Whitehead's battery moved to Laventie in mid-November, remaining there until February. During December he wrote to express his pleasure at the news Sir Douglas Haig was taking over from Sir John French as Commander-in-Chief of the BEF, saying "*One up to S.H., C.C.*". Haig was a former Clifton College student, in the School House with Whitehead senior from 1877-1879. By March the 75th RFA was at St. Jean near Ypres. An incident occurred there that Whitehead did not mention until writing to his brother in November;

A Doctor got a DSO for walking up to dress some men we had wounded last May one night when the roads were rather badly shelled. It was less than a mile to walk there and back. A sergeant of ours and I were out on the road for four and a half hours disentangling some wagons which had got badly strafed that night. We had to pick bits of harness out of mules' guts to get some sort of teams together and get the wagons away. It was quite thrilling, shouldn't have don't it I don't suppose if I hadn't had a good dinner. Only of course I didn't tell anyone what had happened, so no one knows. Don't tell anyone this. But I call that a jolly cheap DSO. What annoyed me was that I got to bed at 2.30 and had to be in the OP by 4.0 o'clock.

That summer Whitehead went on leave to England, travelling to Bournemouth to visit his brother James in a nursing home. He then spent two nights at Clifton, playing cricket against the school and left for France on 12 June to re-join his battery. He did not mention the incident at Ypres to anyone. A memorandum describing the events was found with his belongings on his death, the content being summarised by his family as follows:

The Germans were shelling the roads to prevent supports and ammunition going up. A tree was knocked across the road: in trying to remove it five of his men were hit. He was fetched. The shelling continued for hours with quiet intervals of five or more minutes. Six D.A.C. Wagons came up; ten out of the thirty six mules were killed or badly wounded and six of the drivers. All the wagons had to be unloaded, and turned round, and teams made up as far as possible. He had to shoot two of the mules. He had difficulty with some of the drivers who wanted not to work until the shelling stopped and he had to show them the business end of his revolver: he pitied them but the work had to be done, and when they started they worked well. Altogether he had fifty men sheltering in the farm and fifteen men were wounded on the road: of these two died during the night. The whole affair lasted over four hours before everything was clear. An awful night's work, and not one word did he say. Months afterwards when spoken to he said that "Of course he wasn't going to blow his own trumpet, and he was the only officer present.

In fact, when the commanding officers of 75th Brigade and its A Battery heard of the incident and spoke to Whitehead, he made light of his role and recommended the sergeant with him be put forward for the Distinguished Conduct Medal. It was by then too late to recommend Whitehead for an award, though it was felt he would have plenty of opportunities to earn a decoration later on.

Although not involved in the bombardment designed to soften up the enemy for the main offensive, Whitehead's battery did head to that part of the front later in the summer as the *Somme Continued*. He described their living conditions in a letter dated 20 October 1916;

Our present position is just behind an old Hun trench in which we live. There are a lot of splendid dug-outs further up the trench 30 or 40 feet deep, but unfortunately the Hun left none behind him in the part we occupy. We have had three dug-outs down to about 20 feet, in which some of the men sleep and one is used for a telephone dug-out. I'm sleeping in one end of that now. I started at the bottom of the trench under the open sky when it was fine. Then when it looked like rain I moved to a little communication-trench from one of the gun-pits to the main trench. It had boards and corrugated iron over it, but a couple of nights ago we had some pretty heavy rain and I woke to find myself lying in a pool of water, my blankets wet through, the sides of the trench falling in and threatening to bury me and my bed and clothes. I'm sorry I didn't sleep in my clothes as I should have kept my things moderately dry, but I didn't and the trench fell in over my bags and my coat. I lost all my studs too, so at present, nobody having a spare one, I am wearing a 'British Warm' all day with the collar turned up...

That autumn Whitehead fell ill with appendicitis and, following an operation toward the end of November, he returned to England to recover. He continually pushed to return to the front, but a year passed before he was considered fit enough for General Service. His convalescence had however given him time to think, and he was considering joining the Royal Flying Corps (RFC):

No one who hasn't been out can realise what it is like to sit in a trench from which you can't move and be shelled for hours with heavy stuff.....then to walk home through hundreds of corpses in all stages of decomposition, to a dug-out a foot deep in water, and remember the Gunners are generally in action for a couple of months at a time. If I get into the R.F.C. I shall try to become a pilot…..The danger of spills is almost always due to over confidence and carelessness which is a very good reason why I shouldn't come to grief, if you think of it. Can you ever remember me trying to hit just because I had made fifty, or because I had hit a couple of fours unless there was no need for my side to make more runs? Well, I don't see myself doing unnecessary 'stunts'.

The application to train as a pilot was successful, and Whitehead was posted to Reading in January 1918 where he studied engines, air-frames, theory of flying, Morse, and other subjects relative to the training of a pilot. At the end of March he moved to Stamford for basic flying instruction, and three months later was attached to 35 Wing RAF as temporary 2nd Lieutenant and Honorary Lieutenant. During July he underwent wireless and observer training at Worthy Down, but the next month found time for some cricket, captaining a Public Schools XI against the No1 Royal Fleet Auxiliary Cadet School at Lord's. He scored a well received 66 out of his side's total of 146, and also took 1 for 28 in his six overs.

This photograph of George Whitehead was taken on 10 September 1918, just four days before he departed to join the RAF in Belgium. His uniform still bears his Artillery buttons and markings, to which his Wings have been added. Copyright Clifton College

What became known as the *100 Day Offensive* began during August 1918. The following month Whitehead was transferred to the BEF as an RE8 pilot, and served with 53 Squadron in the Ypres area. On 17 October 1918 at 07.50 he took off from Abeele aerodrome in RE8 D6799 with his observer 2nd Lt. Reginald Hopkin Hill Griffiths, MC, on an artillery patrol to spot German gun positions. Two months later Whitehead's father received a letter from the Mayor of Lauwe, Belgium, describing what happened that day;

My Dear Sir,
On Thursday October 17th, at nine o'clock in the morning an English aeroplane

appeared flying very low and carrying two persons, Lieutenant Whitehead and Lieutenant Griffiths. Your son raised himself in the machine, and with a flag in his hand, amid the cheers of the population, proclaimed our happy deliverance.

The aeroplane flew over the town repeatedly, always saluted by the inhabitants, until when flying near the Railway Station, which is twenty-five minutes walk from the centre of town, it was fired at by German machine-guns. Flying at a low height it was hit by bullets which, alas, wounded your son and his observer. The machine made a steep dive and the lifeless bodies of your brave men were borne into a room in our hospital. They were buried the next day in the Military Cemetery by a party of English soldiers.

The aeroplane crashed in a field of the Farm Verbrugge, and the cemetery they were buried in was the Military Cemetery at Lauwe on Farm Wyseur. The cemetery was on a road which the Municipality renamed "Place George Whitehead", although the road no longer bears that name. This was not to be the last resting place of Whitehead and Griffiths. During 1924-1925 the war graves in the surrounding areas were moved to a central place, the Harlebeke New British Cemetery, and the two airmen now rest there.

[I am grateful to Clifton College for permission to print extracts from the unpublished papers of G.W.E. Whitehead held in the College Archives.]

2ND LIEUTENANT JAMES HUGH EDENDALE WHITEHEAD

James Whitehead had started work in 1914 as a partner in his father's firm, George Whitehead and Chown, and managed to add to his sporting achievements when crowned champion hurdler of the Stock Exchange. He made his application for a commission at the end of October and was gazetted temporary 2nd Lieutenant in the 9th Battalion Royal West Kent Regiment (RWK) on 5 November. The 9th RWK was formed in Chatham the month before, as part of K4 (Kitchener's fourth New Army). During April 1915 the battalion was converted into a reserve battalion and Whitehead moved with it to Canterbury in June 1915, and then to Colchester in July. When he went on leave in September, Whitehead fell ill. It transpired he had tuberculosis, and was so badly affected by it that by March 1916 he had to resign his commission.

In June 1916 George visited him at a nursing home in Bournemouth whilst on leave, and later in the year he moved to Pandyffryn Hall Sanatorium, in Pennaenmawn, Wales, from which place he applied to the War office for a pension as he was unable to pursue his ordinary business, and was dependent on his friends. He was awarded the Silver War Badge in October 1916. His health being undermined, he suffered from influenza in the epidemic of 1918-1919 and after a drawn out illness, borne with great fortitude, he died on 13 March, 1919 at Queen Annes Mansions, St. James Park, London. He was buried in the family vault at St. Michael Churchyard, Wilmington, Kent. A friend wrote "Both at Clifton and Oxford I had every opportunity of recognizing in him an exceptionally fine character, modest, simple, sensitive, and with any amount of grit."

James Whitehead served with the Royal West Kent Regiment. Copyright Clifton College

PRIVATE ERASMUS ALBERT WILLSON

Erasmus Albert Willson was born in Sittingbourne on 13 October 1878 to James George Willson, a dentist, and Catherine Priscilla (née Twort). Having attended Borden Grammar School, where he was in the XI 1893-97, he was engaged on the staff at the Tonbridge Nursery. His debut appearance for the 2nd XI came in August against Sussex at Tonbridge, when he scored 11 runs and he and Arthur du Boulay took four wickets apiece. The next season he played for Gore Court and for Kent as an amateur, making his first class debut in the County Championship at Trent Bridge. *The Times* gave the incorrect initials when they noted that the county was 'trying Mr H Willson, a young fast bowler'. He took what was to be his one and only first class wicket, and played twice more for the 2nd XI that season, scoring 55 against Sussex at Hove, and claimed 2-17 and 5-80 in the return match at Tonbridge.

Willson worked as a bank clerk up until the war, his cricket at club level. He married Nora Beatrice Mary Champion at Wandsworth in February 1903, and the couple later moved to Mitcham in Surrey. On the outbreak of hostilities he was, at 35 years old, outside the age limit and did not attest until December 1915, during the Derby Scheme. At this time he was living in Streatham with his wife and two children. Having attested on 9 December Willson was transferred to the Army Reserve, and went home to await his call-up. He was not called to a medical at the Central London Recruiting Depot until May 1917 and was then mobilized and posted the following month, as a Private in the 2nd Battalion Artists Rifles.

The 1st Artists Rifles had been posted to France in 1914 but, once there, were established as a Training Corps for officers in the field. The 2nd Battalion was subsequently structured along similar lines, organised as a School of Instruction for officers from other Territorial regiments. The regiment was recognised as an Officers' Training Corps, and the Home Battalion became the 2nd Artists Rifles OTC. Half of the battalion was dedicated to providing cadets with preliminary training, and was designated No.15 (Artists Rifles) Officer Cadet Battalion. Having received their basic training, candidates then passed on to the other four companies at Gidea Park for officer training.

No.15 OCB was based at Hare Hall Camp in Romford, where the park had been taken over for use by the Army, and this is where Willson was posted in August 1917. He remained at the camp for the duration of the war, assisting in the training of cadets, who were sent on to the front. After demobilzation at the Crystal Palace Dispersal Centre in February 1919, Willson was transferred to Class Z Army Reserve, liable for recall in the event of a national emergency. He returned to live in Sittingbourne in his later years, and died there on 17 April 1948.

CAPTAIN GEORGE EDWARD CHARLES WOOD

George Edward Charles Wood was born at Blackheath on 22 August 1893, the son of Ernest Wood, and his education started at Shirley House, the same school that Sydney and Arthur Day had attended a few years previously. Wood went on to Cheltenham 1908-1912 and was in the Eleven for the last three of those years. He headed the averages in 1910 and 1911, and was second in 1912 when he had the responsibility of being captain. He also played in the school Rugby XV and joined the College OTC, leaving with the rank of 2nd Lieutenant.

Going up to Cambridge at the end of 1912, he joined Pembroke College and tried for the XI, but had to wait until 1914 for his Blue. He started that year winning his Hockey Blue and then in the cricket match against Oxford he scored 61 and 14, took three catches and made two stumpings, but finished on the losing side. He took part in three Minor Counties matches, two for Surrey 2nd XI in 1913 and one for Kent 2nd XI in July 1914.

George Wood pictured in 1912 in the Cheltenham Cricket XI, reproduced Courtesy of Cheltenham College Archives

Wood applied for a commission just two days after the declaration of war, with a recommendation from the Cambridge OTC even though he had not served with them. He was appointed temporary 2nd Lieutenant in the Infantry on 9 September and temporary Lieutenant in the 7th Gloucestershire Regiment five weeks later, seemingly due to his links with Cheltenham. The battalion had been raised as part of K1, Kitchener's first New Army, and was under the command of 39th Brigade in 13th Division. Wood joined his unit in February, as it moved to Blackdown near Farnborough for final training. Orders were received in June to prepare for a move to *Gallipoli*.

The battalion sailed via Alexandria and Lemnos, and Wood finally landed on V Beach near Cape Helles on 9 July, going into billets at Gully Beach. Three weeks were spent settling in, and then the Gloucesters were suddenly withdrawn to Lemnos. The 13th Division had been selected to take part in an operation to break out of the Allied positions at Anzac Cove, and they left Lemnos for their new destination on 3 August. When the Australian, New Zealand, Indian and Gurkha troops attacked the heights of Chunuk Bair and Hill 971 on 6 August, the 39th Brigade formed part of the left support column. The Brigade Machine-Gun Officer was sick and had to be left behind, and Wood was appointed to that role. He was perhaps lucky not to have gone into the attack with his battalion – every officer was killed or wounded in the fighting on 8 August in which the heights were taken, but not held.

Several days later the Brigade Machine-Gun Officer returned from Lemnos to resume his duties, and Wood was appointed Brigade Staff Captain, the position being vacant following the offensive. He was attached to HQ as the Brigade was moved from Anzac to Suvla, where reinforcements soon arrived for the badly mauled battalions. It proved almost impossible to maintain numbers at a reasonable level with the high sick rate, and Wood himself fell ill in October and was evacuated. He missed the storms in November, and the evacuation from the Peninsula in December, and his position as Staff Officer was taken by another man. When he was fit for duty, it was to the 7th Gloucesters he returned, by this time at Alexandria in *Egypt*. During a period on outpost duties on the eastern bank of the Suez, Wood was appointed battalion Adjutant.

Whereas many Divisions evacuated from Gallipoli remained in Egypt to take part in the campaign in Palestine, the 13th Division was destined to go to *Mesopotamia*, to reinforce the forces attempting to relieve Kut. Wood sailed with his battalion on 16 February, via Suez to Kuwait, and then changed ship to proceed up the Tigris to Basra. There the Gloucesters were left behind until April, quarantined due to several cases of relapsing fever. The Division had joined the fighting up the Tigris on 5 April, and the Gloucesters arrived to take part two weeks later. On Wood's first day in the line, the Turks shelled the Gloucesters trenches, and in the first hour they suffered fifty casualties. During the days fighting he was 'wounded slightly' but stayed at duty. Despite the best efforts of the relieving force, Kut fell to the Turks at the end of the month.

The attempted relief had cost the Allies 23,000 casualties, around three times the number of men they set out to rescue. Reorganisation was needed over the summer months before hostilities resumed in the cooler weather. Wood had left the Gloucesters on 25 April to take up an appointment as Staff Captain with the Brigade again, and would have had a key role in the reorganization of the 39th as they moved to a rest camp to train. He fell sick and was admitted to hospital in June, re-joining the Brigade in July at Gomorrah, not the Biblical city but the name of a post (another was called Sodom). Some time was spent away from the line at Amara due to a lack of hutted accommodation, and training continued into November.

When the Allied offensive was launched in December, Wood was with Brigade HQ throughout the advance. Kut was taken and the Turks retreated back to Baghdad which fell in March, the Brigade establishing a line of defence north of the city. By the time Wood spent a period of leave in Baghdad during July, he had been appointed Brigade Major. Until the final offensive up the Tigris in August 1918, there was little change in the Allied position, and Wood spent a long period of leave in India and Ceylon between April and July. When he returned the Brigade was under orders to head to the *Caucasus* to join Dunsterforce.

As Staff Captain, Wood was involved in organising the move. By 22 August he was boarding a Russian Steamer near Enzeli with Brigade HQ, and soon arrived in Baku. There the Brigade found the line was very vague and held only by a small number of British troops and some 'absolutely unreliable' Russian and Armenian battalions. The Turks were close by and shelling the city, but the Armenians had no proper trench system and made no attempt to organise one. During an inspection of the defences on 26 August the Turks made an attack on that part of the line held by the North Staffordshires. The outnumbered British troops were almost annihilated but held out gallantly whilst every available man was ferried forward in lorries to aid them. Wood joined Brigade HQ as it moved forward to take command of all British troops in the area.

As Brigade HQ set about establishing a new line of defence, Wood had his hands full. The British were given no assistance by the Russians, the war diary noting the Russian commander was 'a completely useless lazy individual'. When the enemy attacked again on the last day of the month, the British were left to it, and had to withdraw to avoid being wiped out. The Armenians were no better. When they were shelled they left the line to shelter in the town, leaving the British flank exposed. The situation became so dire that the Brigade diary entries for 1-14 September were destroyed to avoid them falling into enemy hands. Notes recorded after the event reveal that on 1 September the enemy attacked and the Russians and Armenians fled. The 9th Warwicks covered the retirement until their ammunition ran out and over seventy men failed to return.

In the days that followed, Wood took on the role of Brigade Major when that officer was temporarily transferred. The enemy attacked on 14 September, and the British were compelled to evacuate the town owing to a lack of support. The 39th Brigade was only 892 effective rifles when it left Baku, less than the strength of a battalion. It was on this day that the Brigade diary was destroyed, and Wood joined the retreat through the town, each man carrying as many bombs as possible in case street fighting was encountered. Reaching the port, the Brigade left by sea for Enzeli, and Wood relinquished the role of Brigade Major en route, reverting to Staff Captain.

Enzeli was home to Wood for the latter part of September, and also to the many refugees who fled the massacre of Armenians in Baku. The Brigade Major was among the ten per cent of the Brigade's strength sick in hospital, and Wood took over the role for a fortnight, by now quite familiar with the position. He had reverted to Staff Captain when an Armistice was signed with Turkey at the end of October, and the Brigade soon headed back to Baku. The enemy had slaughtered 30,000 civilians and the British received a warm welcome. Wood left Baku in February 1919, heading for the UK via Constantinople and was demobilized the following month.

George Wood (right) pictured with Kent captain Lionel Troughton in 1921

During October Wood resumed his studies at Cambridge. He was a Rugby and Cricket Blue in 1919 and Cricket again in 1920 when he was captain, and had an average of 39 in his three innings against Oxford. In 1919 against Free Foresters at Fenner's he scored 128 in 140 minutes, his only first class century. He made his Kent debut in 1919 against Hampshire, received his Cap the following year, and represented the county 41 times. In 1921 he top scored with 63 not out against Middlesex, and earlier in the season made six stumpings against Leicestershire. Most of his appearances were made by 1924 with one final appearance against MCC in 1927.

Work at the Stock Exchange limited his ability to play, and prevented him accepting an invitation to tour Australia with MCC in 1920. He did however appear for the Gentlemen against Players on five occasions, kept wicket for England against the Rest and Yorkshire in 1923, and played in three Tests against South Africa in 1924. In 1921 he twice came out on top of the otherwise undefeated Australian tourists, first for AC Maclaren's amateur side, and then CI Thornton's XI, having already played in two drawn games for LG Robinson's XI in May and Kent in August.

In 1924 Wood was married to Monica Virginia Corbet Singleton at St. Paul's, Knightsbridge. In the following years he played for MCC, Free Foresters, and the Gentlemen and also accompanied HM Martineau's XI to Egypt in 1929, the matches in Cairo and Alexandria perhaps stirring memories of 1916. In later years he was founder and President of the Googlies Cricket Club, and he was 77 years old when he died in Hampshire on 18 March 1971.

PRIVATE 1ST CLASS FRANK EDWARD WOOLLEY

Frank Edward Woolley was the youngest of the four Woolley brothers, born to Charles and Louisa Woolley at Tonbridge on 27 May 1887. As a boy he grew up near the Angel Ground, and was soon helping out by fielding during practices at the Nursery, before being taken on the staff in 1903. As a young man Tonbridge was his world. Summer was for cricket, and apparently for going fox hunting with Arthur Fielder, whilst during the winter months he turned to football and helped out with his father's motor business. He played football for Tonbridge along with other players at the Nursery, and also for Tonbridge Half Holidays when Bertie Flemons was one of his team-mates. That is the same BC Flemons whose name appears on picture postcards of Kent players during the early 1900s, and who photographed Woolley on numerous occasions. Frank was of a good enough standard to sign for Tunbridge Wells Rangers in 1906, but was destined to be a household name in the game of cricket.

Woolley's cricketing successes are well recorded, and a brief summary should suffice here. He was awarded his cap in 1906, and from that year on was a regular in the side, instrumental in the Championship wins of 1909, 1910 and 1913. From 1907 until he retired Woolley did not fail to score 1,000 runs in a season, and did so for Kent every year except 1919 when he was not helped by the reduced fixture list. He was named one of Wisden's cricketers of the year in 1911, and in 1914 he scored over 2,000 runs for the first of four occasions. He represented England for the first time in 1909 and went on to play 64 Tests under 14 different captains.

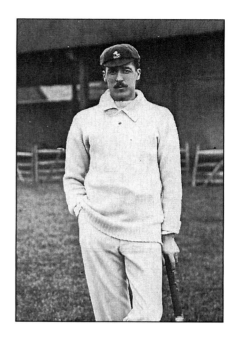

Frank Woolley sporting the moustache he had to remove when he joined the RNAS

Three Woolley brothers joined the Kent Fortress Engineers (KFE) in 1914 and went on to serve overseas, but Frank did not enlist immediately. He was married to Sybil Fordham during September, and the pre-wedding organization, and settling into married life took priority. This put him on the list of players written to by the Committee asking what he was doing to assist the War effort. Woolley promised to join the KFE but on presenting himself for his medical he was surprised to be told he was unfit on account of the compacted toes on both his feet. As the general belief of the public was that the war would soon be over, he contented himself with helping in his father's workshop which had been converted to facilitate the manufacture of munitions.

Jack Hobbs was another cricketer working in munitions, and he was instrumental in recruiting Woolley to the Bradford League at the end of 1915. Hobbs found some animosity in his family because other relations were serving, and there have been the occasional murmurs about Woolley. Whereas Hobbs was a conscript when he joined the RFC in October 1916, Woolley volunteered his services again that same year. The Essex cricketer Richard Keigwin had urged Frank to try the RNAS, and when he did so his application was successful. Woolley was pleased as he had a liking for the Navy, even though they did relieve him of his moustache. His application was made after conscription was introduced but, as he was still under medical exemption, he was not liable for call up and any suggestions he was avoiding service can be put aside.

It was November 1916 before he began training as Aircraftman second class. During March 1917 he was posted to Dover, where the RNAS had a seaplane base on the seafront, and was attached to the Motor Boat section. During his time at Dover Woolley was promoted to Aircraftman first class, and in February of 1918 moved to Felixstowe where he spent time as the coxswain of a rescue launch, tasked with picking up the crews of ditched planes. Whilst Woolley was at Felixstowe the work of the station and its crews became vital to the protection of Britain's merchant shipping due to the U-Boat threat. When the RNAS merged into the RAF in April, he was given the new rank of Private 1st Class, and by July was posted to North Queensferry on the Firth of Forth in Scotland.

Although officially a member of the RAF, Woolley was employed by Admiral Sir John de Robeck, who was a keen cricketer. In this remote station Robeck had Woolley ferry despatches and carry out odd jobs. The base in Scotland had been used throughout the War to help enforce the blockade and deny Germany access to the Atlantic. In his new role Woolley was attached to Robeck's flagship the King George V, which had seen service at Jutland. It was berthed by a kite balloon station and, on their arrival, Frank and his crew tied up their launch and went to their new quarters. The next morning they discovered a crowd of amused sailors studying the launch which was now suspended by its mooring ropes, some ten feet above water after the tide went out. After this initial faux pas, Woolley settled into his new role, and Robeck made life more enjoyable by arranging for some of the men to play cricket at the home of former Surrey captain Lord Roseberry.

Plum Warner gave Woolley several more opportunities to play in the summer of 1918, and as the War came to an end Woolley could look forward to returning to county cricket. He passed through Crystal Palace dispersal centre in January 1919 and was transferred to RAF G Reserve and officially discharged the following year. He played for twenty more seasons post-war, and the success in the first part of his career continued, some highlights being: second in the list of most runs scored in a career with 58,959 at average 40.77; fifth in the list of most runs scored in a season with 3,352 at 60.94 in 1928; only six players scored more than his 145 career centuries, of which 122 were for Kent. He also held more catches than any other non wicket-keeper with 1,018, the nearest to his record being WG Grace with 876.

Woolley lived another forty years after his retirement from the game, reaching the age of 91. His wife Sybil passed away in 1962 and he was married a second time to Martha Wilson Morse, settling in Nova Scotia, Canada with her. It was there he died in the village of Chester on 18 October 1978. Although so far from his country of birth, a memorial service was held at Canterbury Cathedral in honour of one of the greatest cricketers Kent and indeed the world has known.

CAPTAIN CHARLES ROBERT WORTHINGTON

Charles Robert Worthington was born in Surbiton, Surrey on 28 February 1877, the third son of Lucy Ellen (née Oldman) and Richard Burton Worthington, who worked in the Bombay Civil Service for many years. He attended Tonbridge School 1890-1895 where he was in the Football XV in 1894, and the following year was in the Cricket XI and joint winner of the Athletic Points' Cup. He went up to Cambridge in 1895 to study at Caius College, receiving his BA in 1899. Whilst there he played in the Freshmen's match, scoring 66, and then made a single appearance for the Kent 2nd XI against Middlesex at the Angel, Tonbridge. In 1898 he batted with Pinky Burnup and made some useful scores but was not selected for the Oxford fixture. He also made his single appearance for the Kent 1st XI that summer, against Lancashire at Old Trafford, although rain prevented him from batting.

On leaving Cambridge Worthington began studying for a career in medicine, but was interrupted by the Boer War. He joined the Volunteer Company Suffolk Regiment and spent a year in South Africa, earning the Queen's Medal with four clasps, and suffered a bout of malaria as a result. Returning to England he was awarded his MB BC (Bachelor of Medicine, Bachelor of Surgery) in 1903 and took up a position at St. Mary's Hospital in London. Later that year he became Medical Officer in Southern Nigeria under the Colonial Office, and in 1904 became a Surgeon in the Royal Navy. He married Winifred Mary Philips at Builth in Breconshire in 1905, and served seven years as a Navy Surgeon with HMS Powerful. At the end of 1912 he and Winifred emigrated to British Colombia, where he became a rancher.

The first Canadian volunteers came to England as early as October 1914, and as the war continued Worthington chose to join them. He enlisted in April 1916, joining the 102nd (Comox-Atlin) Battalion of the Canadian Expeditionary Force (CEF) with the rank of Private. Following initial training he sailed from Halifax to Liverpool at the end of June, remaining in England for six weeks as the unit was organised for service in France. The 102nd embarked on 11 August, and moved to Godewaersvelde near the Belgian border where Worthington was promoted to Corporal. The men received instructional tours in the St. Eloi trenches, between Messines and Ypres, and soon received their first casualties from heavy shelling. Having been issued with their box respirators at the beginning of October, and probably thankful they had not experienced a gas attack in the meantime, they moved south to Albert where the *Somme Continued*.

Worthington was in the trenches by 18 October, and the battalion was put into the attack three days later, capturing part of Regina Trench, and defending it against numerous counter-attacks. The remainder of the trench was captured in November, although on that day Worthington was on stretcher-bearer duties. At the end of December the 102nd were back in the trenches, and spent New Years' Day in the line at Vimy Ridge. Worthington then set off for the 4th Canadian Divisional School, and was promoted to Sergeant on 12 January. Having returned to his unit a fortnight later, he received orders to transfer to the Canadian Training Depot at Shorncliffe, with a view to being appointed to a commission in the Canadian Army Medical Corps.

After a period of leave Worthington reported at Witley, and was posted to the Assistant Director Medical Service (ADMS) 5th Division. On 24 April, now holding the rank of Captain, he reported for duty with No.14 Canadian Field Ambulance and was attached to a Sick Detention Hut, one of a number set up to deal with milder cases. Having barely settled into his new position, Worthington was given leave to attend the funeral of his brother, Richard Fitzpatrick Worthington, who died from wounds received whilst serving with the Gloucestershire Regiment. The remainder of 1917 was spent in a routine of work and training.

Worthington had a fall whilst horseback riding early in 1918 and, having eventually reported sick, was admitted to hospital. An x-ray revealed a fractured elbow, and he spent a period of time at the Canadian Convalescent Officers Hospital at Matlock, Bath. Once recovered he was attached to the CAMC Reserve and Training Depot at Shorncliffe during July, and on 3 August proceeded overseas for duty with No.2 Divisional Train in France, being one of seven officers leaving the depot that day as reinforcements. He arrived near Saleux in the Somme region on 7 August, about the time the *Hundred Days Offensive* began. Regular moves would have been required to keep up with the advances during the *Battles of the Hindenburg Line*, and the *Final Push*, and he was at Elouges when the Armistice took effect.

Worthington's Division formed part of the Army of Occupation, and he moved into Germany during December, and spent Christmas near Bonn. He did not return to England for demobilization until April, when he was posted to CAMC Casualty Company at Witley, and retired from the forces in September. His papers noted that he was intending to take up residence in England, but he became a temporary Captain in the RAMC on 10 October, and was posted to Egypt in November. He served with the 3rd Egyptian Stationary Hospital until June 1920 when he relinquished his commission and returned to his wife in Cam, Gloucestershire. At some point Worthington did return to Canada. When is not clear, but he was resident at Nanaimo, Vancouver Island when he died on 7 December 1950 in Victoria, British Columbia.

ACTING CORPORAL CHARLES THOMAS WYCHERLEY

Charles Thomas Wycherley was born in West Ham and his family lived in Shenley, Hertfordshire before settling at Linton, Kent. He was son of John Wycherley, a coachman and domestic servant from Lancashire, and Emma Wycherley from Hampshire. His mother ran the Bell Inn at Linton for some years, at least from 1913 to 1922 and possibly longer, and it is likely he worked at the pub, citing his occupation as barman when he enlisted. Wycherley was by all accounts a promising all-round cricketer, engaged at the Tonbridge Nursery and playing for Kent 2nd XI in 1913 and 1914. At the start of the season

the *Kent Messenger* referred to him as a free bat, a useful fast to medium right-hand bowler, and an excellent field. He started the year low down the order, but in his last couple of games had pushed up to number three.

Charles Wycherley died whilst serving with the Royal West Kent Regiment in Mesopotamia

Wycherley enlisted on 24 September 1914 not long after the outbreak of war, as a private in the Royal West Kent Regiment (RWK). What remains of his papers is in poor condition, but we can assume that he was initially with the 3rd (Reserve) Battalion, which was first based in Maidstone, and subsequently moved to Chatham whilst he was trained. He was then posted to the 2nd Battalion RWK as a reinforcement, and ordered overseas to *Mesopotamia*. Having left England in December 1915, Wycherley arrived in Mesopotamia early in January. The 2nd Battalion was situated at Butaniya on the Euphrates, having moved out from Nasiriya to keep the local Arabs in check, other than two Companies which had been attached to the force besieged at Kut.

The battalion at Butaniya was mainly occupied in escorting convoys to and from Nasirya. At that time of year the weather was extremely cold, with blizzards and snow, bad enough that some cattle died from exposure. That, coupled with the distance from Nasirya, resulted in a shortage of supplies and an uncomfortable existence for Wycherley and his fellow soldiers. In February it was decided that the demonstration at Butaniya had served its purpose, and a withdrawal to Nasirya was ordered. Part of the column departed on 5 February with the remainder set to depart two days later, though it is not known which part of the force Wycherley was with. Immediately the second party left, Arab tribesmen appeared and started pressing in to attack. It took the column eight hours to reach Nasirya, six of those spent under attack, sometimes engaged in hand to hand fighting. As they fought a rear-guard action, passing through numerous villages en route, more Arabs joined the attack. In total the column suffered 400 casualties, of which 30 were of the 2nd RWK. They were singled out for praise for their steady courage under fire when one of the Indian Battalions was in disorder. Several days later a column went out to teach the Arabs a lesson, and deter similar attacks, some of the villages involved being destroyed.

Most of the fighting in Mesopotamia took place on the River Tigris, as that river was better suited to carrying troops, but the 2nd RWK remained on the Euphrates through 1916, mainly providing escorts to convoys or supplying detachments to columns for demonstrations. Although more drafts arrived in March and June, the high rate of sickness left the battalion with four very weak Companies. From May onwards they were in camp at Khamisiya, south-east of Nasirya, to keep the Arabs in order in that area, and Wycherley joined the sick list when he was admitted to hospital suffering from Malaria. Conditions were harsh, and the health of most of the men suffered. In his book *The Long Road to Baghdad: Volume I (Candler, 1919: 282)* the author recalled encountering some men of the West Kent Regiment on the Euphrates that summer:

We called at Khamisiyeh on the way back, and took on board eighty sick from this small outpost. They were mostly men of the West Kents. Many of them, too weak to walk, were carried pick-a-back up the companion. They were emaciated with fever, dysentery, scurvy, jaundice, and other ills. As the Euphrates was falling, fresh water no longer reached them by the customary channel, and they had been reduced to the brackish well water of the desert. Their soiled kit added to their exhausted appearance — shirt white with the salt of perspiration, helmets, spine-pads and sun-guards half devoured by locusts, the flake of loose pith and cotton adhesive to their clothes and skin. The locusts were another plague, a local and passing one, of which I heard then for the first time.

Wycherley's woes continued when he was admitted to hospital in January 1917 suffering with rheumatism. In March he was promoted to Lance Corporal Acting Corporal but reverted to Private in April at his own request. The 2nd RWK remained on the Euphrates whilst fighting on the Tigris saw Kut and Baghdad captured, but once the Turks were on the back foot, they were finally able to move to the Tigris line and arrived at Baghdad in June. There they were transferred, as part of 34th Brigade, to the newly-formed Seventeenth Indian Division, which began concentrating around Baghdad in August. Wycherley joined the move up the Tigris and reached Sadiyah in October, part of the overall operations against Tekrit, although he was not involved in any fighting.

In December the Brigade began relieving the Meerut Division, which was transferring to Palestine. Wycherley moved to the outpost lines at Akab on the left bank of the Tigris, where the year ended quietly other than a few deserters handing themselves in. During 1917 he had, at different times, suffered from sand-fly fever, synovitis and a sprained elbow, the conditions continuing to prove very hard. On 11 January 1918 Wycherley was on board troopship S-44 moving along the Tigris, when he accidentally fell overboard and drowned. His name is recorded on the Basra Memorial.

UNCERTAINTY

Some of Kent's cricketers are known to have served, but details have proved frustratingly hard to come by. Their service still deserves mention, although their personal entries that follow are in a shorter format. Horatio Walpole is also included in this section, as although his wartime service can be traced, his cricket pedigree is still to be proved. The obituary Wisden published for him states he played in the Kent 2nd XI, but the Club has no record of that. It is possible he took part in a friendly match, or that the obituary was incorrect. As, at the time of writing, the puzzle has not been solved, the decision to include him seems a better option than omitting him and subsequently finding he did indeed play for Kent.

PRIVATE WILLIAM HENRY ASHDOWN

William Henry Ashdown, better known as Bill, was born at Bromley on 27 December 1898. He was taken on at the Tonbridge Nursery in 1914, and made his first class debut for a Gerry Weigall XI against Oxford University in June, and is the only cricketer to have played first class cricket before WW1 and after WW2.

Bill Ashdown joined the Rifle Brigade

He was too young to volunteer immediately the war began, but is referred to in the General Committee Meeting notes of December 1917 as 'Private Ashdown'. Players who volunteered were granted payments for the difference between their army pay and wages, and the records note Ashdown was to get £2.10.10 as he was on the same level as other members of staff. A newspaper article reveals he served with a reserve battalion of the Rifle Brigade, probably the 5th at Minster or the 6th at Eastchurch, although with no service papers available it is impossible to say more.

Ashdown first played for the Kent 1st XI in 1920 and appeared regularly until 1937. He scored over 22,000 runs for the county at average 30.64 and twice made an individual score of over 300 runs, the highest being 332 against Essex at Brentwood in 1934 when Kent made their record score of 803 for 4. Having retired in 1937 he stepped back to the crease once more ten years later for Morris Leyland's XI vs the Rest. He also took 602 wickets, all but seven of them for Kent, and later became an umpire, coach and scorer.

CORPORAL WILLIAM EDWARD HICKMOTT

William Edward Hickmott was born 10 April 1893 at Boxley and was the nephew of former Kent player Edward Hickmott. Taken on at the Tonbridge Nursery in 1910 he first appeared the in 2nd XI in 1911, and made his first class debut in 1914. He was one of three players making their debut that year (the others being Tich Freeman and George Whitehead), all doing so after war was declared.

Bill Hickmott made his Kent debut weeks after war was declared

Both the Club Committee notes and the *Kent Messenger* refer to Hickmott having enlisted in the West Kent Yeomanry, but he soon transferred to the Royal West Kent Regiment (RWK). His Medal card only refers to his service with the RWK, showing that he reached the rank of Corporal and was awarded the Victory and British War Medals. As he did not receive a 1914 or 1914-1915 Star, it is safe to say he did not serve overseas until 1916 at the earliest. His service papers have not been found, but his entry in the Medal Roll reveals he served with the 6th and 8th battalions RWK, both of which were on the Western Front from 1915 onwards. Although that means he served in France and/or Belgium, nothing further can be said with accuracy.

Hickmott played in the Lancashire League after the war, and although he appeared twice for Kent during 1921, he returned north and played for Lancashire during the 1923-24 seasons. In later years he became a breeder of golden retrievers, and took part in the Crufts competitions. Hickmott died on 16 January 1968 at West Malling.

JAMES SEYMOUR

James Seymour was born on 25 October 1879 at West Hoathly, Sussex and played for the county 1902-1926. Having joined the Nursery in 1902 he made his debut and was capped that season. A fine batsman, he went on to play 536 matches and scored 26,818 runs with a top score of 218 against Essex in 1911. He was one of the players the Club wrote to in 1915 asking what he was doing to support the war effort, and at that time he was serving as a Special Constable. The *Kent Messenger* noted early on that he had marital responsibilities and a motor business in Pembury to look after, and he was certainly over the age limit initially set for military service.

Seymour was a partner with a Mr Rendell in a taxi-cab business, and took over ownership of the garage and cars in October 1915, soon employing an engineer to provide repair services. A few months later conscription was introduced and Seymour received his call up papers. During June 1916 he applied at the Tunbridge Rural Tribunal for exemption, stating that he had invested his capital in his business and if he entered the army he would have to sell the garage and cars at vastly reduced prices. The Tribunal granted him four months exemption to arrange his business affairs.

James Seymour served in the RAF

When the Tribunal sat at the Workhouse in Pembury that November, Seymour returned to request a further exemption and was granted three months and no further appeal without leave. There are no service papers for Seymour, but a post-war newspaper article referred to his serving with the RAF. When he joined is unknown, but he was undoubtedly a conscript. He seems to have had no medal entitlement and any service was presumably Home Service. It is possible he joined the RFC or RNAS and was merged into the RAF in April 1918, or possibly was not called up until after the RAF was formed.

Seymour remained a reliable run-getter post-war and finally retired from first-class cricket at the end of the 1926 season. The legal battle that arose from his benefit in 1920 resulted in a legacy of tax free benefits for those that followed in his wake. Seymour died at Marden on 30 September 1930.

MAJOR KANWAR SHUMSHERE SINGH

Shumshere Singh was born 21 June 1879 in Bahraich, Oud, India. He was at Rugby School 1893-1897 where he kept wicket, and matriculated from Pembroke College, Cambridge where he made the College and University XIs but was not a Blue. His only appearance for the University was against Surrey in 1901 when Sam Day and Dick Blaker also played. After receiving his BA in 1900 he continued his medical studies at Cambridge and earned the MRCS LRCP (the English Conjoint Diploma) at St Bartholomew's Hospital in 1905. During that time Singh also played for Kent, three times in 1901 and once in 1902. His highest score was 45 against Worcester at the Mote, and in total he made 140 runs in his

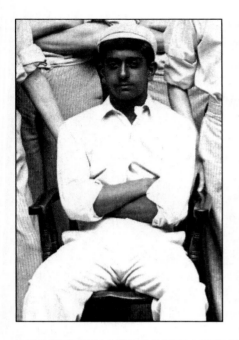

seven innings. Having joined the Indian Medical Service in 1906 he was married at the end of the year to Juliette Alice Maud Anderson d'Auquier.

Shumshere Singh pictured at Rugby. He served with the Indian Medical Service during the Great War. Reproduced by kind permission of the Rugby School Archives

No service papers were found for Singh, and all that is known is that he served in the Indian Medical Service, was promoted to Captain in 1909, Major in 1918 and served in the Great War. He became a Civil Surgeon in 1921 and was promoted to Lieutenant-Colonel in 1926, retiring with that rank in 1937. Singh died on 12 May 1975 in New Delhi.

LIEUTENANT ALEXANDER SMITH

Alexander Smith was born at Beckenham in 1892 and was engaged at the Nursery in 1908, remaining at Tonbridge through to 1912. He then spent a season engaged at Canterbury, but was replaced there by Wycherley for 1914, and returned to Tonbridge. At the start of the 1914 season the *Kent Messenger* referred to him as a six foot 22 year-old, and he bowled medium pace left arm. That year he came third in the bowling averages with 68 at 14.32, only Freeman taking more wickets. He made his first class debut in the same match as Ashdown and James Colquhoun, as Gerry Weigall tried them out against Oxford University.

He is referred to in both the *Kent Messenger* and *The Times* as having joined the Royal West Kent Regiment, and had done so by November if not earlier. An article that appeared in *The Kent & Sussex Courier* during April 1919 referred to him as Lieutenant A Smith, but his service papers have not been found.

RED CROSS DRIVER RICHARD THORNTON THORNTON

Richard Thornton Thornton was born 28 March 1853 at Folkestone and was educated privately at St John's College, Oxford where he was a Football Blue playing as goalkeeper. He was a late starter in first class cricket, being 28 when he made his Kent debut in 1881, going on to play 45 times for the county. He entered Holy Orders and was at one time the acting chaplain to the Royal West Kent Regiment.

A mature entrant into cricket, he also became a mature entrant into the war. In May of 1915, aged 61, he announced that he was converting his car into an ambulance, and enrolled himself in the French Red Cross Society. He proposed to pay his own expenses to get to France where he would rank as an officer in the French Army. In *The Kent & Sussex Courier* he stated "I am hopeful that my going may stimulate some men forty years my junior to come forward to serve their country". In June it was reported that he had reached his destination having travelled some 300 miles across French territory in his converted car, and reported himself 'very fit'. He returned at the end of September after serving a little more than the three months he had volunteered for and said he had been unable to get near the fighting line, and worked instead in a quiet country town to which the wounded were taken. Thornton died at Eastbourne on 30 May 1928.

LIEUTENANT HORATIO (HORACE) SPENCER WALPOLE

Horatio Spencer Walpole is included within this work on the strength of his Wisden Obituary, part of which reads as follows:

WALPOLE, LIEUT. HORATIO SPENCER (Coldstream Guards). Had been wounded. Killed April 9, aged 36. Kent 2nd XI.

He was born in Teddington on 19 July 1881, was educated at Eton from 1894, and went up to New College, Oxford in the autumn of 1900. Having been awarded his BA he sat his Law Society exams and started work with a firm of solicitors. In the summer of 1906 he was married to Dorothea Frances Montgomerie in London. He certainly played cricket for New College, Eton Ramblers, Surrey Club and Ground, Marlow, an HS Vade-Walpole XI and also Kenley. Perhaps a mistake was made over the name of the latter, as Kent has no record of him playing for them.

Horatio Walpole served with the Coldstream Guards, but did he play for Kent?

Walpole was initially over the age limit to volunteer, but was seemingly one of the last to step forward before conscription was introduced early in 1916. He was embodied in the Inns of Court OTC, and on completion of his training Private Walpole was commissioned into the Coldstream Guards. He was posted to join the 1st battalion in France on 25 August and, as the *Somme Continued*, took part in the Battle of *Flers-Courcelette* on 15 September. The Guards suffered very high casualties in the fighting, and practically all the battalion's officers were casualties. Walpole was himself shot in the right forearm.

Following treatment at 8th General Hospital, Rouen, he returned to England to recover, being promoted to Lieutenant at about the same time. He did not return to France until the following year, joining his Battalion at Moule during October 1917. *Cambrai* was launched on 20 November, and the Guards were brought forward when the offensive stalled. Walpole took part in the attack on Bourlon Wood and Fontaine Notre Dame, but the Guards again suffered heavily and were unable to hold the line they captured. During the German counter-offensive on 30 November his battalion was again thrown into the fray near Gouzeaucourt Wood.

On 21 March 1918 Walpole was in the support line at Arras when the battalion was woken by the barrage that signified the start of the *Kaiserschlacht,* and the men hurriedly took shelter in the cellars. He was commanding No.1 Company in the front line at Boiry St. Martin on 9 April. After a heavy bombardment in the morning the afternoon was much quieter, although artillery shells were still being sent over. One landed in Walpole's trench, killing him outright.

CHAPTER FIVE:
ROLL OF HONOUR

Fifteen men of the Kent XI's gave their lives whilst in the service of their country 1914-1918 and one subsequently died from illness contracted on service.

They shall grow not old, as we that are left grow old:
Age shall not weary them, nor the years condemn.
At the going down of the sun and in the morning,
We will remember them.

PLAYER	UNIT SERVED WITH	DATE OF DEATH
Lance Sergeant Fred Stanley Lowe	1st The Buffs (East Kent Regiment)	18/10/14
2nd Lieutenant Leonard Maurice Powell	3rd (attached 1st) Gordon Highlanders	17/06/15
Captain Arthur Corbett Edwards	8th Royal West Kent Regiment	26/09/15
2nd Lieutenant Frank Noel Tuff	1/1st Royal East Kent Mounted Rifles	05/11/15
Captain George Henry Heslop	16th Middlesex Regiment	01/07/16
Lieutenant Kenneth Lotherington Hutchings	12th King's (Liverpool Regiment)	03/09/16
2nd Lieutenant Ernest Herbert Simpson	Royal Garrison Artillery	02/10/17
Sergeant Colin Blythe	12th King's Own Yorkshire Light Infantry	08/11/17
Private (Actg Corporal) Charles Thomas Wycherley	2nd Royal West Kent Regiment	11/01/18

PLAYER	UNIT SERVED WITH	DATE OF DEATH
Major (Bt Lt-Col) Lawrence Julius le Fleming	2nd (commanding 9th) East Surrey Regiment	21/03/18
Lieutenant Horatio Spencer Walpole	1st Coldstream Guards	09/04/18
2nd Corporal David William Jennings	Royal Engineers	06/08/18
Captain Charles Eric Hatfeild	10th (Kent Yeomanry) the Buffs	21/09/18
Lieutenant George William Edendale Whitehead	Royal Field Artillery attached Royal Air Force	17/10/18
Major (Bt Lt-Col) Arthur Houssemayne du Boulay	Royal Engineers	25/10/18
2nd Lieutenant James Hugh Edendale Whitehead	9th Royal West Kent Regiment	13/03/19

As Walpole's Wisden obituary suggests he played for the Kent 2nd XI it seemed right to review him in this book and, as it remains to be proved either way, he has been included in the above list.

THE WOUNDED

In addition to those who died, many more of the cricketers were wounded. Of those who died, le Fleming and Walpole had both been wounded previously and returned to the front, and Heslop had been wounded and treated in France. There are twenty-four men listed, including those who suffered neurasthenia. The list does not extend to cover those who contracted illnesses or suffered accidents in service.

PLAYER	CAUSE OF WOUND	CAUSE OF 2ND WOUND
EM Blair	Neurasthenia	
N Boucher	Aircraft shot down	
JL Bryan	Shell burst	

PLAYER	CAUSE OF WOUND	CAUSE OF 2ND WOUND
JC Colquhoun	Shot	
WS Cornwallis	Shrapnel	
SE Day	Shot	
EW Dillon	Bomb shrapnel	
GH Heslop	Shell	
G de L Hough	Shot	Shell
WEC Hutchings	Shell fire	
CP Johnstone	Shot	Shell
FH Knott	Shot	
HM Lawrence	Shot	
LJ le Fleming	Shot	Shot
CS Marriott	Gas	
WT Monckton	Neurasthenia	
F Penn	Shell	
A Povey	Unknown	
CES Rucker	Shot	Shot
WGM Sarel	Nervous exhaustion	
LHW Troughton	Gas	
HS Walpole	Shot	
GEC Wood	Unknown	
CN Woolley	Shell	

Arthur Povey's papers record that he was wounded and stayed at duty in June 1918, but do not reveal the circumstances. The 39th Brigade War Diary recorded Wood was slightly wounded in Mesopotamia but gave no details of the cause. There is a strong possibility William Hickmott was also wounded, although there is no paperwork to support that. He first served with the 6th Battalion RWK and then the 8th Battalion, and it is possible he was wounded with one and returned to serve with the other. Those men who received Blighty wounds were often posted to a different battalion when they returned to the front, as their places had been filled by drafts. Gerald Hough also served with the 8th RWK and after returning from wounds received at Loos was posted to the 6th RWK.

Of those men serving overseas the casualty rate is approximately 50% killed or wounded. Of the 50 or so Kent cricketers who served on the Western Front, 13 were killed, 17 wounded and 2 wounded a second time. Bearing in mind the Gallipoli campaign was short-lived it still managed to result in 1 killed, 1 wounded, 1 injured and several cases of dysentery amongst twelve cricketers.

NEURASTHENIA

Better known as 'shell shock', neurasthenia was a state of nervous exhaustion that affected a large amount of men. Bill Sarel was diagnosed as suffering from the condition and spent four months resting to get over it. When George Whitehead returned to England to recover from appendicitis, the doctors noted he was showing signs of shell shock and general exhaustion, and he too was ordered to rest. Doctors also spotted signs of shell shock in Charles Marriott after he was gassed in 1917, and he spent months recovering from his ailments in Dublin. Blair suffered neurasthenia whilst organising the laying of the pipeline across the Sinai Desert, the pressure and deadlines of the huge project proving incredibly stressful. Walter Monckton suffered from nervous exhaustion at various times throughout his life, and suffered a bout of it whilst in France in 1917. No doubt others suffered the condition without being diagnosed. Some 80,000 British troops were treated for neurasthenia in medical facilities throughout the war, and the rate of incidents is said to have been four times higher amongst officers, who were expected to hide their emotions, than amongst the rank and file.

MEDALS AND AWARDS

1914 Star

The 1914 Star, unofficially known as the Mons Star, was awarded to those serving with the British and Indian Expeditionary Forces in France and Belgium from 5 August to 22 November 1914 when First Ypres ended. A bar or clasp was issued to those who were under fire during that time. Around 378,000 of the medals and 230,000 clasps were issued. Jack Bryan, Cornwallis, Lawrence le Fleming, Fred Lowe, Francis Marsham and Frank Penn were all awarded the medal and clasps, whilst Barry Cumberlege, Johnny Evans and Herbert Hatfeild also received the medal.

1914-15 Star

The 1914-15 Star was awarded for those seeing service in a theatre of war between 5 August 1914 and 31 December 1915. This could not be claimed by recipients of the 1914 Star, but did allow men serving in other theatres at the start of the war to receive the award. Over two million of the medals were issued of which thirty went to Kent players, many of whom had spent the first months of their war in training prior to being posted during 1915. Charles Wycherley left England in December 1915 and narrowly missed eligibility for the award as he did not arrived in Mesopotamia until January 1916. Frederick Leney and Raymond Bannon did receive the award for their services with the Red Cross, but Bernard Bannon appears not to.

British War Medal

The British War medal was issued to all men of the British and Imperial forces who served during the War, subject to various criteria for each service. Over six million of these medals were awarded, and more than 60 went to our cricketers.

Victory Medal

A version of the Victory Medal was issued by all the Allied nations. The dates on the medal were 1914-1919 the latter being the year the war ended under common law, but the medal for every other nation outside the British Empire showed 1914-1918. There were also over six million of these medals issued, and more than 60 went to Kent cricketers.

The medal awards of each man are recorded on index cards at the National Archive. The cards detail the awarding of the 1914 Star, 1914-1915 Star, the British War Medal and the Victory Medal and generally record what one would expect, although there are one or two curiosities. Bickmore's card does not list his entitlement, and no records were found for Hardinge, Monckton or Worthington, although the latter may reside in the Canadian archives.

Arthur Corbett Edward's medals (l-r) Queen's Mediterranean Medal, 1914-15 Star, British War Medal and Victory Medal

Military Cross

The Military Cross was instituted in December 1914 to recognise the distinguished services, in time of war, of lower commissioned (junior) officers. Mostly they were given for gallantry, but also for 'distinguished and meritorious service', with many given in the New Year and Birthday Honours. In 1917 the criteria was extended to cover temporary Majors, and in 1920 reverted to being a gallantry award for services in action. Just over 37,000 were awarded in WWI, of which thirteen went to Kent cricketers, and Johnny Evans received one of the 2,992 Bars awarded. The majority of the cricketers MCs were awarded for gallantry, the London Gazette announcements typically accompanied by a brief description of their brave actions. These included Evans and Rucker in 1915, Cornwallis and Troughton in 1916, and Blaker, Jack Bryan, Eric Fulcher and Eric Hatfeild in 1918. Evans citation did not appear in the Gazette, although the award reasons were written about elsewhere, and his Bar was awarded for his numerous attempts to escape captivity. The New Year and Birthday Honours MCs included those of Francis Marsham in 1916, Penn in 1917, Knott in 1918 and Wood and Monckton in 1919.

Jack Bryan's Medals, from left to right: the Military Cross, 1914 Star with clasp, British War Medal, Victory Medal, 1939-45 Star, Defence Medal, 1939-45 War Medal (with Oak Leaf denoting MID) and the George VI Territorial Efficiency Medal. Reproduced by the kind permission of Pat Bryan

DSO

The Distinguished Service Order was typically awarded to officers with the rank of Major or higher and 8,981 were awarded during WWI. During the war years it could only be given to someone mentioned in despatches, and was normally given for actions under fire. Between 1914 and 1916, however, it was often awarded for circumstances which were not under fire, typically to Staff Officers. This caused some resentment amongst front line officers and from 1917 it was requested that recommendations revert to being for bravery under fire.

Livesay was awarded his DSO during the Boer War, but four cricketers gained theirs between the years 1914-1918. Tufton was awarded his in January 1916 at the same time he was Mentioned in Despatches. There is no citation accompanying the award to suggest it was for a specific action, and it was presumably part of the New Year Honours. Du Boulay and Francis Marsham were awarded their DSOs in June 1918, again with no citation and presumably part of the Birthday Honours. Hervey Lawrence is the single cricketer to have a citation to accompany his award. Records show he received the DSO for his part in the Battle of Gaza in 1917, and he received a Bar to the award in 1918 for leading the 1st Herefordshire in an attack on Bois de Reugny in which he was wounded.

Mentioned in Despatches

The Commander-in-Chief (C-in-C) of the British forces in any campaign, or theatre of war, was under an obligation to send a despatch to the War Office to keep them apprised of the status of the campaign. The reports often mentioned, by name, those men who the C-in-C believed deserved special mention for their services, although specifics were not given. As we have seen, an award like the DSO was only given if a man was 'mentioned in despatches', often referred to as MID. An 'oak leaf' emblem was issued to wear on a man's medal ribbons, denoting he had been MID. An example of this can been seen in the picture of Jack Bryan's medals, the oak leaf being attached to his 1939-45 War Medal, the emblem granted for Bryan's MID during Dunkirk in 1940. Those men who were MID are as follows, with the number of mentions shown in brackets, although it is possible there were more that have not been unearthed:

Blair (1), Cornwallis (1), Cumberlege (1), du Boulay (6), Evans (1), Friend (4), Harington (3), CE Hatfeild (1), Hough (1), Knott (1), Lawrence (4), LJ le Fleming (1), FWB Marsham (2), JE Mason (1), Monckton (1), Penn (3), Prest (1), Tufton (2).

The corresponding references in the Gazette have all been found, except for Friend (3), Harington, Hough, Knott, Lawrence and JE Mason. The sources of the those MIDs were: Friend – the RE Journal, Harington – the Cheltenham College Register, Hough –

the Wykehamist War Service Roll, Knott – the War Diary of the 7th Battalion Wiltshire Regiment, Lawrence – his DSO entry, JE Mason – the Tonbridge School Register.

The Oak Leaf emblem was only established in 1919, which would explain why Harold Prest's MID Certificate was issued that year for his 1917 MID.

The MID certificate issued to HEW Prest in 1919 has been signed by Winston Churchill, Secretary of State for War. The MID was made shortly after the attack for which Prest was awarded the Croix de Guerre. Reproduced with the kind permission of Hedley Prest

British Orders of Chivalry

Britain has many different orders of chivalry, and Kent cricketers were appointed to a number of these for their wartime service. The following orders are shown in order of their precedence in the chivalric order.

The Most Honourable Order of the Bath

The Order of the Bath is an order of chivalry, established in 1725 and having Civil and Military Divisions, each with three classes; Knight or Dame Grand Cross (GCB), Knight or Dame Commander (KCB or DCB) and Companion (CB). Walter Coote Hedley was appointed to the Order as a Companion (CB) in 1915, and Maurice Bonham-Carter a Knight Commander (KCB) in the Civil Division in 1916.

The Most Distinguished Order of Saint Michael and Saint George

The Order of St Michael and Saint George was founded almost a hundred years before the Order of the British Empire, and named after two military saints. It was established in 1818 by George IV, and appointment to the Order is awarded for extraordinary service overseas. It consists of three classes; Knight or Dame Grand Cross (GCMG), Knight or Dame Commander (KCMG), and Companion (CMG). Three Kent cricketers were made Companions of the Order (CMG). Everard Blair was appointed in 1917 for his service on the pipeline project in Egypt, and Walter Coote Hedley in the same year for his valuable work at the War Office. Robert Livesay was appointed CMG in 1919 for his wartime service.

The Most Excellent Order of the British Empire (KBE, OBE, MBE)

The Order of the British Empire is an order of chivalry that was established during the War, mid-1917, by King George V. The order has civil and military divisions, each with five classes;

- Knight (or Dame) Grand Cross of the Most Excellent Order of the British Empire (GBE)
- Knight (or Dame) Commander of the Most Excellent Order of the British Empire (KBE or DBE)
- Commander of the most Excellent Order of the British Empire (CBE)
- Officer of the Most Excellent Order of the British Empire (OBE)
- Member of the Most Excellent Order of the British Order (MBE)

A large number of appointments to the Order were made during 1919, as the authorities sought to reward those who served the country, and this included the appointment of six of our cricketers to the Military Division. Lovick Friend and Walter Coote Hedley were both rewarded with a KBE, Barry Cumberlege, Hervey Lawrence and James Mason were made OBE, and James Colquhoun was appointed an MBE. In the Civil Division Christopher Hurst was appointed OBE in 1919 and Henry Braybrooke MBE in 1920.

Royal Victorian Order

The RVO is an order of knighthood awarded for service to the monarch, established in 1896 by Queen Victoria. It has five classes: Knight Grand Cross (GCVO), Knight Commander (KCVO), Commander (CVO), Lieutenant (LVO) and Member (MVO). Bonham-Carter was appointed KCVO in the Birthday Honours of 1917.

Foreign Decorations

The warring nations did not give medals and decorations exclusively to the soldiers of their own country, and many awards were made to their allies. In this way British servicemen found themselves eligible for foreign awards, and the cricketers received their share.

Croix de Guerre 1914-1918

The Croix de Guerre was a French medal instituted in 1915 to commemorate any allied soldiers mentioned in French despatches. The laurel branch, or' palme', seen on the medal awarded to HEW Prest, signified an Army Despatch. Other emblems were issued for Brigade, Divisional and Corps Despatches. The letter that accompanied Prest's medal stated that it was for his distinguished actions on 4-5 March 1917 near Moislains when he led his company to clear an enemy trench and then defend it against all counter-attacks. Other Kent cricketers awarded the Croix de Guerre were Arthur du Boulay and Lovick Friend.

HEW Prest's Croix de Guerre flanked by the Victory Medal and British War Medal, reproduced by the kind permission of Hedley Prest

Légion d'Honneur

The Légion d'Honneur was instituted in 1802, and is one of the most prestigious French awards and typically only bestowed on French subjects. Foreign nationals who fought for French ideals or similarly served the country could however receive a distinction of the

Légion, which is practically on a par with membership of the order. It is in this way that five Kent cricketers were made members of the order for their wartime services. There are five classes of members; Grand Cross, Grand Officer, Commander, Officer and Chevalier (Knight). Lovick Friend was awarded the Croix de Commandeur, Troughton and Hedley the Croix d'Officiers, and Livesay and Lawrence the Croix de Chevalier.

Ordre National du Mérite Agricole
The French National Order of Agricultural Merit was established in 1883 to reward services to agriculture. During the war it was given to military members who promoted the development of agriculture for example by the organisation of labour for helping production. John Tufton was made a Knight of the Order in 1919 and although the reason he received the award is not apparent, *The Kent & Sussex Courier* did once refer to him as "heart and soul in agriculture", managing an extensive farm of his own in Kent.

Ordre de Léopold
The Belgian Ordre de Léopold was instituted in 1832 by the then King Leopold I to recognise services to the country. The order has three divisions; Civil, Military and Maritime. Each division has five classes; Grand Cordon, Grand Officer, Commander, Officer and Knight. The Belgian authorities bestowed this award on four Kent players; Lovick Friend was awarded the Commander class, du Boulay and Hedley the Officer class, and Tufton the Knight class.

Ordre de la Couronne
The Belgian Order of the Crown was instituted in 1897 and could be bestowed to reward meritorious military services to the country. There are six classes; Grand Cordon, Grand Officer, Commander, Officer, Knight and Palmes of the Order of the Crown. Walter Coote Hedley and Christopher Hurst were awarded the Officer class in 1919.

American Distinguished Service Medal
The American Distinguished Service Medal can only be awarded to members of the US Armed Forces with the exception of exceptional awards to foreign nationals for wartime services, and only with the express approval of the US President. Robert Livesay was one of the exceptions when he received the Medal in 1919, for the services he provided whilst holding an appointment at the American Staff in France 1917-18.

Order of the Nile
The Order of the Nile was established by the Sultan of Egypt in 1915 as an award for

exceptional services to the country. The Order has five classes; Grand Cordon, Grand Officer, Commander, Officer and Knight. Allan Francis Leach-Lewis was awarded the Officer Class in 1919.

Medal group (missing 1914-15 Star) awarded to Major Allan Francis Leach-Lewis: British War Medal 1914-20; Allied Victory Medal 1914-19; Defence Medal 1939-45; Special Constabulary Long Service Medal, George VI issue; Territorial Decoration George V; Order of the Nile, 4th Class. Courtesy of the Council of the National Army Museum, London

CHAPTER SIX:
WE WILL REMEMBER THEM

Memorials to the victims and heroes of wars have been erected throughout history, but the aftermath of the Great War was different. So many men had fought that almost everyone in the country was affected in some way, families and communities suffering losses alike. Efforts were made by society to preserve the memory of those who had died, believing that the conflict was the 'war to end all wars'. Such memorials will be found on the battlefields overseas, in villages and towns across the British Isles, in local churches, sports grounds, places of work and schools and universities. Rolls of Honour were often mounted on the walls of these establishments, and also put into print, recording the names of those who fell. The Cenotaph is the best known of all the memorials, but Kent cricket supporters will be more than familiar with the Club's own memorial at the St. Lawrence Ground, Canterbury, erected as a memorial fountain to the memory of Colin Blythe and his fellow cricketers of the Kent Elevens.

THE BLYTHE MEMORIAL FOUNTAIN

On 17 April 1918, as the Allies desperately fought to stop the German Spring Offensive, *The Times* carried the following notice:

> *It is proposed to erect to the memory of the late Colin Blythe, the Kent bowler, who lost his life at the front last September, a drinking fountain on the Kent County Cricket Ground at Canterbury. The idea is also entertained of placing a tablet to the memory of Blythe in Tonbridge Church.*

The month of Blythe's death was erroneously given as September, and indeed the date of his death was to be incorrectly engraved upon the memorial. The fact, however, that the idea was being proposed just several months after his death and with the war still in progress, gives an indication of the respect Colin Blythe commanded. A further notice in May stated that the structure would take the form of a drinking fountain to the memory of Blythe and his fallen comrades. The unveiling ceremony took place on 23 August 1919, during a match between Club and Ground and the Band of Brothers.

There were quite a number of Kent's cricketing soldiers playing that day. The Club and Ground side included the Dutnall brothers, Wally Hardinge, Arthur Povey and Ernest Dilnot, and their opponents included Eric Fulcher, Arthur Snowden, Eric Bickmore, Allan

Leach-Lewis and Lord Harris. Blythe's widow was present, as were Lionel Troughton and Tom Pawley, and the ceremony was presided over by the Kent President, Lord George Hamilton, revealing the inscription to the memory of Blythe and ten other men of the Kent Elevens. Prior to the unveiling a small guard of honour of the Buffs, with arms reversed, stood around the memorial, which was veiled with the Union Jack and the Kent flag.

Left: The Blythe Memorial in 2010 – moved into storage during the redevelopment of the St. Lawrence Ground
Right: an earlier picture of the memorial shows the taps which were part of its original function as a drinking fountain. The alterations to the structure are plain to see, the fountain taps and outlets no longer present

The inscription on the fountain gives Blythe's date of death as 18th November 1917, and *The Times* report on the unveiling also gave the incorrect date. However both the *Kent Blue Book 1919* and the *History of Kent County Cricket Appendix F (Kent CCC 1923)* give the correct date of 8th November when describing the memorial. Interestingly Blythe's CWGC War Grave records his age as 39, although he was 38 when he was killed.

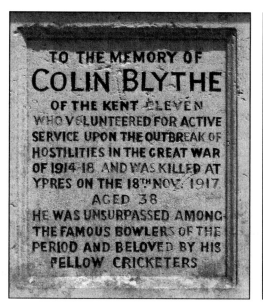

Two of the panels on the Blythe Memorial. The image to the right is reproduced by the kind permission of Shaun Caveney

Newspaper reports of the unveiling recorded that the memorial remembered Blythe and ten others of the Kent Elevens. The photograph above, taken in 1984, shows twelve names. The two additions are Ernest Simpson and James Whitehead, one at the top and one at the bottom. The original listing had officers in alphabetical order, followed by the ranks, and the names of Simpson and Whitehead fall out of sync. Simpson was perhaps overlooked in the immediate aftermath of the fighting, and Whitehead died in 1919 and likely missed the list of names first inscribed.

Two Kent players missing from the list of those killed are George Heslop and Leonard Powell, and then there is Horatio Walpole whose Wisden obituary suggests he might have a claim, although a slim one without further evidence to support it. Other mistakes may have been the errors of prior restorations, as the details in the *History of Kent County Cricket* do not entirely match what appeared on the memorial in later years. The initials of AC Edwards are incorrectly shown as AE and CE Hatfeild's as GE. Wycherley's initial is shown as A, which should be CT, and that was actually recorded incorrectly when the memorial was erected. Lowe's initials are not recorded on the memorial at all.

Tuff's regiment is shown as the REKMR, the Royal East Kent Mounted Rifles, and that was the regiment he was serving with when fatally wounded. Hatfeild was in the same regiment but the last letter is incorrectly inscribed as a P (REKMP), although it should be noted he was serving with the 10th Buffs when killed and that is shown on the headstone of his war grave. George Whitehead is shown as serving with the RFA attached to the RFC, but the RFC was no longer in existence when he was killed, and his war grave references RAF. David Jennings is referred to as serving with the Kent Fortress Engineers (KFE), but when he was posted overseas he served with a Field Company of the Royal Engineers, and it is the RE which is recorded on his war grave. Blythe also enlisted with the KFE, and his war grave records he was serving with the King's Own Yorkshire Light Infantry when killed, although the memorial does not refer to his unit

As can be seen in the pictures of the memorial, it was altered just a few years after the unveiling when the overflow and troughs were persistently blocked with leaves. New stone was added to cover the taps and basin, and the troughs were filled in. At the time of writing the Memorial has been moved to make way for the redevelopment at the St Lawrence, and it is intended it will be restored and re-sited in due course. In addition to the Memorial, the two wallets Blythe had in his pocket when he was killed are on display at the St Lawrence Ground, and it can be seen that the shrapnel that killed him passed through both.

THE CRICKETING WORLD REMEMBERS

The game of cricket lost many men to the war, and the cricketers who returned had lost years of their playing careers. Some, like Charles Rucker, Freddie Knott and Gerald Hough, had suffered wounds that prevented or restricted their ability to play, and the game took quite some time to recover. Wisden has a long tradition of publishing cricketers' obituaries, and was kept busy during the war years. Some players deaths were missed, but the vast majority were remembered in this way. At Lord's a roll of honour was put up by the MCC, naming all its members who fell, and anyone taking the Lord's tour will be able to see the names of Du Boulay, Edwards, Hatfeild, Hutchings, Powell, Simpson, Walpole and James Whitehead – among the many who died.

COMMONWEALTH WAR GRAVES AND MEMORIALS

The Imperial War Graves Commission was established in May 1917, and has been known as the Commonwealth War Graves Commission (CWGC) since 1960. It cares for the graves and memorials to the men of Commonwealth nations who died in two world wars, including those whose bodies remain undiscovered or unidentified. The first memorial the Commission established was at the Menin Gate, Ypres (the modern Ieper) upon which Leonard Powell is named. In the years that followed, the graves of many men who were buried in small cemeteries close to where they died were moved to larger cemeteries where the Commission could more easily tend to them. Some cemeteries established during the war were destroyed in the fighting, the land simply churned up by shells, and those buried there joined the ranks of the undiscovered. The CWGC supports the War Graves Photographic Project, which established a database of images of almost all war graves and memorials from WW1 to the present day. Unfortunately there is not enough space to reproduce images of all those relating to the Kent players, but they can be accessed via the TWGPP website. The CWGC looks after the graves of nine of the cricketers (including Walpole) and six of their memorials have the names of Kent players on them. James Whitehead who died in 1919 is the one exception, having been buried in the family vault at Wilmington, and cared for privately.

The MCC Roll of Honour is headed 1914-1918 although some, like James Whitehead, died in 1919. Under common law the war ended in 1919 and the Victory Medal issued in Britain shows the dates 1914-1919. Copyright Polly Hancock/MCC

COLIN BLYTHE

Blythe, who was killed on 8 November 1917 during the Battle of Passchendaele, is buried in the Oxford Road Cemetery, Belgium grave reference I.L.2. The reference indicates that he was one of the original burials at the site, the cemetery being expanded at a later date to take graves from scattered battlefields to the east and south-east of Ypres. The most famous of Kent's war casualties, Blythe's grave has been visited by many cricket fans making the pilgrimage to Flanders. The inscription on his headstone reads: " **49296 Serjeant C. BLYTHE , King's Own Yorkshire L.I. 8TH November 1917 Age 39 – In Loving Memory of my dear husband, the Kent and England Cricketer.**" Blythe was in fact 38 when he was killed.

ARTHUR HOUSSEMAYNE DU BOULAY

Du Boulay fell victim to the flu epidemic of 1918, succumbing to the disease on 25 October 1918 whilst in a French hospital. His grave is in the Fillièvres British Cemetery, Pas de Calais, France, which was started four months prior to his death by the 46th Casualty Clearing Station and then used by the 6th Stationary Hospital. He is one of 81 Commonwealth burials from WWI, and more casualties from WW2. The inscription on his headstone ends with a quote from Robert Louis Stevenson's *Requiem*: "**Major & Brevet Lt. Col Arthur Houssemayne Du Boulay, DSO, Royal Engineers 25 October 1918 – Glad Did I Live And Gladly Die, And I Laid Me Down With A Will (R.L.S.)**"

CHARLES ERIC HATFEILD

Eric Hatfeild fought at Gallipoli, Egypt, Palestine and finally France, one of three Kent players to fall in the last two months of the war, when killed near Hargicourt on 25 September 1918. He is buried at the Hargicourt Communal Cemetery Extension, site C.11 in the row nearest the Great Cross, one of over seventy WWI casualties buried there. Hargicourt exchanged hands several times during the conflict, and German graves at the site were moved after the war, leaving the British extension isolated. His grave stone reads (apart from the last word which I have unfortunately been unable to decipher): "**Captain Charles Eric Hatfeild, M.C. 10th Bn (Kent Yeo) The Buffs, 21st September 1918 Age 31 – Their Lives for Their Country, Their Souls Together.....**"

GEORGE HENRY HESLOP

George Heslop was one of almost 20,000 British soldiers killed on the first day of the Somme, when his battalion joined the attack near Beaumont Hamel. His body was initially missing, but was recovered at some point, and he is buried in plot B. 40 at the Hawthorn Ridge Cemetery No.1, Auchonvillers in France, started by V Corps who cleared the Ancre battlefields in 1917. The cemetery is home to over 150 Great War casualties, half of which remain unidentified. Heslop's grave bears the inscription: "**Captain G.H. Heslop Middlesex Regiment, 1st July 1916 Age 21 – Pro Patria Pro Deo**" (For Country For God). The grave is shared with Private H Marsden of the Border Regiment who was killed on the same day.

DAVID WILLIAM JENNINGS

David Jennings is one of the two Kent casualties to have died in England. He passed away on 6 August 1918 at St. Mark's VAD Hospital, Tunbridge Wells after returning to England to recover from the effects of gas poisoning. Jennings was buried in the Old Cemetery in his family's home town of Marlborough (grave reference 764). "**40499 2nd Corporal D.W. Jennings, Royal Engineers, 6th August 1918, Age 29 – He fought to guard our country from the foe, His life he gave for one and all**".

ERNEST HERBERT SIMPSON

Ernest Simpson died on 2 October 1917 in a hospital at St. Omer where he was being treated for wounds received from the explosion of an aircraft bomb near Vlamertinghe. He is buried in grave IV. E. 21 at the Longuenesse (St. Omer) Souvenir Cemetery, Pas de Calais, sharing the plot with Royal Fusilier Private H. Coombe. His gravestone inscription reads: "**Second Lieutenant E.H. Simpson, Royal Garrison Artillery, 2nd October 1917, Age 41 – Greater Love Hath No Man Than This, That He Lay Down His Life For His Friends**". St. Omer was the BEF's GHQ for the first half of the war, and the town was home to many hospitals. The cemetery contains 2,784 Commonwealth burials of WWI.

FRANK NOEL TUFF

Kent's single loss to the Gallipoli campaign, Frank Tuff was fatally wounded and evacuated to Malta where he died on 5 November 1915. His grave is plot D. II. 1 in the Pieta Military Cemetery. Over 135,000 casualties of Gallipoli and Salonika were handled on Malta, and Pieta Cemetery contains over 1,300 graves and memorials of Commonwealth casualties. The inscription on Tuff's grave is "**In Loving Memory of Frank Noel Tuff, 2nd Lieut Royal East Kent Mounted Rifles – Wounded Gallipoli 23rd Oct Died at Malta 5th Nov 1915 Age 26 Years – To Be With Christ**".

HORATIO SPENCER WALPOLE

Horace Walpole was killed near Boiry St. Martin during the great German Spring Offensive of 1918, and is buried in grave II. B. 22 of the Bac-Du-Sud British Cemetery, Bailleulval, Pas de Calais. The cemetery was started by several Casualty Clearing Stations in March 1918, just prior to the German offensive, and contains 688 Commonwealth burials. The inscription on Walpole's headstone reads "**Lieutenant H.S. Walpole, Coldstream Guards, 9th April 1918 Age 36 – God Proved Them And Found Them Worthy For Himself**".

GEORGE WILLIAM EDENDALE WHITEHEAD

When George Whitehead's plane was downed over Belgium in October 1918, he was buried by the local residents at the Lauwe Military Cemetery. During 1924 and 1925 a number of graves were moved from smaller cemeteries in the area to the larger Harlebeke New British Cemetery, and Whitehead was transferred to plot I. D. 14. His inscription reads: "**Lieutenant George W.E. Whitehead, Royal Field Artillery attached Royal Air Force, 17th October 1918, Age 23**". Further lettering appears but is obscured by the flowers in the photograph. Harlebeke contains 1,116 Commonwealth burials.

The original graves of George Whitehead (right) and his Observer Lt Griffiths at Lauwe Cemetery, photographed in May 1920 by his family. I am grateful to Clifton College for permission to print this photograph from the unpublished papers of G.W.E. Whitehead

ARTHUR CORBETT EDWARDS

Arthur Edwards was killed during the battle of Loos and is named on Panel 95 to 97 of the Loos Memorial. His battalion did not attack until the 26 September 1915, and that would appear to be the date of his death, although the official date was given as 25 September or after. The Memorial is to 20,000 men who fell in the area but have no known grave. The names are engraved on tablets attached to the fifteen feet high walls, and on the walls of other courts attached. Facing the large Cross of Sacrifice, the panel upon which Edwards is named is on the wall to the right.

KENNETH LOTHERINGTON HUTCHINGS

Ken Hutchings was killed in the attack on Guillemont and Ginchy in September 1916 during the Battle of the Somme, and he is commemorated on Pier and Face 1 D 8 B and 8 C in the south eastern corner of the Thiepval Memorial. The memorial, located near the village of Thiepval, was unveiled in 1932 and remembers 72,000 missing men of the Somme. Colin Blythe's brother Sidney, who died the following month, is also named on the memorial.

LAWRENCE JULIUS LE FLEMING

Lawrence le Fleming was killed on the first day of the German *Kaiserschlacht*, 21 March

1918. His body was recovered but the British lines were pushed back so quickly, that his grave was lost in the chaos of the fighting. He is remembered on the Pozieres Memorial, Panel 44 and 45. The Memorial commemorates over 14,000 men killed on the Somme from March 1917 to August 1918, and surrounds the Pozieres British Cemetery. The panel on which le Fleming's name appears is on the wall to the left of the Great Cross.

FRED STANLEY LOWE

Kent's first casualty of the Great War, Fred Lowe, died near Radinghem, France in October 1914. He is named on Panel 2 of the Ploegsteert Memorial which is located just the other side of the border, in Belgium. The Memorial commemorates over 11,000 soldiers who died in the region who have no known grave. Entering the memorial from the cemetery, the panel upon which Lowe is named is just to the right.

LEONARD MAURICE POWELL

Leonard Powell was killed near Ypres during June 1915 and is named on Panel 38 of the Ypres (Menin Gate) Memorial. The memorial bridges the road, and heading from Ypres to Menin, the panel upon which Powell is named in on the right hand side, in the south-west corner. The memorial is one of four that commemorate the missing of Ypres, and the site was elected because it was a familiar landmark to the thousands of soldiers who passed through the gate as they made their way to the front. Over 54,000 missing men are named on the memorial.

CHARLES THOMAS WYCHERLEY

Charles Wycherley was presumed drowned after falling from a troop ship on the River Tigris in January 1918, and was Kent's only casualty in Mesopotamia. He is named on Panel 29 of the Basra memorial in modern day Iraq, which commemorates over 40,500 Commonwealth casualties in Mesopotamia during WWI. The memorial was unveiled in 1929 on the main quay of the dockyard at Maqil, 8km north of Basra but, due to sensitivities during the Gulf War, was relocated in 1997 to a spot 32 km along the road to Nasiriyah.

FAMILIES AND FAMILY GRAVES

Of the 16 men killed, only one is not marked by the CWGC, that of James Whitehead.

JAMES HUGH EDENDALE WHITEHEAD

James Whitehead died in London on 13 March 1919 from illness contracted whilst serving with the Royal West Kent Regiment. He was buried in the family vault at St. Michael Churchyard, Wilmington, Kent. Memorial Tablets for the Whitehead brothers were unveiled at Wilmington Parish Church on 14 September 1919 and a service held there to dedicate them.

With so many of the war's casualties buried overseas, or in the ranks of the 'missing', the mourning families at home often added the names of their loved ones to family graves, so they had a memorial to visit closer to home. Some were able to visit the battlefields and visit their relatives' graves, or the memorials erected after the war. George Whitehead's parents visited his 'last' resting place in May 1920 where they also found a local road had been named after him by the grateful Belgian residents. Frank Tuff's father was said to have never got over the loss of his two sons, and the files of Ernest Simpson and Arthur Edwards reveal the pain felt by their wives. Violet Simpson, who had only been married during Spring of 1913, exchanged letters with the War Office regarding certain of her husband's belongings which were missing from his personal effects; items that she wanted returned to keep as a reminder of her brave husband. In the aftermath of Loos, Arthur Edwards' wife clung on to the hope that her husband had not been killed and was simply missing or perhaps taken prisoner. She exchanged a number of letters with the War Office, but they were unable to find any record of his being taken by the Germans.

Arthur du Boulay is named on several monuments in England, and his name also appears on his father's grave at Leckhampton whilst Fred Lowe is remembered on his brother's grave in the churchyard of St Stephen's at Hackington near Canterbury. Ernest Simpson is named on his mother's grave at West Norwood Cemetery, and Frank Tuff on the family grave at St. Margaret's, Rochester.

FALLEN COMRADES

Soldiers did their best to respectfully mark the deaths of their fallen comrades throughout the war. The bodies of those killed were collected from the battlefields and given burials, although not all the graves lasted as the ground was fought over time and again. When Lawrence le Fleming was killed, the men he commanded were determined to retrieve his body for burial, and Ken Hutchings' comrades erected a cross to him and his brother officers who were killed during the fight for Guillemont. The men's names were inscribed on a badge that was attached to a white cross at the Ginchy dressing station near the front. After the war the men's relatives brought the cross back to England. Although the wooden cross has since been replaced, the metal badge is the original, and it now resides outside St Peter's Church in Formby, Liverpool. Also near to where Hutchings fell, and Troughton won his MC, a memorial was erected after the war to the memory of those of the 20th Division who were killed in the fighting in that area.

The cross outside St Peter's Church, Formby which bears the name of Ken Hutchings, reproduced by the kind permission of the Vicar of St. Peter's in Formby, the Rev. Paul Ormrod

COMMUNITIES REMEMBER

After the Armistice, as communities took stock of the losses they had suffered, many memorials were erected in towns and villages across the length and breadth of the land. Lord Harris was a member of the Kent War Memorial Committee, as was FSW Cornwallis, the father of the future Kent captain, and both were instrumental in raising the Kent War Memorial. The result of those efforts, positioned in Canterbury between the Precincts and the City Wall, was unveiled in 1921. Harris also supported the raising of memorials in other towns in Kent, and unveiled several of them.

Many of the cricketers had links with Tonbridge and a memorial was erected in the town near St Stephen's Church in 1921. It was removed in the 1950's when the new garden and memorial were created, and the names transferred to this new spot. The Memorial Gardens occupy a quiet spot just off the High Street, and the panels of the brick memorial name the town's fallen sons of both world wars. Colin Blythe is named on the left panel, and Lawrence le Fleming on the right.

Tonbridge Memorial Gardens

Further along the High Street, a small road leads to the well hidden Tonbridge Church. Inside a mural is mounted on the wall to the memory of Colin Blythe. A collection for the mural was started at the same time as the Memorial Fountain at the St Lawrence. Just above is a plaque to the memory of another Tonbridge resident, Frank Woolley.

Not far from Tonbridge is the town of Southborough, where a civic war memorial names those residents who gave their lives. The memorial was unveiled in February 1921 and commemorates 207 casualties of WWI and 44 from WW2. Ken Hutchings was born in the town and his name appears on one face of the base, being one of two named men who died serving with the King's Liverpool Regiment.

Southborough War Memorial

Ken Hutchings name on the Southborough Memorial

356

The Folkestone War Memorial is situated at the eastern end of the Leas, and is now stranded on a traffic island, not far from the seafront. The memorial was unveiled in December 1922, and Arthur Edwards is one of the 578 named on it.

The unveiling of Folkestone War Memorial upon which Arthur Edwards is named

In Margate the town's War Memorial stands proudly on Trinity Hill. When it was unveiled by Lord Harris in November 1922 Trinity Church towered over it, but that building was demolished in 1960 having been damaged beyond repair during the Blitz. Eric Hatfeild is among the 429 WWI servicemen named on the base of the granite cross.

The unveiling of Margate War Memorial by Lord Harris

Margate War Memorial as it looks today

Elsewhere in Kent, Frank Tuff and his brother are both named on the Ifield War Memorial at St Margaret's near Gravesend; at Wilmington the Whitehead brothers' names appear on the War Memorial as well as on the family grave in the churchyard of St Michael's; and George Heslop is remembered on a memorial plaque in the St Nicholas Churchyard, Sevenoaks.

Further afield, the Stevenage War Memorial includes Horatio Walpole among the servicemen remembered; and the name Arthur du Boulay appears on many memorials, perhaps reflecting the impact he had on the communities he lived and served in. These include the Cheltenham War Memorial, West Grinstead Church, St. Botolph's Church War Memorial, Colchester and All Saints Church, Cheltenham.

The Stock Exchange unveiled a memorial in 1922 in memory of its members who died, although since the Exchange relocated, the memorials have been in storage and not on display. A memorial book was published, carrying obituaries of the men, and contains entries for two Kent cricketers, James Whitehead and Ernest Simpson.

SCHOOLS AND UNIVERSITIES

Schools and Universities had spent the War years reading reports of the deaths of former pupils, and many looked to establish a Roll of Service or a Roll of Honour. *The War List Of The University Of Cambridge 1914-1918 (Carey 1921)* and the *Oxford University Roll Of Service (Craig 1920)* both include entries for former students detailing regiments and awards. The Oxford roll contains 14,561 entries for members of the University who served in the forces during the war, and includes all the Kent players who studied there except Percy Baker and Leslie Fawcus. George Whitehead is included as one of the men who had been accepted for admission to a College but lost his life before matriculating. George Heslop who had been accepted to study at Cambridge, is commemorated on the War Memorial in the chapel at Trinity College. His old school Lancing College also received an anonymous gift, by means of which a cricket bat was to be presented annually for the best individual performance in the Brighton College match. Colin Blythe's old school in Deptford also started giving a prize for Patriotism and Athleticism to commemorate their former pupil.

Whilst not War Memorials, readers may be interested to know that inside the cricket pavilion at the Parks, Oxford the walls of the main hall are adorned with wood panelling, upon which previous Blues Cricket XI's are inscribed in gold colouring.

The Oxford Eleven of 1914 as named on a panel in the pavilion at the Parks, included Knott and Rucker who were both wounded. Of the others named, all served on the Western Front and Boswell and Shaw were killed. Reproduced by the kind permission of Neil Harris

The Cambridge Roll includes details of all its Kent players except Marriott and Jack Bryan both of whom studied there after the War. *List of Etonians Who Fought In The Great War 1914-1919 (Eton College 1921)* similarly named all the schools pupils who served in the War including Cornwallis, Edwards, the Hatfeild brothers, the Marsham brothers, Tufton and Walpole. Unlike the Oxford Roll the Eton list does not include Lord Harris. *Tonbridge School and the Great War (Tonbridge School 1923)* includes obituaries for Lawrence le Fleming and Ken Hutchings, and entries for the Bannon brothers, Frederick and William Hutchings, Freddie Knott, John le Fleming, James Mason and Charles Worthington. Powell is named in the Loretto roll, du Boulay the Cheltenham roll, Heslop the Lancing College roll and Hatfeild that of Wye College. There are undoubtedly others elsewhere.

CHAPTER SEVEN:
PEACE

The effects of the war were to be felt for many years to come. Aside from so many players having lost their lives, and the physical and mental scars that others suffered, there had been four years without first class cricket and many players were out of practice. The season's fixtures were limited to two-day matches, and Kent played one home Championship game at each County ground, with extended playing hours as the authorities were unsure what appetite the public would have. When the fixtures were announced in the press the County was still unsure who would be released from the forces in time to play. Just days after the announcement James Whitehead passed away as a result of the illness he contracted when he was serving.

There was no Test cricket that year although the Australian Imperial Forces played a good number of fixtures, Kent drawing with them at Canterbury in August. The professionals who resumed their engagement with Kent ensured there were many familiar faces around in 1919. The season also saw nine players make their debuts for the 1st XI: Bickmore, Jack Bryan, Cornwallis, Frank Dutnall, Eric Fulcher, Lionel Hedges, Hough, Johnstone and Wood. Hedges was the only one of the nine who had not served, having just left Tonbridge School that July.

Kent began their season on Whit Monday against Essex at Leyton. Once they were on the field the players and the umpires stood to attention for two minutes, in silent homage to the Kent players who fell in the war. The unveiling of the Blythe Memorial Fountain at the St Lawrence that August was also a suitable occasion to remember those who did not return. Days later a match was played between a Kent XI and the Next XX, serving as a trial match for the next generation, as the Club tried to look to the future. Some of the youngsters appearing had served in the war (namely Colquhoun, Bickmore, Dutnall, Howlett, Eric Fulcher, Hickmott, Povey and Dilnot) but there was new blood in the form of Godfrey Bryan, Alan Hilder and John Knott. Kent finished in second place after their 14 fixtures, behind Yorkshire who played 26.

Many young men had left university before finishing their studies so that they could join up, or had entered the services straight from school. When they were demobilised, a number wanted to complete their studies to enable them to begin their chosen careers. This resulted in the Universities receiving far more applications than usual in the first few years following the Armistice, and both Oxford and Cambridge allowed the former soldiers different forms of dispensation that enabled them to gain their degrees in a shorter time than usual. This typically meant the scholar could not be given a class, as with an honours degree. Eric Bickmore received his BA but was only at Oxford for two years, and Noel Boucher also completed a shortened course there. Con Johnstone was credited the four terms from October 1917 to Christmas 1918 by the council of the Senate at Cambridge, and he and George Wood were both excused the examination in military subjects. Charles Rucker returned to his studies, as did Charles Marriott who had been at Dublin University pre-war but opted for Cambridge afterwards. Gonville and Caius College, Cambridge did not see the return of either James Colquhoun, who opted to go into business, or Leonard Powell who did not survive the war. Jack Bryan and Charles Fawcus, who had both entered the services from school, chose to attend University after being demobilized.

Others looked to return to the jobs they had before the war, although much had changed. The Army gave references to men being demobilized, and this helped William Dutnall find employment with the GPO. Of those who resumed playing cricket, a number were obviously employed by Kent as professionals.

THE EMERGENCY

When demobilization took place, many men were liable to recall in the event of an emergency. Such an Emergency was declared on 31 March 1921 when a National Strike was threatened by the miners. Tufton and Capes were both recalled to help keep order in the event of trouble, as coal rationing was put in effect on 3 April. When the miners failed to get the support they hoped to, the threatened National Strike was called off, and the two cricketers were stood down.

ANOTHER WAR

'The War to end all Wars'. 'The Great War for Civilisation'. Tyranny had been defeated, and the world looked forward to the peace that followed. The Great War had proved so costly that another war was far from anyone's mind. As we now know that peace lasted all of twenty years, and some of those who fought between 1914-1918 served again between 1939-1945. Of the cricketers serving in WWI, nine had served in the Boer War; Tufton, Livesay, LJ le Fleming, Harington, Hedley, du Boulay, Lawrence, Sarel, Worthington. A further sixteen who served in WWI went on to serve in WWII, mostly in Home Service although the Bryan brothers both joined the BEF and were evacuated from Dunkirk, as was Bernard Howlett who was later killed in Italy. Jack Bryan had joined the BEF in France in the first weeks of the war in 1914, and rejoined the army immediately WW2 broke out. Boucher spent most of the war at sea with the RN. The men who served again were:

N Boucher	RAF Volunteer Reserve
S Boucher	Royal Navy
JL Bryan	Manchester Regiment and Royal Armoured Corps
RT Bryan	Manchester Regiment and Royal Armoured Corps
BS Cumberlege	Royal Observer Corps
AJ Evans	MI9 and IS9
EA Fulcher	Officers Emergency Reserve
CVL Hooman	RAF Volunteer Reserve
B Howlett	Royal West Kent Regt, killed in Italy
FH Knott	Royal Army Service Corps
AF Leach-Lewis	Regional Officer for Midland Civil Defence Region 1940-45
CS Marriott	Home Guard Anti-Aircraft
FWB Marsham	Home Guard GSO1, County Commandant Berkshire Cadets
WT Monckton	Director-General of the Press and Censorship Bureau. Director-General of the Ministry of Information. Under-Secretary of State for Foreign Affairs. UK delegate at Potsdam Reparations Commission.
HEW Prest	Royal Norfolk Regiment.
JR Tylden	General List Infantry 1941-1942

MORE CASUALTIES

The names of those who fell in the 1939-1945 War were added to the Blythe Memorial, and Gerald Hough was instrumental in the addition of the memorial gates and plaque at the entrance of the St Lawrence ground.

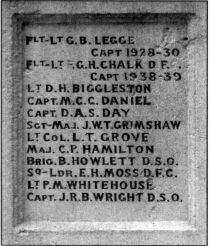

The panel on the Blythe Memorial listing the Club's WW2 casualties

The Bishop of Dover dedicating the WW2 Memorial Gates in June 1951, reproduced by the kind permission of Kent County Cricket Club

Unlike the panel for WW1 the men are not split between officers and ranks, although the two Kent Captains who perished are listed first. Martin Charles Campbell Daniel was not a Kent player, but did play for Rugby School, Butterflies and Broadstairs, and was a Committee member. The three players of the Kent XIs who died, but were not named, are:

Henry Charles Sheffield Armstrong represented the 2nd XI in early 1939. He was a Flight Lieutenant in the RAF, and was killed on 31 January 1944 when the Sunderland Flying boat he was pilot of, came down in Ireland.

Henry Armstrong died whilst serving with the RAF

William Murray Leggatt, DSO, played for the 1st XI in 1926. He served with the Royal Artillery, and died 13 August 1946 from illness contracted on service. Although this is after the war ended, he is listed as a casualty on the CWGC website, and his case is not dissimilar to that of JHE Whitehead who died in 1919 from illness contracted on service, but is named on the WW1 panel.

Geoffrey Phelps Longfield, who played for the Kent 2nd XI in 1928, was the younger brother of first team player Tom Longfield (the father-in-law of Ted Dexter). He was a Wing Commander with the RAF, killed during an operation over Rennes on 26 February 1943.

Geoffrey Longfield, one of Kent's WW2 casualties, reproduced by the kind permission of Ivo Longfield

BIBLIOGRAPHY

Abrahams, H.M., and Bruce-Kerr, J, Oxford versus Cambridge : A record of inter-University contests from 1827-1930, Faber and Faber Limited, London 1931

Arrowsmith, RL, A History of County Cricket: Kent, Arthur Barker Limited, London 1971

Atkinson, Captain C.T., The Queen's Own Royal West Kent Regiment, 1914-1919, Simpkin, Marshall, Hamilton, Kent & Co., Ltd, London 1924

Bakowski, Jane, Leap of Faith, The history of Yardley Court, Gresham Books Limited, Tenterden 2011

Becke, Major A.F., History of the Great War, Order of Battle of Divisions, Parts 1-4, The Naval & Military Press Ltd, Uckfield 2007

Beckett, Ian F.W. and Simpson, Keith (Editors), A Nation In Arms, Pen & Sword Books Limited, Barnsley, South Yorkshire, 1985

Berkley, Reginald, The History of The Rifle Brigade In the War of 1914-1918 Volume I August 1914-December 1916, The Naval & Military Press Ltd, Uckfield, 2007

Blaker, RNR, The unpublished account of an action on the 4th November, 1918, at Louvignies

Bristow, Cyril, History of the Kent Cyclist Battalion: Territorial Force 1908-1920, Privately Published, 1986

Candler, Edmund, The Long Road to Baghdad: Volume I, Cassell and Company Ltd, London 1919

Carey, G.V., The War List Of The University Of Cambridge1914-1918, The University Press, Cambridge 1921

Chaplin, Lieut-Col. H.D., The Queen's Own Royal West Kent Regiment 1881-1914, The Queen's Own Regimental History Committee, Maidstone, 1959

Chesterton, George and Doggart, Hubert, Oxford and Cambridge Cricket, Willow Books, London 1989

Churchill, Winston Spencer, The River War: An Historical Account of the Reconquest of the Soudan, Longmans, Green & Co, London 1899

Coldham, James D, Lord Harris, George Allen & Unwin, London 1983

Craig, E.S., and Gibson, W.M., Oxford University Roll Of Service, The Clarendon Press, Oxford 1920

Creagh, Sir Garrett O'Moore and Humphris, E.M., Distinguished Service Order, 6th September 1886 to the 31st December 1915 (Volume I) and 1st January 1916 to the 12th June 1923 (Volume II), Reprint of the 1924 Original Edition by The Naval & Military Press Ltd, Uckfield 2001

Cull, Ian, *The 2nd Battalion Royal Berkshire Regiment In World War One*, Tempus, Stroud 2005

Dunsterville, Major-General L.C., *The Adventures of Dunsterforce*, Edward Arnold, London, 1920

Edmonds, Brigadier-General Sir James E. (Compiled by), *Official History of the Great War*, Fourteen Volumes published between 1922 and 1948 in London by Macmillan and HMSO

Errington, Lt-Col F.H.L., *The Inns of Court Officers Training Corps During The Great War*, Printing Craft Ltd, London 1922

Eton College, *List of Etonians Who Fought In The Great War 1914-1919*, Printed privately, London 1921

Evans, A.J., *The Escaping Club*, The James A McCann Company, New York, 1922

Evans, A.J., *Escape and Liberation 1940-1945*, Hodder & Stoughton Limited, London 1945

Fair, Capt. A, and Wolton, Capt. E.D., *The History Of The 1/5th Battalion "The Suffolk Regiment"*, Eyre and Spottiswoode, London, circa 1923

Furley, H.D., (Editor), *The Register of Tonbridge School from 1861-1945*, Rivingtons, London, 1951

General Staff Branch, Army Headquarters, India, *The Third Afghan War 1919 Official Account*, Government of India Central Publication Branch, Calcutta 1926

Harris, Lord (Edited by), *The History of Kent County Cricket*, Eyre & Spottiswoode, London 1907 and Appendices E, F and G

Hayes, Dean, *Kent Cricketing Greats*, Spellmount Ltd., Tunbridge Wells 1990

Home, Brigadier General Sir Archibald, *The Diary of a World War I Cavalry Officer*, Costello, Kent 1985

Humphreys, Roy, *The Dover Patrol 1914-18*, Sutton Publishing Limited, Stroud, Gloucestershire, 1998

Igglesden, Sir Charles, *66 Years' Memories of Kent Cricket*, Kentish Express, Ashford 1947

Kent CCC, *Blue Books and Annuals 1899 to 2013*

Kent CCC, *Young Players Minute Book,* extracts provided by David Robertson, Curator, Kent CCC

Kent Messenger, editions published during 1914, accessed at the Kent History and Library Centre, Maidstone

Kerr, Captain R.S. Rait, *A History of Royal Engineers Cricket 1862-1924*, the Institution of Royal Engineers, Chatham, 1925

Lemmon, David, *'Tich' Freeman and the Decline of the Leg-Break Bowler*, George Allen & Unwin, London 1982

London Gazette, *Despatches from the Vice-Admiral, Dover Patrol, on Zeebrugge and Ostend Operations, 22nd-23rd April, 1918, and Ostend Operations, 10th May, 1918*, as recorded in The Gazette, issue 31189, 18 February 1919

Marriott, C.S., *The Complete Leg-break Bowler*, Eyre & Spottiswoode, London 1968

Marriott, C.S., *Unpublished account of the first day of the Somme*, written in December 1964, from the papers held by the Fusilier Museum, Bury

Milton, Howard, *Cricket Grounds of Kent*, The Association of Cricket Statisticians, West Bridgford, Nottingham 1992

Molony, Major C.V., *"INVICTA" With the 1ˢᵗ Battalion The Queen's Own Royal West Kent Regiment In The Great War*, Nisbet & Co. Ltd., London 1923

Moody, Colonel RSH, *Historical Records of The Buffs : East Kent Regiment 1914-1919*, The Medici Society Limited, London 1922

Osborn, T, *The History of the Mote Cricket Club 1857-1981*, Kent County Library, West Malling 1990

Palmer, Alan, *The Gardeners of Salonika, The Macedonian Campaign 1915-1918*, Faber and Faber Ltd, London 2009

Pearse, Colonel H.W. and Sloman, Brigadier-General H.S., *History of the East Surrey Regiment Vol. II 1914-1917 and Vol. III 1917-1919*, The Medici Society, Limited, London 1923

Peebles, Ian, *Woolley: The Pride of Kent*, Hutchinson & Co Ltd & The Cricketer Ltd, London 1969

Petre, F Loraine, *The Royal Berkshire Regiment 1914-1918*, The Naval & Military Press Ltd, Uckfield, undated

Pomeroy, Major Ralph, Collins, Colonel W.F., Duguid-McCombie, Colonel W.M., Hardy, Lt-Colonel S.J., MacDougall, Lt-Colonel A.I., Dewar Gibb, Andrew, *History of The Royal Scots Greys (The Second Dragoons) August 1914-March 1919*, No publisher shown, circa 1928

Ponsonby, Charles, *West Kent (Q.O.) Yeomanry and 10th (Yeomanry) Batt. The Buffs 1914-1919*, Andrew Melrose Ltd, London 1920

Porter, Clive W., *The White Horse and the Kangaroo*, Meresborough Books, Rainham, Kent 1981

Pratt Boorman, H.R., *The Spirit of Kent : Lord Cornwallis*, Kent Messenger, Maidstone, 1968

Radd, Andrew, *100 Greats: Northamptonshire County Cricket Club*, Tempus, Stroud, Gloucestershire 2001

David Robertson, Howard Milton & Derek Carlaw, *100 Greats: Kent County Cricket Club*, Tempus, Stroud, Gloucestershire 2005

Royal Engineers, *History of The Corps of Royal Engineers, Volume V The Home Front, France, Flanders and Italy In The First World War, Volume VI Gallipoli, Macedonia, Egypt and Palestine 1914-18, Volume VII Campaigns In Mesopotamia and East Africa, and the Inter-War Period, 1919-38*, The Institution of Royal Engineers, Chatham 1952

Scoble, Christopher, *Colin Blythe: lament for a legend*, SportsBooks Limited, Cheltenham 2005

Seymour, William W, *The History of The Rifle Brigade In the War of 1914-1918 Volume II January 1917-June 1919*, The Naval & Military Press Ltd, Uckfield, 2007

Smart, John Blythe, *The Real Colin Blythe*, Blythe Smart Productions, Kingsbridge, Devon 2009

Stedman, Michael, *The Somme 1916 & Other Experiences Of The Salford Pals*, Leo Cooper an imprint of Pen & Sword Books Ltd., Barnsley, South Yorkshire, 2006

Stock Exchange, *The Stock Exchange Memorial of those who fell in The Great War 1914-1919*, Philip Lee Warner, London, 1920

Tonbridge School, *Tonbridge School and the Great War of 1914-1919: A Record of the Services of Tonbridgians in the Great War of 1914 to 1919*, published by the school 1923

Wakefield, Alan and Moody, Simon, *Under The Devil's Eye, The Brtish Military Experience In Macedonia 1915-1918*, Pen & Sword Books Limited, Barnsley, South Yorkshire, 2011 (first published by Sutton Publishing 2004)

Warner, Oliver, *Cricketing Lives: Frank Woolley*, Phoenix House, London 1952

Wenyon, Lieut-Col. H.J. and Brown, Major H.S., *The Eighth Battalion The Queen's Own Royal West Kent Regiment 1914-1919*, Printed Privately for the Battalion 1921

Whitehead, *The unpublished papers of G.W.E. Whitehead* as held in the Clifton College Archives

Wilson, H.W., *HUSH or The Hydrophone Service*, Mills & Boon, Limited, London 1920

Woolley, Frank, *The King of Games*, Stanley Paul & Co. Ltd, London 1936

Original papers that were accessed at the National Archives were in the following series:

Officers' service records: WO 339 and WO 374 series: K Barlow, AF Bickmore, EM Blair, RNR Blaker, CJ Capes, DW Carr, JC Colquhoun, BS Cumberlege, AP Day, SE Day, EW Dillon, AC Edwards, AJ Evans, EA Fulcher, EJ Fulcher, GH Heslop, FV Hutchings, KL Hutchings, WEC Hutchings, CP Johnstone, J le Fleming, AF Leach-Lewis, CS Marriott, CHB Marsham, JE Mason, WT Monckton, LM Powell, CES Rucker, WGM Sarel, EH Simpson, GA Simpson, LHW Troughton, FN Tuff, JSR Tufton, HS Walpole, GJV Weigall, GWE Whitehead, JHE Whitehead, GEC Wood

Service records for the RFC/RAF in AIR 76 and AIR 79 series: N Boucher, AJ Evans, HTW Hardinge, CS Marriott, CHB Marsham, PE Morfee, WGM Sarel, FE Woolley

Service records for the RN/RNAS/RNR/RNVR in ADM 188, ADM 196 and ADM 337
series: RB Bannon, S Boucher, SW Brown, HTW Hardinge, E Humphreys, JE Mason,
JR Mason, FE Woolley,

War Diaries for numerous service units as held in the WO 95 series.

Service records for Other Ranks, now accessible on the 'ancestry' website, in the WO 363
series: PC Baker, EW Dilnot, F Dutnall, W Dutnall, DW Jennings, FS Lowe, A Povey,
HJB Preston, AO Snowden, HJ Taylor, EA Willson, CN Woolley, CT Wycherley

Medal Index Cards in the WO 372 series and Medal Rolls in the WO 329 series

Service records made available by Library and Archives Canada for CR Worthington

Files held with the MOD for soldiers serving beyond March 1922, of which copies were
consulted: JL Bryan, RT Bryan, WS Cornwallis, HS Hatfeild, FH Knott, F Penn, HEW
Prest, JR Tylden,

ONLINE RESOURCES

The following online resources were accessed to obtain information:

Ancestry (ancestry.com): birth, marriage and death records, census forms and also some
military detail of medal records and entries in originally published in De Ruvignys
Roll of Honour 1914 1918 (5 Vols.)

Commonwealth War Graves Commission (CWGC.org): casualty details

Cricketarchive.com : cricket records

Fosters Of Malvern (thefostersofmalvern.co.uk) : background information on the Fosters

London Gazette (London-gazette.co.uk) : public notices of appointments, promotions
and awards

Oxford Dictionary of National Biography (oxforddnb.com) : biographical details

Rolls of Honour (roll-of-honour.com) : casualty details

The British Newspaper Archive (britishnewspaperarchive.co.uk) : obituaries and other
articles

The Long Long Trail (1914-1918.net) : The British Army in the Great War of 1914-1918
and the website forum

The Times Digital Archive 1785-2008 (galegroup.com) : obituaries and other articles

The War Graves Photographic Project : (twgpp.org) : casualty details

Who's Who (ukwhoswho.com) : biographical details

Wisden (espncricinfo.com) : obituaries

The following schools, colleges and universities provided information from their registers
and records that was used in the writing of this book:

Schools: Aldenham; Bradfield; Charterhouse; Cheltenham; Clifton; Dulwich; Durham;

Glenalmond; Lancing College; Loretto; Malvern; Marlborough; Radley; Rugby; St. Andrew's; St. Colomba's; St. Edmund's; Sevenoaks; Sutton Valance; Taunton; Tonbridge; Uppingham; Wellington; Westminster; Winchester.

Universities Trinity College, Dublin; Oxford University; Cambridge University.

Colleges of Oxford University: Brasenose College; Christ Church College; Magdalen and University Colleges; New College; St John's College; Worcester College.

Colleges of Cambridge University: Jesus College; Pembroke College; St. John's.